Analyzing Policy

Also by MICHAEL C. MUNGER

Ideology and the Theory of Political Choice (with Melvin J. Hinich)

Analytical Politics (with Melvin J. Hinich)

Empirical Studies in Comparative Politics (coedited with

Melvin J. Hinich)

Analyzing Policy:

Choices, Conflicts, and Practices

MICHAEL C. MUNGER
DUKE UNIVERSITY

W·W·NORTON & COMPANY
New York   London

The text of this book is composed in Galliard
with the display set in Modern 216 Light
Composition by PennSet, Inc.
Manufacturing by The Courier Companies, Inc.
Book design Jacques Chazaud

Library of Congress Cataloging-in-Publication Data
　　Munger, Michael C.
　　　　Analyzing policy : choices, conflicts, and practices / Michael C. Munger.
　　　　　　p. cm.
　　　　Includes bibliographical references and index.
　　　　ISBN 0-393-97399-9 (pbk.)
　　　　　　1. Policy sciences.　　2. Evaluation.　　I. Title.
　　H97.M86 2000
　　320´.6—dc21　　　　　　　　　　　　　　　　　　　　　　　99-047240

Editor: Stephen Dunn
Associate Managing Editor: Jane Carter
Production Manager: Ruth Dworkin
Project Editor: Kate Barry

W.W. Norton & Company, Inc., 500 Fifth Avenue, New York, N.Y. 10110
www.wwnorton.com

W. W. Norton & Company Ltd., 10 Coptic Street, London WC1A 1PU
1　2　3　4　5　6　7　8　9　0

For Donna Gingerella, with Love

Contents

Preface

Human societies seem complex. People who study them compare differences, and try to figure out why people do what they do. This is the task of the social sciences, including psychology, sociology, political science, economics, and history. Though the social sciences, in their current form, have existed for only about a century, we have made considerable progress toward understanding many pieces of the puzzle of human behavior.

Another social science profession, called policy analysis, draws on some of the best features of the main disciplines listed above. In addition to studying what people actually do, and why, policy analysts establish benchmarks for evaluating those actions. Policy analysis tries to answer two practical questions: First, *what would be the best thing to do?* Second, *what is the best result that can actually be achieved?* This book is an introduction to both questions. We will examine the way policy analysts conceive of the "best" policy choice, using the concepts of efficiency and equity. We will also look at the limits and constraints that restrict real policy choices.

As with any nascent science, some of the news I will be reporting will be bad. At times, it may appear to the student that real policy analysis is impossible. But don't be dismayed. Good policy analysis is *not impossible*; it is just *hard*. I hope the difference will become apparent. In any case, let me be clear from the outset: There is no more important task, in any of the social sciences, than identifying what a good policy would look like. With some idea of what is good, we have some hope of knowing bad, or mediocre, when we see it.

We can start with some broad alternatives. Though governments, and nations, are complicated, in fact there are only three ways for humans to organize activity:

- *Markets*, or decentralized actions by many individuals, whose aggregate implications may be hard to predict or reconcile.
- Leadership by *authority*, or people who by virtue of insight or ex-

perience know more than the rest of us. Of course, the basis of
authority may be simple military power, or savage repression, but
even in these cases the authority generally touts his or her vision,
intelligence, or judgment.
• Some collective choice mechanism, or *democracy*, where all enfranchised citizens register beliefs about what society should do. These
beliefs are recorded in sum and the aggregate "will" of the people
is revealed.

It appears that something like the market form of organization
dominates almost every society in the world. Most activity, after all,
takes place in a setting where government acts to limit, rather than to
direct, human choices. Markets happen almost spontaneously, requiring only a rudimentary set of property rights definitions, some
reasonably accepted medium of exchange, and a legal system for
adjudicating disputes.

Without any central plan or direction, something mysterious can
happen, something not well understood from a scientific perspective.
A dizzying array of conventions, informal rules, or other means of reducing the costs of transactions emerge. These nongovernmental institutions for facilitating exchange may be imperfect, but they are
neither haphazard nor ineffective. The marketplaces of the ancient
Egyptians or Aztecs, the "law merchants" of the middle ages, and the
present-day diamond markets of Antwerp and New York are all examples of the spontaneous emergence of institutions which reduced
transactions costs and permitted a wide variety of welfare-enhancing
exchanges which would have been impossible without markets.

On the other hand, the fact that effective "private" institutions
might emerge spontaneously, if we wait and have faith, is hardly
proof that we should always count on the deus ex machina of the
market's invisible hand. Sometimes, as in Italy in the eighth and
ninth centuries, or Russia in the late twentieth century, the organizations that emerge in the absence of government control are far from
optimal. Incentives are pathological, outcomes are disastrous, and
people lose faith in markets.

To avoid such missteps, every government in the world manages
its markets. In deciding how to set and monitor these regulations,
decision makers rely for guidance on either authorities (the "experts"
in all but the most primitive societies) or democracy in choosing the
form that management should take. Some societies manage markets
very intensively, taking over many of the market's functions in broad

sectors of citizens' activities. Others rely on something much closer to the *laissez faire*, or "let (the people) do (as they will)," ideal of classical liberalism. Few nations stay with precisely the same set of policies regarding the management of markets for very long, instead adjusting and "reforming" their regulatory policies almost every year.

Policy analysis helps explain why are there so many differences in the way we organize productive activity. It also helps us judge if some policies are good, and others are bad, by creating benchmarks for comparing the results we observe in one country, or at one point in time, with others. These benchmarks are hypothetical, because perfect policies are never observed, but without a standard of comparison evaluation is impossible.

Themes

My goal is for the reader to take away from this book two apparently conflicting perspectives about policy analysis: optimism and skepticism. The conflict between these two perspectives drives much of the debate we see in Congress, on talk shows, and in the newspapers.

Optimism can mean one of two things. *Market-oriented* optimists tend to believe that the world we live in is the best of all possible worlds (a variant of the view espoused by Liebniz and mocked by Voltaire in *Candide*). *Regulation-oriented* optimists tend to believe that all will turn out well, and expect the best, rather than the worst, outcome from any attempt to redirect market activities so as to make everyone better off.

Neither of these two extreme forms of optimism is a satisfactory guide to policy choice. As the skeptic Voltaire said through his artless naïf, Candide, optimism of the laissez-faire sort "is the mania of maintaining everything is well when we are wretched." (1977; p. 73). Many government policies, on the other hand, harm rather than help, but regulation-oriented optimists keep trying anyway to reform and improve policies. As Hegel(1832) said, "What experience and history teach is this—that people and governments never have learned anything from history, or acted on principles deduced from it."

The first theme of this book is simple: The best policy analysts are skeptical optimists. They believe, in principle, that better policies are possible, but they view any particular proposal with a strong presumption of doubt. More simply, a good policy analyst hopes for the best, but assumes the worst unless her skepticism is disproved. The use of analytic techniques described in this book, including models of incentives, discounting with respect to time, and discounting to account for uncertainty, are all crucial tools for evaluating the claims of optimists.

The second theme, obvious from the title as well as the sequence of chapters, is that I believe there are three conflicting sources of power and legitimacy in policy processes. The power bases, corresponding to the ways of organizing activity, are markets, politics, and expertise/authority. Policy conflicts tend to be dyadic, with one or another pair of these decision bases clashing over the right course of action. The result is that a policy which answers a conflict between politics and markets may appear irrational or harmful when viewed by policy experts; policies that reconcile expert-market conflicts may be politically infeasible. Consequently, the first step in understanding a particular policy is to understand what sort of conflict gave rise to the policy in the first place. We will consider each of the three power bases at some length in later chapters.

Policies and Institutions

Suppose we could establish that some kinds of results, the "outcomes" of choosing policies for managing markets and directing resources, are better than others. Then we have to face the fundamental dilemma: *How should we choose how to choose?* Are good outcomes more likely if we rely on the institutionalized judgments of experts, or on the aggregated voices of citizens, expressed through votes or surveys? This book describes advantages and drawbacks in using expertise and democracy in choosing outcomes, as well as giving the reader some important tools for deciding whether a particular attempt at management, or "policy," is good or bad.

If this sounds like "policy analysis" has too many meanings . . . well, it may! Policy analysis defies easy definition, because it is hard to pin down as belonging to any one social science discipline. The simple reason is that no one discipline has all the answers. In fact, no one discipline even has all the right *questions*, and asking the right questions is the heart of good policy analysis. Policy analysts get blamed for asking hard questions, because they are skeptical. They worry about how much a policy will cost, who will pay those costs, and whether the benefits promised by the policy will ever be delivered. They worry about unintended, and unanticipated, consequences of policy choices.

On the other hand, being a policy analyst is one of the best jobs there is. Providing advice to key decision-makers is scary, but it is also exhilarating. Rather than sitting in a room pondering theories, or analyzing data, policy analysts have to know about every aspect of the policy being considered. They might start with theory, or the history of similar programs in other states, or other countries. They might look at the process of implementation and the evaluation of the nuts and bolts of the policy itself. At the end of the day, elected officials and appointed bureaucratic leaders have to make decisions. If you, the policy analyst, don't know the answers, or don't have the information they need, they are going to make decisions anyway. Worse, decision makers under pressure may end up listening to some crackpot who has even less information, but lots more confidence. Everything you know, and everything you think, adds up to make you a better policy analyst. Good luck!

Aims of the Book

This book is targeted at undergraduates in public policy programs or political science departments, as well as master's programs in public policy or public administration programs. Such courses have three discrete goals:

- Help students to understand the different roles that policy analysts play. I have served as both an administrator and an instructor in professional policy analysis programs, and will admit the following dirty little secret: Students come in believing that they will learn how to make policy, yet they leave with little knowledge of how policy is made! I know from my own experience as a policy analyst in Washington, D.C., and as a consultant in a variety of state and local government analysis projects, that "analysis" is often an afterthought. Policy analysts have at least two roles, and it is important not to confuse them: Analysts serve sometimes as advocates for a particular perspective, and sometimes as objective searchers for truth. But even if you think you have found the truth, that doesn't mean anyone will believe you. They may not even listen. The reason students must learn the language, tools, and roles of policy analysis is not that by learning they can make policy, but rather, that if they don't learn policy analysis they will be ignored, and excluded from the debate altogether.

- Teach students the basics of the welfare economics paradigm. This includes basic microeconomic theory, the theory of consumer surplus as a metric for measuring welfare gains and losses, and the effects of policy intervention (taxes, subsidies, price restrictions, and standards- or rules-based regulations). This field has evolved rapidly in the last ten years, and right now there is no text that provides an accessible treatment and overview for students just getting started.

- Give a well-grounded introduction to cost-benefit analysis. For students to do cost-benefit analysis on their own, as professionals, they must be intimately familiar with two types of "discounting": First, they must understand the idea of expected value, and be able to account for risk. Expected value puts alternatives with different risks and payoffs on a common footing, so that they can be compared and judged. Second, students need to be able to account for time, using the concept of present value, so that accurate judgments can be made in comparing streams of costs or benefits in the future with spending or income today. Accounting for both risk and time allows the professional to arrive at the appropriate discount rate for a project, policy, or activity. Further, a sensitivity analysis, allowing for varying assumptions, can be used to judge how sensitive a conclusion is to particular assumptions.

Acknowledgments

I tried out many of the arguments, and examples, in this book over more than a decade of teaching policy analysis and public administration classes at the University of Texas at Austin and the University of North Carolina at Chapel Hill. While there were too many students with helpful suggestions to name, I should acknowledge just how useful their responses and comments have been in teaching me about policy analysis.

Several faculty colleagues have been particularly helpful in guiding me toward useful ideas and away from foolish ones. Perhaps the most influential are Duncan MacRae, at UNC, and Murray Weidenbaum, at Washington University. Their views of what constitutes good policy are very different, but each has a level of insight that leaves me feeling both admiration and envy. Further, each conducts himself in a way that sets a high standard for intellectual discourse. Michael Ensley and Melissa Harris provided first-rate research assistance in several parts of the process of writing and rewriting, as well as finding obscure information that had eluded me completely. Michael also wrote a draft of the case on social security, and much of the end-of-chapter material. Rebecca Lewis and Kevin Munger read several chapters, and helped me clarify the ideas I was trying to get across. Brooke Barton read the entire manuscript, and made many useful suggestions for clarification. Joan Benham did an outstanding job copyediting the manuscript. Jay Hamilton, Brian Sala, and one anonymous reviewer were the most helpful readers of all, carefully criticizing the whole project as well as many of its parts. Thanks to all.

Finally, for Kevin and Brian Munger: Yes, now we can go outside and play baseball. I get to pitch first, though.

Analyzing Policy

～1～

Policy Analysis as a Profession and a Process: An Overview

Policy: *[1] A definite course or method of action selected (as by a government, institution, group, or individual) from among alternatives and in the light of given conditions to guide and usually determine present and future decisions; [2] A projected program consisting of desired objectives and the means to achieve them.*

Analysis: *(1) Separation or breaking up of a whole into its fundamental elements or component parts; (2) A detailed examination of anything complex (as a novel, an organization, a race) made in order to understand its nature or to determine its nature or to determine its essential features; a thorough study.*

—Webster's Third International Dictionary

Policy analysis is as old as policy. Everyone has an opinion on policies; everyone wants to believe their conclusions are the result of careful and objective analysis. But they are often wrong. As William Fulbright said, "We are handicapped by policies based on old myths rather than current realities."[1] Fulbright was referring to U.S. foreign policy in Vietnam, but the same could be said about welfare policies, prison reform, or dozens of other problems. You may have noticed the problem: on most policies, most people think the answer is obvious. But they sometimes disagree about what the "obvious" answer is.

Fulbright's "myth" may really just be whatever someone *else* believes. One's own beliefs, by contrast, are "the truth." Clearly, that is no basis for having a debate: we have to be able to say more than you have your opinion and I have mine. We have to say what is right, and what is wrong, or at least make a good guess. Are there good policy analysts? How would we know one if we saw one? Shakespeare praised Henry V as many things, but not least was old Henry a policy analyst of the first rank:

> Hear him debate of commonwealth affairs,
> You would say it hath been in all his study:
> List his discourse of war, and you shall hear
> A fearful battle rendered in music:
> Turn him to any cause of policy,
> The Gordian knot of it he will unloose,
> Familiar as his garter; that, when he speaks
> The air, a charter'd libertine, is still."[2]

"Unloosing the Gordian knot" is a perfect metaphor for the practice of policy analysis. After all, "analysis" comes from a Greek word meaning to loosen, or to break up a complex whole into parts that can be understood.

The problem is that for most causes of policy, the Gordian knot resists loosening. In Greek legend, Gordius was a King of Phrygia who tied an intricate, incomprehensible knot. But the knot was of great importance, because the Oracle at Delphi revealed that whoever untied the knot would be the future king of all Asia. Alexander the Great tried, for a time, to untie the knot. Before long, though, he gave up and angrily whacked at the thing with his sword. The rope fell in pieces, Alexander went on to become king of the whole region, and now we all rush out to elect politicians who grossly oversimplify our policy problems.

The ability to seem to cut through problems still matters. Ross Perot got lots of attention for saying, "Look, it's simple!" in response to almost any question about policy problems in the 1992 and 1996 presidential elections. In June 1999, wrestler-governor Jesse Ventura told the U.S. Chamber of Commerce that his main principle of governing is K.I.S.S.: "Keep It Simple *AND* Stupid."

The point is that we admire those who can "cut the Gordian knot." This is just a colorful way of saying such a person can come up with a quick, simple solution for what seems to be a complex problem. As we shall see, however, this is a fundamental problem in a democracy, because the same sword appears to "work" for all knots: just cut the darned thing, and get on with it. But every knot is a little different, and if you want to untie the knot, to *understand* it, you have to have a process for simplifying complex problems, for focusing on parts to get an idea of the nature of the whole.

Unfortunately, many of our difficulties, as cities, states, or a nation, will not be solved by impatient knot-whacking. Shakespeare was giving Alexander a not so subtle jibe, because King Henry "unloosens" the knot, actually solving the problem, rather than just slicing through it, which gets rid of the knot but ruins the rope.

And there you have the essence of policy analysis: We try to understand the knotty problems of policy, rather than propose simple, universal solutions. This means that policy analysts are not very popular with politicians. Political leaders often feel they were elected to make problems go away, fast, and get on to the next task. A politician elected for a two-year term is not likely to have the patience to want to appreciate the uniqueness, depth, and difficulty of the policy being analyzed.

Consequently, there is a natural conflict between elected officials, who (probably rightly) see themselves as the delegates of the people, and policy experts, who think they know what is right because of an abstract, and in some cases highly developed, theory of cause and effect. All politicians, not just Ross Perot or Jesse Ventura, would like to apply simple, universal principles, because politics rewards the ability to offer consistent reasons and explanations. It is tempting to think that one should ignore the complex "analyses" of experts, and get back to underlying fairly simple reality.

On the other hand, expert policy analysts often think of problems in odd ways, because they reconceive a problem as they analyze it. Someone familiar with a given problem, or with the politics of coalition building, may find the recommendations of policy analysts ludicrously naive. For example, in the mid-1980s, some analysts who worked for the Social Security Administration, and some Congressional staff analysts, realized that many elderly people would not be able to afford hospital stays in the event of a long-term illness. Because of the federal budget deficit, it was decided that the government could not help for free; some charge for the "service" would have to be levied.

For people with annual incomes under $30,000, the charge would have amounted to about $4 per month. For those who had high incomes, a maximum fee of $67 per month would be charged. The "advantage" of the program (or so the analysts thought) was that mandatory membership among the elderly would make the "catastrophic coverage," as it was called, a very effective, inexpensive insurance program with benefits that far exceeded the fees paid by most seniors.

Well, as soon as the Medicare Catastrophic Coverage Act of 1988 was passed, there was a firestorm of protest. Surprisingly, the protest did not come from young people, whose social security taxes would have been subsidizing the below-cost benefits received by the elderly. Instead, it was the supposed beneficiaries, the people the policy analysts thought they were going to *help*, who raised a ruckus. Seniors were not much concerned with hospital stays; they wanted the government to help pay for long-term care, in nursing homes or in their own homes. Further, the fact that the program was (a) mandatory, and (b) not free, was very upsetting to senior citizens on tight, fixed budgets.

The act was repealed, in its entirety, in 1989. The very people who figured to be helped by catastrophic coverage were the ones who killed it. Not surprisingly, the politicians caught in this politically misguided policy imbroglio were furious at the analysts. It seemed as if the analysts had no idea what real people actually wanted or thought, but just used abstract theory as a guide to what *should* be done, based on what a "rational" person *should* want.

In the next section, we will begin to consider the process of analyzing policy. To the outsider, used to the political system of simplifying and moving on, policy analysis may seem quite foreign. I will present an abstract version of the process first, and then will consider some examples.

The Process of Policy Analysis

Policy analysis is the process of assessing, and deciding among, alternatives based on their usefulness in satisfying one or more goals or values. Generally, the policy recommendation is made by one person, a decision is made by another entity, and enforcement of the policy actually chosen is left to yet a third person or group.

For the sake of clarity, let's consider an example. Suppose you are a policy analyst for a governor of a state in the United States. Your state has a problem: There are nearly twice as many prisoners as there are normal beds in the state penitentiaries. Until now, the situation has been handled by putting in temporary cots, so that prison rooms designed for two inmates hold three, or even four, people. But that has to change: A federal court has ordered that prison overcrowding in your state has to be reduced within thirty days.

The governor asked you to do an analysis, and make recommendations. It is useful to think of the process of analysis as having five stages.[3]

1. Problem formulation
2. Selection of criteria
3. Comparison of alternatives and selection of the policy
4. Consideration of political and organizational constraints
5. Implementation and evaluation of the program

Let's consider each stage briefly.

Problem Formulation

The analyst must create a statement of the policy problem to be addressed. The "problem formulation" often includes, at least implicitly, a theoretical model of causation. This stage includes the listing of available alternatives. One important task for the analyst is the redefinition, or *creative* restatement,[4] of the problem in such a way that new alternatives become available. Often, the context that gives rise to the analysis is much broader than the analytical problem formulation, if the analyst is doing her job right.

In our prison-overcrowding example, the *context* is simply too many prisoners per room. But the *problem formulation* may be elusive, and controversial. Are there too few prisons? If so, more should be built. Are there too many prisoners? If so, programs are needed to improve economic opportunities, educate underprivileged children, and rehabilitate prisoners to reduce recidivism. There are other possibilities, of course, including a mismatch of sentencing practices and type of crime, or prisons that are too comfortable and attractive to provide deterrence.

The point is that the analyst has to be careful. By saying, "The problem is that [statement]", some alternatives are advantaged, others impaired, and still others ruled out completely. Psychologists call this "framing," and it has been shown that the way one frames the question may determine the type of answer you get. Later, we will consider the difference between objective analysis and advocacy; for now, just remember that the problem formulation, or the way the policy is conceived or framed by the analyst, has a lot to do with the direction the analysis takes.

Selection of Criteria

"Criteria" are the bases for judging or choosing. The word comes from the Greek *krites*, a judge. The way you have selected to frame the problem immediately suggests some alternative solutions. Criteria are the premises for analysis, for saying that one alternative is better than another. The difficulty, of course, is that one alternative may be superior in satisfying one criterion, but another alternative may be better in other ways. Consequently, in the criteria stage the analyst must first specify the list of criteria that are relevant, and then define the trade-offs, or relative importance, of those criteria.

This is in many ways an ethical problem, rather than a purely analytic one. Criteria, and their relative importance, are statements about the ethical worldview of the analyst, or of the society the analyst serves. There have been many attempts to guide analysts in choosing criteria. The clearest, yet most useful, guidelines come from MacRae (1993), and MacRae and Whittington (1997). They argue that criteria should themselves satisfy five meta-criteria, which can be paraphrased as follows:

- Criteria should focus on *ends*, not *means*.
- Each criterion should be stated clearly and precisely enough to imply a *measure* for how well it is satisfied by an alternative.
- All else being equal, a set of criteria is better if *trade-offs* can be *quantified*.
- The set of criteria should be *complete*, accounting for all the concerns of all citizens.
- Criteria should address separate aspects of the policy problem, so that satisfaction of each criterion is *mutually exclusive*.

To continue our example of prison overcrowding, imagine that we select four criteria:

cost (where less is better, all else equal)
justice (the sense that the incarcerated person is neither mistreated nor coddled, but is being appropriately punished)
space (number of prison beds freed up by the policy choice)
recidivism (fewer repeat offenders is better)

Comparison of Alternatives and Selection of the Policy

The notion of alternatives implies, by definition, at least two courses of action. In terms of our example, we could:

- Build more prisons
- Rent prison space from a nearby state
- Slate "nonviolent" offenders for early release after they have finished a "rehabilitation and job placement" program

This conception of alternatives implies that the choices must be mutually exclusive: the selection of one course of action rules out the alternatives. One immediate difficulty with this idea of discrete choice is that the actual choice could be some *combination* of these policies. For example, we could build one small new prison, rent a little prison space, and focus most of our attention on the rehabilitation program.

The choice among alternatives (whether the choice is mutually exclusive, or some combination) requires some assumptions about the trade-offs between criteria. No question about it, this is the hard part. The framing of the problem, identification of alternatives, and choice of criteria are all functions that trained analysts can handle. But the choice of one alternative, one policy, requires a knowledge of the values of the polity. Trade-offs now have to be explicit, because it often happens that one alternative does well on one criterion, but some other alternative is preferable on other grounds. How can we know how much better is enough?

There is no magic answer, but a good place to start is the "criteria-alternatives matrix,"[5] or CAM. As you can see in Table 1.1, this matrix is a way of organizing the process of analysis. The CAM sets up a comparison of the performance of alternatives in satisfying different criteria. Alternatives are *columns*, and criteria are *rows*.

You need to find a lot of information to fill out the criteria-alternatives matrix. Each box, or "cell," contains a value describing the performance of that alternative (the *column* in the matrix) for the particular criterion (the *row* in the matrix). For example, the cell in the third row and second column in Table 1.1 is the number of prison beds made immediately available for the alternative "rent prison space from other states." You would need to find out exactly how many beds could be rented, and put the number in this cell. Then you would put the cost for the rental option in the cell for *that* information: row 1, column 2.

In general, the cells in any criteria-alternatives matrix contain entries measured at one of three levels of precision: **categorical**, **ordinal**, and **interval ratio**. It is useful to consider just what each of these levels of precision in measurement implies.

TABLE 1.1
Criteria/Alternatives Matrix (CAM) for Problem of Prison Overcrowding

Criteria	Alternatives		
	Build More Prisons	*Rent Prison Space from Other States*	*Early Release/ Rehabilitation*
Cost	?	?	?
Justice	?	?	?
Prison Beds Freed Up Immediately	?	?	?
Recidivism	?	?	?

- *Categorical measures.* Values fall into categories, such as "male" and "female," or "rural" and "urban." A CAM analysis is generally not possible with categorical-level measures, because there is (by definition) no basis for saying one category is better than another. You need to be careful, because sometimes categorical measures look like numbers (e.g., rural = 1, suburban = 2, small city = 3, large city = 4). Not so; these numbers are really just names, or shorthand for the categories. You can't say a large city "4" is really four times as much of anything as a rural "1," yet that is what the numbers seem to say.
- *Ordinal measures.* Values can be ranked from worst to best. However, statements about the size of the difference between alternatives cannot be made. For example, if a group of experts rank one technology for waste disposal as best, you might assign it a 10. The second best gets a 9, and so on. CAM analysis is possible with ordered, or ordinal, measures, but it can be deceptive. Is a 10 twice

as good as a 5, or five times as good as a 2? No; all we know is that a 10 is better.

- *Interval/ratio measures.* Values have specific, numeric meanings. In particular, the difference (for example) between 20 and 21 is the same (has the same analytic meaning) as the difference between 167 and 168. Further, for ratio measures, the zero point is meaningful, so that if the variable changes from 10 to 11 we can say the level of the concept being measured increased by 10 percent.[6]

To compare, you have to be able to aggregate the good and bad aspects of each alternative, and determine which is best overall. If there are *n* different criteria, what you are looking for is the alternative with the highest rating on the criteria, given the relative importance you have assigned those criteria. In equation form, using *i* to represent an arbitrary criterion, that goes something like this:

$$Rating = \sum_{i=1}^{n} a_i V_i = a_1 V_1 + a_2 V_2 + \ldots a_n V_n \tag{1}$$

where:

a terms are weights of the alternatives. They give the relative importance of the criteria in the decision process. That is, if $a_2 = 0$, then criterion 2 is not important. If $a_7 < 0$, then the seventh criterion is a "bad" in the decision. An example of such a criterion would be cost: usually, more cost means the alternative is less preferred. If $a_3 > 0$, then criterion 3 is a "good." In our example, justice would be such a criterion.

V terms are the values of the alternatives measured by satisfaction of the criteria. It is worth saying again: these values must have some mathematical meaning in order for the CAM approach to work. Categorical values are not "measures;" they may be important, but they cannot be shoehorned into this approach. Don't do it, and don't let other people do it in your presence!

To clarify the abstract content of equation (1), let's go back to our prison overcrowding example. Suppose you had filled in Table 1.1 as shown in Table 1.2, using estimates from published studies from other states, interviews with experts, and some of your own educated "guesstimates."

TABLE 1.2
Completed CAM for Problem of Prison Overcrowding

Criteria	Build More Prisons	*Alternatives* Rent Prison Space from Other States	Early Release/ Rehabilitation
Cost	$105 million	$29 million/year	$25 million/year
Justice	Best (3)	Poor (1)	Moderate (2)
Prison Beds Freed Up Immediately	None	2,000	5,000
Recidivism	4%	4%	11%

Now, before you can continue, you have to assign weights to the criteria. You could assign equal weights (e.g., a_i = 0.25 for all four criteria, though with a negative sign for "cost"). You could assign all weight to one criterion ("space" is the only concern, so that a_{space} = 1, and all the other weights are zero). But what is the *right* thing to do?

This is not a technical question, but an ethical one. For decisions to be accepted as legitimate (at least in democracies), the idea of trade-offs needs to capture the relative weights placed on the criteria by the public. The dilemma of choosing a set of weights is a problem of democracy, or "social choice," which will be considered at length in chapter 6. For now, I will simply point out that the choice of weights in the CAM is almost exactly the same problem as the use of a voting procedure to select policies. In both cases, information is required about voter preferences and values. This information might be acquired through surveys, public meetings, voting, and so on, but it has to come from somewhere.

Suppose you decide on equal weights. Then the results of your analysis might look like the first panel in Table 1.3. Note that all the "ratings" are negative, because cost is large, and has a negative weight (i.e., more costs are bad). But we can still judge the highest rating: it is for the "early release" program. Early release is not very costly (at least in terms of the governor's budget!), and frees up lots

TABLE 1.3
Total Rating Comparison for Alternative
in Prison Bed Example

Alternative	Rating (Equal Weights)
Build More Prisons	$Rating = -.25 \times 105 + .25 \times 3 + .25 \times 0 - .25 \times 4 = -26.5$
Rent Prison Space	$Rating = -.25 \times 29 + .25 \times 1 + .25 \times 2 - .25 \times 4 = -7.5$
Early Release	$Rating = .25 \times 25 + .25 \times 2 = .25 \times 5 - .25 \times 11 = -7.25*$

Alternative	Rating (40% on Recidivism)
Build More Prisons	$Rating = -.20 \times 105 + .20 \times 3 + .20 \times 0 - .4 \times 4 = -22$
Rent Prison Space	$Rating = -.20 \times 29 + .20 \times 1 + .20 \times 2 - .4 \times 4 = -6.8*$
Early Release	$Rating = -.20 \times 29 + .20 \times 1 + .20 \times 2 + -.4 \times 4 = -8$

Note: *implies highest rating, given weights.

of beds immediately. There are recidivism problems, of course (in this example, nearly three times as high as the other alternatives), but it looks like early release is the way to go. You can go to the governor now, and make your recommendation.

Or can you? Recidivism is a real problem; maybe you should give it more weight in the decision analysis. How about if we try a weight of 40 percent on recidivism, and 20 percent each on the other criteria? That set of weights, [.2, .2, .2, .4], is not so different from the "equal weights" [.25, .25, .25, .25] used earlier. Disturbingly, we get a different answer. "Rent prison space" is now the best alternative, by quite a bit.

Let's make some observations about the choice of weights.

1. *The decision about the best alternative may depend on the choice of weights on the criteria.* To the extent that this is true (and it always is, in any decision process where the answer is not so obvious that analysis is a waste of time), policy analysis using the CAM is weak. More precisely, you are only as sure about your conclusion as you are about the weight assignments. You had better have good reasons for choosing one set of weights over another.

2. *The units of the measures are extremely important.* Without warning you, I have used "millions" as the units for costs, "thousands" as the units for beds, an ordinal scale for "justice,"

and "percentages" as the units for recidivism. This amounts to a weighting scheme, all by itself! For example, notice that the "justice" scale only can change 2 units, as it goes from 3 ("best") to 1 ("poor"). That means that, *in terms of units,* justice "counts" (at most!) as much as a $2 million difference in costs. The implied substantive justice difference between "best" and "poor" may be large, but a $2 million cost difference is relatively small. Why? Why should they count the same? They shouldn't! We should have been more careful to standardize units, so that the criteria are counted on a more equal basis. The problem is that it is not clear how to "standardize," *unless we know the weights!*

3. *The CAM approach is much better conceived as a means of organizing a decision, rather than being a decision itself.* The discipline imposed by laying out alternatives, coming up with criteria, and then deciding on weights to describe the trade-offs among criteria, is very useful. But if we had stopped after the first round of measurement in Table 3.1, we would have been making a mistake.

I don't mean to be too negative in my description of the CAM approach, because it really is useful. Often, analysts use something like the procedure I have discussed without calling it a "criteria-alternatives" matrix, or even realizing they are doing a formalized analysis at all. The main value of writing down the matrix, and thinking hard about the cell contents, is that one can identify the sensitivity of the "answer" the analyst comes up to small changes in assumptions, or to difficulties in quantification. Further, if you can get good, accurate measures of the levels of satisfaction of the criteria for each alternative, the CAM approach is a genuinely scientific approach to decision analysis. I have seen groups of people, ranging from faculty deciding on curriculum reforms to a collection of scientists debating technical aspects of hazardous waste reform, change their minds about the best course of action after doing a CAM analysis. It really works, because of the structure it imposes on the decision process, and the discipline it imposes on the analyst to reveal and justify assumptions about trade-offs in values.

Consideration of Political and Organizational Constraints

Once the analyst has decided on a policy recommendation, two kinds of "constraints" come into play. These constraints have to do with the acceptability of the policy to other participants in the process. The first is *political feasibility*; will *elected* officials *vote for* the proposal and make it law? The second is *organizational feasibility*: will *appointed* officials support the law and *implement* it in a way that makes its success possible?

It is tempting to merge stage 4 into stage 3, adding political and organizational feasibility as new criteria in the criteria-alternative matrix. That would be a mistake, however, for two reasons. First, these are not criteria for judgment, in the sense that more or less of the quality is a "good" for the policy. Remember: policy analysis starts with a benchmark for the best policy, and then considers how real policy may be different. Political and organizational feasibility are *constraints*, not criteria. If the legislature, city council, or other relevant elected body won't convert the policy proposal into law, then it is time to stick a fork in the thing: it's done! Likewise, bureaucrats charged with implementing the policy are fully capable of foiling an otherwise well-designed initiative, either by a lack of enthusiasm or by actual sabotage.[7]

Second, the analyst generally cannot get accurate information on the likely reaction to a proposal until it is proposed. Predicting the reaction of elected officials, or bureaucrats, to a proposed policy is at best an inexact science. As we will see in chapter 6, there is some basis for predicting how legislators may vote, but lots of things can happen to change the mind of policy makers.

In general, there is only one way to ensure that politicians and bureaucrats are more likely to favor, or at least not oppose, a policy. It seems obvious, but it is often overlooked: *Get them involved from the beginning.* There are at least two places where their participation is most important: at the stage of framing the problem, and at the stage of selecting alternatives. Since politicians and bureaucrats have different kinds of veto power over many policies, it is important to get their views on each alternative before you go too far down the road toward selecting that alternative.

For example, if one of your alternatives is to eliminate a cabinet-level agency, and transfer the associated budget to another agency, you have to recognize that you are activating powerful forces whose interest is in maintaining the status quo. You will need to anticipate their response, and offer the affected employees, managers, interest groups, and their elected supporters in Congress some compensation. It doesn't matter if your policy is the "right thing to do" from an analytic perspective, because the costs of transition to your ideal policy will be all the affected parties can see.

On the other hand, even if you do everything right, you may run afoul of the feasibility constraints. Even if you have asked questions, invited comment, and thought everyone had said they would support you, when the policy proposal is actually introduced, it is as if you are starting over. Carefully crafted compromises, and detailed, interdependent portions of the proposal may be selectively changed, modified completely, or reworded in such a way that your goals for reform are no longer met. Once the proposal leaves the analyst's desk, it is a whole new world.

Consider the misadventures of the Clinton administration with "health care reform." Health care and the economy had been the two central issues of the 1992 U.S. presidential election. After the election, the administration began a series of meetings focused on developing a proposal for reform. The goals of the reform effort were complex, and the kind of information necessary for evaluating alternatives was just not available. The first lady, Hillary Rodham Clinton, was appointed by the president to head the so-called Health Care Reform Task Force, a large group of analysts and departmental representatives with a stake in the outcome of the reform process. Another central figure in the process of developing a policy proposal was Ira Magaziner, a Rhodes Scholar turned business consultant.

What happened over the next eighteen months was a case study in how *not* to do policy analysis. Listen to Woodward's (1995) description, which is worth quoting at length.

> Magaziner's strategy on health care reform had been to run two tracks of briefings. First, he held a series of briefings attended by [the entire Task Force]. For the second track, Magaziner met with just the president and Hillary alone. . . . One day at one of the larger group meetings on the fourth floor of the Old Executive Office Building, Bob Boorstin [another staff member] was summoned away . . . Magaziner said not to worry. The meeting was not that significant. [Magaziner] was having regular private, confidential meetings with the Clintons. . . . A regular series of secret meetings was explosive, Boorstin felt. "If they find out, you're a dead man. You're digging your own grave. Not only will the policy be dead, but it will be dead for less than a good reason. It will be because these people [from eight different federal agencies, all affected by health care reform] feel cut out." Magaziner ignored Boorstin's warning. The private briefings for the Clintons continued. (pp. 188–89)
>
> [In a meeting a year later, in August, 1994, Treasury Secretary Lloyd Bentson] was disturbed that health had not been subjected to the collegial deliberative process of the economic plan [now passed into law, in

modified form], but was handled back channel with Magaziner trying to keep all the information to himself. He argued that the resulting plan was not politically attainable in Congress . . . Magaziner felt that by proposing a plan that was left of center, Clinton would eventually win something in the center. But Magaziner did not fully grasp that the health plan, *no matter how wonderfully configured or academically sound,* would get dropped in the same caldron as the economic plan. The Congress, the media, and the interest groups would all have their spoons in the brew stirring at his creation. . . . (pp. 372–73, emphasis mine).

[President Clinton said "I am] like the captain of a ship," grasping for the metaphor of a very old ship with oars. "That is, I can steer it, but a storm can still come up and sink it. *And the people that are supposed to be rowing can refuse to row. . . .*" In the fall of 1994 . . . Congress killed any and all proposed health care reform—no compromise, no half measures, none of the meagerest changes. *Nearly two years of work went down the legislative drain. . . . Clinton, his wife and Magaziner had designed an unwieldy monster of a plan. . . .* (p. 389, p. 398, emphasis mine)

In devising a health care proposal, Magaziner seemed to believe that there were only three steps in the policy process, ending with the proposal itself. By denying a role in the process to others with a stake in the outcome, he had doomed the whole enterprise. The Clintons, by allowing an analyst to dominate the process of drafting the proposal, seemed to forget that all policies eventually have to satisfy the legislature who must vote on the program, and the bureaucrats who must implement the program. The key to success (and I am not saying it's easy!) is to get information about political and organizational feasibility built into the proposal itself.

Implementation and Evaluation of the Program

After the program is passed by the legislature and implemented by the bureaucratic agency, it can be evaluated. MacRae and Wilde (1985, pp. 266–68) point out that there are three types of evaluation built into social processes:

1. *Market accountability.* Citizens decide whether they like the goods and services provided by firms. Firms that fail the "market test" (i.e., do not provide quality service, deliver inferior quality goods, or charge exorbitant prices) will not survive, as citizens express their dissatisfaction by taking their dollars elsewhere. Market accountability is an evaluation by many different

citizens, but it affects the firm by giving information on the firm's performance. Bad products mean bankruptcy, good products mean profits. Obviously, market accountability has significant subjective elements, because it relies on the aggregation of the tastes of consumers choosing products.

2. *Political accountability.* Citizens decide whether they like a particular policy or activity. If citizens oppose the policy, they can use "direct" democracy (such as a referendum) or "indirect" democracy (vote in elections where representatives are chosen) to express this opposition. If enough (often, but not always, a majority of the citizens) oppose a policy, it will be changed. Political accountability may be either decentralized (if primarily a grassroots, citizen-led phenomenon) or centralized (if organized by the president, or by leaders of the legislature). Furthermore, it can be just as subjective as market accountability, as voters decide whether they like or don't like a policy. That is, the reasons why a voter doesn't like a policy don't matter: if enough oppose the policy, for whatever reason, the policy is dead.

3. *Expert analysis.* Experts use some objective, scientifically grounded, set of criteria to decide if the policy or activity is a success. Many of the tools we will consider later in this book, such as cost-benefit analysis, discounting to account for time, and indirect valuation, are intellectual devices for analysis by experts. However, unlike both market accountability and political accountability, expert analysis purports to be objective. It may be centralized, in a "blue ribbon" panel or commission. Or it can be decentralized, as experts debate policy consequences in refereed professional journals and at conferences.

Consider how these three types of social accountability would work in an everyday example. Are "Beanie Babies"[8] a good product?

- Do Beanies pass the market test? You bet they do! It has been estimated that Ty Inc. has grossed over $600 million since it started manufacturing and selling Beanie Babies. Lots of people love Beanie Babies, so much so that a substantial secondary market has developed, in which buying and selling Beanies has become a highly speculative business.
- Do Beanie Babies pass the test of political accountability? Apparently. We could outlaw them, just as we outlaw heroin or other ad-

dictive drugs. But we haven't (though some parents I know have
been heard to mutter support for prohibition after waiting in line
for hours for some new little beansack with arms). Interestingly,
there are import restrictions on Beanies, created by Ty, Inc., and
enforced by the U.S Customs Service.[9]
• Would Beanie Babies pass an expert analysis? That is, do Beanies
serve a social purpose? Are Beanie Babies, in the final analysis, the
best use of the resources employed in this way? Should Ty be allowed to manufacture, and people be allowed to purchase, this
product? What are the alternatives? What criteria should be established to judge the alternatives? How would we evaluate the performance of the status quo (i.e., Beanies are legal), compared to
other alternatives?

Now, it should be pointed out immediately that there has been no
"Ban Beanies!" movement among policy experts. Further, if there
were, such a recommendation would clearly fail the political accountability criterion above (i.e., the experts would be overruled by politicians, for fear of being trampled to death by waves of Beanie-loving
moppets).

But we evaluate things all the time, by some combination of market test, political test, and expert analysis. Most of the time, we do
this without giving it much thought, but sometimes the way we evaluate matters, because we apply different criteria. The choice not to
evaluate using expert analysis is tantamount to selecting the status
quo (usually the market outcome), or risking subjective and perhaps
poorly informed change (resulting from the vagaries of democratic
politics). Still, I will use "evaluation" in the narrower sense of expert
analysis, because that is the usual sense of the word in the policy
analysis literature.

Evaluation thus is a different process from the policy analysis performed in problem formulation, selection of criteria, and comparison
of alternatives. Evaluation entails an analysis of whether the *program
or policy that was implemented* has achieved its stated goals. The analyst may use some of the same information, and ask some of the
same questions, as in the original analysis, but in evaluation the set
of alternatives, and the scope for creative problem redefinition, are
sharply circumscribed.

There have been many descriptions of "types" of evaluation within
the policy analysis literature. The one presented here is adapted from
the discussions of Trisco and League (1978) and Bingham and Fel-

binger (1989).[10] Before giving the general format for an evaluation, it is useful to offer a qualification: There are many types of programs, and many dimensions of programs that can be evaluated. You have to know what kind of evaluation you are performing if you are going to complete the job successfully. To clarify these differences, consider Trisco and League's typology of "levels of evaluation," which have to do with the types of objectives being evaluated:

Types of Evaluations
Purely formal evaluation: monitoring daily or routine tasks. Are contracts met? Are budgets balanced? Are procedures followed? An answer of "yes" doesn't mean that the program is a good one, but "no" almost certainly means trouble.
Client satisfaction evaluation: performance of primary functions. Do employees understand who is the client, or customer, for the program? Are clients satisfied? Again, passing this type of evaluation is not necessarily a sign that the program is successful, but failing this test is a bad sign.
Outcomes checklist: satisfaction of a list of measurable desired outcomes. How many of the program's objectives have been met?
Expense and effectiveness: cost-benefit analysis, measuring both the costs and impact of the program. Was the program cost effective? What would have happened to the target population in the absence of the program?
Long-term consequences: impact on the core problem, rather than the symptoms alone. Has the program, in the long run, achieved its goals of curing the social problem it was designed to address? If the cure was not achieved, is the program worth continuing? Notice that a program might "pass" most of the other types of evaluation, yet still be found wanting in the long run.

All of these types of evaluation are important, but the first three are relatively straightforward to carry out. These evaluations (formal rules, client satisfaction, and outcomes checklist) can be accomplished by the careful collection of data using surveys and interviews, and a study of the rules and procedures that are supposed to govern the program's functioning.

It is with the fourth and fifth types of evaluations (cost-benefit analysis, and the long-term evaluation of program effectiveness) that we will be concerned later in this book. These are the types of evaluation where analysis, of both the theoretical and statistical types, is most important. And it is for these types of analysis that the following process of evaluation, originated by MacRae and Wilde (1985), is most appropriate.

Process of Evaluation
1. Identify the goals and objectives of the program or policy in a way that makes measurement, and evaluation, possible.
2. Construct an analytic model of what the policy or program is expected to accomplish. This model will embody a set of theoretical propositions about means-end relationships, based on the accumulation of knowledge from research on the subject.
3. Develop a research design capable of distinguishing (a) what is expected from the program (*goal*), (b) what is actually observed (*data*), and (c) the range of outcomes that might be observed if the variation of outcomes is simply random, or unaffected by the policy (*null hypothesis*).
4. Collect the data, or actual measurements that describe the phenomena of interest.
5. Analyze and interpret the results. In particular, do the data imply that actual performance is at or above the goal? For example, suppose the goal was the improvement in some measurable indicator (such as prison recidivism). Is there a difference observable in the data? Is this difference statistically significant, in the sense that it is unlikely to have been generated by chance variation?

Review of the Process of Analysis

At the beginning of this section, I claimed that the process of analysis can usefully be divided into five parts:

1. Problem formulation
2. Selection of criteria
3. Comparison of alternatives
4. Consideration of political and organizational constraints
5. Evaluation

To illustrate the first three steps, we considered a specific example, a decision about making a recommendation to your boss, the governor of a state facing a court order to make its prisons less crowded. The political and organizational constraints may simply overwhelm any policy recommendation you make, of course. For example, if a court order says that the prisons have to be less crowded by *tomorrow*, then early release might be your only option. You would have to stay up all night coming up with criteria for the classes of criminals, or types of crimes, for which release would likely result in the least damage (on average) to the state's citizens. And you won't be able to perform the fifth step, "evaluation," until enough time has passed to decide what the effects of your decision have been.

Most of the rest of this book will be devoted to elaborating parts of this process of analysis and evaluation. Don't worry if portions seem unclear now; this chapter has served only to give an overview of what will be developed at length in later chapters. This chapter will close with a look at the profession of policy analysis in the broader context of expert advice to decision makers generally.

Policy Analysis as Part of a Broader Profession: Expert Advice on Policy

Because policy can be analyzed in many ways, from a variety of theoretical and ethical perspectives, it is useful to consider policy analysis in terms of the results it is designed to generate: advice to decision makers on policy. In some cases the experts may themselves be decision makers, but the two functions can be separated analytically.[11]

Experts who advise policy makers are part of a broader community. This aspect involves research regarding the design of policy alternatives and the decision to choose one among several possible alternatives. Broadly construed, "advice" includes both policy-relevant research (theory about causal connections; empirical research about the magnitudes of the cell entries in a particular CAM), and research designed to improve the way policy is designed. Improvements in policy design might focus on its ethical or procedural basis (metapolicy analysis), or on specific institutional rules such as voting.

Consequently, expert advice on policy could encompass both a political scientist's research on committee decision-making and an environmental scientist's research on the implications of lead levels in sumac leaves on a gradient away from an interstate highway. In other words, "expertise" is difficult to define, because the term is used in many ways. The discussion given by MacRae and Whittington (1997) may be the most useful for present purposes.

The quality of "expertness" here refers to a claim by a specially trained group to contribute knowledge or advice. An expert group's claim of authority can be based both on their collective training and on group members' quality control over one another's work. Disciplinary definitions of expertise are not, however, transferred to expert advice on policy because most policy problems extend beyond the domain of any one discipline. Moreover, the extension of analytic capacity to citizens and the media can blur the boundaries of "expertise." (MacRae and Whittington, 1997, p. 12)

In this view, then, an "expert" is someone whose advice is likely (at least on average) to improve the outcomes of a policy choice, from the perspective of the society. This is a much broader definition than would be implied in a discussion of "policy analysis" as conceived in this book. In the broader sense MacRae and Whittington intend, an expert is anyone who has something useful to say, because of their high level of training or experience.

The process of policy analysis is primarily the gathering of data and the measurement of various values achieved by different alternatives. Policy analysis ideally is performed when a problem is first recognized, but more commonly is done only when the problem becomes acute. Expert advice, in the broadest sense, may be sought at any time, and may be performed quite independently from any specific "problem" or policy concern. Ideally, expert advice assists decision makers by providing courses of action that prevent the more crisis-oriented kind of policy analysis from ever happening!

Looking Ahead

The rest of the book develops and extends the themes we have glimpsed in this first chapter. Chapter 2 describes some sources of conflict between the three institutional sources of accountability already described: markets, politics, and expert analysis. The next section examines the performance of each of these institutions separately. Chapters 3 and 4 consider the performance, and potential failures, of markets. Chapter 5 outlines the difficulties, and advantages, of focusing on expertise as a basis for policy decisions. Chapter 6 is a brief introduction to the performance of governments and the limits of collective choice.

We then move to the nuts and bolts of how policy analysis is practiced. The "welfare economics paradigm," in many ways the methodological center of policy analysis, is the subject of chapter 7. Chapter 8 identifies three conflicting metacriteria in the choice of regulatory form: efficiency, equity, and politics. Chapters 9, 10, and 11 introduce the concept of cost-benefit analysis. After a description of discounting for risk (in chapter 9) and discounting for the rate of time preference (in chapter 10), examples and techniques of cost-benefit analysis are presented in chapter 11. Chapter 12 then offers some caveats, and other perspectives, on cost-benefit analysis in particular and policy analysis in general.

As I noted above, this introduction will hardly make you an expert in policy analysis. But for students interested in finding out what policy analysis really is, or for experts in other fields who need to learn how policy analysis is performed, this book will prove very useful. And I promise that we will try to have some fun along the way.

SUMMARY OF KEY CONCEPTS

PROCESS OF POLICY ANALYSIS

1. *Problem formulation* is the redefinition or restatement of the problem. The problem formulation often includes an implicit or explicit theory of causation.
2. Criteria are the bases for analysis and thus provide the means for comparing and evaluating alternative solutions. The *selection of criteria* has two stages. First, the analyst must specify the criteria. Second, the analyst must define the relative importance of the specified criteria.
3. After the problem has been formulated and the criteria have been chosen, the policy analyst must perform a *comparison of the alternatives.* The policy alternatives are evaluated using the criteria and the relative importance of those criteria. The *selection of policy* is made after the alternatives have been compared.
4. Policy analysts must consider the *political and organizational constraints* that affect the acceptability of the selected policy. Policy analysts must ask whether elected officials will adopt the policy and whether appointed officials will implement it.
5. *Implementation and evaluation of the program* is the final stage in the policy analysis process. This stage requires assessing whether

the policy recommendation obtained in the first four steps has achieved the stated goals. There are three types of evaluation: *market accountability*, *political accountability*, and *expert analysis*.

6. *Market accountability* is the process by which citizens evaluate firms by purchasing or not purchasing a firm's products.

7. *Political accountability* is the process by which political actors—voters, interests groups, or political leaders—evaluate a policy or program by using their political power, such as the vote.

8. *Expert analysis* is the evaluation of a policy or program by a set of scientifically grounded criteria. Expert analysis is often claimed to be objective.

CRITERIA-ALTERNATIVES MATRIX

9. The *criteria-alternatives matrix* (*CAM*) is a convenient method for comparing the performance of different policies.

10. The rows of CAM are the alternatives. The columns of CAM are the criteria.

LEVELS OF MEASUREMENT

11. A *categorical* measure uses numbers to classify different kinds or types of objects. The numerical values assigned to each category do not have a substantive interpretation.

12. An *ordinal* measure utilizes values to rank objects. Although an ordinal measure can indicate whether one object is better than another object, it does not indicate the degree to which one object is better or worse than another object.

13. An *interval* or *ratio* measure utilizes values to rank objects and (unlike an ordinal measure) indicates the degree to which one object is better or worse than another object.

TYPES OF EVALUATIONS

14. A *formal* evaluation of a program entails the monitoring of routine tasks.

15. A *client satisfaction* evaluation requires that the agents are aware

of whom the relevant customers or clients and assessing whether the clients are satisfied.

16. An *outcomes checklist* is a list of outcomes that are desirable and measurable.

17. An *expense and effectiveness* evaluation assesses the benefit of a program using cost-benefit analysis. This process involves assessing the welfare of the target population with and without the program.

18. Evaluating the *long-term consequences* involves assessing the impact of a program on the core problem and not just the symptoms of the problem.

EXPERT ADVICE TO POLICY MAKERS

19. An *expert* is someone who may improve the welfare of society by providing advice on policy choice.

20. Expert policy analysis is often used for curing problems but can also help prevent problems before they develop.

PROBLEMS AND QUESTIONS

1. Choose a problem that concerns policy makers. State the problem *situation* (for example, "Our prisons are overcrowded") clearly, and then give at least three different problem *formulations* (for example, "Criminals don't fear imprisonment enough," or "Underprivileged people have no economic opportunities, and so turn to crime." Notice that the problem situation simply claims that we have a problem, while the problem formulation makes an implicit argument about why we have a problem. How would you go about deciding which of your problem formulations is better?

2. Choose a problem that policy makers have attempted to solve in the past. Discuss how the policy performed for the following types of evaluation: purely formal evaluation, client satisfaction evaluation, outcomes checklist, expense and effectiveness, and long-term consequences.

Criteria	Alternatives		
	A. Aaron's HMOs	Fly-Buy Knight's Health Service	Fee-for-Service (private)
Cost	$55/mo., no deductibles on hospital stay	$16/mo., $1,000 deductible on each hospital stay	No fixed fee; if you get sick, you pay $250 per office visit, plus $5,000 per hospital stay
Quality	Good	Moderate	Good
Waiting Period for Appointments	1 week	6 weeks	No waiting

3. Consider the following criteria-alternatives matrix, which describes the problem of which health plan to choose at your new job. Suppose you expect to get sick enough to require an office visit to the doctor two or three times per year, and have never had to go to the hospital. What additional information would you need to choose a health plan? In particular, what weights would you assign to the three criteria in the CAM? Choose a set of weights that would imply that A. Aaron is better, and another that makes Fee-for-Service preferable. Which set of weights seems more plausible to you? Why?

4. Give an example of a policy variable that can best be measured categorically. What sort of analysis can be performed on such variables? If we assigned each category a numerical value, what would this mean? For example, suppose you find the following information in a report: Trees in a public park were counted and recorded, with an oak tree assigned a 1, a pine tree assigned a 2, and a birch tree assigned a 3. The average value of all trees in the park is a 2.05; if you took a walk in that park, would you expect to see lots of pines, or no pines and lots of oaks and birches?

5. Consider the following news story (from "The Worst of 1998 Scandals," *Time*, December 21, 1998):

BEANIE BROUHAHA: U.S. Trade Representative Charlene Barshefsky sparked a mini-scandal when she returned from the presidential trip to China with a stash of 43 coveted Beanie Babies—42 more than U.S. Customs regulations [at that time] allow. Republicans bashed her, prompting Barshefsky to apologize to reporters, offering the defense: "I'm a mother." She surrendered the booty to authorities.

Ms. Barshefsky was clearly trying to influence the criteria that observers use to evaluate her action. As an official representative of the U.S. government, charged with negotiating trade and customs agreements, and certainly knowledgeable of the law, her action is hard to defend. But as a parent, she did something that many parents would have tried to do, if their child loves Beanies. This difficulty in deciding which criteria to apply, and how to weigh them, is typical of policy analysis problems, especially those involving ethical dilemmas. Do a policy analysis of the Barshefsky case from the U.S. government's perspective. What are the alternatives for official government reaction? What are the criteria for evaluating those alternatives, and how should they be weighted?

TAKE IT TO THE NET!

Go to: http://www.wwnorton.com/college/polisci/analyzingpolicy for additional problems, data sets, and course materials.

NOTES

1. William Fulbright, in a speech in the U.S. Senate, March 27, 1964.
2. William Shakespeare *King Henry V*, act I, scene 1.
3. Several scholars have outlined the process of policy analysis in these terms. For example, see MacRae and Wilde (1985, pp. 7–11); MacRae and Whittington (1997, p. 13); Stokey and Zeckhauser (1978, pp. 5–6).
4. Wildavsky (1979, p. 386) calls this step "problem crafting." MacRae and Whittington (1997), chaps. 2 and 3, present the most complete discussion of the importance of this step in policy analysis.
5. The origin of the criteria-alternatives matrix is shrouded in mystery; I won't pretend to take a definitive position on who used it first, or best, in this context. However, it is orthodox (see, for example, Weimer and Vining, 1992, p. 228; or MacRae and Whittington, 1997, p. 25n) to credit Easton (1973), Lichfield, Kettle, and Whitbread (1975), Zeleny (1982), Quade (1982), or Patton and Sawicki (1986) with independently conceiving, or advancing, the technique. I am partial, on sentimental grounds, toward the account of Quade (1982), who credits Bruce Goeller, an employee at the Rand Corporation in the early 1970s, with using just this sort of matrix to guide policy makers in identifying trade-offs and highlighting the importance of values. In my mind, the "criteria-alternatives" matrix will always be the *Goeller matrix*, because that is how I learned it.
6. Measures can be interval, but not ratio, scales. For example, temperature in degrees Fahrenheit is clearly an interval scale (the change from 35 to 36 degrees

represents the same change in energy as the change from 108 to 109 degrees). But you can't sensibly say that an increase from 50 to 60 degrees is a 20 percent increase in heat energy, because the zero point of the Fahrenheit scale is arbitrary.

7. The "sabotage" idea comes from Brehm and Gates (1997). The three categories Brehm and Gates talk about are "working, shirking, and sabotage."

8. "Beanie Babies" is a registered trademark of Ty Inc., Westmont, IL, U.S.A. The company is named after its CEO, "Ty" Warner.

9. According to a newspaper story (Albany, New York, *Times Union*, December 18, 1998, p. E4), U.S. Customs seized nearly six thousand Beanies which had been illegally imported from Canada, hidden in a large shipment of cocaine. Just kidding: the Beanies were hidden in boxes containing computer games. The current restriction is thirty Beanies, per person, per month. Like the "speculative bubble" in tulip bulbs in the seventeenth century, one wonders how long this can continue. There is certainly no discernible basis in value for the transactions. Kudos for finding this to my sharp-eyed friend Jay Hamilton, who has a taste for economic oddities.

10. In particular, while these four authors came up with the taxonomies I started with, they should not be blamed for my uses in adapting them.

11. The term "Expert advice on policy" choices comes from MacRae and Whittington (1997).

2

Deciding How to Decide: "Experts," "The People," and "The Market"

Government is a contrivance of human wisdom to provide for human wants. Men have a right that these wants should be provided for by this wisdom.
—Edmund Burke, *Reflections on the Revolution in France*

What should government do? What do you *want* it to do? What does everyone else want? Do the desires of the people have anything to do with the "wisdom" that Edmund Burke cites? How should we discover what is wise?

Policy analysis is mostly about the last question: *Which policy is wise?* That is, given a proposed policy, or a policy actually in operation, what tools of analysis can guide us in identifying and evaluating the effects of the policy? How can experts improve what government does? What policies can experts propose that will improve the functioning of markets?

Of course, policy analysis does not take place in isolation. Instead, there are many groups in the political process who think that *they* know what wisdom is. These groups may have little use for "experts" or "evidence." Furthermore, as was argued in the previous chapter, the market has a logic, and a kind of wisdom, of its own. These three kinds of wisdom—*markets, politics,* and *experts*—are constantly in conflict. This chapter considers the sources of this conflict, and how it affects the practice of policy analysis by experts.

To understand the nature of this conflict, it is useful to consider the overview depicted in Figure 2.1. To the casual observer, it often seems that policies are in conflict with one another, or that policy makers are just confused. This may be true, but the panoply of policies we see can only be understood as ways of reconciling the various conflicts depicted in the figure.

FIGURE 2.1
Tensions Among Sources of Wisdom, and Accountability

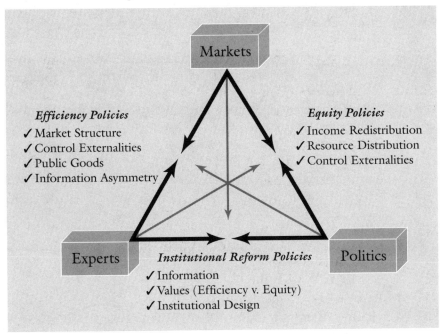

We can consider each pairwise conflict separately.

Experts versus markets. As we will see in later chapters, markets have an internal logic of operation. However, without management and support of experts, markets can fail, sometimes spectacularly. While there is debate about the extent of intervention required, there is substantial agreement about the categories of intervention that can improve market performance. Although in principle an expert could have any imaginable goal, in this chapter I will use the term "expert" to mean someone who has the goal of improving the functioning of politics or markets. What is meant by "improve" should become clear as we proceed, but I am intentionally leaving the goals of experts unspecified for now.

The categories of "market failure" are (1) "market structure" regulation, including management of natural *monopolies* (such as utilities), or antitrust policies to control concentrations of economic power; (2) policies to control *externalities*, such as pollution, through regulation or internalizing costs; (3) the systematic undersupply of *public goods*, due to the related problems of "free riding" (if privately provided) or "demand revelation" (if publicly provided, but financed by tax shares revealed by the individual); and (4) information problems, such as drug approvals or physician licensing, to reduce the costs of fraud or simple confusion.

The conflict between markets and experts will be analyzed in chapters 3 and 4. We can call policies to resolve these conflicts **efficiency policies**, because the guiding value is efficiency. While we will consider efficiency much more deeply later on, it is worth pointing out now that efficiency, for the policy analyst, is defined a little differently than you might expect. The dictionary[1] definition of "efficient" includes: "producing the desired effect or result with a minimum of effort, expense, or waste, working well; competent; able; capable." We will use the following definition, applying the concept of efficiency to the allocation of resources:

> *A particular matching of resources to uses is* **efficient** *if and only if there exists no better alternative allocation of those same resources.*

One obvious problem with this definition is that "better" is hard to specify precisely when there are two or more people involved. Suppose person 1 likes allocation A, and person 2 likes allocation B; which allocation is better for the pair? To "solve" this problem, we will simply ignore it: if there is disagreement, we will not be able to apply our concept of efficiency! More precisely, we will apply the so-called Pareto criterion, which requires unanimous agreement.

To see how the concept of efficiency based on the Pareto criterion would work, imagine that both allocation A and allocation B are technically feasible, in the sense that society can marshall the resources and apply them to the uses required in those two allocations. Now, suppose person 1 likes A, and then imagine that person 2 prefers A. That is, both agree that A is better than B.

Then forcing allocation B on our two-person society would be inefficient. What is meant by "inefficient" in this context is a lot like "wasteful." It would be wasteful to choose allocation B, because A is feasible and because both person 1 and person 2 prefer A. In this case, we say that A is "Pareto superior," or unanimously preferred, to B.

It is worth remembering, however, that efficiency is not the only consideration in expert management of markets. It is as if the analyst, in focusing on efficiency, is saying, "Ignoring politics, and for a given distribution of income . . ." That is, the distribution of gains is an important, but separate, question. As the dotted line in Figure 2.1 indicates, there may be substantial influence from political actors. In some sense, this influence is secondary, because it does not directly involve the management of markets. But political considerations may distort, or even rearrange, attempts by experts to manage markets.

Politics versus markets. The nature of politics in a democracy inevitably creates a tension between markets and collective decision-making. Markets are decentralized, operate with little central direction, and (most importantly) recognize power based on wealth. If you have more dollars than someone else, you have more "votes" in the market. Democratic politics operates on a much more egalitarian basis: each person gets only one vote, so that in the ballot box, at least, the poor person and the rich person have the same power.

Consequently, conflicts between politics and markets often take the form of disagreements over the outcomes of market processes, such as the redistribution of income or the use of publicly held resources such as national forests or fisheries. In a larger sense, since markets are the engines of growth in capitalist economies, but politics is the process by which property rights, tax rates, and social programs are decided, this conflict may be the most fundamental of all. There are those who portray the conflict between collective decision-making and market processes as a battle of good versus evil, but this view is simplistic. The fact is that both markets and politics provide us with a useful way of deciding; the conflict has to be managed, because it isn't going to go away. Attempts to solve this type of conflict can be called **equity policies**.

Another word for equity is "fairness." One meaning of "fair," of course, is average, as in the following scale you might find on a survey about food service on your campus:

The food at the cafeteria was _____.
Pick one: (a) poor (b) fair (c) very good

The other meaning is more complimentary: fair means honest, just, or unprejudiced. It is the second meaning that makes "fair" a synonym for "equitable," but the first meaning sometimes creeps in when we are thinking of politics. As we shall see, some people argue that the distribution of income implied by the use of markets is not fair, and requires political intervention. But the standard for fairness seems to be that we all get the average, with no deviations allowed. This conflict between the two notions of fairness as definitions for equity is a microcosm of the policy conflicts between politics and markets. People who favor markets tend to think that "equitable" and "equal" are unrelated concepts, at least for descriptions of the distribution of wealth among the members of society. People who favor political redress for the inequities they perceive in markets appear to think "equitable" and "equal" are very nearly the same word.

Once again, the source of wisdom not directly involved in the conflict may have an influence. Experts may try to affect the debate in equity policy by proposing solutions, or new problem definitions. We will consider expert analysis of equity policies in chapters 5, 6 and 7.

Experts versus politics. The *way* that we decide influences *what* is decided. As we will see later in this book, the particular "institutions" of choice, given public opinion, make a big difference. Consequently, experts often have advice for politicians on how the political process itself should be reformed. However, these reforms may not be popular with elected officials. The reason may seem obvious, but it is worth remembering: Whatever else politicians may differ on, they share *incumbency*. Incumbents were all elected under the current system, every one of them! Consequently, efforts at "improvement" by experts may be met with skepticism, or open hostility. Attempts to resolve this final type of conflict, between experts and popular politics, can be called **institutional reform policies**.

This brings us to the third dotted line in Figure 2.1, the one where markets may influence institutional reforms. Depending on your point of view, this influence can be fairly benign, or completely evil. The choice of institutional form for public choices is fundamental to the functioning of any democracy. Most importantly, whatever the institutions of collective choice, it is crucial that the public perceive the government selected by this process to be legitimate and fair.

Markets, by injecting considerations of wealth and economic power into political choice, may distort choices and threaten the legitimacy on which the whole system depends. In some ways, this problem is outside the scope of policy analysis, but we will consider it briefly in chapters 6, 8, and 9.

Let's summarize what has been said so far in this chapter. There are three bases of wisdom, or sources of accountability, in policy processes: markets, politics, and experts. In choosing the wise policy, there is inevitably conflict about which of these to follow. If the primary conflict is between markets and experts, the result is an *efficiency* policy. If the primary conflict is between markets and politics, the result is an *equity* policy. Finally, if the primary conflict is between expert and politics, the result is an *institutional reform* policy.

The State of Nature: No Policies

In the previous section, I argued that the context of a policy debate is the key to determining what kind of policy results. Different policies seem to be contradictory, but that is because they resulted from different conflicts. Efficiency policies often seem in conflict with equity policies; institutional reforms may seem to serve neither efficiency nor equity very well. Each policy arena has its own logic, where policies may seem rational given the problem the participants think they are trying to solve. From a larger perspective, of course, the whole thing may seem messy and incoherent.

Before we start thinking about trees, we should take a step back and think about the forest, and where it came from. This step back must take the form of a thought experiment: What would policy look like without any political, market, or expert context? Precisely *because* the context of policy analysis is so important, it is useful to imagine what things would be like if we *removed* context, at least as far as is possible.

In the United States, we live in a democracy, in an advanced industrial society, with well-developed norms of choice and an elaborate system of expertise in almost every field. Suppose that none of this were true. How would we make decisions?

Philosophers and social scientists call this idea the "state of nature," a thought experiment considering what life would be like without institutionalized markets, politics, or experts. Different people have had very different ideas about what "natural" life would be like. One of the most famous is Thomas Hobbes, who was not (to say the least) optimistic:

. . . the nature of War, consisteth not in actual fighting; but in the known disposition thereto, during all the time there is no assurance to the contrary. . . . Whatsoever therefore is consequent to a time of War, where every man is Enemy to every man; the same is consequent to the time, wherein men live without other security, than what their own strength, and their own invention shall furnish them withall. In such condition, there is no place for Industry; because the fruit thereof is uncertain; and consequently no Culture of the Earth; no Navigation, nor use of the commodities that may be imported by Sea; no commodious Buildings; no Instruments of moving, and removing such things as require much force; no Knowledge of the face of the Earth; no account of Time; no Arts; no Letters; no Society; and which is worst of all, continuall feare, and danger of violent death; And the life of man, solitary, poore, nasty, brutish, and short. (Hobbes 1968, Chap. 13, p. 186)

Hobbes recognizes that his dark portrayal of the condition of humankind in the state of nature may not be realistic ("It may peradventure be thought, there was never such a time . . ." p. 187). But that is not his point. What Hobbes is analyzing are the conditions or conventions that enable a society to avoid the cataclysmic "war of every man against every man" (p. 188).

In Hobbes's view, societies are able to avoid the state of nature by vesting power, and the legitimate ability to focus force, in the person of the *sovereign*. As democratic theory has progressed, we have adapted Hobbes's notion of sovereignty into something more abstract, and at the same time more concrete. That "something" is the *will of the people*. This is really quite an astonishing intellectual achievement. We start with (1) a *state of nature*, move to (2) the *person of the sovereign*, who embodies the power and legitimacy of the state, and then (3) mentally divorce the literal person (king, sultan, or chieftain) from the function of that office, which is to carry out the *will of the people*. In this construction, the sovereign is the will of the people, which (in theory, at least) is the anthropomorphised ruler of the society.

Not everyone would accept this formulation; not by a long shot. For some, it is the rule by the general will that should be most feared. Edmund Burke, speaking perhaps ironically,[2] makes this argument most clearly:

In vain you tell me that Artificial Government is good, but that I fall out only with the Abuse. The Thing! The Thing itself is the abuse! Observe, my Lord, I pray you, that grand Error upon which all artificial legislative power is founded. It was observed, that Men had ungovernable Passions, which made it necessary to guard against the Violence they might offer to each other. They appointed governors over them for this Reason; but a worse and more perplexing Difficulty arises, how to be defended against the Governors? (Burke 1982, pp. 64–65)

In this passage, Burke would appear to argue that nature, or "natural society," may be preferable to government, since there is no way to ensure that the will of the people is obeyed. "The thing" is government; saying "the thing itself is the abuse" means that Hobbes had it all wrong, and humans in the natural state would be just fine. It is the power of unjust government we should fear, and guard against.

I am not going to pretend to offer an answer in this debate, but it is useful to think about where governments, and societies, come from. Consider Aristotle's account, from Book I, chapter 2 of the *Politics*:

> When several villages are united in a single complete community, large enough to be nearly or quite self-sufficing, the state comes into existence, originating in the bare needs of life, and continuing in existence for the sake of a good life. And therefore, *if the earlier forms of society are natural, so is the state. . . .* Hence it is evident that the state is a creation of nature, and *that man by nature is a political animal.* And he who by nature and not by mere accident is without a state, is either a beast or a god. (emphasis added)

This passage leads to a hard question: Is it true that "man by nature is a political animal"? If the answer is yes, then institutions of collective decision are required. More simply, humans will have to make decisions as a group that somehow embody, or at least account for, the desires of the individuals who make up the group.

Many people have worked on the problem of how to make collective choices out of individual desires. One of the most important early efforts was by Jean-Jacques Rousseau. Rousseau's thought was complex, so any attempt at brief summary will not do it justice. However, it is clear that Rousseau believed in the superiority of some idealized "natural" condition of humanity, where people are free to delight in liberty and nature.

On the other hand, he recognized that some mechanism is required for generating binding collective choices, and for governing the otherwise unavoidable tendency for inequalities among citizens to arise. These two ideas (complete freedom of the individual, and the need for submission of the individual to the general will) are not fully reconciled in Rousseau, but he certainly recognizes the problem. In a celebrated and controversial passage, Rousseau makes his argument:

> As long as several men in assembly regard themselves as a single body, they have only a single will which is concerned with their common preservation and general well-being. . . .
>
> A State so governed needs very few laws; and, as it becomes necessary to issue new ones, the necessity is universally seen. The first man to propose them merely says what all have already felt. . . .
>
> There is but one law which, from its nature, needs unanimous consent. This is the social compact, for civil association is the most voluntary act in the world. Since every man is born free and master of himself, no one can, under any pretext whatsoever, subjugate him without his consent . . . Apart from this primitive contract, the vote of the majority is always binding on all the others; this is a consequence of the contract itself. But it may be asked how a man can be free while he is forced to conform to wills that are not his own. How are the opponents free while they are bound by laws to which they have not consented?
>
> I reply that the question is not put properly. The citizen consents to all the laws, even to those that pass against his will, and even to those which punish him when he dares violate any of them. The unchanging will of all the members of the state is the general will; through it they are citizens and free. When a law is proposed in the assembly of the people, what they are being asked is not precisely whether they approve or reject the proposal, but whether or not it is consistent with the general will that is their own; each man expresses his opinion on this point by casting his vote, and the declaration of the general will is derived from the counting of the votes. When, therefore, the opinion that is contrary to my own prevails, this proves neither more nor less than that I was mistaken, and that what I thought to be the general will was not so. If my private opinion had prevailed, I would have done something other than what I had willed; it is then that I would not have been free. (Rousseau, 1973, pp. 150–51).

This reasoning may seem a little tortuous, but the argument is important. As a citizen, you want government to do the right thing. However, citizens may disagree about what the right thing is. We could vote, as a way of deciding what "we" think, as opposed to insisting that we must all think the same thing. Provided each of us renders a judgment about what is best for society, rather than just what is in our self-interest, this process of voting is a means of discovering the collective wisdom, or general will. Each member of a society must agree, in the abstract, to accept specific decisions we may not agree with. Rousseau is arguing, then, that this submission to the general will is the price of freedom.

In mentally creating the general will out of some combination of individual desires, we have also created something else, the "society." In fact, the very essence of the general will is the notion that there is some group larger than the individual whose welfare we can measure, or at least compare across different policy choices.

The comparison of the welfare of the individual and the welfare of some larger entity, whether it is a rural community, a city, or the entire nation, is at the heart of many policy questions. You have probably seen media accounts of attempts by cities to expand a road system, where one old house (owned in our example by Grandma Filinda Blank) stands in the way. The city offers to pay the "market value" of the house, but the property and the family farm are worth much more than that to Ms. Blank. What should the city do? It can use its right of "eminent domain," and force Grandma Blank out of the house. Or it can spend millions of extra dollars to reroute the road, delaying completion of the highway by six months. How should we decide? What is the wise policy, in a situation where the welfare of one individual is clearly in conflict with the welfare of most, or even all, other citizens?

We will consider, in chapters 10, 11, and 12, some potential ways to address the question, accounting for risk, time, and the use of cost-benefit analysis. While these techniques aren't perfect, they offer at least a starting point for measuring values and organizing our thinking. The set of techniques called cost-benefit analysis are some of the most widely used, and valuable, tools a policy analyst can possess. But like any potent tool, cost-benefit analysis can be misleading or even dangerous if it is used improperly.

One word of caution, however. My mother, who grew up on a farm, always said "You can't make chicken salad out of chicken feathers." (Yes, I am paraphrasing; she didn't say "feathers"). Cost-benefit analysis is a way of coming up with measures of the values of certain actions, but it can't tell you what the fundamental values of a society are, or should be. If you believe that the society has interests, and rights, that are superior to those of any one individual, or even groups of individuals, then some very aggressive actions by government on behalf of that collective interest may be justified. On the other hand, if you think that the rights of individuals are paramount, the ability of government to function in the face of disagreement may be severely curtailed. One can't rely on cost-benefit analysis to answer the really fundamental questions, or to create consensus where there is profound disagreement. Policy analysis generally works best for societies that have already agreed, among themselves, on most of the hard questions of collective choice and values.

Let us now turn back to the notion of a state of nature, and see how policies may have originated in the simplest sorts of human cultures.

The Hun-gats: Choosing and the Wisdom of the Group

Let us consider the simplest case of collective choice, and see if it has some lessons for larger societies. Suppose we lived in a small extended family group, or clan, of hunter-gatherers. Imagine we had only rudimentary role definitions and rules of behavior to guide us, but that we faced problems of deciding what to do. How would we conduct the business of society? How would we make decisions?

Each person's membership in the clan is initially conferred by birth, or marriage. But as life continues, each person has the option to leave, to strike out on their own and abandon the "we" to live as "I." The fact that tribes stay together, and try to decide as a group, tells us the first thing we need to know about policy analysis. *Policies are "public"*: once a policy is chosen, all of us have to live with it, whether we agree with it or not. Consequently, policy analysis is different from any other problem you are likely to encounter when making decisions. You aren't just deciding what you want, or what is best for you. Somehow, you have to figure out what is best for other people.

Let's make the example more specific. Suppose you are a member of a hunter-gatherer tribe (I will call them the "Hun-gats," as in an earlier book, Hinich and Munger, 1997) You, and the clan, have hunted (and gathered) all of the food in the area that you know is safe to eat. Now everyone is hungry, and everyone is starting to look at other plants, strange animals, and maybe even Cousin Gombog, in a whole new way. These are all things that the tribe does not normally consider to be food, but hunger has made them define potential food sources more broadly. What "policy" should the tribe adopt about eating?

The first thing the Hun-gats would have to decide is how to decide. It is by no means obvious that the "What do we eat?" question is a collective one. So, step one is to decide whether we need a *policy* at all, or whether it is okay to let a more private or "market" oriented solution (i.e., each of us tries whatever we want) work itself out.

Let's suppose the Hun-gats decide they need a policy, for two reasons. The first is the chance that lots of members of the tribe will eat

FIGURE 2.2
Decision Problem of the Hun-gats:
Should We Have a Policy?

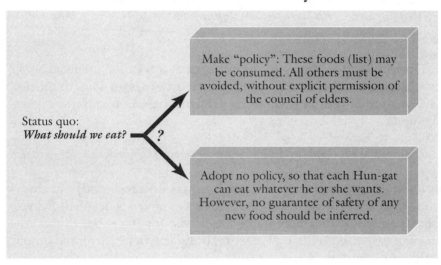

Status quo:
What should we eat? ◀ ?

Make "policy": These foods (list) may be consumed. All others must be avoided, without explicit permission of the council of elders.

Adopt no policy, so that each Hun-gat can eat whatever he or she wants. However, no guarantee of safety of any new food should be inferred.

something poisonous, and then die. This is a waste of effort, because more people are exposed to risk than is necessary to find out if the food is safe. This is a problem of too *much* risk. The Hun-gats' ancestral enemies, the fierce Raouli tribe, would likely find out about widespread food poisoning, and use the Hun-gats' weakness as an opportunity to attack.

Second, there is a "free rider" problem: someone found an oyster, opened it up, and then looked at his companion: "Hey, this looks like food. Oooh . . . why don't *you* try it?" Free riding creates a problem of too *little* risk: some foods would not be sampled, because everyone is waiting for someone else to try it first, especially if it looks bad.

The two problems (too much risk from uncontrolled experimentation, and too little risk from free riding) are not likely to cancel out. Instead, the two problems will both hurt the effort to find new foods to relieve the impending famine. The tribe has two choices: It can try to use theory, or it can use empirical experimentation to determine what is safe. The sort of "theory" they might use is not based on knowledge of germs and poisons, of course. Rather, for primitive peoples theory is more likely to be religious law, applied by the use of analogy.

Suppose someone finds a beaver, and brings it back to camp. The shaman, the Hun-Gat's chief religious official, makes a policy pronouncement based on theory:

Our laws say that pigs are unclean, and you may not eat them. Beavers look like pigs, albeit with large teeth and funny, flat tails. Therefore, beavers (like pigs) are unclean.

Obviously, theory may have problems as a tool for policy analysis, especially if the theory was really designed to explain something else.

The alternative might be an experiment, based on empirical investigation:

Let's roast up this bad boy, and see how he tastes. Here, you take the first bite.

If the person who takes the first bite says it tastes good, and shows no ill effects in the next day or so, then the policy is decided: Beavers can be added to the "acceptable foods" list for the tribe. In fact, the shaman may even update his theory, using the newly acquired empirical knowledge:

Animals that look a lot like pigs are okay to eat, provided that (unlike pigs) those animals have big teeth and funny flat tails.

My example has been rather silly, of course, but theory and analogy can play an important role, even when cause-and-effect relationships are poorly understood. In fact, it may be precisely in those instances where little is known about the mechanics of cause and effect that people are likely to use "theory." This is a very conservative (in the sense of avoiding risk) approach to policy analysis, but it can work pretty well. Consider Table 2.1, which gives a comparison between the rules for handling meat in a kosher butcher shop, and the 1998 version of USDA procedures for doing the same tasks.

The similarities are striking, yet the approach to creating the "policy" in each case was dramatically different. Kosher rules were "designed," but not by scientists. Kosher rules are a set of religious practices; "keeping kosher" is a moral imperative, not a health con-

TABLE 2.1
Science and Religion as a Source of "Policy"

Item	USDA Requirement[a]	Kosher Dietary Laws[b]
Blood	Poultry shall be slaughtered in accordance with good commercial practices in a manner that will result in thorough bleeding of the carcasses.	Meat must be rid thoroughly of blood before being consumed.
Blood	Blood from the killing operation shall be confined to a relatively small area.	Blood from the killing of an animal shall be covered up under certain circumstances.
Cadavers	Carcasses of poultry showing evidence of having died from causes other than slaughter shall be condemned.	Only animals killed through the ritual slaughtering are fit for consumption.
Receptacles	Receptacles used for handling inedible products shall be of such material and construction that their use will not result in adulteration of any edible product or in unsanitary conditions at the establishment, and they shall bear conspicuous and distinctive markings to identify them as only for such use and shall not be used for handling any edible poultry products.	Vessels used to cook forbidden meat may not be used to cook kosher meat. Also forbidden to use vessel in which meat has been salted for eating hot food
Utensils	Equipment and utensils used in the official establishment shall not be used outside the official. Equipment used in the preparation of any article (including, but not limited to, animal food), from inedible material shall not be used outside of the inedible products department. Exceptions may be prescribed or approved by the Administrator in specific cases.	An instrument used to slaughter an unclean animal must be rinsed in cold water and wiped with a rag. Knives used to slaughter animals for consumption as food must be sharp, and straight, so no undue pain is caused to the animal. Some exceptions are granted, but only for emergencies.

[a] Information regarding the Food Safety and Inspection Service (FSIS), a division of the United States Department of Agriculture (USDA), standards obtained from the U.S. Government Printing Office via GPO Access (http://www.access.gpo.gov/nara/cfr/index.html).
[b] Information regarding Jewish Dietary Laws obtained from *The Code of Maimonides, Book Five, The Book of Holiness*, translated from the Hebrew by Louis I. Rabinowitz and Philip Grossman. New Haven: Yale University Press, 1965.

cern. Yet it seems obvious that the kosher rules have a strong basis in science, or at least in health. In many ways, the "religious" kosher food-handling rules approximate the "scientific" USDA guidelines. The USDA requirements (presumably) are based on science; their sole goal is to promote health. The USDA has the benefit of significant experience, and a well-developed germ-based theory of contamination of food products.

In a primitive society, adopting a policy such as orthodox Jewish rules for keeping kosher has important health benefits. You could imagine how the policy might be adopted: People notice that if one eats chicken prepared according to the rules, one is less likely to get sick. Without a germ theory of disease, or an understanding of food parasites, the people may misattribute this sickness to the anger of spirits or deities that control our health. Consequently, "policies" about food might start out as religious rules. If the rules adapt over time to record safe, and outlaw unsafe, foods and practices, the power of the shamans will increase, because they really do appear to speak for the gods.

For example, suppose the shamans say,

> *Don't eat pork, as it is unclean. If you eat pork, you will die; demons will possess your stomach.*

You flout the policy, and eat pork in a hot environment where cleanliness and cooking procedures are (at best) inconsistent. Before long, parasitic trichinae from an undercooked piece of pork enter your intestines. Untreated, the trichinosis becomes acute, affecting your viscera and then even some of your voluntary muscle groups. You die, screaming. The shamans, shaken by the power of God to punish the wicked, redouble their efforts to ensure that God's will is both universally known and obeyed.[3]

This leads us to a problem: How are we to evaluate the opinions of experts, or (alternatively) the democratic decision processes that use majority rule? Our Hun-gats don't *know* what foods are safe to eat; they are very uncertain, and afraid. Their votes would be meaningless on this question, because they have no basis for making good choices. The shamans only have laws based on accumulated experience, codified as religious dietary restrictions. These rules do not apply to new foods, because it is not clear where new comestibles fit into the existing system of safe and unsafe foods. Without a scientific understanding of what causes disease, or of what foods are safe, we have no means of making a decision. Neither expertise, nor democracy, is equipped to handle this problem.

But being a policy analyst means you never get to say "I don't know." The Hun-gats have to do something, because their children are crying from hunger. And Gombog, who is a bulky man, is starting to get nervous at the way people stop talking, but keep staring, when he approaches. Suppose you are a consultant, whose job it is to help the Hun-gats decide what policy they should adopt for new foods. What would you recommend? What are the alternatives?

There is a general process of policy decision, which you need to understand to get through the rest of this book. We will spend quite a bit of time fleshing out this process later, but for now we'll just give the outline, as depicted in Figure 2.3.

FIGURE 2.3
The Three Stages of Policy Choice:
First We Decide How to Decide

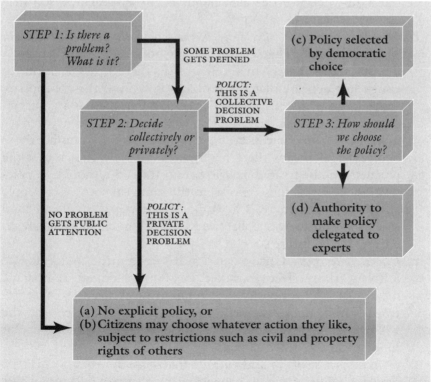

Step 1: Is there a problem? What is it?

Step 2: Should we decide collectively, or privately, how to solve the problem?

Step 3: If a collective decision is required, should we decide using democracy, or should we delegate policy-making authority to experts?

The outcomes of this process have three broad categories, the figure shows. In the broadest sense, the alternatives are those listed in Figure 2.3:

a. *Allow the problem to remain outside the scope of collective control.* This might occur because no one cares, or because the issue is not deemed important. Alternatively, this "nondecision" may be an aspect of civic or religious culture: it never occurs to citizens to have government intervene. In practical terms, citizens may choose whatever action they like, subject to other restrictions the society has placed on individual action. In the case of our Hun-gats, if no explicit policy is chosen, each person may eat, or not eat, new foods.

b. *Decide the problem collectively, but choose to allow citizens to make their own choices.* This seems a lot like option (a), but there is an important difference. In the first case, there is no decision, or else it just appears that the problem is beyond the appropriate scope of government action. For option (b), there is an affirmative act, an actual decision that citizens must be allowed to make their own choices, even if the collective may not like those choices. This means there has been a *collective* choice that the problem will be treated *as if* it were private. So, though in practical policy terms these two seem the same (in each case, people choose), in fact there is a world of difference (in the second case, the choice was collective, so it is much more likely to change in the future).

c. *Choose collectively.* Once a decision has been made to decide collectively, the collective choice is often made by democratic means, such as voting in a referendum or choosing representatives. Within the prescribed limits of the collective choice, the will of the majority (or whatever other decision rule is in use) is binding on the other citizens.

d. *Delegate authority to make a collective choice to experts.* This type of outcome has different properties from option (c), democratic choice. In some ways, it may be better, if the choice is made by well-informed, highly trained people. On the other hand, the decision may appear less legitimate, because it seems imposed. The people did not consent to the choice, as in majority rule; they delegated the choice. What this all means is that the basis of the grant of "expertise" is crucial. If expertise comes from knowledge of reading goat entrails or star portents, there are likely to be problems. The biggest problem, of course, is that nonexperts have a hard time judging expertise. Experts have to judge themselves, with peer review and licensing requirements.

For most of the rest of this book, we will consider some of the implications of delegation to experts, and look at problems with markets and democracy. The technical tools we consider in the later chapters are all designed to ensure that the reader, as an expert policy analyst, will get things right, or will recognize when others have things wrong. Before we can do that, however, it is useful to consider the biggest question that societies have to face, one that we have already mentioned but have not yet addressed in any fundamental way. That question is the choice of the public or private arenas for decision making.

Public Decisions versus Collective Decisions

So far, I have talked about public and private decisions as if there were clear and obvious differences. But this is hardly the case. In fact, the rhetoric of many policy conflicts is about precisely the problem of whether the public has any business telling individuals what to do. While I can't offer a general solution to that problem, I can point out a subtlety that is often missed in policy debate: There is a difference between *public* decisions and *collective* decisions.

The easiest way to appreciate this distinction is to consider Figure 2.4.

- Public decisions can be defined as those where my choices affect your welfare.
- Private decisions are then choices that affect only my welfare.

This "affect welfare" standard is subjective, of course. It may "affect my welfare" that you wear an ugly (in my opinion) tie, or use racial epithets, or enjoy pornographic films and books. In the extreme, "you have offended me" could be an almost universal excuse for forcing my will on others. Alternatively, the idea of "private" actions

FIGURE 2.4
Collective Decisions and Public Decisions

	Individual Decision: I can choose, alone and without interference	**Collective Decision:** Choices are made by a group, and are binding on all
Private Decision: My choice has no consequence for your welfare	*Liberty of the individual:* • What socks should I wear? • Whom should I marry?	*Tyranny of the majority:* • Invasion of privacy • Theft of property rights
Public Decision: My choices affect your welfare	*Underinvestment, or else theft by the minority:* • Air or water pollution • Education	*Liberty of the group:* • How much to spend on defense? • How to take care of the poor?

is hard to define, or sustain. I have said that marriage is a private act. Yet the potential that gay men or lesbian women may want to marry is an important political issue, because at present that right is not established. In some ways, "public" decisions are simply those that other people care a lot about, which is a subjective matter. Still, some objective criteria for "externalities," or the effects of my actions on your welfare, can be devised, as we will see.

The difference between individual and collective decisions, by contrast, can be defined in practical, measurable terms, as a question of the power to choose.

• Individual decisions are those where I can choose on my own.
• Collective decisions are made by a group, using some choice rule, and are binding on all.

As can be seen, there is a difference between the public-private and individual-collective conceptions of choice. Certainly, many of the decisions a society faces fall along the main diagonal (top left and bottom right boxes) in Figure 2.4: private decisions are made by individuals, and public decisions are made collectively. But that is not always true. There is *nothing* about the machinery of democracy that prevents private decisions from being made collectively. This result is usually identified as "tyranny of the majority" over an individual, or smaller group.

Conversely, public decisions may be made by individuals: I may choose to pollute common pool resources such as air or water, or I may undertake activities that affect others positively (such as seeking an education) without being able to capture the full gains from the activity. These "negative externalities" (if the activity is harmful to others) can effectively result in theft of value from the rest of society. "Positive externalities" (when the activity results in uncompensated benefits to others), may explain why there is underinvestment, or too little of such activities undertaken privately.

The final point worth noting about Figure 2.4 is that it identifies rhetorical strategies in policy debates. In most cases, the default "policy" is the top left box: individual decisions made on private matters. Earlier, in Figure 2.3, we saw that the first two steps in a public policy process are identification of a problem, and then a decision about whether the problem is public. The rhetoric of the debate will focus on the question of whether the problem is really more appropriately in the bottom right box, or public decisions, collectively reached. So the point of the debate is whether the decision should be made *collectively*, but the words of the debate will be a contest over whether the decision has *public* implications. It turns out that the concept of "externality" is a powerful rhetorical tool, as well as a legitimate analytical concept.

Summary

The quote from Edmund Burke at the beginning of this chapter is worth repeating: "Government is a contrivance of human wisdom to provide for human wants. Men have a right that these wants should be provided for by this wisdom." Using human wisdom to provide for human wants is not easy, but it is what policy analysis is all about.

In this chapter, there were three separate themes of introduction to policy analysis. It is useful to summarize each so the reader can see how they fit together, because I will refer back to them in later chapters.

First, as the title of the book suggests, policy outcomes are the results of policy conflicts. I argued that there are three main dyadic conflicts in the policy world, with three different types of associated policies. The reason why policy may seem contradictory or incoherent is that the result a particular policy conflict produces is an answer to a very specific question. If the goals or interests of the observer are different, then the result may be hard to explain.

The three main policy conflicts are as follows:

- Markets versus experts: efficiency policies
- Markets versus politics: equity policies
- Politics versus experts: institutional reform policies

Second, the origins of many policies may be obscure. We tend to use things that work, even if we don't understand quite why. Just as dietary laws had to be based on accumulated trial-and-error knowledge from the past rather than a scientific theory of epidemiology and disease, our understanding of policy from a theoretical perspective is primitive. This makes policy analysis frustrating, since so little is known about cause and effect. It also makes policy analysis exciting, because it is possible to make lots of progress very quickly on fundamental problems.

Third, it is important to recognize that there may be "policies" even when we haven't decided anything, or even when we haven't decided whether to decide. I proposed a three-stage process for conceiving the policy process:

Step 1: Is there a problem? What is it?
Step 2: Should we decide collectively, or privately, how to solve the problem?
Step 3: If a collective decision is required, should we decide using democracy, or should we delegate policy making authority to experts?

In many cases, the fact that there is no formal policy is not the result of any failures in steps 2 or 3. Rather, we never got past step 1, realizing that there is a problem or agreeing on its nature. The notion that a problem exists is logically antecedent to the conclusion that something should be done. Generally, we hope that "something should be done" about what I have called "public" problems which involve "externalities" where the actions of one person affect the welfare of others. The difficulty is that what is decided is not whether the problem is *public*; rather, what is decided is whether the authority to delegate power is held *collectively*. This contest, over what is legitimately within the purview of the society to decide for its citizens, may be the biggest policy conflict of all. In the next chapter, I will outline the workings of markets, which make private and public decisions in ways that are definitely not collective.

SUMMARY OF KEY CONCEPTS

1. A *market* is a set of institutions for reducing transactions costs of the exchange of goods and services.
2. *Politics* is the process of deciding on policy and the distribution of benefits of public programs.
3. An *expert* is someone who may improve the welfare of society by providing advice on policy choice.
4. The conflict between experts and markets is resolved by efficiency policies. Markets may fail and experts may suggest how to correct these market failures.
5. A *market failure* is an outcome produced by the market that is not efficient, or that does not satisfy the Pareto criterion.
6. An allocation of resources is *efficient* if there does not exist another allocation of the same resources that leads to a more desirable result. Markets may fail to allocate resources in an efficient manner.
7. The *Pareto criterion* is useful for assessing whether a policy is efficient. By the Pareto criterion, an allocation of resources is efficient or optimal unless there exists an allocation of resources that everyone prefers.
8. Conflicts between markets and politics are resolved by equity policies. The tension between markets and politics is over the outcomes of market processes and is the result of the different distributions of power in the two arenas.
9. Conflicts between experts and politics are resolved by institutional-reform policies. The manner in which policies are chosen

affects the result of those decisions. Experts may offer advice on how collective decisions should be made.

10. The thought experiment known as *the state of nature* is the contemplation of what life would be like without institutionalized markets, politics, or experts. The state of nature is useful for assessing the importance of context in policy analysis.

11. *Public decisions* involve individual choices that can impact the welfare of other individuals, whereas *private decisions* impact the welfare of individual decision-maker. *Collective decisions* are choices that are made by a group and are binding on all members of the group, whereas *individual decisions* our made by an individual.

12. The distinction between public and collective decisions is important for identifying problems and the possible solutions.

13. An *externality* is the effect of one individual's actions on the welfare of other individuals. These effects can be *positive* or *negative*.

14. A good for which (a) use by an individual does not diminish the value or amount available to other individuals, and (b) consumption cannot be withheld, is a *public good*.

15. *Free riding* is the act of receiving the benefits of an action while not contributing any resources or exerting any effort to support that action.

16. A *monopoly* is a market with many buyers and a single seller.

PROBLEMS AND QUESTIONS

1. In Figure 2.4, two kinds of potential "tyranny" were identified. One of these occurs when a group decides a private matter for an individual, as when I am told how I must act, dress, eat, or think. This is "tyranny of the majority." The other type occurs when an individual imposes his or her will on the group, as when one person pollutes the atmosphere or steals public property. This is "tyranny of the individual." Obviously, societies face an important problem in deciding how to balance these two types of tyranny: Giving the collective more power helps control tyranny of the individual, but encourages tyranny of the majority. Write an essay to answer each of the following questions.

a. In this chapter, we saw that some philosophers (e.g., Rousseau) thought that the power of the collective is most important, and others (e.g., Burke, at least in the quoted passage) that that freedom of the individual is paramount. Who is right?

b. More importantly, how should society divide the public and private spheres of our lives, identifying what should be decided collectively and what should be chosen by individuals without government interference?

c. Finally, should the answer to this question be taken from economic theory and the notion of public goods, or from theories of justice and the good society? If neither tells us everything we need to know, how should we approach the problem?

2. Define, and give an example of, each of the following categories of policy. Describe also the policy conflict that gives rise to such policies.
  a. Efficiency policies
  b. Equity policies
  c. Institutional reform policies

TAKE IT TO THE NET!

Go to: http://www.wwnorton.com/college/polisci/analyzingpolicy for additional problems, data sets, and course materials.

NOTES

1. Webster's *New Universal Unabridged*, 1979.
2. This passage is from a work of fiction, published anonymously by Burke, as a very young man. It is not clear that Burke is arguing in his own voice here. Still, the point is simply and starkly stated, and therefore serves the purpose of exposition well.
3. I certainly don't mean to claim that the Jewish religious dietary rules, or any other religious practices, are without basis in spiritual fact. For all I know, they may be the revealed will of God. The discussion of Jewish dietary laws is intended only to convey the similarities between what many believe is God's will and scientific rules of hygiene based on a germ theory of infection. If this is God's will, he or she certainly got it right.

~ 3 ~

A Benchmark for Performance: The Market

Overview of Markets

The first two chapters have described the profession of policy analysis, given a little background on the problem of making collective and private decisions, and identified the key tensions or conflicts that shape real policy debates. Now it is time to turn to the form of organization most commonly used to direct human activity: the market. This chapter and the next are devoted to an outline of basic economic concepts. Let there be no mistake, however: This introduction is no substitute for a real course of study in economics. Economics is central to the study of markets, and to the analysis of policy in general, so if you are serious about becoming an analyst you will have lots more work to do.

On the other hand, it is possible to give a quick, and hopefully intuitive, overview that will take you a long way toward appreciating the value of economic reasoning. A "market" is a set of institutions, rules, or informal norms, that promote exchange. On the most concrete level, a market is a physical place, or setting, where exchange takes place. If I say, "I'm going to the market," you imagine a place with merchandise and people trying to sell the merchandise. But there are other, more abstract, institutions of exchange that may be harder to locate physically or to conceive of as part of a market. These include, for example, a *medium of exchange*; a *mechanism for conveying information about prices* accurately and cheaply; and a *concept of property that allows for both possession and sale* of items without a lot of arguing over who owns what. Interestingly, it is not unusual for these complex institutions to emerge spontaneously, without any central plan or conscious act of collective creation. Put simply, markets happen.

That doesn't mean that what happens is always good. Precisely because a market is likely to break out in almost any context, sometimes markets perform well and sometimes they perform poorly. Any one of the following conditions is likely to give rise to the set of exchange institutions we think of as a "market."

Preconditions for the Existence of a "Market"

1. Differences in goals, tastes, or desires (*diverse preferences*)
2. Differences in endowments of productive resources and personal talents (*diverse endowments*)
3. Declining average costs as more output is produced (*economies of scale*)
4. Declining average costs as the scope of action of one producer is decreased (*specialization*)

If people were clones in terms of their preferences and endowments, and production processes were linear in scale and scope, then markets would be irrelevant. It would be just as easy (efficient) to produce everything we wanted on our own. This "go it alone" kind of economic organization is called *autarky*, or a "Robinson Crusoe" economy, after the famous Daniel Defoe character.

The fact that markets are widely observed is a hint about their function: Markets make human beings better off. Not all human beings are better off, perhaps, and some of us are helped more than others, but by and large markets improve the human condition. There are three aspects to the benefits of markets. Any action by experts, or by politics, to suppress or distort the functioning of markets can cause harm by denying citizens these three advantages.

The Three Benefits of Markets

• **Gains from trade.** Differences in endowments, or differences in preferences, result in improved welfare for all participants, as long as trades are informed and voluntary. This is a benefit in consumption, since by rearranging the consumption bundles among citizens, we can make everyone better off, even though there is no increase in the total amount of goods available for consumption. Magic? No, just markets.

• **Gains in productive efficiency.** By allowing entrepreneurs to take advantage of economies of scale, or economies accruing to increased specialization, markets foster economic growth. An increase in the level of economic activity means growth in the total amount of consumption goods available to citizens. Increased efficiency in production means that more can be produced with the same resources, again creating the potential for everyone to be better off.

• **Reductions in transaction costs using information transmitted by prices.** Quite separate from efficiency in the allocation of consumption goods (i.e., ensuring all gains from trade are exhausted) and efficiency in the allocation of productive resources, markets also provide the important service of providing information. Prices convey information about the relative scarcity of resources in a concise yet effective way.

To see how these aspects of markets work, it is useful to consider a historical perspective of market processes.

Nearly 2,500 years ago, the Greek philosopher Aristotle made some accurate and important observations about the origins of money, and of markets, that are no less true today.

> Of everything which we possess there are two uses: both belong to the thing as such, but not in the same manner, for one is the proper, and the other the improper or secondary use of it. For example, a shoe is used for wear, and is used for exchange; both are uses of the shoe. He who gives a shoe in exchange for money or food to him who wants one, does indeed use the shoe as a shoe, but this is not its proper or primary purpose, for a shoe is not made to be an object of barter. The same may be said of all possessions, for the art of exchange extends to

all of them, and it arises at first from what is natural, from the circumstance that some have too little, others too much. Hence we may infer that retail trade is not a natural part of the art of getting wealth; had it been so, men would have ceased to exchange when they had enough. In the first community, indeed, which is the family, this art is obviously of no use, but it begins to be useful when the society increases. For the members of the family originally had all things in common; later, when the family divided into parts, the parts shared in many things, and different parts in different things, which they had to give in exchange for what they wanted, a kind of barter which is still practiced among barbarous nations who exchange with one another the necessaries of life and nothing more; giving and receiving wine, for example, in exchange for coin, and the like.

This sort of barter is not part of the wealth-getting art and is not contrary to nature, but is needed for the satisfaction of men's natural wants. The other or more complex form of exchange grew, as might have been inferred, out of the simpler. When the inhabitants of one country became more dependent on those of another, and they imported what they needed, and exported what they had too much of, money necessarily came into use. For the various necessaries of life are not easily carried about, and hence men agreed to employ in their dealings with each other something which was intrinsically useful and easily applicable to the purposes of life, for example, iron, silver, and the like. Of this the value was at first measured simply by size and weight, but in process of time they put a stamp upon it, to save the trouble of weighing and to mark the value. . . .

When the use of coin had once been discovered, out of the barter of necessary articles arose the other art of wealth getting, namely, retail trade; which was at first probably a simple matter, but became more complicated as soon as men learned by experience whence and by what exchanges the greatest profit might be made. Originating in the use of coin, the art of getting wealth is generally thought to be chiefly concerned with it, and to be the art which produces riches and wealth; having to consider how they may be accumulated. Indeed, riches is assumed by many to be only a quantity of coin, because the arts of getting wealth and retail trade are concerned with coin. Others maintain that coined money is a mere sham, a thing not natural, but conventional only, because, if the users substitute another commodity for it, it is worthless, and because it is not useful as a means to any of the necessities of life, and, indeed, he who is rich in coin may often be in want of necessary food. But how can that be wealth of which a man may have a great abundance and yet perish with hunger, like Midas in the fable, whose insatiable prayer turned everything that was set before him into gold? (Aristotle's *Politics*, Book I, section 9).

The paradox that Aristotle points out is interesting. Money clearly is not wealth, because a person with nothing but money would starve. The answer, of course, is that money *represents* all other commodities. The medium of exchange is a measure of value, or the unit of account, of the barters people would negotiate if money were not available. Instead of my trading you two bottles of wine for a sheep, we can exchange money. I give you $10 for a sheep. You give me $5 each for bottles of wine, and end up buying two bottles. The $10 has gone back and forth, to no net effect; for this reason, some economists say that money is a "veil," disguising but not really affecting the contours of trade.[1] In our example, money was an artifice: the real exchange was the trade of wine for mutton.

Having a currency, however, reduces the frictions or **"transaction costs"** of the exchange, making it easier for both of us. Furthermore, if we have money the exchange need not be directly a barter between two people. If my only option is trading wine for sheep, but you don't like wine, I can't get any sheep, even if each sheep is "worth" two bottles of wine! Money breaks the dyadic relations of barter into separate exchanges, allowing me to obtain abstract command over goods and services (i.e., units of money) instead of having to take physical possession of a commodity I don't value or can't use. Money allows us to focus on an important aspect of scarcity, the "opportunity cost" of a commodity. It is worth pausing to consider opportunity cost more closely.

Opportunity Costs and Scarcity

Using a resource—time, gold, wood, a drill press, or labor—for one purpose means you cannot use it for something else. We all want more things (more leisure, more consumption, more savings), so there can't possibly be enough to go around. Consequently, societies have to find ways to allocate limited resources in the face of unlimited wants. This is what economists mean when they talk about the problem of "scarcity": How do we allocate limited resources to satisfy unlimited human wants? This may seem strange, since you are likely used to thinking of scarcity more narrowly, as when we say, "In the desert, people face a terrible scarcity of water." Economists think of scarcity much more broadly, as you will see.

To understand scarcity better, we first need to define the related concept of opportunity cost.

> **Opportunity cost:** the cost of forgone alternatives, or uses given up if a resource is used in a particular way. If a resources can be used for activity A or activity B, the opportunity cost of using it for B is the value of its use for A. In an idealized, perfectly functioning market system, the opportunity cost of a resource is greater than or equal to its price. In practice, however, the relation between opportunity cost and price has no necessary sign or magnitude. More simply, the opportunity cost of a resource is rarely the same as what you paid for it.

Opportunity cost can be illustrated fairly simply, but it is a subtle concept. Consider this: If you found a valuable diamond, and I wanted it, would you give it to me? Suppose that you don't know me, and that I am not a member of your family, and so have no claim on your affections. Then I suspect you would not give me the diamond for one penny less than its market value, despite the fact that the diamond was "free." The price you paid to obtain a commodity is *completely irrelevant* to its value to you, or to the opportunity cost of using it or giving it away.

As an illustration, ponder a test question I asked in an intermediate microeconomics class while teaching at Dartmouth College. I was surprised then how many people missed it; see if you get the "right" answer.

Mental Exercise on Opportunity Cost: What Would You Do?

Suppose you are a big fan of the rock star, Mickey Martin. You especially like his number-one hit about root canal surgery without anesthesia, "Living, But Need a Local!" You hear he is coming to town to give a concert in two weeks. Seating at the concert is "festival" style, so that there are no reserved seats: one ticket is just like another, since you have to stand in line at the gate to get seats. Tickets cost $25, and you want two, so you can take your friend along.

Arriving to buy tickets when they go on sale a week before the show, you see that you have underestimated how popular Martin is in your city. The line stretches around the block. You wait in line, and inch slowly toward the ticket window. When you are only about thirty people from the front of the line, with hundreds now standing behind you, you hear the ticket window slam shut, and a loud murmur ripples back along the line: "Sold out? SOLD OUT!" Oh, no.

Days later, back at home, you read that "scalpers" (assume re-selling tickets, or scalping, is legal in your state) are asking, and get-ting, $200 or more for a ticket to the show. As you walk out to your car, you hear snatches of Martin's songs from a nearby fraternity house. You think to yourself how much you want to see that show. You have more than $1,000 in your checking account, and still have no plans for the night of the concert. But there is just no way that it is worth $400 for two tickets! Heck, for that much money, you can buy a CD player, and every Mickey Martin CD ever made!

As you start to get in the car, you notice a scuffed envelope on the sidewalk. Looking around, you don't see anyone. You pick up the en-velope and inside, *mirabile dictu*, you find two tickets to the Martin show. You make a legitimate effort to see if anyone lost the tickets, but of course you can't just go ask random people, because they would say, "Yeah, sure, hand 'em over. I lost those. You bet I did!" Deciding the tickets really are yours now, here is the question:

Do you go to the concert?

The answer, as any economist will tell you, is "no."[2] After all, you can scalp the tickets, which means you should value the tickets at their "opportunity cost": $200 each. But we have already established that the concert was not worth $200 per ticket, at least not to you, because you had a chance to pay that price to a scalper and decided against it.

This turned out to be a bad test question: all my students missed it. It is not that I am a bad teacher; the student seemed to understand opportunity cost as an abstract concept, and could recite the formal definition without a hitch. But when it came time to apply the con-cept, they had no intuition. They all had some version of the same answer: "Of course I would go. Free tickets: cool!" No, no, *NO*! The tickets are not free, because using them costs you the $400 you could have obtained by selling them. It *doesn't matter* what you *pay* for something; the "price" is *what you give up by using* the *resource*. The real price of something is its opportunity cost. Obtaining something for free is very different from valuing that thing at zero. If you found a diamond, you would not give it away.

Having defined opportunity cost, it is immediately possible to de-fine scarcity:

Scarcity: The condition in which a resource has an effective op-portunity cost that exceeds zero. Generally, this means that any resource with a price greater than zero is scarce. If a resource has a zero effective price it may still be scarce, however, because property rights to the resource may be imperfectly specified.

Notice that "scarce," by this definition, and another adjective, "valuable," are certainly not synonyms. Air to breathe is not *scarce* for most of us, because it can be obtained for free. But it is of paramount *value*. If property rights to air are poorly specified (if the air is what is sometimes called a "common pool resource"), the market *price* of air might be zero. Yet the *opportunity cost* of using the air as a dumping ground for industrial waste may be far higher than zero.

One of the main goals of experts working in policy analysis is to find ways to make the price to an individual of using a resource equal to its true social opportunity cost. It is useful to state the reason explicitly, in a form I will call "Pigou's conjecture," after A. C. Pigou's famous argument in *The Economics of Welfare*.[3]

> **Pigou's conjecture:** Markets are inefficient, as a means of allocating resources, to the extent that the (social) opportunity cost of a resource diverges from its price, or private cost to the user.

The inefficiency derives from the overuse (if social cost is greater than price) or underuse (if social cost is less than price) of the resource. To return to the air pollution example, if the cost to me of using the air to dump wastes is small, but the costs to society are large, then I will overuse (in terms of efficiency, to say nothing of justice) the atmosphere as a trash can.

The policy prescription that arises from this conjecture is the need to use a system of taxes or subsidies to make the opportunity cost of the resource equal the effective price as nearly as possible. That is, if the amount I pay is equal to the full social cost, I will take all of those social costs into account when making decisions on resource use. Consequently, I will use the resource only if the advantages to me exceed the full social costs.

There is a counterclaim that questions Pigou's conjecture; I will call it Coase's counter-conjecture," from R. H. Coase's (1960) "The Problem of Social Cost."

> **Coases's counter-conjecture:** If property rights are clearly and exclusively defined, and the cost of writing and enforcing

contracts is not too high, market forces will make the opportunity cost and the price of a resource converge.

Why are these two claims "conjectures"? Because neither is proven! In fact, each claim is "true," in some deductive sense. The debate turns on the question of which approach makes better public policy: an expert-managed approach (Pigou) or a decentralized market-oriented approach (Coase). In the terms of policy conflict developed in the previous chapter, we are in the arena of markets versus experts, with attempts by political actors to manipulate the outcome to their benefit. In later chapters, the bases of this debate will be considered in more detail. For now, a brief introduction to the logic and function of the market system will help us to evaluate the two conjectures.

How Do Markets Work?

Markets are mysterious. Friedrich A. Hayek once said that if, rather than just arising *naturally*, markets had been consciously *invented*, then the market system would be proclaimed mankind's greatest achievement. There are two reasons, why markets are celebrated, and nearly universally used, as a mechanism for organizing large-scale human activity: **information** and **incentives**.

- A market system uses prices to convey very accurate, yet very cheap, *information* about the value of different activity.
- A market system relies not on ethics, but rather on *incentives*. A properly functioning market system brings into alignment the self-interest (even naked greed) of individuals and the collective interests of the entire society.

In short: Markets give thousands and thousands of people both the information and the incentives to do what an omniscient social planner would want them to do!

As we begin to consider how markets direct scarce resources to the uses that society values most, it is useful to bear in mind the alternative means for handling the fundamental problem of scarcity. As a matter of institutional technology, there are four major ways to allocate resources in the face of scarcity.

Means of Allocating Scarce Resources

1. **Price system (market).** Resources are directed to their highest-valued use, so that whoever is willing to pay the most (either in terms of other valuable goods, or in currency) gets to control the resource. *Big winners:* People with lots of money, or with talents or resources the society values highly. *Disadvantages:* There are two. (1) Poor people may get too little, creating ethical problems of equity. (2) Independently of their basis in justice, market allocations may be politically untenable, if democratically based authority is in a position to impose redistributive or confiscatory taxes.

2. **Queuing.** A queue is a line.[4] Queuing is a system of allocation based on waiting your turn. So, first in line is first in priority. If all the resource is used up before your turn, you lose out. *Big winners:* People with lots of time (or rather, a low opportunity cost of time spent waiting in line). *Disadvantages:* There are two. (1) People standing in line incur "deadweight losses," or time wasted, for no gain in consumption or productivity. (2) There is no reason to believe that resources are directed to their highest-valued uses. As evidence, consider that queue-based allocations often evoke secondary, or "black," markets, where allocations initially dictated by queuing are reallocated by prices.

3. **Chance.** Lotteries, drawings, or other random selection processes mean everyone has an equal chance of winning. *Big winners*: No individual is a winner from the process, because in terms of expected value everyone is treated the same. From an ethical perspective, however, this may be an advantage. *Disadvantage*: By definition, allocation is random. The person who actually gets the resource may value it at only a fraction of its worth to someone else. Opportunity cost is explicitly ignored in random processes. Consequently, chance allocations evoke secondary markets for reallocating by price.

4. **Authority/discretion.** Allocations can be made by experts, party officials, elected leaders, or central planners. This sort of allocation process is also called a "command" system. *Big winners:* Guess who: the party officials, leaders, and planners, their friends, and family! Alternatively, the beneficiaries of the policy may be those targeted by the policy, if discretion is used to avoid corruption and follow the rules. *Disadvantages:* There are two. (1) It is very difficult to obtain

the information required to make accurate judgments about scarcity and opportunity cost, without some mechanism for measuring intensity. In effect, command systems often fall back on queuing, as people are forced to stand in long lines for products "sold" far below their opportunity cost values. (2) Command systems present almost irresistible opportunities for corruption and favoritism, because the central authority can't monitor all the officials with the ability to hold up products in exchange for bribes or in-kind payoffs.

The distinguishing feature of a market system of allocation is the reliance on prices. You are used to prices; you have dealt with them all your life. Some prices are stated in terms of goods, as when you decide whether to trade baseball cards: Is a Ken Griffey rookie card worth a Mark Lemke plus a Dave Stieb, or would it take a third card to make the values equal? (Hint, non–sports fans: it would take a third card!) Some prices are quoted in terms of dollars, like when you go into a store and see a candy bar in a display rack. The price is on a sticker on the candy, or on a sign above the rack: "75 cents." Have you ever thought about what this price means, what it *really* means?

The Two Informational Functions of Prices

The price is what you give up to get something else. If you spend the 75 cents on the candy, you won't have it anymore. But there are other prices operating here, in ways that are less obvious but just as important. The store owner decided to display that candy bar, and not some other; another display choice might have resulted in increased sales. The candy maker uses her machines, buildings, and distribution network to put that candy bar, and not some other one, in the stores. Just as price affects your decision to buy the candy bar, price influences the store owner and the manufacturer in their choices about what to display, and what to produce.

More broadly, in a market system, the prices of resources serve two very different, and very important, functions.[5] First, prices are signals about the relative scarcities of resources. Second, prices determine wealth by giving information on the value of the resources owned by individuals. Let's consider each of these functions in turn.

Prices are scarcity signals. Suppose you aren't just worried about candy bars anymore. Suppose you were put in charge of planning a very large number of activities. In fact, you must make all production decisions and consumption choices in an entire nation. What is the right set of choices? You must first allocate all of your productive resources among myriad alternative uses. Then you have to decide who gets to consume all these different outputs, and how much they get.

Start with farmland: Should you grow corn, wheat, or soybeans? Should you grow cotton? Should you use the land for cows for dairy products, or pigs for food, or sheep for wool to make warm clothing? After all these production decisions are made, your storehouses are full of clothes, food, and machines; how do you dole them out? What allocation rule would give you the "best" result? You could give everyone an equal share, or you could use some other rule to assess each person's needs.

Obviously, in a market system this is not the way things work, because there is no central planner who directs resources to their highest valued use. A farmer in central Illinois doesn't wait for a letter from the government to decide how to use his land. Instead, he makes forecasts of the results of different courses of action, and then chooses the one course of action that results in the largest excess of revenue over costs. What information is available to make these forecasts? How does the farmer know what to do, if he is not given instructions from a central planner?

The farmer uses prices as a signal. Notice how cheaply, and yet elegantly, price signals the value of different resources for the society. The farmer looks at a newspaper, and sees that soybean prices (let's keep this simple, and ignore futures markets) have risen by more than $2.00 per bushel, from $6.20 per bushel to $8.25 per bushel. If he is a reflective man, he may wonder why. If he is a compassionate man, he may feel sorrow for the hardships that the scarcity of soybeans is imposing on consumers. But suppose he is neither reflective nor compassionate. Suppose this farmer is a terrible, selfish man, not at all given to altruistic impulses. What does he do? He immediately drives to the seed store, and plants every inch of land he owns in soybeans!

So the selfish, narrow-minded, "only out for himself" farmer hurries to do what an omniscient, benevolent central planner would have wanted the farmer to do from the perspective of benefiting the entire society. This should give you goosebumps: the selfish farmer (1) didn't need to know the source of the scarcity, and (2) doesn't need to care about the welfare of those harmed by the scarcity. All he needs to do is care about himself, and the scarcity is very effectively addressed. This feature of markets has been extensively analyzed, by

F. A. Hayek (in his 1945 article "The Use of Knowledge in Society") and others, but the best-known statement of the function of prices is the earliest. In his 1776 *The Wealth of Nations*, Adam Smith resolved the problem of how resources are directed to their highest-valued use without resort to any central direction whatsoever:

> Every individual is continually exerting himself to find out the most advantageous employment for whatever capital he can command. It is his own advantage, indeed, and not that of the society, which he has in view. But the study of his own advantage naturally, or rather necessarily leads him to prefer that employment which is most advantageous to the society.
>
> . . . As every individual, therefore, endeavours as much as he can both to employ his capital in the support of domestic industry, and so to direct that industry that its produce may be of the greatest value; every individual necessarily labours to render the annual revenue of the society as great as he can. He generally, indeed, neither intends to promote the public interest, nor knows how much he is promoting it. . . . By preferring that industry in such a manner as its produce may be of the greatest value, he intends only his own gain, and he is in this, as in many other cases, led by an invisible hand to promote an end which was no part of his intention. By pursuing his own interest he frequently promotes that of the society more effectually than when he really intends to promote it. . . .
>
> What is the species of domestic industry which his capital can employ, and of which the produce is likely to be of the greatest value, every individual, it is evident, can, in his local situation, judge much better than any statesman or lawgiver can do for him. The statesman, who should attempt to direct private people in what manner they ought to employ their capitals, would not only load himself with a most unnecessary attention, but assume an authority which could safely be trusted, not only to no single person, but to no council or senate whatever, and which would nowhere be so dangerous as in the hands of a man who had folly and presumption enough to fancy himself fit to exercise it. (Smith, 1994, pp. 484–5)

In these passages, Smith is making two rather astonishing claims: (1) In a properly functioning market system, actions based on self-interests are identical with those actions implied by altruism (ignoring problems of the distribution of wealth). (2) The net value (i.e., the benefits minus the costs of operation and of transmission of information) of a price system for signaling scarcity, and directing resources, is so great that no expert-driven central planning regime could possibly duplicate it. With hindsight, and two hundred years of economic analysis of markets, we now know that there are a number of important qualifications and corrections that weaken these claims. In some cases, as we will see in later chapters, one or both claims are simply not true.

Still, the basic structure of Smith's reasoning has stood the test of time. Markets are uniquely suited to foster the organization of large numbers of decentralized production and consumption decisions. Not only is no central plan required to create this happy result, but even the most draconian repression of market processes is unlikely to snuff out a "black market" system of exchanges based on the self-interest of the participants. This is the "efficiency" argument for market processes, and it is a powerful argument indeed.

Prices determine wealth in a market system. As I noted above, prices have two functions in a market system. The first, directing economic activity in production and consumption by producing signals of relative scarcity, is the one proponents of the market point to when they advocate the use of markets. What about the second function, the determination of wealth?

Wealth has two very different definitions, and it is important to keep them distinct. In a material sense, wealth might simply mean possession of a surplus of consumption goods. Robinson Crusoe, alone on his island, might have been wealthy in this sense, if he were able to provide for his own needs very comfortably by farming and by using the flotsam washed up from the wreck of his ship.

But we usually mean something different by "wealth," because we live in a society where there are markets, with production and exchange going on all around us. In this setting, wealth means the possession of command over lots of resources, and the ability to sell these resources to others, to direct their use, or to store them for use in the future. So one can no longer measure wealth by how much stuff one has. Instead, wealth is determined by the *monetary value* of all that stuff. And value means that we need prices.

Suppose that there are n different products or resources one might own, and let us use i as an index for some unspecified resource. Let x represent resources, and let p represent prices. Then, for example, x might be acres of land (suppose the person has four acres), and p is the price of one acre (each acre is worth \$15,000). The value of land the person owns would then be $x \times p$ (in this case, $4 \times \$15,000 = \$60,000$) so that part of the person's wealth could be measured this way. Formally, total wealth can be defined as follows on page 68:

$$Wealth = \sum_{i=1}^{n} x_i p_i$$

This may seem disturbing, when you think about it. If prices change, your wealth changes, *even though the amount of stuff you own hasn't changed at all*. To put it another way, you aren't wealthy unless the society you live in places a high value on the resources you control. Most disturbing of all, a significant part of most people's wealth is their own labor, which they offer in the market in exchange for wages. If the value of your labor is very low, you are poor. This may happen because your skills, though significant, are obsolete, as in the case of a buggy whip maker, or are in excess supply, as with a migrant farm field worker.

The reason this creates difficulty is that, in a market system, the "demand" each of us has for consumer products is based not on how much we want the product, subjectively, but rather on how much our want is made effective by wealth. For example, consider this problem: How much does a starving person want a sandwich? The answer is hard to swallow: If the starving person doesn't have any money, he doesn't want the sandwich at all, not one bit! From a practical perspective, this is nonsense, of course: the starving man is desperate for food. But market systems operate on the premise that human desires have to be made effective by an offer of wealth, of one form or another.

If the working of market processes leaves some people with too little wealth to survive, society may decide that the distribution of wealth needs to be changed. There are many ways of effecting this redistribution, but the premise is always the same: Markets may operate efficiently, in the sense of directing resources to their highest-valued use. But that conception of "value" relies on the prices of resources possessed by individuals, and on the demands made effective by the value of those resources. To the extent that this definition of *monetary value* (based on scarcity) does not correspond to the *ethical values* (in terms of a theory of justice) of the society, then the distribution of wealth needs to be adjusted. The particular value which is generally invoked to justify income redistribution from the wealthy to the poor is "equity," or the sense that all citizens are entitled to a certain standard of living.

The performance of markets in terms of scarcity signaling (*efficiency*) is well established; the performance of markets in terms of ethical values (*equity*) is much more hotly debated. Furthermore, just to make everything a little more interesting, it turns out that expert-driven regulatory policies to improve performance on one dimension of performance may hurt performance on the other dimension. For example, an income tax designed to redistribute wealth from the rich to the poor can hurt efficiency, because it distorts the signal sent by effective (after-tax) income. The conflict between efficiency arguments and equity arguments is one of the central themes in policy analysis, as we will see.

Looking Inside Market Processes

In the previous section, I claimed that the functions of transmitting information and creating appropriate incentives are the hallmarks of properly functioning markets. But what does "properly functioning" mean? And if markets are so wonderful, where do they come from? These are difficult questions, and this chapter can only make a start at answering them. The question of proper function, and of market failure in particular, won't be answered in full until chapter 4.

To crack open the notion of "markets," and see what is inside, three smaller questions will occupy the discussion for the remainder of this chapter:

- How do markets originate?
- How does a pure barter system (i.e., exchange of goods, with neither currency nor production) serve to improve aggregate welfare?
- What are the functions of money, and how does money affect market processes?

Market Origins

Earlier in this chapter, I claimed that markets are likely to arise, spontaneously and without conscious decision on the part of any central authority, under any one or more of four conditions. It is useful to repeat those four conditions, because it is easy to forget how general and flexible markets can be. These four conditions have to do with preferences, endowments, economies of scale, and division of labor (specialization).

Diverse preferences. This means my likes are different from your likes. Suppose we all got an identical initial endowment of fruit to eat: four oranges and four apples. Imagine I like oranges better than apples, but your likes, or "preferences," are the reverse. Then, if I give you an apple and you give me an orange, we are both better off. This may seem like magic, because we are both better off even though the total amount of resources (eight apples and eight oranges) in our little society is unchanged. It isn't magic, of course. Instead, fostering exchange at low cost is the primary reason markets, or something like markets, are universal in human societies, even those which had no contact with other groups. Resort to the market, or exchanges among people, improves the allocation of resources by directing each resource to it highest-valued use. In this case, each person gets to eat more of the fruit he or she prefers.

Diverse endowments. My likes are the same as yours, but we have different resources. Using the fruit example again, suppose that both of us like the same thing, fruit salad! Imagine our resource endowments are distressingly monochrome, however: I have eight oranges, and you have eight apples. If what we really like is fruit salad (sliced oranges mixed with sliced apples), we are mutually benefited by exchanging apples for oranges. If I trade four of my oranges for four of your apples, we each have four of both kinds of fruit, and we are both better off with our mixed fruit salad.

Economies of scale. An economy of scale is a technical condition, meaning that the cost per unit of producing an output falls as more output is produced. Suppose you had to hammer a nail, and bought a hammer for $10 to do it. Hammering that nail cost you $10.00, plus a nickel for the nail and a quarter for your time. So your cost per nail is $10.30. Now suppose you were hired to hammer ten nails; your average cost is ($10 + $.50 + $2.50)/10, or $1.30 per nail. This situation is common in the use of expensive "capital," or equipment for jobs. Because markets allow us to exchange services, one person who is pursuing nothing but his own self-interest will purchase tools which he could not justify for his personal use alone. But this results in a lower price for the service for everyone. As Adam Smith notes:

> It is the maxim of every prudent master of a family, never to attempt to make at home what it will cost him more to make than buy. The taylor does not attempt to make his own shoes, but buys them of the shoe-

maker. The shoemaker does not attempt to make his own clothes, but employes a taylor. The farmer attempts to make neither the one nor the other, but employs those different artificers. All of them find it for their interest to employ their whole industry in a way in which they have some advantage over their neighbours, and to purchase with a part of its produce, or what is the same thing, with the price of a part of it, whatever else they have occasion for. (p. 485)

As a market system becomes more highly developed, enterprises spring up that can realize enormous economies of scale. Consider the cost per automobile if each automobile, or personal computer, had to be made separately, from a unique plan. If each of us had to rely on our own resources, we would enjoy very few of the technological marvels that now fill our homes. The reason we see these amenities, and are able to buy them at low prices, is that markets have developed to exploit the profit potential of economies of scale.

Specialization. Efficiency gains from specialization are different from decreasing average costs. Adam Smith was the first to recognize this important feature of production processes in his famous example of the "pin factory":

To take an example, therefore, from a very trifling manufacture, but one in which the division of labour has been very often taken notice of, the trade of the pin-maker; a workman not educated to this business (which the division of labour has rendered a distinct trade), nor acquainted with the use of the machinery employed in it (to the invention of which the same division of labour has probably given occasion), could scarce, perhaps, with his utmost industry, make one pin in a day, and certainly could not make twenty. But in the way in which this business is now carried on, not only the whole work is a peculiar trade, but it is divided into a number of branches, of which the greater part are likewise peculiar trades. One man draws out the wire, another straights it, a third cuts it, a fourth points it, a fifth grinds it at the top for receiving the head; the making of the head requires two or three distinct operations; to put it on, is a peculiar business, to whiten the pin is another; it is even a trade in itself to put them into the paper; and the important business of making a pin is, in this manner, divided into about eighteen distinct operation, which, in some manufactories, are all performed by distinct hands, though in others the same man will sometimes perform two or three of them. I have seen a small manufactory of this kind where ten men only were employed, and where some of them consequently performed two or three distinct operations. But though they were very poor, and therefore but indifferently

accommodated with the necessary machinery, they could, when they ex-
erted themselves, make among them about twelve pounds of pins in a
day. There are in a pound upwards of four thousand pins of middling
size. Those ten persons, therefore, could make among them upwards of
forty eight thousand pins in a day. But if they had all wrought separately
and independently, and without any of them having been educated to
this peculiar business, they certainly could not each of them have made
twenty, perhaps not one pin in a day. (Smith, 1994, pp. 4–5)

It is important to understand the distinction between the two types
of productive efficiencies fostered by markets. *Economies of scale*
mean products in capital-intensive industries are cheaper, as more
output is produced. The gains to *specialization* derive from the division of labor into a larger number of smaller, discrete tasks. But both
economies of scale and the division of labor are limited by the extent
of the demand for the product.[6] By rewarding increases in scale, and
specialization, markets tie us all closer together, and create links, first
across families, then across communities, and eventually across nations, as entrepreneurs seek out larger markets.

Barter and Pure Exchange

A "barter" system is created, or may just emerge spontaneously, as a
means to capture gains from trade. As was pointed out in the apples,
oranges, and blueberries examples earlier in this chapter, diversity in
either preferences or endowments creates the surprising opportunity
for doing magic: Exchange improves *everyone's* welfare, just by rearranging consumption bundles. That is, allowing trade, without increasing the total quantity available for consumption, can increase the
value each person places on his or her consumption.
    We could start at a simpler level, of course. A true "Robinson Cru-
soe" economy, with just one person, is still an interesting problem.
Our Robinson has complex analysis to perform, as he decides how to
allocate his effort in growing, hunting, and gathering food, finding
water, and building shelter. Each minute spent in one activity "costs"
Robinson whatever he could have done with that minute in some
other activity. Suppose he spends a month working on a garden, instead of fishing and preserving the fish he catches by salting and
drying them. If the garden fails, Mr. Crusoe may starve. There are incentives, because there are costs, in Robinson Crusoe's world.
    But the fact that there are costs doesn't mean that there is a mar-

ket. The distinctive feature of markets is their use of a price system to allocate resources and send signals of relative scarcity. As F. A. Hayek (1945) argued,

> The economic problem of society is . . . how to secure the best use of re-sources known to any members of society, for ends whose relative impor-tance only these individuals know . . . the knowledge of the particular circumstances of time and place. . . . To know of and put to use a ma-chine not fully employed, or somebody's skill which could be better uti-lized, or to be aware of a surplus stock which can be drawn upon during an interruption of supplies, is socially quite as useful as the knowledge of better alternative techniques. (pp. 520–22)
> . . . It follows from this that central planning based on statistical infor-mation by its nature cannot take direct account of these circumstances of time and place. . . . (p. 524)
> Assume that somewhere in the world a new opportunity for the use of some raw material, say tin, has arisen, or that one of the sources of supply of tin has been eliminated. It does not matter—and it is very significant that it does not matter—which of these two causes has made tin more scarce. All that the users of tin need to know is that some of the tin they used to consume is now more profitably employed elsewhere, and that in consequence they must economize tin. . . . The most significant fact about [market processes] is the economy of knowledge with which it op-erates, or how little the individual participants need to know in order to be able to take the right action. In abbreviated form, by a kind of symbol, only the most essential information is passed on, and passed on only to those concerned. It is more than a metaphor to describe the price system as a kind of machinery for registering change, or a system of telecommu-nications which enables individual producers to watch merely the move-ment of a few [prices] . . . in order to adjust their activities to changes of which they may never know more than is reflected in the price move-ment. . . . The marvel is that in a case like that of a scarcity of one raw material, without an order being issued, without more than perhaps a handful of people knowing the cause, tens of thousands of people whose identity could not be ascertained by months of investigation, are made to use the material or its products more sparingly; i.e., they move in the right direction. (pp. 526–27)

Put simply, markets are useful to societies because they can orga-nize the activities of members of society, even in the absence of any central plan or direction. That is why even the most primitive market requires at least two people. Hayek is claiming that, especially in huge markets with thousands or millions of people, the organizing and directing function of prices is more important than one might think.

Indifference curves: analyzing bargaining and the gains from trade. People have tastes that drive their consumption choices; exchange is perhaps the most important way for people to satisfy these tastes. To see how this works, let's consider a simple example. Economists talk about the trade-offs between guns and butter; let's not be so boring. We will analyze the trade-off between guns (more broadly, defense) and roses (representing the arts and other cultural amenities). Consider a representative citizen in the society where roses and guns are the only products available for consumption, and assume the following four statements are true:

• More guns are better.[7]
• More roses are better.
• The fewer guns I have, the more I value an additional gun.
• The fewer roses I have, the more I value an additional rose.

If these statements are accepted, we can depict a "map" of the value the citizen places on different combinations of roses and guns. More technically, we can represent the citizen's preferences, using what are called **indifference curves**. Pick any point in the nonnegative quadrant of consumption space, depicted in Figure 3.1. Restricting ourselves to the nonnegative quadrant simply means that the citizen must consume quantities of roses, and guns, of at least zero: there can be no negative consumption.

Suppose that, when I said "pick any point," you picked B. There are then three types of alternative consumption bundles in the picture. Some, like D, with fewer roses and fewer guns, the citizen likes less than B. On the other hand, if the consumption bundle has more guns and more roses, as with point E, the citizen likes it better. If there are some points the citizen likes better, and some the citizen likes less, than B, there must be some boundary between these two sets. This boundary is the **indifference curve**, or the set of consumption bundles the citizen likes just as well as B. All we know for sure is that there are some points with more guns and fewer roses, and others with more roses and fewer guns, such that the citizen is indifferent between these points and B. For the sake of example, I have arbitrarily chosen points A and C, and drawn the indifference curve implied by this preference profile.

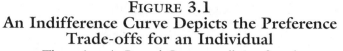

FIGURE **3.1**
**An Indifference Curve Depicts the Preference
Trade-offs for an Individual**
The points A, B, and C are equally preferred

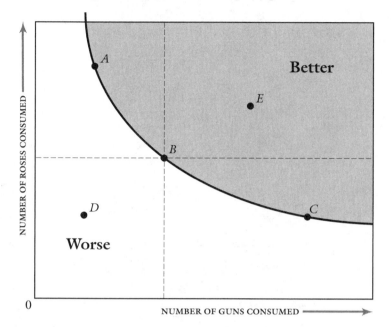

Indifference curves are very useful for analyzing bargaining and the gains from trade. The fact that every point "above" an indifference curve (i.e., all consumption bundles with no less of both, and more of at least one, of the commodities compared to the points on the curve) is strictly preferred to any point on the curve, and that points "below" the curve are strictly inferior, allows us to depict problems of commodity exchange very precisely.

To see this, consider Figure 3.2. Panel A depicts an exchange problem for two people, Mr. 1 and Ms. 2. Suppose there is a total of forty guns and thirty roses available for allocation for consumption for the two people, and that Mr. 1 starts out with thirty guns, five roses—[let's write this "(30, 5)"—and that Ms. 2 starts with (10, 25)].

The Edgeworth box and the contract curve. The box in Figure 3.2 is called an **Edgeworth box**, after its creator, Francis Ysidro Edgeworth. The clever thing about an Edgeworth box is that its dimensions depend on the *total* amount of the resources available (the box

FIGURE 3.2
Gains from Exchange
Everyone is better off, though the total quality of
guns and roses is unchanged.

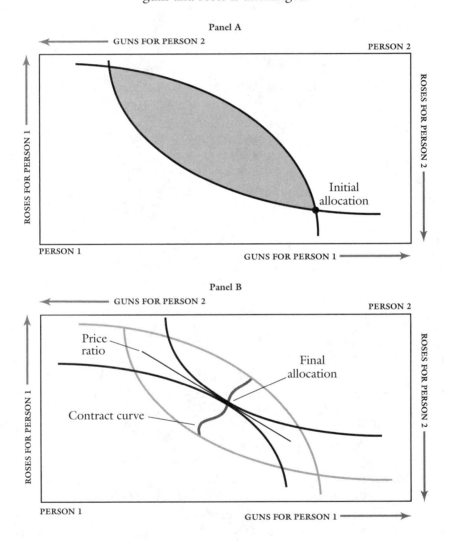

is thirty roses high, and forty guns wide). But each position in the
Edgeworth box depicts the way this total quantity of resources is divided up. So, any point in the interior of the box actually has *four* coordinates: an allocation for Mr. 1—in this case, (30, 5)—, and an allocation
for Ms. 2—here, (10, 25). Notice that the allocations are assumed to
have no waste, or leakage, so that 30 + 10 = 40, and 5 + 25 = 30.

The top right corner of the box is the "origin," or (0,0) point, for Ms. 2; it is also the point where Mr. 1 gets everything: (40, 30).

The question the Edgeworth box provokes is obvious, but it is important: Are there any allocations that are *stable*, in the sense that if such an allocation is ever achieved, at least one party will refuse to exchange any of the commodities he possesses for a quantity of some other commodity his trading partner is willing to give? A stable allocation of this sort is called an **equilibrium**, because it does not change. Is the initial allocation, where Mr. 1 has (30, 5) and Ms. 2 has (10, 25), an equilibrium?

The answer depends, of course, on whether there are any feasible trades that make both parties strictly better off. As you recall, any allocation "above" the relevant indifference curve is strictly preferred by the citizen to any point on the curve. This is true for both people, so the determination of whether there are any mutually beneficial trades amounts to a simple graphical question: is there a non-empty intersection of the sets of consumption bundles preferred to the initial allocation?

You bet there is! The hatched area, called the **lens** for its resemblance to an optical glass in side view, is the set of points both parties prefer to the initial allocation. The edges of the set—the two indifference curves—represent the boundaries of the set of mutually beneficial trading outcomes. So, the initial allocation is not an equilibrium, and we might conclude (rightly) that any division of the commodities is not an equilibrium if the intersection of preferred bundles is nonempty. But then it seems like you could draw a figure analogous to panel A over and over, without ever establishing what we really want to know: What allocations *could* be equilibria?

The answer is actually fairly easy, when you think about it. Panel B shows an example of an equilibrium consistent with trading starting at the initial allocation of (30, 5), (10, 25). That equilibrium occurs at (22, 16) for Mr. 1, and (18, 14) for Ms. 2. How do we know that this is an equilibrium? Consider the set of points Mr. 1 prefers to this "final allocation": the points above and to the right of the indifference curve through (22, 16). Likewise, for Ms. 2: she likes points below and to the left of (18, 14) (where the coordinates are measured out from her origin, at the top right corner). What is the overlap of the two sets of preferred bundles? There is none, except the allocation itself: the indifference curves are tangent to each other. Tangency means, by definition, that the curves intersect at only point: the equilibrium itself.

There are many such points of tangency for different pairs of indifference curves, of course. Depending on the preferences of the traders, the points of tangency can lie near the straight 45-degree line connecting the two origins, or these points can wander around, as shown in the heavy dotted line in panel B. Regardless of the shape of the line connecting the points of tangency, this set of potential equilibria is called the **contract curve**, because we expect that fully informed trading partners will always ultimately write a contract that puts them somewhere on this curve. Later in this chapter, I will introduce some measures for evaluating performance, but it is worth pointing out that we have already discovered one, the "Pareto optimum." (In chapter 2, we discussed the Pareto criterion as a means for assessing whether a policy is efficient; we'll now move on to a more precise measure.)

> **Pareto optimum**: An allocation of resources such that any trade
> or exchange makes at least one party to the trade worse off.

It follows immediately that all points on the contract curve are Pareto optima. It also follows immediately that the concept of Pareto optimum is not a very strong criterion for evaluation. Notice that the following allocation (one endpoint of the contract curve) is a Pareto optimum: Mr. 1 gets everything, Ms. 2 gets nothing. So is the opposite endpoint on the contract curve, where Mr. 1 gets nothing and Ms. takes it all. In a broader sense, we might want to say that neither of these is terribly "optimal," from the perspective of society.

Still, it is clearly true that points off the contract curve (i.e., allocations that are not Pareto optima) are poor candidates for selection as policy "solutions." By definition, points off the contract curve allow reallocations such that both parties can be made better off. So, the intuition of the Pareto optimum has more to do with efficiency (the absence of waste), than with any normative criterion of equity in distribution.

One final point: What about price? I have argued that the essence of the market system is the use of price to allocate resources. Yet it doesn't seem that prices appear anywhere in the analysis of exchange I have presented. Well, that's wrong: prices lurk at each point on the contract curve in the Edgeworth box. We are all accustomed to thinking of prices in terms of money, but the example in Figure 3.2 involves only pure exchange. That is how prices started out: to get something you wanted, you had to give up something in exchange.

Consequently, the price of a gun (in our example) is the number of roses you have to pay. In our example, it appears that (at the equilibrium) two guns exchange for three roses; that means that the price of a gun is 1.5 roses. Graphically, the price is the slope of the line through the point of tangency which intersects the indifference curves only at that point.

The Functions of Money

Why do we need money at all? What's wrong with barter? After all, as we saw from the Edgeworth box in the previous section, it is possible to arrive at a Pareto optimum through barter alone. The price ratio implied by that equilibrium reflects the relative scarcity of the commodities available for consumption, given the preferences of the market participants. If I have to give up one apple to get half an orange, the opportunity cost of consuming that half orange is clear: I don't get to eat the apple.

But prices are usually stated in terms of an abstraction: money. You may never have given money much thought (unless you were trying to get more!), but money is an astonishing creation. Without money, large societies as we know them could not exist. Let's start with a definition.

> **money**: a generally accepted medium of exchange, representing
> abstract command over any goods and services available in
> the market.

But that doesn't help very much, and is very nearly circular: if I will accept something in exchange for my goods, that means I must believe it has value as a medium of exchange. Why would I believe that it has such value? Because I think other people will accept it in exchange for their goods. This is all rather upsetting, because we would like to have a better definition. But there really isn't one; we can only list the characteristics that make for "good" money, or currency.

Characteristics of a Good Currency

1. Widely accepted as a *medium of exchange*, for any kind of transaction
2. Clear, consistent *unit of account* (one unit is identical with another)

3. *Store of value* (does not deteriorate if unspent)
4. *Durable* (does not wear out)
5. *Difficult to counterfeit* or create (not easily debased)
6. *Divisible* into small units (so you can make change)

Now we can answer the "Why not barter?" question. Suppose that we had not two, but three people, and three commodities. This is still a pretty simple society, but the added complexity in negotiating exchanges is considerable. With three people and three commodities, you may not be able to exchange your goods directly for what you want. Instead, you may have to conduct intermediate exchanges, and visit both other traders, to reach a Pareto optimal distribution of resources.

Suppose Mr. 1 has apples, doesn't like oranges, and wants to get some bananas. Mr. 1 goes to Mr. 3, who has lots of bananas. However, Mr. 3 doesn't like apples; he will only trade his bananas for oranges. So Mr. 1 has to go over to Ms. 2, the orange grower, and trade apples for oranges. Then, but only then, can Mr. 1 go back to Mr. 3 and effect the trade Mr. 1 wanted to make all along, securing bananas for his supper.

Notice that this is true even if there is universal agreement (or a law) that the "price" of any one fruit is any other fruit—that is, an apple exchanges for an orange exchanges for a banana exchanges for an apple. If I have an apple, and you have a banana, I would like to trade. But you hate apples, and insist on an orange. I could walk over to the neighbor's house, a mile away, and trade my apple for an orange, but that is too much trouble. More simply, the difference in my satisfaction between the banana I love and the apple I like is not enough to make me walk two miles. The essence of barter is, then, not "haggling," or the separate negotiation of price, but rather the act of physically exchanging one commodity for an agreed-on amount of another commodity.

The inconvenience and time wasted in making trades through barter dissipates much, or all, of the value of the trade. Economists call this friction in making exchanges **transaction costs**. Transaction costs are pure deadweight losses, because no one gets any value or advantage out of the waste of time and energy. Reducing transaction costs is Pareto superior, because you are (in effect) getting something for nothing.

And there is our answer: People use money, instead of barter, because money reduces the transaction cost of exchange. Our three fruit-lovers might agree to create a "fruit note," with the understanding that one unit of fruit note exchanges for an apple, a banana, or an orange. Then the holder of a note has abstract command over fruit of any type; Mr. 1 can immediately obtain his bananas, without the intermediate exchanges.

There are other advantages, of course. Mr. 1, who has apple trees, could plausibly borrow against his nearly ripe, but not yet edible, apple crop, obtaining fruit notes on loan from Mr. 2, with the understanding that the fruit notes will be paid back when it becomes possible to sell the apples. In effect, Mr. 1 is just exchanging apples in the future for bananas now, but the institution of a currency facilitates this exchange.

In nearly all human societies, most economic activity is concerned with the making and spending of money incomes. Historically, many different objects have served as money, including stones, shells, ivory, wampum beads, tobacco, furs, and dried fish, but it appears that even from the earliest times precious metals (especially gold and silver) have been preferred because they satisfy the characteristics of "good" money listed above.

To a larger and larger extent, however, money does not depend on its value as a commodity. Paper currency was first issued about three hundred years ago, but until recently it was almost universally "backed" by some standard commodity of intrinsic value into which the currency could be freely converted on demand. By contrast, *fiat money* is inconvertible money made legal tender by the decree of the government. The Australian government has introduced a plastic money, lighter and cheaper than metal, and more durable than paper.

But most money in the world does not exist at all, at least not in any physical sense. More than 90 percent of the world's "money" exists only as a binary code on some electromagnetic medium, with an electronic tag identifying who owns it. The increasing use of credit cards, ATM debit cards, and other "paperless" forms of transactions appears destined to eliminate the last 10 percent of money held as currency or commodities. Why? Because eliminating the physical aspect of money reduces transaction cost even further. Aren't markets wonderful?

Well, yes, markets are wonderful. Immediately following this chapter is a case study excerpted from a fascinating account of the spontaneous emergence of a set of institutions of exchange, showing how a "market" based on a cigarette currency allowed a group of prisoners of war to improve their lives. But the market system of organization is not perfect, and sometimes it is downright bad. In chapter 4 we will consider failures of markets, and difficulties in evaluating market processes.

Summary

Let us retrace the main argument of this chapter. Markets are a very efficient means of organizing large groups of people for activities that do not harm, and often advance, the interests of society. By using a price system, markets give signals as to the relative scarcity of resources, and determine the wealth of market participants. Providing that people work to increase their wealth (that is, act selfishly), the incentives afforded by prices direct the actions, and resources, of citizens toward creating the most value. A social planner with perfect information and the most honorable intentions, trying to match desires with resources, could do no better. In fact, in many circumstances the social planner might do worse. Without a price system to provide information and incentives, the task of planning is very difficult.

We also began to develop the analytic machinery for understanding some of the shortcomings, and outright failings, of markets. The origin of markets, defined as a set of institutions for fostering exchange, lies in primitive systems of barter. Differences in preferences, differences in resource endowments, and conditions on production such as economies of scale and division of labor, give rise to the potential for markets. But the actual institutions of markets arise only when people try to capture the gains from trade associated with these conditions. The way to gauge the extent of potential gains from trade is to analyze preferences, using indifference curves. We will use indifference curves a lot in the next chapter, so be sure you understand how to use them.

The final piece to the puzzle of how markets work is one of the most important innovations in human history: money. Most people don't think much about money; they just use it, and want more of it. But money is the lubricant that allows modern market economies to work efficiently. The case that follows this chapter gives an account of the spontaneous emergence of a surprising "currency" in a rather strange economy. All the elements that I have laid out in this chapter, including gains from trade through barter, the origin of market institutions, and the use of money, can be found there.

SUMMARY OF KEY CONCEPTS

1. A *market* is a set of institutions for reducing transactions costs of the exchange of goods and services.
2. In a *barter* economy, goods or services are directly exchanged, without the use of money, and usually for the purpose of consumption or immediate use, without plans for further exchange.
3. An *autarky* is a type of economic organization in which it is efficient to produce all goods by oneself.
4. A market system produces *information* cheaply and accurately about the relative scarcity of goods.
5. A market system utilizes *incentives* or self-interest instead of ethics or altruism to organize markets.

PRECONDITIONS FOR MARKETS

6. Although markets spontaneously emerge in many contexts, there are a set of preconditions that must be satisfied for a market to emerge and persist. These preconditions are *diverse preferences, diverse endowments, economies of scale,* and *specialization.*
7. Diverse preferences refer to differences in tastes, goals, or desires.
8. Diverse endowments refer to differences in resources and abilities.
9. If the average cost of producing a good declines with an increase in the quantity produced, then there is an economy of scale.
10. Specialization results if the average cost of production declines with a decrease in the scope of activity of a producer.

BENEFITS OF MARKETS

11. Diverse preferences and diverse endowments are preconditions for a market because they create the potential for *gains from trade.* There are gains from trade because the rearrangement of consumption bundles through voluntary and informed exchange increases the welfare of those involved.

12. Economies of scale and specialization lead to *gains in productive efficiency*. The gains result because the increase in production means that there are more goods to consume.
13. *Prices* help convey information about the relative scarcity of goods.

THE PROBLEM OF SCARCITY

14. The *opportunity cost* is the uses and benefits of a resource that were given up by using the resource for another purpose.
15. *Scarcity* results if the effective opportunity cost of a resource exceeds zero. Thus any resource with a price greater than zero can be considered scarce.
16. *Pigou's conjecture* is the idea that a market is inefficient in terms of allocating resources if the social opportunity cost of a resource diverges from the price or the private cost to the user.
17. *Coase's counter-conjecture* is the idea that market forces will lead the opportunity cost and price of a resource to converge if property rights are clearly and exclusively defined and the cost of writing and enforcing contracts is not too high.
18. *Transaction costs* are the foregone value of the next best alternative use (i.e., opportunity costs) of the resources expended in controlling or exchanging property rights.

MEANS OF ALLOCATING SCARCE RESOURCES

19. The *price system* (market) is a method of allocating scarce resources. The price system allocates resources to their highest-valued use through the exchange of valuable goods or currency.
20. *Queuing* is a method of allocating scarce resources through waiting in line.
21. *Chance* is a method of allocating resources through a random selection process such as a lottery that affords all an equal chance of obtaining the scarce resources.
22. Resources can be allocated through the discretion of an *authority* figure or group, such as policy experts, political parties, or central planners.

INFORMATIONAL FUNCTION OF PRICES

23. The price of a resource is a relative *scarcity signal* because it represents the value of the resource in relation to other resources in society. Therefore, prices help direct production and consumption through a decentralized process.
24. Wealth in the context of a market system is measured by the monetary value (given prices) of the resources an individual possesses. Therefore, decreases in the prices of the resources an individual possesses imply a decrease in that individual's wealth.

EDGEWORTH BOX

25. An *indifference curve* represents the set of consumption bundles that produce equal amounts of welfare for the individual.
26. The *Edgeworth box* provides a method for representing a barter economy with two parties and two resources. The bottom (top) of the box represents the allocation of resource A for party 1 (2). The left (right) of the box represents the allocation of resource B for party 1 (2). Any point in the box represents four allocations: the allocation of resources A and B for parties 1 and 2.
27. The *lens* represents the set of points or allocations of resources in an Edgeworth box that both parties prefer to the initial allocation.
28. An allocation of resources is in *equilibrium* or stable if there does not exist another allocation of resources that all parties prefer.
29. The *contract curve* is the set of points or resource allocations that are potential equilibria. The curve consists of the points in the Edgeworth box where the indifference curves for parties 1 and 2 are tangent.
30. A *Pareto optimum* is an allocation of resources such that any reallocation of resources makes at least one party worse off. All points on the contract curve are Pareto optima.

MONEY

31. *Money* or *currency* is a generally accepted medium of exchange that represents abstract command over any goods and services available in the market.

32. Money is used as a medium of exchange because it reduces the transaction costs of exchange.
33. Money is also a *store of wealth or value* because it does not deteriorate if unspent.

CHARACTERISTICS OF A GOOD CURRENCY

34. A good currency is *widely accepted* as a medium of exchange.
35. A good currency is a *clear, consistent* unit of account. If one unit of currency is identical to another, then the currency is clear and consistent.
36. A good currency is nonperishable and *durable*. If the currency did not last, it would not be an effective store of value.
37. A good currency is *difficult to counterfeit*. If a currency is easily counterfeited, then its value can easily be debased and therefore would not be an effective store of value.
38. A good currency is easily *divisible* into small units. Divisibility facilitates exchanges.

PROBLEMS AND QUESTIONS

1. Suppose that a society has a total of two people (Xerxes and Zenobia), and the following quantities of two commodities: fifty pomegranates and thirty wheels of goat cheese. Draw the Edgeworth box for the society, assuming the origin for Xerxes is at the bottom left and the origin for Zenobia is at the top right.

2. In this same diagram, draw a set of indifference curves for Zenobia, and a set for Xerxes. (Remember that higher levels of utility are down and to the left for Zenobia!) Make sure that no two indifference curves representing the same person cross each other, and be careful that you don't violate the "more of both is better" rule.

3. Given the indifference maps you have constructed for Xerxes and Zenobia, draw in the contract curve with a heavy black line. By definition, every point on the contract curve is a Pareto optimum; every point off the curve is therefore inefficient, because it is Pareto inferior to at least one point on the contract curve. Make an argument for why any point not on the contract curve is wasteful, in the sense that it is not the best use of resources available to the society.

4. Identify the point (call it P_1) in the box where Xerxes gets fourty pomegranates and five cheeses, and Zenobia gets ten pomegranates and twenty-five cheeses. Is this point on the contract curve, as you have drawn it? (Hint: The answer will be no, unless you have drawn some *very* unusual indifference curves).

5. Redraw the section of the diagram you have already constructed to identify the lens, or bargaining space, associated with P_1. Be careful to place P_1 first, then draw one indifference curve that passes through P_1 for Xerxes, and one for Zenobia. The lens will then be the overlap of the points preferred to P_1 by Xerxes and the points preferred to P_1 by Zenobia.

6. Consider the four means for allocating scarce resources (price, queuing, lotteries, and authority). Give at least one example in the real world where this allocation scheme is used, and offer an explanation why. Is one of these allocation schemes inherently better than the others, or is each useful in the right situation?

7. How does money help reduce the transaction costs of exchange? Discuss one of the good characteristics of good money and suggest why it is important to facilitating exchange.

TAKE IT TO THE NET!

Go to: http://www.wwnorton.com/college/polisci/analyzingpolicy for additional problems, data sets, and course materials.

NOTES

1. On the other hand, the "money is a veil" perspective is probably too narrow. Like other institutions, a monetary system can perform more or less well, depending on expectations and transparency. As Gurley (1961) said, in reviewing a book by Milton Friedman, "Money is a veil, but when the veil flutters, real output sputters." (Quoted in George Selgin's introduction to Yeager, 1997).

2. Actually, the answer *could* be yes, in either of two circumstances: (1) An "income effect" might push you past the threshold to attend the concert, if attendance is not inferior. But this means that you would have gone to the concert if you had found $400 instead of two tickets. (2) You are so close to the threshold of buying anyway that the transactions cost involved in selling the tickets make it more sensible to attend. But this means that those same transaction costs were an important reason why you didn't buy the tickets in the first place. Transaction costs change the problem.

3. A. C. Pigou, *The Economics of Welfare*, 4th ed. (London: MacMillan and Co., 1932).

4. The word "queue" is French in origin, itself deriving from the Latin *cauda*, for "tail."

5. Many authors have pointed out this distinction between the allocative and distributive functions of prices. For background on the distinction, see Meade (1964; p. 11).

6. This intuition was formalized by George Stigler in "The Division of Labor is Limited by the Extent of the Market."

7. This is actually the conclusion of the recent study by Lott (1998): more guns really are better. Again, thanks to Jay Hamilton for making this point.

Case 1: A Prison Camp Economy*

This article was written by R. A. Radford, an English economist who was captured by the Germans while serving in the British Army during World War II. It is a famous account of the apparently "spontaneous" emergence of institutions for fostering exchange in order to capture gains from trade. As you read, consider this: The exchange market that developed, complete with a well-established currency and price system, appears to have made everyone, or nearly everyone, in the camp better off. Yet the market itself produced *nothing*; it simply rearranged the holdings of the prisoners, in a way that better accorded with their preferences. This (nothing new produced, but all are better off) may seem like magic, but it is a common feature of market processes.

Introduction

After allowance has been made for abnormal circumstances, the social institutions, ideas and habits of groups in the outside world are to be found reflected in a Prisoner of War Camp. It is an unusual but a vital society. . . . One aspect of social organisation is to be found in economic activity, and this, along with other manifestations of a group existence, is to be found in any P.O.W. camp. True, a prisoner is not dependent on his exertions for the provision of the necessaries, or even the luxuries of life, but through his economic activity, the exchange of goods and services, his standard of material comfort is considerably enhanced. . . . Everyone receives a roughly equal share of essentials; it is by trade that individual preferences are given expression and comfort increased. All at some time, and most people regularly, make exchanges of one sort or another.

. . . A P.O.W. camp provides a living example of a simple economy which might be used as an alternative to the Robinson Crusoe economy beloved by the text-books. . . . But the essential interest lies in the universality and the spontaneity of this economic life; it came into existence not by conscious imitation but as a response to the immediate needs and circumstances. Any similarity between prison organisation and outside organisation arises from similar stimuli evoking similar responses.

The following is as brief an account of the essential data as may render the narrative intelligible. The camps of which the writer had experience were Oflags[1] and consequently the economy was not complicated by payments for work by the detaining power. They consisted normally of be-

---

*Excerpted from R. A. Radford, "The Economic Organisation of a P.O.W. Camp" (*Economica*, November 1945, pp. 189–201).

tween 1,200 and 2,500 people, housed in a number of separate but inter-communicating bungalows, one company of 200 or so to a building. Each company formed a group within the main organisation and inside the company the room and the messing syndicate, a voluntary and spontaneous group who fed together, formed the constituent units.

Between individuals there was active trading in all consumer goods and in some services. Most trading was for food against cigarettes or other foodstuffs, but cigarettes rose from the status of a normal commodity to that of a currency. RMKs [Reichmarks] existed but had no circulation save for gambling debts, as few articles could be purchased with them from the canteen.

Our supplies consisted of rations provided by the detaining power and (principally) the contents of Red Cross food parcels—tinned milk, jam, butter, biscuits, bully,[2] chocolate, sugar, etc., and cigarettes. So far the supplies to each person were equal and regular. Private parcels of clothing, toilet requisites and cigarettes were also received, and here equality ceased owing to the different numbers despatched and the vagaries of the post. All these articles were the subject of trade and exchange.

The Development and Organisation of The Market

Very soon after capture people realised that it was both undesirable and unnecessary, in view of the limited size and the equality of supplies, to give away or to accept gifts of cigarettes or food. "Goodwill" developed into trading as a more equitable means of maximising individual satisfaction.

We reached a transit camp in Italy about a fortnight after capture and received ¼ of a Red Cross food parcel each a week later. At once exchanges, already established, multiplied in volume. Starting with simple direct barter, such as a non-smoker giving a smoker friend his cigarette issue in exchange for a chocolate ration, more complex exchanges soon became an accepted custom. Stories circulated of a padre who started off round the camp with a tin of cheese and five cigarettes and returned to his bed with a complete parcel in addition to his original cheese and cigarettes; the market was not yet perfect. Within a week or two, as the volume of trade grew, rough scales of exchange values came into existence. Sikhs, who had at first exchanged tinned beef for practically any other foodstuff, began to insist on jam and margarine. It was realised that a tin of jam was worth ½ lb. of margarine plus something else, that a cigarette issue was worth several chocolate issues, and a tin of diced carrots was worth practically nothing. In this camp we did not visit other bungalows very much and prices varied from place to place; hence the germ of truth in the story of the itinerant priest. By the end of a month, when we reached our permanent camp, there was a lively trade in all commodities and their relative values were well known, and expressed not in terms of one another—one didn't quote bully in terms of sugar—but in terms of cigarettes. The cigarette became the standard of value. In the permanent camp people started by wandering through the bungalows calling their offers—"cheese for seven" (cigarettes)—and the hours after parcel issue were Bedlam. The inconveniences of this system soon led to its replacement by an Exchange and Mart notice board in every bungalow, where under the headings "name," "room number," "wanted" and "offered" sales and wants were advertised. When a deal went through, it was crossed off the board. The public and semi-permanent records of transactions led to cigarette prices being well known and thus tending to equality throughout the camp, although there were always opportunities for an astute trader to make a profit from arbitrage.[3] With this development everyone, including non-smokers, was willing to sell for cigarettes, using them to buy at another time and place. Cigarettes became the normal currency, though, of course, barter was never extinguished.

The unity of the market and the prevalence of a single price varied directly with the general level of organisation and comfort in the camp. A transit camp was always chaotic and uncomfortable: people were overcrowded, no one knew where anyone else was living, and few took the trouble to find out. Organisation was too slender to include an Exchange and Mart board, and private advertisements were the most that appeared. Consequently a transit camp was not one market but many. The price of a tin of salmon is known to have varied by two cigarettes in 20 between one end of a hut and the other. Despite a high level of organisation in Italy, the market was morcellated[4] in this manner at the first transit camp we reached after our removal to Germany in the autumn of 1943. In this camp—Stalag VIIA at Moosburg in Bavaria—there were up to 50,000 prisoners of all nationalities. French, Russians, Italians, and Jugo-Slavs were free to move about within the camp: British and Americans were confined to their compounds, although a few cigarettes given to a sentry would always procure permission for one or two men to visit other compounds. The people who first visited the highly organised French trading centre, with its stalls and known prices, found coffee extract—relatively cheap among the tea-drinking English—commanding a fancy price in biscuits or cigarettes, and some enterprising people made small fortunes that way. . . .

The permanent camps in Germany saw the highest level of commercial organisation. In addition to the exchange and Mart notice boards, a shop was organised as a public utility, controlled by representatives of the Senior British Officer, on a no profit basis. People left their surplus clothing, toilet requisites and food there until they were sold at a fixed price in cigarettes. Only sales in cigarettes were accepted—there was no barter—and there was no higgling. For food at least there were standard prices: clothing is less homogeneous and the price was decided around a norm by the seller and the shop manager in agreement; shirts would average say 80, ranging from 60 to 120 according to quality and age. Of food, the shop carried small stocks for convenience; the capital was provided by a loan from the bulk store of Red Cross cigarettes and repaid by a small commission taken on the first transactions. Thus the cigarette attained its fullest currency status, and the market was almost completely unified.

It is thus to be seen that a market came into existence without labour or production. The B.R.C.S. [Red Cross] may be considered as "Nature" of the text-book, and the articles of trade—food, clothing and cigarettes—as free gifts—land or manna. Despite this, and despite a roughly equal distribution of resources, a market came into spontaneous operation, and prices were fixed by the operation of supply and demand. . . .

There were also entrepreneurial services. There was a coffee stall owner who sold tea, coffee or cocoa at two cigarettes a cup, buying his raw materials at market prices and hiring labour to gather fuel and to stoke; he actually enjoyed the services of a chartered accountant at one stage. After a period of great prosperity he overreached himself and failed disastrously for several hundred cigarettes. . . .

Middlemen traded on their own account or on commission. Price rings and agreements were suspected and the traders certainly co-operated. Nor did they welcome newcomers. Unfortunately the writer knows little of the workings of these people: public opinion was hostile and the professionals were usually of a retiring disposition. . . .

One trader in food and cigarettes, operating in a period of dearth, enjoyed a high reputation. His capital, carefully saved, was originally about 50 cigarettes, with which he bought rations on issue days and held them until the price rose just before the next issue. He also picked up a little by arbitrage; several times a day he visited every Exchange or Mart notice board and took advantage of every discrepancy between prices of goods offered and wanted. His knowledge of prices, markets and names of those who had received cigarette parcels was phenomenal. By these means he kept himself smoking steadily—his profits—while his capital remained intact.

Sugar was issued on Saturday. About Tuesday two of us used to visit Sam and make a deal; as old customers he would advance as much of the price as he could spare then, and entered the transaction in a book. On Saturday morning he left cocoa tins on our beds for the ration, and picked them up on Saturday afternoon. We were hoping for a calendar at Christmas, but Sam failed too. He was left holding a big black treacle[5] issue when the price fell, and in this weakened state was unable to withstand an unexpected arrival of parcels and the consequent price fluctuations. He paid in full, but from his capital. The next Tuesday, when I paid my usual visit he was out of business.

Credit entered into many, perhaps into most, transactions, in one form or another. . . . A treacle ration might be advertised for four cigarettes now or five next week. And in the future market "bread now" was a vastly different thing from "bread Thursday"; Bread was issued on Thursday and Monday, four and three days' rations respectively, and by Wednesday and Sunday night it had risen at least one cigarette per ration, from seven to eight, by supper time. One man always saved a ration to sell then at the peak price: his offer of bread now" stood out on the board among a number of "bread Monday's" fetching one or two less, or not selling at all—and he always smoked on Sunday night.

The Cigarette Currency

Although cigarettes as currency exhibited certain peculiarities, they performed all the functions of a metallic currency as a unit of account, as a measure of value and as a store of value, and shared most of its characteristics. They were homogeneous, reasonably durable, and of convenient size for the smallest or, in packets, for the largest transactions. Incidentally, they could be clipped or sweated by rolling them between the fingers so that tobacco fell out.

Cigarettes were also subject to the working of Gresham's Law.[6] Certain brands were more popular than others as smokes, but for currency purposes a cigarette was a cigarette. Consequently buyers used the poorer qualities and the Shop rarely saw the more popular brands: cigarettes such as Churchman's No. 1 were rarely used for trading. At one time cigarettes hand-rolled from pipe tobacco began to circulate. Pipe tobacco was issued in lieu of cigarettes by the Red Cross at a rate of 25 cigarettes to the ounce and this rate was standard in exchanges, but an ounce would produce 30 home-made cigarettes. Naturally, people with machine made cigarettes broke them down and re-rolled the tobacco, and the real cigarette virtually disappeared from the market. Hand-rolled cigarettes were not homogeneous and prices could no longer be quoted in them with safety: each cigarette was examined before it was accepted and thin ones were rejected, or extra demanded as a make-weight. For a time we suffered all the inconveniences of a debased currency.

Machine-made cigarettes were always universally acceptable, both for what they would buy and for themselves. It was this intrinsic value which gave rise to their principal disadvantage as currency, a disadvantage which exists, but to a far smaller extent, in the case of metallic currency—that is, a strong demand for non-monetary purposes. Consequently our economy was repeatedly subject to deflation and to periods of monetary stringency. While the Red Cross issue of 50 or 25 cigarettes per man per week came in regularly, and while there were fair stocks held, the cigarette currency suited its purpose admirably. But when the issue was interrupted, stocks soon ran out, prices fell, trading declined in volume and became increasingly a matter of barter. This deflationary tendency was periodically offset by the sudden injection of new currency. Private cigarette parcels arrived in a trickle throughout the year, but the big numbers came in quarterly when the Red Cross received its allocation of transport. Several hundred thousand cigarettes might arrive in the space of a fortnight. Prices soared, and then began to fall, slowly at first but with increasing rapidity as stocks ran out, until the next big delivery. Most of our economic troubles could be attributed to this fundamental instability.

Price Movements

Many factors affected prices, the strongest and most noticeable being the periodical currency inflation and deflation described in the last paragraphs. The periodicity of this price cycle depended on cigarette and, to a far lesser extent, on food deliveries. . . . In August, 1944, the supplies of parcels and cigarettes were both halved. Since both sides of the equation were changed in the same degree, changes in prices were not anticipated. But this was not the case: the non-monetary demand for cigarettes was less elastic than the demand for food, and food prices fell a little. More important however were the changes in the price structure. German margarine and jam, hitherto valueless owing to adequate supplies of Canadian butter and marmalade, acquired a new value. Chocolate, popular and a certain seller, and sugar, fell. Bread rose: several standing contracts of bread for cigarettes were broken, especially when the bread ration was reduced a few weeks later.

In February, 1945, the German soldier who drove the ration waggon was found to be willing to exchange loaves of bread at the rate of one loaf for a bar of chocolate. Those in the know began selling bread and buying chocolate, by then almost unsaleable in a period of serious deflation. Bread, at about 40, fell slightly; chocolate rose from 15; the supply of bread was not enough for the two commodities to reach parity, but the tendency was unmistakable. . . .

Enough has been cited to show that any change in conditions affected both the general price level and the price structure. It was this latter phenomenon which wrecked our planned economy.

Paper Currency—Bully Marks

Around D-Day, food and cigarettes were plentiful, business was brisk and the camp in an optimistic mood. Consequently the Entertainments Committee felt the moment opportune to launch a restaurant, where food and hot drinks were sold while a band and variety turns performed. Earlier experiments, both public and private, had pointed the way, and the scheme was a great success. Food was bought at market prices to provide the meals and the small profits were devoted to a reserve fund and used to bribe Germans to provide grease-paints and other necessities for the camp theatre. Originally meals were sold for cigarettes but this meant that the whole scheme was vulnerable to the periodic deflationary waves, and furthermore heavy smokers were unlikely to attend much. The whole success of the scheme depended on an adequate amount of feed being offered for sale in the normal manner.

To increase and facilitate trade, and to stimulate supplies and customers therefore, and secondarily to avoid the worst effects of deflation when it should come, a paper currency was organised by the Restaurant and the Shop. The Shop bought food on behalf of the Restaurant with paper notes and the paper was accepted equally with the cigarettes in the Restaurant of Shop, and passed back to the Shop to purchase more food. The Shop acted as a bank of issue. The paper money was backed 100 per cent. by food; hence its name, the Bully Mark. The BMk. was backed 100 per cent. by food: there could be no over-issues, as is permissible with a normal bank of issue, since the eventual dispersal of the camp and consequent redemption of all BMk.s was anticipated in the near future. Originally one BMk. was worth one cigarette and for a short time both circulated freely inside and outside the Restaurant. Prices were quoted in BMk.s and cigarettes with equal freedom—and for a short time the BMk. showed signs of replacing the cigarette as currency. The BMk. was tied to food, but not to cigarettes: as it was issued against food, say 45 for a tin of milk and so on, any reduction in the BMk. prices of food would have meant that there were unbacked BMk.s in circulation. But the price of both food and BMk.s could and did fluctuate with the supply of cigarettes.

While the Restaurant flourished, the scheme was a success: the Restaurant bought heavily, all foods were saleable and prices were stable. . . . In August parcels and cigarettes were halved and the Camp was bombed. The Restaurant closed for a short while and sales of food became difficult. Even when the Restaurant reopened, the food and cigarette shortage became increasingly acute and people were unwilling to convert such valuable goods into paper and to hold them for luxuries like snacks and tea. Less of the right kinds of food for the Restaurant were sold, and the Shop became glutted with dried fruit, chocolate, sugar, etc., which the Restaurant could not buy. The price level and the price structure changed. The BMk. fell to four-fifths of a cigarette and eventually farther still, and it became unacceptable save in the Restaurant. There was a flight from the BMk., no longer convertible into cigarettes or popular foods. The cigarette re-established itself.

But the BMk. was sound! The Restaurant closed in the New Year with a progressive food shortage and the long evenings without lights due to intensified Allied air raids, and BMk.s could only be spent in the Coffee Bar—relict of the Restaurant—or on the few unpopular foods in the Shop, the owners of which were prepared to accept them. In the end all holders of BMk.s were paid in full, in cups of coffee or in prunes. People who had bought BMk.s for cigarettes or valuable jam or biscuits in their heyday were aggrieved that they should have stood the loss involved by their restricted choice, but they suffered no actual loss of market value.

Price Fixing

Along with this scheme came a determined attempt at a planned economy, at price fixing. The Medical Officer had long been anxious to control food sales, for fear of some people selling too much, to the detriment of their health. The deflationary waves and their effects on prices were inconvenient to all and would be dangerous to the Restaurant which had to carry stocks. Furthermore, unless the BMk. was convertible into cigarettes at about par it had little chance of gaining confidence and of succeeding as a currency. As has been explained, the BMk. was tied to food but could not be tied to cigarettes, which fluctuated in value. Hence, while BMk. prices of food were fixed for all time, cigarette prices of food and BMk.s varied.

The Shop, backed by the senior British Officer, was now in a position to enforce price control both inside and outside its walls. Hitherto a standard price had been fixed for food left for sale in the shop, and prices outside were roughly in conformity with this scale, which was recommended as a "guide" to sellers, but fluctuated a good deal around it. Sales in the Shop at recommended prices were apt to be slow though a good price might be obtained: sales outside could be made more quickly at lower prices. (If sales outside were to be at higher prices, goods were withdrawn from the Shop until the recommended price rose: but the recommended price was sluggish and could not follow the market closely by reason of its very purpose, which was stability.) The Exchange and Mart notice boards came under the control of the Shop: advertisements which exceeded a 5 per cent. departure from the recommended scale were liable to be crossed out by authority: unauthorised sales were discouraged by authority and also by public opinion, strongly in favour of a just and stable price. (Recommended prices were fixed partly from market data, partly on the advice of the M.O.)

At first the recommended scale was a success: the Restaurant, a big buyer, kept prices stable around this level: opinion and the 5 per cent. tolerance helped. But when the price level fell with the August cuts and the price structure changed, the recommended scale was too rigid. Unchanged at first, as no deflation was expected, the scale was tardily lowered, but the prices of goods on the new scale remained in the same relation to one another, owing to the BMk., while on the market the price structure had changed. And the modifying influence of the Restaurant had gone. The scale was moved up and down several times, slowly following the inflationary and deflationary waves, but it was rarely adjusted to changes in the price structure. More and more advertisements were crossed off the board, and black market sales at unauthorised prices increased: eventually public opinion turned against the recommended scale and authority gave up the struggle. In the last few weeks, with unparalleled deflation, prices fell with alarming rapidity, no scales existed, and supply and demand, alone and unmellowed, determined prices.

Public Opinion

Public opinion on the subject of trading was vocal if confused and changeable, and generalisations as to its direction are difficult and dangerous. A tiny minority held that all trading was undesirable as it engendered an unsavoury atmosphere; occasional frauds and sharp practices were cited as proof. Certain forms of trading were more generally condemned; trade with the Germans was criticised by many. Red Cross toilet articles, which were in short supply and only issued in cases of actual need, were excluded from trade by law and opinion working in unshakable harmony. At one time, when there had been several cases of malnutrition reported among the more devoted smokers, no trade in German rations was permitted, as the victims became an additional burden on the depleted food reserves of the Hospital. But while certain activities were condemned as antisocial, trade itself was practised, and its utility appreciated, by almost everyone in the camp.

More interesting was opinion on the middlemen and prices. Taken as a whole, opinion was hostile to the middleman. His function, and his hard work in bringing buyer and seller together, were ignored; profits were not regarded as a reward for labour, but as the result of sharp practices. Despite the fact that his very existence was proof to the contrary, the middleman was held to be redundant in view of the existence of an official Shop and the Exchange and Mart. Appreciation only came his way when he was willing to advance the price of a sugar ration, or to buy goods spot and carry them against a future sale. In these cases the element of risk was obvious to all and the convenience of the service was felt to merit some reward. Particularly unpopular was the middleman with an element of monopoly, the man who contacted the ration wagon driver, or the man who utilised his knowledge of Urdu. And middlemen as a group were blamed for reducing prices. Opinion notwithstanding, most people dealt with a middleman, whether consciously or unconsciously, at some time or another.

There was a strong feeling that everything had its "just price" in cigarettes. While the assessment of the just price, which incidentally varied between camps, was impossible of explanation, this price was nevertheless pretty closely known. It can best be defined as the price usually fetched by an article in good times when cigarettes were plentiful. The "just price" changed slowly; it was unaffected by short-term variations in supply, and while opinion might be resigned to departures from the "just price," a strong feeling of resentment persisted. A more satisfactory definition of the "just price" is impossible. Everyone knew what it was, though no one could explain why it should be so.

As soon as prices began to fall with a cigarette shortage, a clamour arose, particularly against those who held reserves and who bought at reduced prices. Sellers at cut prices were criticised and their activities referred to as the black market. In every period of death the explosive question of "should non-smokers receive a cigarette ration?" was discussed to profitless length. Unfortunately, it was the non-smoker, or the light smoker with his reserves, along with the hated middleman, who weathered the storm most easily.

The popularity of the price-fixing scheme, and such success as it enjoyed, were undoubtedly the result of this body of opinion. On several occasions the fall of prices was delayed by the general support given to the recommended scale. The onset of deflation was marked by a period of sluggish trade; prices stayed up but no one bought. Then prices fell on the black market, and the volume of trade revived in that quarter. Even when the recommended scale was revised, the volume of trade in the Shop would remain low. Opinion was always overruled by the hard facts of the market.

Curious arguments were advanced to justify price fixing. The recommended prices were in some way related to the calorific values of the foods offered: hence some were overvalued and never sold at these prices. One argument ran as follows—not everyone has private cigarette parcels. Thus, when prices were high and trade good in the summer of 1944, only the lucky rich could buy. This was unfair to the man with few cigarettes. When prices fell in the following winter, prices should be pegged high so that the rich, who had enjoyed life in the summer, should put many cigarettes into circulation. The fact that those who sold to the rich in the summer had also enjoyed life then, and the fact that in the winter there was always someone willing to sell at low prices were ignored. Such arguments were hotly debated each night after the approach of Allied aircraft extinguished all lights at 8 p.m. But prices moved with the supply of cigarettes, and refused to stay fixed in accordance with a theory of ethics.

Conclusion

The economic organisation described was both elaborate and smooth-working in the summer of 1944. Then came the August cuts and deflation. Prices fell, rallied with deliveries of cigarette parcels in September and December, and fell again. In January, 1945, supplies of Red Cross cigarettes ran out and prices slumped still further: in February the supplies of food parcels were exhausted and the depression became a blizzard. Food, itself scarce, was almost given away in order to meet the non-monetary demand for cigarettes. Laundries ceased to operate, or worked for £s or RMk.s: food and cigarettes sold for fancy prices in £s, hitherto unheard of. The Restaurant was a memory and the BMk. a joke. The Shop was empty and the Exchange and Mart notices were full of unaccepted offers for cigarettes. Barter increased in volume, becoming a larger proportion of a smaller volume of trade. This, the first serious and prolonged food shortage in the writer's experience, caused the price structure to change again, partly because German rations were not easily divisible. A margarine ration gradually sank in value until it exchanged directly for a treacle ration. Sugar slumped sadly. Only bread retained its value. Several thousand cigarettes, the capital of the Shop, were distributed without any noticeable effect. A few fractional parcel and cigarettes each, led to momentary price recoveries and feverish trade, especially when they coincided with good news from the Western Front, but the general position remained unaltered.

By April, 1945, chaos had replaced order in the economic sphere: sales were difficult, prices lacked stability. Economics has been defined as the science of distributing limited means among unlimited and competing ends. On 12th April, with the arrival of elements of the 30th U.S. Infantry Division, the ushering in of an age of plenty demonstrated the hypothesis that with infinite means economic organisation and activity would be redundant, as every want could be satisfied without effort.

Discussion Questions

1. What is the role of self-interest, as opposed to altruism, in the creation of markets?
2. Who was in charge of setting up the market for exchanging food and other amenities?
3. Who was in charge of establishing cigarettes as a currency? Who was in charge of establishing the BMk.? What were the advantages, and disadvantages, of these two very different mediums of exchange?
4. Suppose the rumor about the "itinerant priest" is true; does this mean that markets are unfair? More generally, is arbitrage ("middlemen") a legitimate and moral practice?
5. One of the interesting ideas that Radford identifies is the doctrine of "just price." This is a doctrine that many, if not most, prisoners seemed to accept as valid and moral. But what is the

"just" price of a commodity? How could it be determined? Is it ever ethically defensible to charge something other than the just price?

NOTES

1. "Oflags" were military prisoner of war camps, as distinct from internment camps (for foreign civilians) or concentration camps (where people were imprisoned based on their ethnicity). For some reason, the Germans treated their military prisoners somewhat more uniformly, and substantially better, than prisoners in the other types of camps.
2. "Bully" is short for "bully beef." The name is derived from the French *bouilli*, or boiled meat. Bully beef was a large step below modern SPAM, and was something one would only consider eating if one were very hungry indeed.
3. "Arbitrage" is making profits through exploiting price differences in markets separated by distance or (more often) some barrier of information or rule. The arbitrageur buys at the lower price and then sells at the higher price.
4. "Morcellated" is synonymous with "fragmented" or "separated."
5. "Treacle" is molasses—high in calories and more nutritious than sugar.
6. "Gresham's Law" is named after Thomas Gresham, 1519–1579, though the phenomenon itself is described by Thomas Aquinas, in *Summa Theologica*, question 77, and was probably recognized even earlier. Gresham's law holds that if there are two kinds of money in circulation, with the same denominational value but different intrinsic values, the money with higher intrinsic value will be hoarded and eventually driven out of circulation by the money with lesser intrinsic value. More simply, bad money drives out good money. Gresham apparently became concerned with the problem after observing a collapse of currency and bills of debt in France after the civil war precipitated by the massacre of Huguenots at Vassy, March 1, 1562. The problem is particularly severe for commodity moneys, as we see in the prison camp example, but it was recognized very early that Gresham's law also plagues monetary currencies. See, for example, the discussion of "bank money" from Amsterdam, Hamburgh, and Venice in Book 4, chap. 3, part 1 of Adam Smith's *Wealth of Nations*.

"Evaluation and Market Failure": Criteria for Intervention

Tools for Evaluating Policy

Market institutions are uniquely powerful mechanisms for organizing enormous quantities of capital and labor. Market processes may seem ideal, even for providing for diverse needs of large numbers of consumers. But markets aren't perfect. In fact, sometimes the performance of an unregulated market may be politically unacceptable. Later chapters will consider mechanisms for managing markets.

To decide whether such management works, we first need some benchmarks for evaluation. With these benchmarks laid out, we will then turn to the "failure" of market systems, and rationales for public sector intervention. This chapter introduces five tools policy analysts use to measure, and evaluate, the performance of policies, taxes, and regulatory practices. These evaluation procedures are widely used in economics and policy analysis. They may seem strange at first, but it is important to understand the perspective of evaluation within the welfare economics tradition. The five evaluation tools considered here include: (1) the Pareto criterion; (2) the Kaldor-Hicks compensation principle; (3) consumer surplus; (4) the Bergson-Samuelson social welfare function; and (5) the first and second welfare theorems.

As with most tool kits there may not be a single theme that motivates tool use in every case. The five different tools allow us to try to solve different problems. But virtually all procedures of evaluation will invoke one or more of these tools for measuring and comparing welfare. In chapter 7 (on basic analytics), and again in chapter 11 (on cost-benefit evaluation) later in this book, we will apply these tools and see what we can build.

The Pareto Criterion

It is time to be more precise about the Pareto criterion mentioned in chapter 2. Consider two situations S_1 and S_2. It doesn't matter what those states, or conditions, represent. We just want to be able to compare them.

- If all citizens strictly prefer S_1 over S_2, we say "S_1 is *strongly Pareto superior* to S_2."
- If no citizen prefers S_2 over S_1, and at least one person likes S_1 better, we say "S_1 is *weakly Pareto superior* to S_2."
- If there is no other state of the world that everyone likes as well as, or better than, S_1, we say "S_1 is a *strong Pareto optimum*."
- If there is no other state of the world that everyone likes better than S_1, we say "S_1 is a *weak Pareto optimum*."

In policy analysis, we use both **positive** (what *is*) and **normative** (what *should be*) tools. The Pareto criterion is normative, but only in the weakest sense. A Pareto optimum is efficient, in the sense that it implies there is no waste, or unrealized gains from trade or group action. But what if some people like S_1 better, and others like S_2? The Pareto criterion tells us nothing about situations where there is disagreement, because *Pareto comparisons require unanimity*. As we saw in the "roses and guns" example earlier, there are many Pareto optima, so imposing the restriction that we should strive for some Pareto optimum doesn't reduce our choices very much.

The Kaldor-Hicks Compensation Principle

The "compensation principle" is not widely known outside of the policy analysis community, yet you have been dealing with it, and using it, all your life. You just didn't know it until now. The Kaldor-Hicks[1] criterion is an elaboration of the Pareto criterion, and is designed to address comparisons among states of the world that are all Pareto optimal. So, the Kaldor-Hicks criterion might be thought of as having two parts:

- Compare two states of the world, S_1 and S_2. If one is Pareto superior, no further analysis is needed: the Pareto superior alternative is preferred.
- If both states are Pareto optima,[2] add up the gains and losses to all citizens from choosing each alternative. Select the policy that maximizes the difference between the gains to the gainers and the losses to the losers. Importantly, *it is not required that the gainers compensate the losers,* but only that the excess value created by the policy choice is maximized.

Kaldor-Hicks is the basis for all of cost-benefit analysis, so if you think cost-benefit analysis is a good idea you are implicitly supporting Kaldor-Hicks as an ethical system. All that matters is that the final outcome is a Pareto optimum and that the gains to the gainers exceed the losses to the losers. It doesn't matter who the gainers, or the losers, are. As Jenkins-Smith (1990) puts it,

> The Kaldor-Hicks criterion allows redistributions that increase net welfare such that those who gain from the distribution could compensate those who lose, restoring the losers to their prior level of well-being, while the winners retain enough of their gains to be better-off than they would have been without the redistribution. In this case individuals' utilities need not be compared; as long as a common value of the good redistributed is available, such as the *money value of the gains and losses* to the individuals involved, it is possible to determine just how much of the improvement to the gainers must be given in compensation to the losers to assure that no one is worse off than they would have been without the redistribution. . . . In the comparison of policies, the relevant criterion is: which policy option serves to create the *largest net gain in social well-being?* (Jenkins-Smith, 1990; p. 22).

Consider an example. In Raleigh, the capitol of North Carolina, the leaders of Wake County wanted to build a new children's museum, called "Exploris," a celebration of multiculturalism with exhibits designed to teach children about other nations and other peoples. Exploris was universally admired as an innovative concept, and a site was chosen in downtown Raleigh, not far from some state museums and city parks.

The county managed to acquire all the land it needed, except one parcel. This parcel belonged to the Singleton family (mother Ruth and son Gary), who owned an acre of land and operated the Disabled American Veterans' Thrift Store, a nonprofit organization selling used goods and clothing as a way of providing an income to handicapped veterans who might otherwise have had to live on the street.

The museum was expected to cost about $25 million.[3] The assessed (i.e., tax) value of the thrift store was about $540,000. The county, in determining that this was the best location for the museum, was trying to take the wishes and goals of many citizens into account. The Singletons, who were running a business, had been paying taxes for years, and were not interested in selling the land to the county. The county offered a little more than $520,00 for the property, and the Singletons said no. The Singletons probably had a point: Wake County uses a proportional assessment policy, so that tax assessments are generally lower (sometimes much lower) than market values. Since the county's offer was $20,000 lower than even its own tax assessment on the property, it is not surprising that the Singletons said no.

A personal note: I have worked, as a consultant and fellow professional, with the man who was the Wake County attorney at the time. A finer public servant you could not find anywhere. His motives were perfectly clear: he was implementing the wishes of the county commissioners to build the museum at the best place available, from the perspective of the people of the county.[4] He was quoted in the Raleigh *News and Observer* as saying, "It's not uncommon for people not to want to sell. The [Raleigh city government also] condemns property constantly for public projects. It's just what they have to do. . . . We are not in the market of taking advantage of folks."

Eventually, the Singletons refused to sell at the price offered by Wake County, and the county forced the Singletons off the land using the perfectly legal procedure of condemning, then taking, the property through "eminent domain." Eminent domain is the traditional right of governments to declare that the public interest supercedes private interests in property within the boundaries controlled by that government. This means that the government can take private lands for public use, even without the owner's permission or cooperation, provided just compensation is given.

In a letter to the county commission, Gary Singleton made a last desperate appeal. "Honoring and supporting our handicapped veterans is certainly equal, if not superior, to celebrating Third World cultures, especially when one considers that as private property, it pays its own way; as public property, it does not."[5] No matter; the county took the land, the Singletons were paid about $525,000, and the Disabled American Veterans' Thrift Store is now operating at a very nice location on Crabtree Boulevard in Raleigh.

A final personal note: I have two little boys, and live in Wake County. I was excited about the Exploris museum, and was glad that it was being built. But I had to wonder about the ethical basis of taking the Singletons' land away from them, when they didn't want to sell. Yes, that was a good (let's be honest, perfect!) place for a museum. *But the Singletons didn't want to sell.* Who says that the public interest can dominate private property rights in this way? When is it legitimate for government to use force to take property it can't obtain through market processes?

That is where the Kaldor-Hicks principle comes in. If we decide to operate under the "compensation principle" Kaldor and Hicks advanced, then that is the way things work. If, in the judgment of elected officials, the benefits to the society of the public activity are large, and the costs of moving the public activity somewhere else are high, then the government can take the land for public use. They don't have to ask, and they don't have to explain; they can just take the land and pay the owner the market value, as determined by a real estate appraiser and (if the current owner wants to resist) a state court.

The same logic can be applied to decisions to build a new dam, or to impose new regulations, or to create almost any new public policy. The gains to the gainers, and the losses to the losers, may be hard to compute accurately, but the basic ethical perspective is perfectly straightforward: The "compensation principle" holds that losses and gains can be measured and balanced, even if they are imposed on different people. Consequently, we can choose among Pareto optima, because (in principle) the excess of gains over losses means that those who are opposed could be compensated, converting disagreement into unanimity.

The problem with all this is obvious: How are we to measure the gains and losses, and who will do the measuring? We have two choices, neither of them very good: (1) We can use participants' own estimates of the costs and benefits, recognizing that these estimates may be misrepresented or distorted; or (2) we can use experts' estimates, recognizing that the experts are likely to use market-derived averages rather than individual value systems. Since one of the most important bases for expert-generated estimates is the concept of "consumer surplus," that is where we should turn next.

Consumer Surplus

The concept of "consumer surplus" is central to many problems in economics, not only as a device for measuring performance, but also as an analytic tool for explaining economic phenomena. The definition is deceptively simple:

> **Consumer surplus:** The difference between the maximum value the consumer would be *willing to pay* and the amount s/he *actually has to pay* in the market.

The reason the simplicity of this definition is deceptive is that we can only observe one part of the definition, the amount the consumer *must* pay, or the market price. The amount the consumer would be *willing* to pay is summarized by economists in a conceptual device called the **demand curve**. As shown in Figure 4.1, the vertical axis of the demand curve is the price (in dollars, in this case), and the horizontal axis is the quantity purchased.

The demand curve slopes downward, illustrating the so-called law of demand: *The quantity purchased varies inversely with price.* This claim, that people buy less if the price goes up, can be derived from two assumptions: First, as in the previous chapter, more is preferred to less, and the more I have of one commodity the less I value additional units. Second, the consumer has a fixed budget, so that the opportunity cost of purchasing one product is the other products forgone.

Regardless of the price, however, many consumers will still keep some "consumer surplus," or difference between the maximum the commodity was worth and the price. This becomes clearer if we think of the demand curve in Figure 4.1 as a schedule relating willingness to pay. The consumer is willing to pay a high price for the first unit, and then less and less for successive units. But assuming there is no price discrimination (that is, a single price is charged), the total difference between the amount the consumer *would* have paid and the amount he *had* to pay can be very large. If we imagine that the

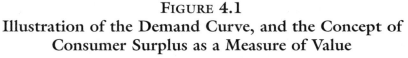

FIGURE 4.1

Illustration of the Demand Curve, and the Concept of Consumer Surplus as a Measure of Value

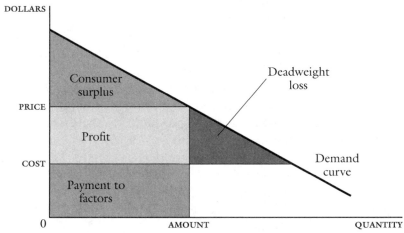

"price" is at the point shown in Figure 4.1, then the total consumer surplus is the dark triangle. More generally, the consumer surplus is the area under the demand curve, between zero units and the quantity actually purchased, minus the total payments the consumer gives up to acquire the commodity.

Let's examine Figure 4.1 more carefully, and consider things from the producer's perspective. Notice that, in the example depicted in the figure, price exceeds cost. That means that, for whatever reason, the firm selling the product is able to charge a price higher than the opportunity value of the resources that go into production.[6] In that case, the area under the demand curve represents several important quantities. The *total revenue* of the firm is the price multiplied by the quantity purchased. The *total costs* of the firm are all the expenses incurred in producing the output. In this case, using a very simplified view of the world where marginal costs are constant, we can say that total costs equal cost per unit multiplied by the number of units. The definition of profits is then obvious: *Profit* is total revenue minus total cost.

More simply, the value of the transaction between consumer and firm can be divided into three parts: *consumer surplus, profits,* and *costs* (payments to factors of production). But there is one more shaded area in Figure 4.1, representing a controversial concept that has been the basis of countless policy decisions. That area, the triangle to the right of amount purchased, above costs and below the demand curve, is labeled **deadweight loss**.

A deadweight loss, as the name suggests, is the loss of value from pure waste. Payments to factors are clearly a necessary part of production; there may be some debate over the equity of the distribution of profit and consumer surplus, but at least nothing is wasted. Deadweight losses are different, because the value is simply thrown away.

What is the source of the value that is wasted? Consider the shaded triangle in Figure 4.1: the consumer is willing to pay more for each unit of output than the unit costs to produce, yet these units are not offered. The consumer keeps the money, or uses it in some less-valued way. Factors of production are underemployed. The producer, however, cannot lower his price to capture this marginal consumer surplus, because doing so would mean that all units would be sold at the lower price. Firms are usually assumed to maximize *profits*, not revenues.

Deadweight losses can arise from any distortion that causes a divergence of price and cost of production. Taxes, regulations, subsidy programs: all these can cause significant deadweight losses under the right circumstances. The advantage of the consumer surplus measure is that it is explicitly monetized, to allow immediate comparisons among different courses of action. The disadvantage of the consumer surplus measure, as with the Kaldor-Hicks criterion, is that it requires a comparison of values based on measures that may be incommensurable. The requirement that value is monetized is an advantage only if the values thus represented are accurate. Economists have measured, and argued about, the concept of consumer surplus for more than a century. Modern policy analysis couldn't do without consumer surplus, but you should be careful not to rely on its accuracy absolutely.

The Bergson-Samuelson Social Welfare Function

Recall from chapter 3 the discussion of the Edgeworth box as a device for depicting gains from trade, and for making predictions about equilibrium allocations of resources. The Edgeworth box turns out to be the first building block toward a much more general graphical model of the distribution of resources in the entire society.

To describe the model fully, two other analytical tools need to be defined. The first is the "production possibilities frontier," the second is the "social welfare function." The **production possibilities frontier (PPF)** is a menu of choice for the productive resources of a society. Notice that this is fundamentally different from, and logically antecedent to, the question of how to allocate consumption commodities (which is where we use the Edgeworth box). The production possibilities frontier is an illustration of total *potential* productivity of all of the society's resources. Let's return to our roses and guns example from the previous chapter, and consider the PPF shown in Figure 4.2.

FIGURE 4.2
The Production Possibilities Frontier (PPF)
The production possibilities frontier provides a menu of choice among allocations of productive resources: *A* is inefficient, *B* and *C* are both efficient, and *D* is infeasible.

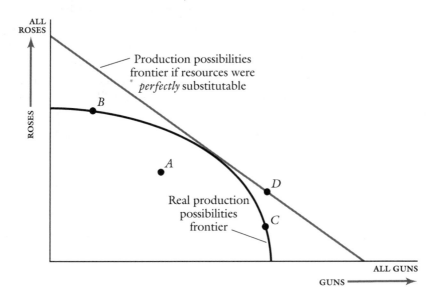

If resources were *perfectly substitutable*, the production possibilities frontier would be a straight line connecting the "all roses" and the "all guns" points on the axes. But that could never happen: If all of society's productive resources were devoted to producing roses, some of those resources would not be very useful. Machine tools and production lines don't transfer over into rose production very well. Likewise for guns; even the largest, most fertile fields won't grow heavy howitzers. Consequently, the PPF is concave to the origin.

Only in the middle of the PPF, where all of society's resources are devoted to their most productive (in the physical, not financial, sense) uses, is the real PPF close to the PPF implied by perfect substitutability.

Point A in Figure 4.2 is feasible, but represents unemployment of some of society's resources. We know this because A is inside the PPF, implying that it is possible to produce more of both roses and guns. Point D is infeasible. Even if this pattern of production were desirable, it is not possible with the resources the society has available. Only points B and C are feasible, and efficient. But the PPF provides no guidance as to which of the two points are better, because the PPF represents only the technological production *possibilities*.

To choose among the points on the PPF, which represent efficiency in production, we need a device for representing the consumption preferences of the society. One possible answer was the **Bergson-Samuelson social welfare function**."[7] The social welfare function assumes that the society is somehow able to aggregate the welfare of individuals, so as to be able to evaluate different technologically efficient alternatives. In effect, the SWF is an analogy to the individual consumer's **utility function**, represented by the indifference curves we have seen in chapter 3. The difference is that the indifference curves now represent the boundary between the "more preferred" and "less preferred" allocations of resources for the entire society.

The social welfare function is a simple concept: it requires only that a set of weights can be attached to the utilities of all individuals, so that the sum of the weighted utilities is the total utility of the society. More formally, the social welfare functions (represented by F) might be written out as follows:

$$F(U_1, U_2, \ldots U_n) = \sum_{i=1}^{n} w_i U_i \qquad (1)$$

where U_i is the utility of the ith citizen, and w_i is the weight attached to the utility of the ith citizen. More simply, the SWF uses two pieces of information: (a) How well off is each person in the society? (b) How much we should care about (i.e., what weight should be attached to) each person's welfare?

When we recall that we have claimed that the utility of each person depends on the resources they have available to consume, the problem to be solved becomes clear: Each allocation of productive resources implies a set of consumption goods to be produced. Each division of these consumption goods implies a particular level of utility for each individual. The question is: How do we choose the *best* division of consumption goods, produced by the *best* allocation of productive resources?

The simplest answer, for which economists in the 1940s and 1950s had high hopes, was a kind of materialistic deism. Deism was a rationalistic philosophical-religious view of the eighteenth century which held that physical processes could be precisely worked out, and that the integration of these processes could be understood as if the world were a giant watch. There may have been a "watchmaker," but all He had to do was wind up the world and everything else happened naturally and predictably.

In the context of the social welfare function, all the "policy authority" (presumably the government, rather than God) had to do was choose the point on the production possibilities frontier implied by the social welfare function (see Figure 4.3), and then use a system

FIGURE 4.3

The Choice among Pareto Optima in Production and Consumption: The Social Welfare Function, Tax Policy, and the Market

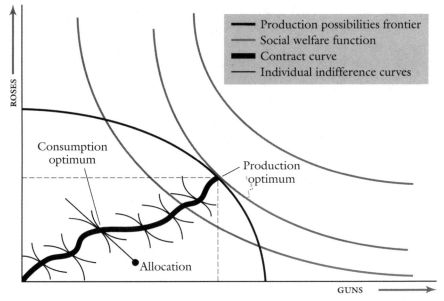

of taxes and subsidies to ensure the appropriate allocation of resources among consumers. The natural workings of the market would then take over, ensuring that all gains from trade would be exhausted, and that all would be well with the world.

This view of the policy analyst as God can be depicted, in the case where there are but two consumers, in Figure 4.3. The overall allocation of productive resources is implied by the tangency[8] of the production possibilities frontier with the highest attainable social indifference curve of the social welfare function. Once this (technologically efficient) production allocation is chosen, there immediately springs up an Edgeworth box with the appropriate dimensions (i.e., with the quantities of roses, and guns, implied by the resource allocations). Then some point along the contract curve must be selected, but this choice among Pareto optima is once again implied by the maximum value of the SWF. All that is necessary is to divide resources optimally, even if the division is off the contract curve, and trade will lead ("by an invisible hand") the citizens to select the optimal point on the contract curve.

The First and Second "Welfare Theorems"

We can build from the social welfare function by addressing the problems of welfare maximization. In this section, I briefly introduce two new concepts, **welfare economics** and **general equilibrium** theory. Welfare economics is the study of the normative properties, or "goodness," of economic outcomes. More simply, welfare economics tries to answer the question "How can we tell if one economic policy, or type of regulation, is better than another?"

General equilibrium theory is the study of the consistency and coherence of disparate economic decisions that people make. Consumers buy goods based on their expectations of income earned from working, and producers decide what workers to hire based on what they expect to sell to consumers. It is by no means obvious that these separate decisions (consumption, investment, hiring, saving) are mutually consistent. If all of these separate economic decisions "add up" (for example, supply equals demand), this is a situation the general equilibrium theorists call **equilibrium**, or a situation with no inherent tendency to change. The key question for general equilibrium theorists is this: "Under what circumstances does general equilibrium exist for the entire economy?"

Welfare economics and general equilibrium theory meet in the so-called welfare theorems. There are two; not surprisingly, they are called the first and second welfare theorems. They go like this:

First welfare theorem: All general equilibria in perfectly competitive markets are Pareto optima.

Second welfare theorem: General equilibria exist. Furthermore, all Pareto optima can be achieved in perfectly competive markets through the appropriate initial division of productive resources, and through optimizing behavior on the part of citizens.

More simply, Adam Smith was largely correct about the ability of markets to lead to mutually beneficial outcomes, and the choice of which outcome is best can be made by the central policy authority using the power to tax and subsidize.

Now, let's pause a minute. I can just hear the questions forming in your head as you read. "*Not so fast, policy boy!* There are at least two obvious problems with this optimistic presentation. First, how do we arrive at the appropriate 'social welfare function?' Second, the welfare theorems explicitly assume 'perfect competition'; what does that mean? If competition is not perfect, do the welfare theorems still hold?"

The question of the social welfare function is part of the more general problem a society faces in making collective choices. We call that problem "politics," which will be treated in chapters 5 and 6, so let's put the first question off for now.[9] But the second question, perfect competition, is clearly a "market" topic. What are the assumptions of pure, or perfect competition, and what are the implications of violating those assumptions in real markets?

The Rationale for Government Intervention: The Market Failures Perspective

The assumptions of perfect competition are fairly straightforward. They are also fairly unrealistic. For that reason, it is important to be careful about just what is being assumed, and to establish what the breach of the assumptions implies. Unfortunately, to give a full development would take too much machinery. But I do want to distinguish two very different things:

- *Sufficient* assumptions, or conditions strong enough to ensure the results described in the first and second welfare theorems
- *Necessary* assumptions, or the minimum set of conditions where the welfare theorems still apply

There are many different phrasings of the assumptions in the literature; I will present an intuitive version that captures much (but not all) of the technical content of the sufficient conditions. Remember, sufficient conditions are stronger (i.e., more restrictive) than necessary conditions.

Perfect competition has the following four major characteristics:

- *Perfect and free information:* All market participants have free and immediate access to accurate information about prices, the quality of products, and the implications of present actions for future welfare.
- *Price taking:* No market participant is large enough, in the sense of controlling a significant proportion of transactions, to influence the price either up or down. The price is simply "taken" as given. This means that all consumers are price takers, that all resource owners are price takers, and in particular that all output is sold by firms that are price takers.
- *Private decisions:* Choices by individuals do not affect the welfare of others. This requires that there are no externalities in production and no externalities in consumption.
- *Private goods:* No goods are public, in the technical sense of having zero marginal cost of production and costly exclusion.

If these are the assumptions that the first and second welfare theorems must follow, it is obvious that the failure of these assumptions to hold can cause the welfare theorems to be false. The focus of policy analysis has often been to consider "market failures" (i.e., violation of one of the assumptions above to hold) to be a sufficient cause for government intervention in the workings of the markets. Note that there are three parts to this chain of logic:

1. Markets are the primary mechanism for ensuring and achieving Pareto efficient outcomes, where all gains from trade are exhausted.
2. Violations of the "perfect competition" assumptions mean that

observed outcomes diverge from Pareto efficiency in predictable ways.

3. Government policy makers have the correct goals, and have accurate enough information, to redirect the functioning of the
economy back to the correct Pareto optimum, where "correct"
is defined in terms of the distribution of welfare that maximizes
the social welfare function.

Any one of the steps in this logical chain might be incorrect, of
course. Certainly there are people who decry the notion that markets, with their emphasis on self-interested action, are the "best" way
to organize human activity. It might be argued that the implications
of violations of perfect competition are hard to gauge, and that we
don't know enough about the effects of information problems, or
market power, or public goods to be able to solve the technical problems involved. Finally, there is a significant body of scholarship which
argues that policy makers either have the wrong incentives, or rarely
have accurate enough information, to be able to select the ideal re-
distributions of resources and consumption goods.

I will have something to say on a few of these points in later chapters. For now, let's just be satisfied that the chain of logic is coherent
from a pure "if-then" perspective: *if* the market failures perspective is
correct, *then* we can analyze and correct market failures to improve
the outcomes of market processes, and restore the economy to the
ideal Pareto optimum.

It is time for a more detailed consideration of the primary forms of
market failure.

Information Perfect and Free

The first of the "sufficient conditions" for pure competition is perfect
information, meaning that all consumers can be assumed to know the
implications of choices for their welfare, to be aware of all prices and
products available in the market, and to be capable of judging the
quality of those products costlessly. Obviously, this assumption is not
true, but the implications of the violation of this assumption are not
so obvious.

On the one hand, there is the tradition in English common law,
the basis for much of the commercial practices and statutes that govern markets in the United States and many other countries. In

the common law, the presumption is generally **caveat emptor**, or "let the buyer beware." This standard is actually quite complex, since the requirement is that the seller of a product does not need to tell all he knows, but cannot misrepresent information or disguise material defects in the product. So, if the buyer fails to ask the right questions, and the quality is different from what the buyer expected . . . well, the buyer should have been more careful.

This situation, where the seller has more information or better information than the buyer, is the problem of **asymmetric information**. If every (potential) buyer, each of whom would benefit from purchasing goods actually available in the market, has to pay the search costs of finding the product, and discovering if the product is wholesome, effective, or usable, many mutually advantageous transactions may not be arranged. The result is a significant deadweight loss, as many transactions do not take place.

There are several ways around the asymmetry of information problem, and not all of them involve government action. Reputation, or "brand name," constitutes a mechanism for creating (in effect) an economic hostage. A recognized brand name is a signal to potential buyers that the product is of high quality. Reputation is a potential solution for what Akerlof (1971) called the *lemons problem*: If you can't tell whether you are buying a "lemon" (a bad used car), you won't pay as much.[10]

On the other hand, government action in situations of asymmetric information can be very effective. For example, licensing requirements provide some assurance that a person who claims to be a doctor, or an airplane pilot, really is qualified to provide that service. Reputation might be able to distinguish good doctors, or pilots, from bad ones, but only after the information that some are bad is revealed in the form of dead patients or smoking wreckage from a plane crash. Firing, or refusing to hire, the incompetent doctor or pilot once the incompetence has resulted in death or injury is too costly to be a useful mechanism for sorting out the good from the bad. Similarly, drug safety regulations are designed to ensure that products are both safe (cause no harm) and effective (perform the advertised function).

The problem, of course, is that we don't know how far to push this "asymmetric information" rationale for regulation. If it works for drugs, how about food? We already regulate health standards at restaurants, of course, just as we regulate drug safety. But why not go all out and regulate quality, too? Some restaurants are good, some are great, and some are just awful. Why not a chop checker, a scrod scrutinizer, an examiner of escargot? We could establish a Federal Burrito Bureau, and close down restaurants that serve stale tortillas, moldy cheese, or rancid cilantro ("Sir, move away from the tapas bar! And put down that margarita! Slowly!").

You see the point. If you go to a restaurant and don't like the food, you just don't go back. You tell your friends, and they tell others. Newspapers publish a review of restaurants, and the places with bad food get panned. Successful restaurants may establish franchises, and the brand name both ensures quality and communicates information about cuisine type. The decision whether to regulate, or license, appears to be based more on the potential for avoiding harm than for realizing gains, since markets can handle the problem of realizing gains of their own.

Price Taking

A wheat farmer goes to the grain elevator in town, and checks the price list. He notices that wheat is trading at $5.31 per bushel. Shocked, he shouts, "That is highway robbery! It costs me $5.35 a bushel to grow and harvest the stuff!" The elevator employee nods sympathetically, and says, "Yup, too much wheat this year. Everybody had a bumper crop." As the farmer drives home, he considers his options. Maybe he should just not sell the wheat this year; that'll show 'em!

No, refusing to sell wouldn't accomplish anything. The farmer is a "price taker": he has to accept the price determined by aggregate demand for the wheat. His farm, a well-tended section[11] of fertile North Dakota prairie, produces a huge quantity of wheat: 24,000 bushels per year. But this produce is only a trivial part of U.S. annual production of more than 2.5 *billion* bushels in the 1998–9 growing season. The farmer's threat to withhold the wheat draws no reaction from anyone, and has no effect on price. He is better off selling the wheat for what he can get, and making whatever payments he can on his loans.

Market participants of all sorts can be price takers. Owners of resources, such as labor, or wood, or mineral rights, can be price takers. Producers, like our wheat farmer, can be price takers. And consumers, or people who buy bread and apples in the store, can be price takers.

What if some market participants are not price takers? That means that they control enough of a market, for resources, for production, or for consumption. It turns out that "price taker" means exactly the same, technically, as "faces a flat, or horizontal, demand curve." Consider Figure 4.4. In panel A, we see a horizontal demand curve, like that faced by the wheat farmer. There is a price offered in the market, and you can buy, or sell, at that price. The amount of wheat the farmer has available is not enough to affect the price. Of course, it

FIGURE 4.4
The Size of the Deadweight Loss Depends on Whether All Parties Are "Price Takers"

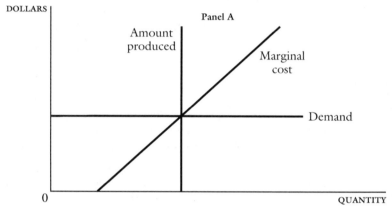

Panel A Demand is horizontal, and deadweight loss is negligible.

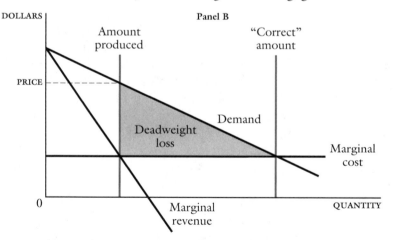

Panel B Deadweight loss from "monopoly": Downward-sloping demand curve for the firm implies Pareto inefficient allocation of productive resources (amount produced is much less than the "correct" amount).

must be true that the demand curve has some downward slope, even in a competitive market. After all, it couldn't be true that the market demand curve slopes downward (as it must, since an increase in wheat prices makes people buy less bread, cake, and pancake flour) but that the demand curve individual farmers face is truly flat. But the demand for the single farmer's wheat is practically flat, even if he bought up all the wheat in the whole county.

The demand curve does slope down, even in the perception of the individual producer. Examples include electricity and other utility services, long distance telephone providers, and automobile producers. If we assume that each producer tries to maximize profits, then it must be the case that there are some deadweight losses due to market power if the demand for that producer's product slopes down. This is obvious when you look at panel B of Figure 4.4.

First of all, it is easy to show that if the demand curve slopes downward, the profit-maximizing firm should charge a price that exceeds marginal cost.[12] This means that monopoly, in and of itself, can cause significant inefficiencies.[13] As a consequence, we in the United States have some of the tightest regulation of monopoly power in the world.[14] Both the Federal Trade Commission and the Justice Department have "antitrust" jurisdiction, and veto power, over the decision by firms to merge or otherwise affect market structure.

There is one situation, however, where monopoly is nearly unavoidable. Industries with long-run declining costs, at least over the relevant range of production, present a difficult problem for regulators. On one hand, it is cheaper to spread large **fixed costs**, such as building a hydroelectric power generator, over more units. In the case of an electric utility, the costs of building a generation facility, and a transmission grid to deliver the power to homes and businesses, is very high, before a single kilowatt is used. For example, suppose it costs $10 million per year just to rent the power plant and pay to maintain the wires strung to all the houses. If there are 100 houses, and each uses just 5 kilowatt hours per year, the **average cost** (that is, total costs divided by units produced, or the charge necessary to cover total costs) is $20,000 per kwh. If there are 10,000 houses, and each uses 5,000 kwh per year, the cost is only 20 cents per kwh. The point is that if you have to pay a lot of "fixed" costs, or costs required even to start providing the service, the average cost of service falls dramatically as more of the service is provided.

The solution from an efficiency standpoint, is to spread the high fixed costs over more units. Consequently, rather than having many small firms, technological efficiency is better served by having a single large firm capable of realizing the **economies of scale** inherent in a production activity with high fixed costs. But this leads to a different problem: The larger the firm in relation to the total market to be served, the greater the firm's market power. More specifically, a single firm producing electricity would face a sharply downward-sloping demand curve. If the firm charged the profit-maximizing price, the deadweight losses might be enormous.

Thus, in the case of industries with high fixed costs and declining average costs, such as electric power, we are presented with a dilemma: Accept the technological inefficiency of many firms competing, or suffer the economic inefficiency of monopoly output restriction and overpricing. There is, of course, a third way out: Regulate the monopoly, by mandating rates to be charged and the return that can be earned on investment.[15] Nearly all private utilities in the United States are regulated in this way, because policy makers are unwilling to accept the consequences of this type of market failure.

Private Decisions

The assumption that all choices, in consumption and in production, have only internal consequences is central to the perfect competition model. The reason is obvious: An individual takes only his or her own, "internal" costs, and benefits, into account. If there are other effects, for which no compensation is made, then the individual incentives may diverge from those leading to a Pareto optimum.

Suppose, for example, I have a large quantity of toxic liquid wastes in barrels on my property. The barrels have started to leak, and I notice that my crops planted near the barrels look brown and wilted. I need to get rid of this waste; what should I do? Imagine that there is a river nearby, and that I can transport the barrels there without too much trouble. Since the river flows away from my property, I can be sure that I will suffer no ill effects from dumping my barrels. However, the *society* may suffer significant ill effects, from fish kills and increased cancer incidence in people downstream.

My use of the river, which many people value, for a place to dump my poison, is an example of an **externality**. The problem is not that there are no benefits. In fact, I get big benefits, because clearly I am better off for having rid my property of the toxic liquids. The problem is not even (necessarily) that the costs are bigger than the benefits, since it is possible that the benefits to me are larger than the costs to the people downriver from the highly diluted waste.

No, the real problem is the fact that *my action affects others, but they have no say in my action.* I keep all the benefits, and impose costs on the people downriver. More technically, I consider the benefits to me (which are large), and also the costs to me (which are only the costs of dumping the barrels of toxic waste into the river), but am not forced to consider the total, or "social" costs of my actions.

In chapter 3, I described "Pigou's conjecture." A. C. Pigou (1932; pp. 183–4) argued that externalities could cause market failures, as people responded to individual incentives different from those facing the entire society. The beauty of the welfare theorems is the claim that individual and group optimality are both served by market processes. But externalities may break this nexus of private motive and public good. In particular, self-interested people engage in too much of certain activities (such as pollution) if they don't have to pay the full cost of the action. Alternatively, people may engage in too little of other activities (such as installing sprinkler systems to stop fires from spreading to other buildings) if they don't receive the full benefit of the action.

Pigou's solution to the market failure problem is shown in Figure 4.5. Notice that there are *two* "marginal cost" curves—one paid by

FIGURE 4.5
Pigou's Conjecture
A system of taxes will bring incentives back in line with Pareto optimality.

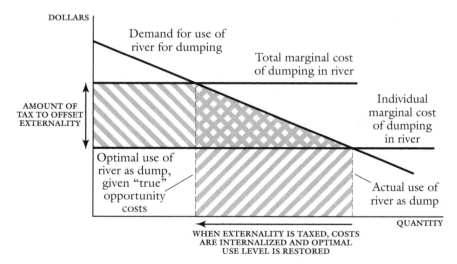

the individual considering the action, and another summarizing the total societal opportunity cost of resources used up by the action. Since the demand for use of the river is assumed to slope downward, this means that a person facing only the individual (i.e., lower) costs will overuse the river as a dump. Pigou's solution, elegant in its simplicity, is to impose a tax on the use of the river as a dump, with the amount of the tax (in dollars) calculated precisely to account for the otherwise uncompensated externality.

The tenacious reader will recall that I compared Pigou's conjecture—a system of taxes and subsidies is the best way to eliminate the problem of externalities—with another view: Coase's conjecture. Coase noted a difficulty with Pigou's statement of the problem, a difficulty that is fundamental to an understanding of the workings of a market system. The only way that there could be "externalities," in the sense Pigou seems to intend, is if the other parties damaged by the action of production or consumption have no recourse. For this to be true, at least one of two things would have to be true:

1. Property rights to the affected resource must be poorly specified, or else the legal system must not be functioning well. Otherwise, the damaged party could recover damages through a tort action, in court. Since the court is at least as able to judge harm as a policy maker charged with calculating the tax rate, this private action is fully capable of solving the externality problem, with no direct government intervention other than provision for a system of law.
2. Property rights to the affected resource must be diffuse, so that the resource is held in common and no one individual is responsible. In this case, the "transaction costs" of organizing all the affected parties and bringing a suit may be prohibitive. If transaction costs are significant, it is possible that government action (i.e., a **Pigouvian tax**) will be required to internalize the externality.

Coase argued, however, that if property rights are clearly specified, if the legal system functions smoothly, and if some mechanism for reducing transaction costs (such as a class action suit, or an action by just a few affected individuals) can be found, the notion of "externality" is simply wrong: externalities either don't exist, or they will be internalized by private action through the court system. Coase's reasoning, if correct, leads to a surprising conclusion: The best way to solve problems of externalities may not be government action to tax or regulate. Instead, the solution may simply be to facilitate private action by reducing transaction costs and ensuring clearly specified property rights.

Nonetheless, government regulations in the case of externalities is a central feature of nearly every national, state, and local government. Restrictions on pollution, dumping, or noise; zoning restrictions to protect property values; fire and safety restrictions to prevent injury to others—the list is long indeed. While the measurement of externalities is difficult, the idea that government action is required to solve the problems they cause is here to stay. **Coase's conjecture's**[16] is one of the most controversial parts of policy analysis.

Yet it is clear that the Coase theorem is simply an argument for the result Kaldor and Hicks favored. The only difference is the mechanism by which the resource allocation is achieved. As Coase (1960) argued:

> The problem which we face in dealing with actions which have harmful effects is not simply one of restraining those responsible for them. What has to be decided is whether the gain from preventing the harm is greater than the loss which would be suffered elsewhere as a result of stopping the action which produced the harm. In a world in which there are costs of rearranging the rights established by the legal system, the courts, in cases relating to nuisance, are, in effect, making a decision on the economic problem and determining how resources are to be employed. . . . Courts . . . often make, although not always in a very explicit fashion, a comparison between what would be gained and what lost by preventing actions which have harmful effects. (pp. 26–7)

The reason for Coase's skepticism of government intervention is stated later in the same paragraph: "There is a real danger that extensive governmental intervention in the economic system may lead to the protection of those responsible for harmful effects being carried too far" (p. 27). That is, though the Kaldor-Hicks approach might lead to the same (efficient) outcome if it were carried out well, the real-world political process may be prone to errors in measurement, or simple corruption.

Private Goods

The assumption that goods are not "public" is similar to the idea that there are no externalities. But there are also important differences. Externalities affect the welfare of others; public goods are simply impossible, or very difficult, to produce successfully in a purely competitive market setting. The reason is simple: Pure public goods will be underproduced, or not produced at all, in a market system.[17]

Suppose you go into a movie theater, at 2:15 on a Tuesday afternoon. You pay $3 for your ticket (it's a matinee), and notice that the person behind the ticket window looks like she just ate something sour. "What's wrong?" you ask. She replies, "Well, now we have to show the gol-darned movie!"

Walking into the theater, you understand: you are the only patron! The movie starts up, and during the promos for other films, you think about how little it would cost for other people to see this movie. There are more than two hundred empty seats around you, the air conditioning is running, there is a security guard near the exit, and two people working the popcorn stand. It seems awfully wasteful to run all this for just one person.

And you are right: it is wasteful. Even if you allow that a completely crowded theater is bad, it is still true that another fifty, or seventy-five, or one hundred people could watch this movie with you at something close to zero cost to you, to the theater, and to society. Since they (the absent viewers) would enjoy the movie, that means that there are significant deadweight losses from excluding them. Further, if the theater always operated with such sparse crowds, it would go bankrupt.

Zero marginal cost of production is one of the key characteristics of public goods. The movie theater, up to the point of "congestion," clearly satisfies that criterion. So, is the movie theater a public good? No: The other characteristic of public goods is *costly exclusion*, meaning that it is difficult to prevent others from enjoying the benefits of the public good if any is produced. This leads to a consideration of degrees of "publicness" of goods produced for consumers, as can be seen in Table 4.1.

As the table shows, the idea of "publicness" is complex.

- There are commodities with high marginal costs and costly exclusion. These are not public goods, but are rather much closer to

TABLE 4.1
Public Goods Have Zero Marginal Cost and Costly Exclusion

	Exclusion Is Costly	*Exclusion Is Cheap*
Negligible Marginal Costs	Pure public goods	Movie theaters Airplane seats
High Marginal Costs	Common pool resources	Pure private goods

what are known as "common pool resources."[18] Examples include fisheries, pools of petroleum underground, public forests, or watersheds. In any of these cases, a unit that I harvest or consume is not available for you, so marginal cost is significant. On the other hand, it is difficult to prevent me from harvesting or consuming from the "common pool": If no one owns open waters outside territorial boundaries, then the fish belong to whomever can catch them. If I sink a well and find oil under *my* property, then drawing it out may cause the oil under your property to flow over in my direction, too.

- There are commodities with negligible marginal costs (up to endogenously determined thresholds of "crowding"), where exclusion is inexpensive. Once an airplane is making a trip, the marginal cost of filling unsold seats is small. The movie theater example, above, works the same way: one person at the door can easily exclude people who don't pay the full price of a ticket, even though the marginal cost of the seat is only a small fraction of that price.

- Many commodities, such as the things we buy in the grocery, at the drugstore, or the car dealer, are for all practical purposes pure *private* goods. That means that they have high marginal costs of production, and exclusion (barring theft) is cheap. Markets are likely to work well for these commodities, and as we have already seen, market outcomes in such a setting are Pareto optimal.

- Pure public goods, however, are a different story. *Public goods have both high costs of exclusion and low marginal cost of production.* The canonical (pun intended) public good is national defense: the cost of defending the United States is unaffected by an increase in population, and it is difficult to withhold the benefits of defense from anyone who refuses to pay their taxes. So, any firm which tried to go into business providing national defense would go bankrupt. For one thing, it would have a hard time collecting for its services, because exclusion is nearly impossible. Furthermore, if the firm charged the marginal cost of national defense, the price would be zero. But the firm has to cover its *average* costs (including all those big shiny tanks and airplanes), which are much higher than zero. On both counts, private provision of public goods is doomed, even though citizens all recognize that they would be better off if the service were provided. This means that there is a **prisoner's dilemma** aspect to the public goods problem. In brief, the prisoner's dilemma is a strategic setting where self-interested action leads to a Pareto-inferior result. Technically, a prisoner's dilemma is a game where each participant has an identical strategy set consisting of two elements, "cooperate" and "defect." The structure of the payoffs is such that "defect" is the dominant strategy for all participants, and the resulting outcome for the group is worse—for *all*—than if everyone had cooperated. For now, it is enough to point out that private provision of public goods leads to a market failure, because the result is not Pareto optimal.

There are other instances of "near" public goods that are the focus of debate among policy analysts. Roads and highways are one example. Clearly, marginal costs are negligible (again, up to crowding constraints; the marginal cost of one more car may matter at peak rush hour). So, the question is whether exclusion is costly. It is easy to envision private roads, where cars pay at toll booths. But in most cases this involves queuing; if you have ever driven on the Garden State Expressway in New Jersey at rush hour, you know that costs of exclusion can be very high, as you and hundreds of others wait ten minutes or more in line to pay a 35-cent toll.

It is hard to imagine a toll booth at every entrance to every road, but that is what once would have been required to have a pure private road system. Still, changes in technology have made the idea of private roads much more plausible: a computerized system of billing codes for each car, with electronic sensors embedded in the roadways to measure use, raises the possibility that roads are not pure public goods after all. There are private highways in portions of Los Angeles, and in Hong Kong, a fact which illustrates once again that "publicness" is as much a technological issue as a political one.

Summary

In the previous chapter, I argued that markets have properties that make them uniquely suited to organize and direct large groups of people without any obvious central plan or strategy. But what are the limits of this value? Are there circumstances where markets perform poorly, or even disastrously? And how can we measure actual results against the theoretical benchmark of perfect performance within the ideal of pure competition?

This chapter has tried to answer both questions. The market failures rationale for government intervention in the market was discussed, with the conditions for poor performance (natural monopoly, externalities, public goods, information asymmetries) defined and described. Several types of measurement or evaluation were also presented, ranging from the notion of consumer surplus to the Bergson-Samuelson social welfare function and the two welfare theorems of economics. The chapter started by expanding the set of comparisons that the analyst can make by redefining the Pareto criterion to account for "potential" efficiency gains, allowing for compensation. This approach, the Kaldor-Hicks compensation principle, will occupy much of our time in later chapters on cost-benefit analysis.

SUMMARY OF KEY CONCEPTS

1. A *normative* proposition describes what ought to be.
2. A *positive* proposition describes what is.
3. *Utility* is a means for representing the level of satisfaction or well-being of consumers and citizens. The *utility function* is a means to measure and rank consumers' preferences for the allocation of resources.
4. The *total revenue* of a firm is the price multiplied by the quantity purchased.
5. *Costs* are payments to factors of production. The *total cost* of a firm is the sum of all of the expenses incurred in producing the output.
6. The cost of producing one more unit of a good is the *marginal cost.*
7. The cost per unit produced is the *average cost.* It is calculated by dividing the total costs by the number of units produced.

8. The cost of starting to provide a service or producing a good is the *fixed cost*.

9. *Profit* is the total revenue minus total cost.

10. *Price discrimination* is the practice by a firm of charging consumers different prices for the same good.

11. A good is *perfectly substitutable* with another good if there is one-to-one relationship between the utility and the total amount of the two goods: I like (10,0), (5,5), and (0,10) equally well.

TOOLS FOR EVALUATING POLICY

12. By the *Pareto criterion*, an allocation of resources is efficient or optimal unless there exists an allocation of resources that everyone else prefers. The comparison of alternatives using the Pareto criterion requires the principle of unanimity.

13. The *Kaldor-Hicks compensation principle* is useful for comparing two states of the world that are both Pareto optimal. This principle entails choosing the policy from the set of Pareto optimal states that maximizes the difference between the gains for the winners and losses for losers.

14. The *consumer surplus* is the difference between maximum value a consumer would be willing to pay for a good and the value that she actually paid for it in the market.

15. A *demand curve* is an analytic tool employed by economists to assess the maximum value a consumer would be willing to pay for a good or service. The demand curve demonstrates the *law of demand:* the quantity purchased varies inversely with the price.

16. A *deadweight loss* is the value of waste in the exchange of goods and services. A deadweight loss can result from any force that causes a divergence between the price and the cost of production.

17. The *Bergson-Samuelson social welfare function* is a potential method for choosing among points on the production possibilities frontier. This social welfare function assumes that society can aggregate the welfare of its individuals, and therefore evaluate the set of alternatives, just as an individual consumer can. The social welfare function requires that the utility of all individuals can be weighted, which allows the utility of the society to be calculated by summing the individual utilities.

18. The *production possibilities frontier* is the set of choices that rep-

resents a society's total potential productivity of all of the resources.

19. *Welfare economics* is the study of the normative properties of economic outcomes.

20. *General equilibrium theory* is the study of the consistency and coherence of economic outcomes.

21. Welfare economics and general equilibrium theory are the bases for the first and second welfare theorems. The *first welfare theorem* states that all general equlibria in perfectly competitive markets are Pareto optima. The *second welfare theorem* states that these general equlibria exist and these Pareto optimal outcomes can be achieved through the appropriate initial allocation of productive resources.

22. A *sufficient* assumption is a condition that is strong enough to imply a specified result. A *necessary* assumption is the minimum set of conditions required implying a specified result. A sufficient assumption is stronger, or more restrictive, than a necessary assumption.

23. A market is *purely* or *perfectly competitive* if it meets the following sufficient assumptions: information is perfect and free, all consumers and firms are price takers, all decisions are private, and all goods are private. A *market failure* exists when these assumptions are not met.

THE MARKET FAILURES PERSPECTIVE

24. The assumption that *information is perfect and free* requires that all participants have free and immediate access to information about the quality of products and about the implications of present actions for future welfare.

25. The assumption of *price taking* requires that no market participant controls enough of the market transactions to influence the price of the good or service. In a *monopoly*, or a market with many buyers and a single seller, the seller influences the price of the good or service. Therefore, the existence of a monopoly precludes the existence of pure competition.

26. The assumption that *all decisions are private* requires that the choices of individuals do not affect the welfare of others, or in other words, that there are no externalities in production or consumption.

27. An *externality* is the effect of one individual's actions on the welfare of other individuals. These effects can be *positive* or *negative*.
28. *Costly exclusion* implies that it is difficult to prevent others from consuming a good.
29. The assumption that *all goods are private* requires that there are no goods with the following two characteristics: zero marginal cost of production and costly exclusion. A good with these characteristics is referred to as a *public good*.
30. A *property right* is the control over the use and sale of a resource, commodity, or idea.
31. A *common pool resource* is a good with costly exclusion and high marginal cost of production.
32. The *prisoner's dilemma* is a strategic setting where self-interested action leads to a Pareto-inferior result. The provision of public goods is an example of this type of situation.
33. *Pigou's conjecture* is that market failures in the form of externalities can be corrected through the imposition of taxes and subsidies on the use of the public goods.
34. *Coase's conjecture* is that externalities do not exist if property rights are clearly specified, if the legal system functions properly, and if there exists a method of reducing transaction costs.

PROBLEMS AND QUESTIONS

1. Suppose that a society faces the following problem: Most citizens want to build a road from city A to city B, where no road now exists (see art on page 131). Imagine further that there will be no other exits on the road, and that it is inexpensive to place electronic sensors in the highway and usage meters in cars. The road could in principle be "private."

a. Evaluate Coase's conjecture: Under what circumstances could the road be privately financed, built, and operated? In particular, what problems will the citizens of city A and city B have to solve to make sure "the road goes both ways"? (Ignore the question of which route to choose, and focus only on whether the road will be built at all).

b. The road is not, strictly speaking, a public good, since by assumption exclusion is possible. But there are conditions under which the society (say, the state in which city A and city B are located) might provide road services at lower total cost, and finance the costs out of tax revenues. What are those conditions? More to the point, if you were a consultant for the A-B Regional Planning Commission, what information would you want? What, specifically, would you recommend they do?

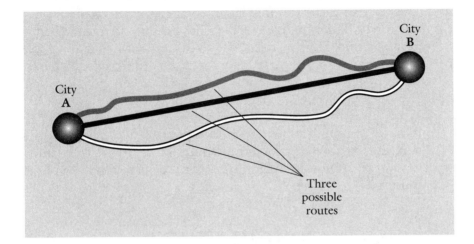

2. Now, suppose that the citizens have decided to build a *public* road, regardless of what you recommended above. Suppose that land will have to be purchased, and that various topographic features (hills, rivers, etc.) of the land affect the cost of road construction significantly. Which of the three routes depicted in the figure in question 1 will be chosen, assuming that public officials apply the Kaldor-Hicks criterion honestly and with full information?

3. Is there any difference between the route chosen by applying the Kaldor-Hicks criterion and building a public road, and the route chosen by applying the Coase theorem and building a private road?

4. Suppose that a consumer's demand for rutabagas (R), given the price (P) is given by the following equation: $R = 50 - 2P$.

a. Assume the price of rutabagas is 7; what is the consumer surplus the consumer enjoys on the fourth rutabaga? That is, what is the numeric difference between the highest price the consumer would have been willing to pay, and the price s/he actually had to pay for delicious tuber number 4?

b. Given the demand schedule for the consumer, and the fact that $P = 7$, what is the total consumer surplus of the consumer? More simply, how much is the maximum amount the consumer would pay for admission to the marketplace?

5. The social welfare function (SWF) involves the assignment of weights, to the utilities of each citizen. In broader terms, the SWF reflects the value of each citizen in the society. List three or more principles that you think should guide this assignment, based on a definition of justice. In particular, does justice require that all people be treated equally, or are there some occasions (differences in *need*, differences in *ability*, differences in *wealth*) when some people "count" more than others?

6. What is a common pool resource? Provide two examples of a common resource. What problem surrounds the use of a common pool resource? How does Pigou's conjecture relate to a common pool resource?

TAKE IT TO THE NET!

Go to: http://www.wwnorton.com/college/polisci/analyzingpolicy for additional problems, data sets, and course materials.

NOTES

1. See Kaldor (1939), and Hicks (1939).
2. In fact, we can rarely be certain that an alternative is a Pareto optimum, except in the restrictive sense of comparison to the other alternative. The search for a global optimum that all might prefer if offered is precluded by lack of information and political obstacles. So, when I say "both are Pareto optima" I mean that neither alternative is unanimously preferred to the other.
3. It ended up costing a little more than $30 million.
4. Actually, of course, from the perspective of the elected representatives of the citizens. But that is the way things usually work in representative democracies; the will of the officials is as close to the will of the people as we are likely to get, for most everyday questions.
5. Raleigh *News and Observer*, April 11, 1996, in a story authored by Matthew Eisley, "Thrift Store Owner Fighting Condemnation Over Museum."
6. The question of how costs are computed is not treated here. In most cases, however, a "normal" rate of profits would be included in the accounting definition of costs. In that case, the kind of profits depicted here (over and above the opportunity cost rate of return) would require some kind of regulation, or scarce resource, to prevent entry.

7. The Bergson-Samuelson social welfare function was originally developed in Bergson (1938) and Samuelson (1947). For a review of the history, and intellectual development, of this concept see Mueller (1989), chap. 19.
8. "Tangency means that two lines intersect, but do not cross."
9. A historical note: Samuelson (1967) derided Arrow's notion that a nation even should, much less could, have an analytic notion of politics. The idea that political values are somehow ineffable, or oracular, being delivered in some inscrutable yet definitive way, is common in the early policy analysis literature. Since I come from the "public choice" perspective, it has always seemed to me that arriving at political values is at the very heart of the problem, and yet we now know that there is no obvious way of solving that problem.
10. The "lemons" problem has to do with a prospective buyer's inability to judge the quality of a car, or of any other product. Since the buyer cannot distinguish among different quality levels, the price for a used car will represent the value of the *average* quality for a car of that age and type. But then high-quality used cars will be withheld from the market, or exchanged privately. This drops average quality, and causes the price (which is tied to average quality) to fall also. The result is a market that unravels, to the point where only very low quality cars ("lemons") are traded, at low prices.
11. For those not from the Midwestern United States, a section is 640 acres, or 1/36 of a township.
12. The argument is straightforward: Profits equal total revenues minus total costs. But then, using calculus, it must be true that $d\pi \, / \, dx = d(\text{TR} - \text{TC}) \, / \, dx = \text{MR} - \text{MC}$. Setting this expression equal to zero, we find that the firm should produce where $\text{MR} = \text{MC}$. This production level will always be less than the Pareto optimal level. In other words, deadweight losses always exceed zero if the firm perceives a downward-sloping demand curve, and cannot perfectly price discriminate.
13. There are numerous arguments about the actual size of deadweight losses from monopoly. See Harberger (1954), Stigler (1956), and Posner (1975).
14. Sherman Act, Robinson-Patman Act.
15. There have been arguments that regulation of utilities is not necessary, provided a careful bidding and contracting process is followed in choosing a provider in the first place (Demsetz, 1968).
16. The Coase conjecture can be stated more precisely as follows: If (a) property rights are clearly specified, (b) transactions costs are negligible, and (c) wealth effects on consumption and production can be ignored, then the initial allocation of property rights is irrelevant to the final allocation. Further, the final allocation will be a Pareto optimum, exhausting all potential gains from exchange. Finally, there is a close relationship between the Coase result and the Kaldor-Hicks compensation principle: in each case, the imperative is to choose the efficient allocation of rights (Coase) or resources (Kaldor-Hicks). The chief difference is that Coase argued for private negotiation and settlement of claims, while the Kaldor-Hicks approach usually involves the estimation or measurement of costs and benefits by analysts. This also means that Coase believed that the compensation should actually take place, because the agreement is a contract. For Kaldor-Hicks, the question of compensation is much less important.
17. One important source for the theoretical basis of this claim is Samuelson (1954), who solved a problem already identified in the "just taxation" literature, including Wicksell (1958, original 1896) and Lindahl (1958, original 1919).
18. For a discussion of common pool resources, or the "commons" problem, see Ostrom (1990).

~ 5 ~

Experts and "Advocacy": The Limits of Policy Analysis

An expert is one who knows more and more about less and less.
—Nicholas Murray Butler, Commencement Address,
Columbia University, 1926.

The previous chapter described circumstances where most analysts agree that public policy makers should intervene in market processes. In terms of the triangle of policy conflict introduced in chapter 2, this tension between freewheeling market activity and regulation designed by experts results in "efficiency" policies.

But do real policy analysts follow anything like the abstract model from the previous chapter? The answer may surprise you: You bet they do! Or at least, many do, in the way they describe problems, and in the way they characterize solutions. The single most important problem-solving tool in policy work is the Kaldor-Hicks compensation principle, or cost-benefit analysis. Furthermore, the focus of much of "scientific" policy analysis really is efficiency to the exclusion of other concerns. I am not saying this is good, or bad. It is just true, so if you want to learn about policy analysis you need to gain some insight into how policy analysts really think. This chapter attempts to give you that insight.

Is Policy Analysis "Value Neutral"?

Many policy analysts consider their enterprise to be value neutral. There are two ways to justify this claim of objectivity:

1. *Policy analysis focuses on means-ends relationships: Y = f(X).* That means that, if a society wants to accomplish outcome Y_i, it should pull policy lever X_i. There is no intimation that Y_i is good, or bad. Analysis is just a tool for evaluating the chance that X_i will lead to Y_i, and not some other outcome Y_j. Suppose you want to reduce prison overcrowding. Some people say we need more prisons, and more police. Others say that we need more rehabilitation, and job training in poor communities.

   It is possible to dismiss the whole debate as "ideological," or not really about evidence, but there is in fact a purely objective component lurking here: one policy, or the other, actually is more likely to lead to the desired outcome. Generally, then, the "objective" perspective would claim that policy analysis is not about choosing outcomes. Instead, policy analysis deals with advising decision makers *which policy is most likely to lead to the outcome the decision makers have chosen*, without in any way judging whether that outcome is "good."

2. *Pareto efficiency is the core concept of welfare economics*, and it has been adopted by policy analysts who take an economics-driven approach. This means politics, and the (re)distribution of income or resources, can be ignored as a separate question. Policy analysts can take as their goal the capture of unrealized gains from trade, or the elimination of deadweight losses. Even if the Pareto criterion is expanded to include the Kaldor-Hicks compensation criterion, and consequently we take account of total gains and losses, the need for making the implied compensation is played down. The reason is that this is an "equity," or political, question—once again, outside the field of study for policy science.

I am being intentionally reductionist, and provocative, of course. But it is common to find the "economics is solely about efficiency" ideology in research about policy analysis. The argument can be structured this way: It is the job of the analyst to try to move the workings of the economy as nearly as possible toward efficiency. Some of the required changes will benefit certain groups; other policies will benefit other groups. It will be easier to estimate, and to compensate for, the *aggregate* net distributional effects than to try to keep track of the distinct effects of each policy change, and compensate for them one at a time.

Further, the policy authority is better qualified to make judgments about the income requirements of individuals, because distributional issues involve the values of the community. Any policy analyst who focuses exclusively on the market failure rationale for regulation or other government action in the marketplace is, intentionally or not, explicitly choosing a purely efficiency-based view of the world. Many policy analysts view this neutrality, or apolitical perspective, as an advantage. Consider the argument of Stokey and Zeckhauser (1978).

> One of the great virtues of the benefit-cost approach is that the interests of individuals who are poorly organized or less closely involved are counted. (This contrasts with most *political* decision-making procedures.) Even when pushed by powerful interest groups, projects whose benefits do not outweigh their costs will be shown to be undesirable. The benefits and costs accruing to all—to the highway builders, the environmentalists, the "little people," the users and providers of services, the taxpaying public—will be counted on a dollar-for-dollar basis. *Benefit-cost analysis is a methodology with which we pursue efficiency and which has the effect of limiting the vagaries of the political process.* (Stokey and Zeckhauser, 1978, p. 151; emphasis added)

Alternatives to the Value-Neutral Focus on Market Efficiency

As we have seen, the advantage of the efficiency paradigm is that it centers all attention on Pareto optimality, which by construction is value neutral: alternative A is better than alternative B if, but only if, literally everyone agrees that A is better than B. The Kaldor-Hicks criterion, or potential Pareto comparison, follows the same logic, since if some people like B better but those who like A could compensate the losers, unanimous consent is still attainable.

The limitation of the Pareto criterion, or compensation principle, is that it takes markets and monetary value as presumptive starting points. Any changes in resource use or consumption patterns must be justified as deviations from the market-driven status quo. Within the policy analysis community there are a number of alternatives to the narrow focus on market efficiency. The remainder of this section considers four such perspectives.

- Technical command economies (Can expertise substitute for prices?)
- Interest groups, "advocacy," and political power
- Roles and resources of the policy analyst
- Standards versus incentives in the regulation of markets

Technical Command Economies: Can Expertise Substitute for Prices?

Markets "fail" in a variety of ways, but there is a larger potential failure that has led many observers to call for an alternative mechanism for organizing productive activity: This failure is the potential for chaos, or collapse of the market system. Analysts have tried to offer better solutions for the following four basic problems with prices and market systems:

1. *The market system is too unpredictable, with wild swings in employment and prices, leading to social chaos and even revolution.* Most (in fact, all) economies in the world are heavily "managed." In less developed nations, such as Colombia, Uganda, or Brazil, this management may take the form of price controls, resource use restrictions, or "commodity boards" that purchase products within the country and then sell them abroad at a profit, which the government takes as revenue.[1]

In many industrialized nations, the management of markets takes the form of sophisticated (well, complex) fiscal and monetary policy designed to limit the frequency and severity of downturns in economic activity. In the United States, the Federal Reserve system manages the money supply, and tries to direct interest rates. The Congress manages overall employment through fiscal policy (such as the Humphrey-Hawkins "Full Employment" Act of 1976), and influences economic decisions in hundreds of ways through federal regulatory agencies.

The "social safety net" of welfare programs, providing for those who cannot provide for themselves, is the largest public expenditure in the United States after national defense. Consequently, whether you believe that American government is addressing equity concerns

about income distribution, or just trying to keep the lid on social un-
rest caused by "contradictions" in market processes, much of the
government activity we see in the market is clearly motivated by concerns other than pure efficiency. Should policy analysis really remain
outside this debate completely?

2. *The market system inevitably involves the exploitation of labor, for
the sake of profit for "capital," or the owners of the means of production.*
Many economies, especially in the Scandinavian countries, are heavily
managed through state, or collective, ownership of capital-intensive
industries such as steel, automobiles, or medicine. Consequently,
while there are very few extremely wealthy people in these societies,
there are also few desperately poor people. Still, these "market socialism" countries use the market to direct goods to consumers, and to
determine which products are in greatest demand. Socialism has
more to do with the distribution of wealth, and productive resources,
than it does with suppressing the market completely.

3. *The market system is incoherent, because prices do not accurately
represent the scarcity value of resources.* This is an argument that the
market system is incapable of gauging true scarcity values because externalities are so pervasive. In particular, (a) markets cannot give accurate present values for future use, so we are denying future
generations the use of resources squandered today; and (b) markets
cannot give accurate values for amenities, or other collective goods,
which are damaged by pollution, traffic, and other by-products of
economic development. This is a difficult argument to evaluate, because it rests on the presumption that value ≠ price. The definition of
value becomes a problem whenever the price system does not give an
accurate measure. Value becomes determined by experts, or by politics, in ways that may be different from the market. The problem is
deciding whether the difference is really an improvement. Earlier, we
saw Pigou's argument that value ≠ price in the face of externalities.
But then the compensating tax, or subsidy, has to be estimated somehow. As we will see in later chapters, this sort of estimation may give
a point of purchase for a number of arguments about "true" scarcity.

4. *The market system is incoherent, and dangerously unstable, because there is no reason to believe that the quantity of goods supplied will
match up with the effective demand of consumers.* This is an interesting
point: since markets operate on effective demands, and consumers

must rely on their abilities as laborers (i.e., producers) to earn incomes, why would the quantity of goods produced always be purchased by consumers at prices that will allow producers to avoid going bankrupt? In the early part of the twentieth century, this was one of the most important questions in all of economics. Perhaps the earliest formulation was that of Karl Marx:

> Since the production of commodities is accompanied by a division of labor, society buys these articles by devoting to their production a portion of its available labor-time. Society buys them by spending a definite quantity of the labor-time over which it disposes. That part of society, to which the division of labor assigns the task of employing its labor in the production of the desired article, must be given an equivalent for it by other social labor incorporated in articles which *it* wants. There is, however, no necessary, but only an accidental, connection between the volume of society's demand for a certain article and the volume represented by the production of this article in the total production, or the quantity of social labor spent on this article, the aliquot part of the total labor-power spent by society in the production of this article. (Karl Marx, 1972, vol. 3, p. 220; emphasis in original)

Marx's distinction between actual, and social, labor echoes Pigou's discussion of actual, and social, costs. The point is that intentions to produce, and to buy, may not match up well because the price system may adjust too slowly, or even perversely.

Well, do prices and intentions match up, or adjust? Interestingly, and perhaps disturbingly, no one knows for sure. Economists have shown that, under certain fairly general conditions, abstract models of the economy always converge to a "general" equilibrium where quantity supplied matches up with the quantity consumers wish to purchase, at the prices which imply stable, sustainable wealth positions for owners of capital and suppliers of labor. But do these abstract models apply to real economies, where the assumptions are not met? Or is there the constant potential for instability and economic crises such as the world witnessed during the Great Depression of the 1930s?

Each of the four claims above is a reason to be skeptical of the "start with markets, then fix failures" approach. Each claim may, on its own merits, be true or false. But the larger problem is that, if we were to choose some alternative organizational system, there really has to be an *alternative*. There is an old saying in policy analysis:

"You can't beat something with nothing." Any alternative to the market must perform the *same functions* as the market (directing resources toward their highest-valued use, creating incentives for increasing production of things consumers want, reducing deadweight losses by encouraging competition, and creating incentives for innovation and invention), with fewer drawbacks or "failures."

Hundreds of economists, especially in nations where economic activity was organized around Marxist-Leninist principles instead of market philosophy, worked on this problem, particularly in the decades of 1930s through the 1950s.[2] If the market is suppressed by giving ownership of the means of production to the state, and then offering consumer goods at "prices" far below their resource scarcity cost, the state's central planners face two grave difficulties.

First, *information:* How many sugar beets should be produced, and how many cabbages? You have to guess, and there is no reason to expect that your guess will match up with actual desires a year from now. Further, because planned economies are hierarchical, and organized from the top down, they respond only very slowly. Farmers can't look at futures prices to see which crops to grow in response to increasing scarcity. Instead, they have to wait for a letter from the central authority. If the cabbages rot because of excess production, but there aren't enough sugar beets, the deadweight losses can be enormous. The fact that the losses aren't measured in monetary terms (remember, no prices!) doesn't mean that the opportunity cost isn't significant.

Somehow, planners have to account for opportunity cost without using the concept of price. No real solution was ever found: if you went to the butcher shop in the former Soviet Union, the price posted for pork was very low. But there was never any pork to buy, because the opportunity cost of pork was far higher than the price the government had mandated.

Second, *incentives:* Why should anyone care how much gets produced, or how good it is? The sugar beet producers, and the cabbage producers, are going to get paid their pittance regardless of what happens. If the cabbages are small from lack of proper care, or the beets spoil because the fields were plowed in patterns that prevent drainage, why should the workers be upset? Those cabbages, and those beets, didn't belong to them anyway. Somehow, planners have to find a way to make people care about their work, and make them work hard, when compensation is completely divorced from output.

Otherwise, the economy is led to the difficulties summarized by the old joke about the "pretend" economy in the Soviet Union: "We pretend to work. They pretend to pay us."[3]

Of course, there aren't many people working on the problem of alternatives to the market in the 2000s. Many of the economies where markets were suppressed, including those in Central Europe, Russia, and Africa, have disappeared, to be replaced by some form of market system with at least a rudimentary currency and notions of exclusive property rights. This apparently unconditional surrender has raised an important question: Are markets the only solution? At this point, the answer seems to be a provisional yes, if we place the burden of proof on proposing a viable alternative. It appears that the "markets first, then regulate" approach has carried the day.

Interest groups, "Advocacy," and Political Power

This chapter addresses the real world of policy analysis, rather than the analysis found in economics textbooks. In the abstract, the debate over "efficiency policies" concerns only the problem of ensuring that markets work as well as possible. In reality, politics (the excluded force in pure efficiency policies) intrudes in many ways.

This is hardly news, but many who "do" policy analysis appear to ignore the constraints placed by the political process on the policies that can be legislated, and implemented. One of the first to recognize the problem with politics and markets was the high priest of markets, Adam Smith. He said: "People of the same trade seldom meet together, even for merriment and diversion, but the conversation ends in a conspiracy against the public, or in some contrivance to raise prices" (Smith, 1994, p. 148). The problem is a simple one, but Smith's insight is profound: Firms seek profits, but competitive markets are the enemy of profits. Competition forces profits down to the opportunity cost rate of return. Consequently, the "invisible hand" works only if firms can somehow be prevented from reaching price-fixing agreements, or making arrangements to divide markets.

In pure competition, of course, fixing prices and excluding competitors is not easy: high profits will attract new investment. By what means could existing firms possibly protect themselves, and insulate their markets from competitive pressures? Government! After all, as George Stigler (1971) points out,

The state—the machinery and power of the state—is a potential resource or threat to every industry in the society. With its power to prohibit or compel, to take or give money, the state can and does selectively help or hurt a vast number of industries. That political juggernaut, the petroleum industry, is an immense consumer of political benefits, and simultaneously the underwriters of marine insurance have their more modest repast. The central tasks of the theory of economic regulation are to explain who will receive the benefits or burdens of regulation, what form regulation will take, and the effects of regulation upon the allocation of resources.

. . . As a rule, regulation is acquired by the industry and is designed and operated primarily for its benefit. . . . We propose the general hypothesis: every industry or occupation that has enough political power to utilize the state will seek to control entry. In addition, the regulatory policy will often be so fashioned as to retard the rate of growth of new firms. (p. 1).

Pursuing, and expanding, this theme, Stigler avers:

The state has one basic resource which in pure principle is not shared with even the mightiest of its citizens: the power to coerce. . . . These powers provide the possibilities for the utilization of the state by an industry to increase its profitability. . . . The most obvious contribution that a group may seek of the government is a direct subsidy of money. . . . The second major public resource commonly sought by an industry is control over entry by new rivals. . . . A third general set of powers of the state which will be sought by the industry are those which affect substitutes and complements. Crudely put, the butter producers wish to suppress margarine and encourage the production of bread. . . . The fourth class of public policies sought by an industry is directed to price-fixing. Even the industry that has achieved entry control will often want price controls administered by a body with coercive powers. (pp. 3–4)

If Stigler's argument contains even a grain of truth, there is a real problem with the idealized model of public-interest-oriented market failure regulation. If market failures having to do with industry structure, information asymmetry, or externalities are regulated, the "regulations" are designed by the industries ostensibly bound by the new rules. This may be rather like setting the wolf to guard the henhouse.

Interestingly, this so-called Chicago view of regulation is very similar, at least in terms of its premises, to the Marxist view.[4] Both take as a starting point the claim that public attempts to intervene in private market processes are likely to be "captured," or subverted, by the very economic agents whose behavior was to be regulated and controlled. That is, *concentrations of economic power can be translated into (illegitimate) concentrations of political power.* Such political power can then be used to consolidate, protect, and even expand the economic power. For both these sets of theorists the bottom line is that private interests will taint regulatory policy. The difference is that Chicago economists tend to conclude that we should get rid of the regulation, while Marxists conclude we should get rid of the private interests.

There may be some truth in both views. The belief that politicians and bureaucratic agencies will simply accept and implement a program without changes is profoundly naïve (remember Ira Magaziner and the health care fiasco). Interest groups cannot, and probably should not, be denied a voice in the political process. But it is frustrating to watch a program with general reforms be whittled away and changed piece by piece.

Consider this account of an attempt at tax reform in the late 1970s, from Birnbaum and Murray's (1987) description of the Tax Reform Act of 1986:

> [President Jimmy] Carter made tax reform a cornerstone of his election campaign, calling the existing tax system "a disgrace to the human race" and "a welfare program for the rich." In an interview with Fortune magazine, the president said he thought the nation was "ready for comprehensive, total tax reform." While not divulging details, he said his plan would "eliminate hundreds of tax breaks and greatly reduce the tax rate." After taking office, Carter's treasury secretary, Michael Blumenthal, began publicly discussing some of the provisions under consideration, and they did indeed sound bold and sweeping. He floated the idea of eliminating the preferential treatment of capital gains, for example.
>
> The response of interest groups to Carter's trial balloon was fierce and swift, and the administration's resolve was indeterminate. In the fall of 1977, Carter aides said they were "reshaping" the tax proposal to reflect changing budgetary, economic, and political realities. When the plan was finally unveiled in January 1978, Carter's grand rhetoric boiled down to a few exceedingly modest reforms, such as cutting back on the "three-martini-lunch" deductions for business meals and entertainment. Even those modest measures were quickly ripped apart by Congress.
>
> The bill finally enacted in 1978 was a complete renunciation of the Carter proposals and of any notion of tax reform. It included a host of new tax benefits. The Senate proved to be particularly generous, voting to expand many existing tax breaks and adding numerous new provisions targeted to help farmers, teachers, Alaskan natives, railroads, record

manufacturers, the Gallo winery of California, and two Arkansas chicken farmers.

. . . Tax reform was out; "capital formation" was in. The influence of special interests had reached new heights. (pp. 15–16)

What had happened was this: President Carter promised to reform the tax system by cutting loopholes and lowering rates, but the result of the "reform" efforts was exactly the opposite of what was intended, as many more features of the tax system were changed to encourage tax breaks and subsidies on particular kinds of investment. I am not interested in passing judgment on the value of the tax changes themselves (though most were probably bad, from a public policy viewpoint, and good from the perspective of persons whose taxes were reduced or eliminated). Rather, I offer this example to illustrate the unintended, but probably predictable, consequence of public interest "reforms:" far from eliminating "loopholes" and special preferential provisions, the new tax code had more loopholes than before.

This is not to argue that policy analysis is useless, or that reform is impossible. Instead, I want the reader to understand that the process of policy formulation is complex, and that analysis is only one part of the process. Analysts play a variety of roles, and a good analyst recognizes which role he or she is playing. Let's now consider what some of those roles look like, and how to recognize them.

Roles and Resources of the Policy Analyst

In chapter 1, I argued that policy analysis has five steps (*problem formulation*, selection of *criteria*, comparison of *alternatives*, consideration of political and organizational *constraints*, and *implementation* and *evaluation* of the program). These five steps, when applied to the study of markets and the activities of economic agents, should allow any analyst to draw the same conclusion when presented with the same set of facts. That is, any policy analysis will be conducted in the same way, though there may be differences in emphasis.

But the way the five steps will be carried out will differ depending upon the context or particular institutional constraints within which the analyst is working. There are important conflicts that make the real process of policy analysis different from the idealized process I have outlined:

- The conflict between loyalty to the clients and loyalty to one's own principles
- Client-imposed restrictions on the criteria-alternatives matrix
- The conflict between the need for certainty and the need for an immediate decision
- The requirements of the "guild," the profession of policy experts
- Resource constraints

These conflicts are well known to anyone who has worked in a policy job. The question is how to reconcile competing goals and satisfy multiple constraints, and still have the sense that you are honorable and ethical. The answer may not be very satisfying from a global ethical perspective, but any policy analyst would agree: Your ability, and desire, to be objective and "fair" depends on the context in which you find yourself.

Loyalty conflicts: clients or principles? Suppose that after settling on a problem definition (or having been given a problem formulation by your client), you realize that a different problem formulation is more sensible. Of course, your client may insist on sticking to the original formulation, because changing the definition of the problem may fundamentally change the set of alternatives being considered. This kind of conflict is very difficult for the analyst, but it is nearly always resolved in favor of the client, because the client controls the funding, or can fire the analyst.

Restrictions on the criteria-alternatives matrix. Even if the analyst and the client agree on the problem formulation, the contents of the criteria-alternatives matrix may be hard to agree on. First, the weights placed on different criteria by the client may differ from what the analyst discovers through research or surveys to be the value criteria of the relevant portion of the population. This means, of course, that the conclusions the analyst reaches may point to a policy different from what the client wants, or different from what would best serve the client politically. What should you do? Under what circumstances should you follow the client's wishes, and under what circumstances should you do what you think is right?

The need for certainty versus the need for an immediate decision. The pace of the policy process is very different from the pace of research and evaluation. Policy analysts are trained to consider evidence, to research possible alternatives, and to consider the implications of being wrong. Surveys, or other forms of data collected by other researchers, are often not quite (or not remotely!) applicable to the particular questions that the analyst needs to answer. Yet because of the pressures of the political process, and the need to know right now, inappropriate data may be the best you can get. The analyst who insists on certainty, and time for research, probably won't have a voice in the decision, which will simply be made without his or her input. But the analyst who shoots from the hip, and makes a guess, runs the risk of being wrong, with potentially disastrous consequences.

A famous example is the Reagan administration's budget deliberations in 1982, as described by David Stockman (1985). Meeting nearly around the clock, White House economic analysts and top staff were trying to hammer out a budget proposal. Estimates and assumptions were flying around, and the sources and accuracy of these numbers were very hard to gauge. In deciding the defense procurement budget projections, Casper Weinberger requested a very large set of increases in future years. Some analysts balked, saying that the increases were far too large, and would cause a budget deficit of enormous proportions. But the top economic staff, with little time to do the research required to be certain, backed Weinberger's estimates. As it turned out, of course, the inflation estimates were much too large, and the real increases built into the defense budget were gigantic. This mistake under pressure was not the only cause of the budget deficits of the 1980s and 1990s, of course, but it was a very significant contributing factor.

Requirements of the "guild": The profession of experts. It is for just this reason that agencies tend to sort themselves, over time, by the political views of their overseers. Many kinds of problems are resolved according to the type of people an organization hires and retains. Different organizations have different cultures, or norms about honesty and accuracy. If you are considering a job at an agency, think tank, or private consulting firm that does policy analysis, you need to ask questions to find out if the organization approaches problems, and sticks to values, in the areas of policy that really matter to you. A pure advocacy organization may be willing to argue any conclusion or to select only evidence that tends to advantage its side in a debate which is actually very difficult. There is nothing inherently immoral or evil about this type of organization, because our legal system is *adversarial*, requiring that each side in a conflict gets an advocate, or exclusive representation of their position.

Government agencies tend to value objective evidence, care in analysis, and accuracy of conclusions, but even here there is plenty of room for advocacy as opposed to analysis. In my experience as a policy analyst with an economic regulation agency in Washington, D.C., I found repeatedly that the process I had expected was reversed. Instead of starting with analysis, and then using evidence to reach conclusions, it was often the case that the "conclusion" (reached for political reasons) was handed to the analyst. As Jenkins-Smith (1990) points out, "A primary use to which analysis has been put is the *legitimation* of policy choices made by politicians. In this role, the analyst is employed for the aura of dispassionate, objective rationality that he or she can impart to politically motivated policy initiatives. The analyst's contribution is largely symbolic."

In such a situation, the analyst is really an advocate, in much the same way that a defense lawyer's job is to emphasize evidence that supports a particular conclusion. Of course, it is much easier, practically and psychologically, if the conclusion is one the analyst happens to believe.

That also means, of course, that the most difficult time for an analyst working for a government agency is the period following a significant change in political leadership. Someone who was hired when (for example) the Democrats controlled the Congress, or the presidency, may find herself in a difficult ethical position when the Republicans take over. The problem is that the analyst may perceive her client (the "person" she works for) to be the public, or members of some underprivileged group, but her boss (the person she reports to) may have very different ideas of what is right.

Jenkins-Smith points to three organizational characteristics that influence the analyst's "organizational allegiance": conditions of employment, proximity to the client, and availability of feedback from client. In general, the more the analyst works directly for the client, especially if there is daily personal contact, the more likely the analyst is to act as an advocate.

Resource constraints. As Jenkins-Smith argued, the first important type of constraint on the analyst is organizational. But resource constraints may be just as important. I have depicted these two types of constraints as dimensions in Figure 5.1. The vertical axis is *eco-*

FIGURE 5.1
The Roles of the Analyst

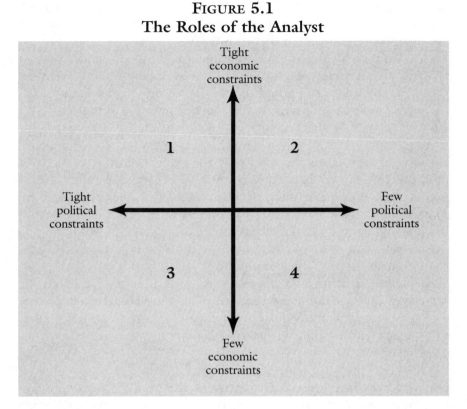

nomic: how many resources (including time, staff, and money) does the analyst have to carry out the task? The second (horizontal) dimension is *political resources*: is the analyst free to reach her own conclusions, or is this primarily an exercise in advocacy, where the conclusions are given with the assignment, and the analyst's job is simply to support the conclusions? For simplicity, in this figure the three organizational features Jenkins-Smith identified collapsed into one: *the extent of advocacy*. The four quadrants in the figure, numbered 1 through 4, then identify different "roles" played by the analyst.

Quadrant 1 is standard "staff" analyses done in-house for a client/employer. It involves a routine, long-term kind of advocacy by employees such as a federal department or commission, or state agency. There is little freedom to choose a subject, or to redefine the question, and the analyst has little time, or extra resources, to complete the work.

Quadrant 2 is volunteer work or work for some "public interest" nonprofit organization. The analyst here has wide latitude for creative definition, but usually little time or money to go beyond the most rudimentary analysis. Consequently, though there are few external political constraints, the work may not be "objective," if objectivity is understood to mean that the analyst reaches a conclusion *after* doing the analysis. Instead, analysts in this situation tend to sort themselves into organizations that advocate causes they already believe in. The conclusion is known in advance, and analysis is simply supportive fact-finding.

Quadrant 3 is likely to be some kind of consulting work or preparation of expert testimony for trials. There may be very substantial resources available, but the analyst is a hired gun whose task is to justify a position known in advance. That is not to say that the analyst is selling out, because she may well believe that her arguments are true. But analysts in this role should recognize that they have been selected for the content of the conclusions they will argue, not for their ability to do analysis.

Quadrant 4 is pure academic or think tank work. The results are either published as basic research or as policy/position papers designed to influence the opinions of the community of experts. Analysts who work in such positions are likely to have academic credentials such as a doctorate, a license, or some other signal of standing as an expert. Research papers written by analysts playing this role likewise face hurdles, such as peer review, to establish their veracity. The peer review process, in which anonymous referees approve or deny access to publication outlets, is supposed to enhance objectivity, of course. But its real function may be to enforce orthodoxy: a new or revolutionary idea may be hard to publish. As a result, the perspective in academic journals is inherently cautious and conservative.

Standards versus Incentives

Suppose you have just studied policy analysis from the welfare economics perspective. You know that a pure efficiency rationale for regulation to counteract market failures would hold that government action should minimize (or ideally, eliminate) deadweight losses, or departures from Pareto optimality. On the other hand, there are other concerns faced by a democratic society, such as fairness and equal treatment before the law. In fact, in the United States, the interpretation given by the Supreme Court to the Fifth Amendment (due process) and the Fourteenth Amendment (equal protection) is often taken to mean that the use of such policy analysis standards as incentives-based regulation, or cost-benefit analysis, is strongly suspect.

Consider the following two situations.

Situation 1. It is decided that the best way to solve the problem of externalities created by dumping raw sewage and chemical waste into the Gloppe River is to tax polluters, according to the marginal harm caused by the pollutants. Some pollutants (cyanide, carcinogens) are so harmful that damage equal to $1 million per fluid ounce results from dumping them in the river. Others, such as treated sewage, are comparatively benign and will be taxed at 10 cents per gallon. Producers respond to this regime in two ways: (a) They modify their production processes to produce less of the pollutants that are the most expensive. If the taxes are set correctly, "expense" will correspond to those pollutants that do the most harm to the environment. (b) They invest in cleaners, scrubbers, and treatment plants, up to the point where it is cheaper to process the waste themselves rather than dump it in the river.

There may remain, however, some producers who dump waste in the river, and have to pay the tax. What does this mean? It means (assuming the pollution taxes were set correctly, at exactly the marginal harm to the environment) that the commodity being produced by these firms is so valuable to society (in terms of the effective demands of consumers) that it is worth more to society to produce the output, and pay the full social costs of the consequent pollution, than to shut down the operation. Further, it must mean that dumping the waste is cheaper than cleaning it up.

Situation 2. It is decided that the best way to solve the problem of externalities created by dumping raw sewage and chemical waste into the Gloppe River is to prohibit such dumping. A "standard" is imposed on each type of pollutant, based on a level of harm that is equalized across substances. That is, no one can cause more than a certain, very minimal, amount of harm to the ecosystem of the river and the downstream users of the water. A system of fines is used to enforce the standards, with higher fines associated with violations involving more dangerous pollutants.

Which is the better approach incentives or standards? As an objective policy analyst, which would you recommend to decision makers?

More generally, should democratic societies use the incentives-based approach of situation 1, or the standards-based approach of situation 2? The quick and easy answer is . . . there is no quick and easy answer! Let's see why.

First, it isn't clear that there is really a difference. If the fines in situation 2 really correspond to the marginal harm, and there is no other enforcement mechanism, the two systems are indistinguishable, save that in the first case the charges are called "taxes" and in the second they are "fines."

Second, there are both advantages and disadvantages with the incentives approach. Stokey and Zeckhauser (1979) give the classic statement of the broad advantages of incentives:

> Two major classes of adverse consequences result when the government attempts to mandate private behavior: (1) individual freedom of action is restricted, carrying with it an implied threat, although possibly remote, to other liberties; and (2) the government may require behavior that is inefficient or inappropriate. These adverse consequences suggest a tension between government efforts to compensate for the inadequate workings of the market and the desire to allocate society's resources in an efficient manner without infringing on basic liberties. This tension can be reduced or avoided in many important situations if the government employs incentives that attempt to influence individual actions rather than directives that specify them. (p. 312)

In the case of environmental regulation, the problem may be simpler: regulatory agencies lack good information. Kneese and Schultz (1975) argue it this way:

> A regulatory agency cannot know the costs, the technological opportunities, the alternative raw materials, and the kinds of products available for every firm in every industry. Even if it could determine the appropriate reduction standards for each firm, it would have to revise them frequently to accommodate changing costs and markets, new technologies, and economic growth. (p. 88)

But hold on a minute: there is a little more to the story. If it is really so hard for the regulatory agency to make accurate judgments about *standards*, why would we think they can estimate *taxes*? Further, the decision about how much "pollution tax" to charge would presumably be open to the kind of industry manipulation Adam Smith and George Stigler warned about. There is no reason to believe, when millions or even billions of dollars are at stake, that the "invisible hand" of economic selfishness will lead polluting firms to advocate the "correct" (i.e., Pareto efficient) tax rates.

Finally, the specter of the Kaldor-Hicks compensation (i.e., simple utilitarianism) principle pervades this whole discussion, although the reason may not be obvious at first. Who benefits from allowing pollution to be dumped into the river, and a price charged to account for the externality? The answer is: consumers of the output produced by the polluting firm.[5] The people who benefit (consumers of product) may be different from the people who are harmed (users of the river). Now, who pays the costs of the pollution? Answer: downstream users of water, and people who value the ecological quality of the river environment. Are these two groups the same? Not necessarily. So, we are once more brought up short by the curious distributional consequences of cost-benefit analysis: the "efficient" amount of pollution implies certain benefits, which exceed the implied costs, *but the losers and gainers are different people.* Downstream water users are unlikely to be mollified by the argument that the amount of pollution is "Pareto optimal."

Of course, the compensation could be made: the revenues from the pollution tax could be earmarked for pollution abatement, water treatment, or compensation of downstream users. But this is a distributional requirement, and that smacks of politics! Furthermore, the advocates of the incentives-based approach perceive themselves as value-neutral, and purely objective, because the advantages of incentives are largely in the realm of efficiency (though, as Stokey and Zeckhauser pointed out, there are larger ethical questions also). The real point is that incentives are often politically infeasible, because the policy analysis rarely addresses the mismatch between gainers and losers.

Third, to be fair, there are also disadvantages with the standards approach. The most obvious is that, in fact, most standards-based regulatory systems are not based on fines calculated to capture the marginal harm from flouting the standard. Instead, the polluting firm is shut down, and further economic activity is enjoined. This is certainly effective for preventing the pollution, but there is the potential for serious distortions of relative prices and signals about scarcity. Simply put, *standards enforced by the threat of injunctions put a marginal value of infinity on the resource in question.* It doesn't matter how much it would cost the firm to stop polluting, or how much consumers value the product. The pollution must stop, or the firm will be put out of business and it employees turned out on the street.

This all-or-nothing aspect of standards can have pernicious effects. For one thing, firms are encouraged to operate illegally, dumping or disposing of waste secretly (and dangerously), because they may have no other option. In addition, firms that are caught simply disappear. Their assets, if there are any, are tied up in bankruptcy proceedings, while the polluted field, river, or warehouse is left unused. The pollutants, unprotected and unguarded, are no one's responsibility. The result is a new hazardous waste site for which we will all have to pay.

What Is the "Best" Alternative?

Facing the many constraints that we've just reviewed, how should a policy analyst choose the "best" alternative? Are there other factors that guide the policy analyst? There generally isn't time, or money, to do a complete study of alternatives and criteria in the way that the subject is taught. An important stage in policy analysis is therefore *prescreening*, where the relevant or most important alternatives and criteria are chosen.

Generally the analyst can do no more than set up the criteria-alternatives matrix, having to rely on the basic research of others to fill in the cells. The analyst must possess methodological skills sufficient to evaluate the quality of the basic research, and may have to choose among competing measures or construct an average if the cell entry is controversial. Such cells are also good candidates for sensitivity analyses: if a conclusion relies on one particular measure of a cell, when there are other competing estimates that would change the conclusion, the analyst must make a choice based on professional judgment. This means analysts cannot simply accept the results of experts, but must have enough methodological expertise to judge their validity.

It may not be possible to choose a single "best" alternative, since one alternative rarely dominates all others on all criteria. Instead, the best the analyst can do is make clear the value trade-offs she accepts and highlight the best alternative given those trade-offs.

Still, it may be possible to eliminate certain alternatives using the Pareto criterion (in either the strong or weak form, where "ignorance" equals "indifference"), or to make some imputation of what people would want if they were informed. This is an important result because it simplifies the public agenda and raises significantly the lowest value of what alternative is chosen.

In the likely event that the best that can be achieved, with confidence, is the reduction of the alternative set to two or three elements, some further recommendation can be made, though with a lower level of certainty, by following these options:

- Combine all the cells into some common unit (do the best you can with dollar estimates, for example), and then compare the options on this basis. The most common technique is cost-benefit analysis, based on the Kaldor-Hicks criterion. The disadvantages? First, you may be forced to accept **false specificity**, or numbers that appear to embody an exactness of measurement far beyond what the data can actually support. Averages or indices generated by complex calculations may often be quoted to several decimal places, when in fact the reliability of the estimate doesn't plausibly go beyond plus or minus the nearest ten. Second, the results may exhibit extreme **sensitivity to assumptions**, so that assumption A may lead to one conclusion, but assumption B leads to an entirely different set of predictions. If there is no obvious means for saying one assumption is better than another, but the choice among assumptions dramatically affects the predictions, then any conclusions the analyst draws should be qualified, and a caveat about assumption sensitivity should be included in the analysis itself.

- Leave the criteria in their respective units, but then come up with explicit trade-off ratios for comparing criteria, based on public opinion research, surveys, or voting. Trade-offs may be qualitative or quantitative, but the more explicit they are, the better. If you don't know the trade-offs, try three different levels and be explicit about the fact that you are uncertain. The disadvantage is that you may get contradictory answers to the same question, as we will see in chapter 10. The answer to the question, What is the value of a human life? could be based on (a) the law to require child safety seats on airplanes, (b) a law to require safety belts, or (c) expenditures on welfare programs such as WIC. You get different answers—$18 million, $250,000, or $2,000—depending on which basis you use.[6]

- Make no comparison beyond a fair description of the strengths and weaknesses of each alternative. Leave the task of devising relative weights and trade-offs to the client, though you may make recommendations based on research. The disadvantage is that your results may be (mis)interpreted for political purposes. You don't force any interpretation, but at the same time you lose the chance to prevent incorrect interpretations.

Professional Standards and Norms

At one time, almost anyone could work as a policy analyst. All that was required was some experience, knowledge of a policy area, or just a lack of self-doubt. In the past thirty years or so, however, there has been a professionalization of policy analysis as the policy sciences (law, economics, political science, and the parts of the hard sciences charged with liaison with government and the public) have codified procedures and requirements. Today, it is quite likely that you will need a credential, such as a master's degree, a law degree, or even a doctorate, to be taken seriously as an analyst.

As with any profession, there are norms of behavior in any of these fields. Extreme violations, such as criminal misconduct, may cause you to lose your license to practice the profession, as when an attorney is disbarred for malpractice. Beyond avoiding such egregious transgressions, professionals are more often motivated to pursue the achievements required to be taken seriously, and to have the respect of their peers.

In policy analysis, these requirements are not always clear-cut, because anyone whose analysis seems to have an impact on real policy decisions is "important." But the internal standards revolve around the adjectives you would expect: Careful. Objective. Fair-minded. Well-trained. Anytime you act too little like a policy analyst, from whatever part of the guild claims you as its own, you run the risk of losing respect. This is an important consideration, and should be a significant (and valuable) check to how far a policy analyst is willing to go to make a claim for his or her employer.

Summary

This chapter began by pointing out that "real" policy analysis often really does follow the abstract model, based on welfare economics, that was laid out in the previous chapters. One reason analysts find the abstract model and its focus on "efficiency" attractive is that it is value neutral: the goal of policy analysis is to make recommendations to decision makers, not to choose which outcome is best. The centrality of efficiency implies that the analyst can make choices based on facts, not values. Though this claim of objectivity is probably too strong, it is widely encountered in the policy analysis profession.

We then discussed four alternative perspectives to the "markets first" approach: These perspectives were: (1) technical command economies: can expertise substitute for prices? (2) interest groups, "advocacy," and political power; (3) roles and resources of the policy analyst; and (4) standards versus incentives in the regulation of markets.

The chapter concluded by offering some observations about the possibilities for the real-world policy analyst to choose the "best" approach. What makes policy analysis unique, and separate from economics, political science, or any other single discipline is its focus on multiple criteria. This may lead to problems, of course, such as extreme sensitivity to assumptions, or susceptibility to pressures for advocacy rather than objectivity. On the other hand, the lack of disciplinary affiliation also frees the policy analyst to select methods and approaches from a wide variety of sources.

This chapter is subtitled "The Limits of Policy Analysis" to emphasize the difficult choice analysts face in the way they treat markets. One alternative, the classic policy analysis paradigm for economists and for those who take the approach of economists, makes the market form of organization the starting point, and then considers regulations and policy initiatives as a way of adjusting or reforming market outcomes. The advantage of this "markets first," status quo approach is that it is often the most realistic and feasible: in practical terms, incremental changes from existing market processes are at the heart of most policy debates. But this may present serious limitations for the policy analyst, since the capacity to reconceive or redirect policy is focused so much on markets.

Non–market alternatives are often simply beyond the practical reach of the proposals the analyst can hope to have taken seriously. A suggestion that the market process be suppressed completely, or that resources be used in a way that violates the logic of the market, is very difficult to advance politically. I pointed out that one barrier to creative thinking is the orthodoxy imposed on academic discourse, ostensibly the freest and most open forum for debate, by the peer review process. The burden of proof of the value of any alternative approach is very much on the proposer, and the limits of the ability of analysts to satisfy this burden has been frustrating to those who wish to turn policy analysis away from a near-exclusive focus on economics. For now, however, economics remains central, because of the centrality of market systems as the organizing principle in economies in nearly every nation in the world.

SUMMARY OF KEY CONCEPTS

1. The *efficiency* paradigm of policy analysis is based on the concept of Pareto optimality from welfare economics. The concept of Pareto optimality is value neutral.
2. The claim of *objectivity* in policy analysis has two justifications. The first objectivity justification is that policy analysts evaluate which means or policies help achieve specified ends. The second objectivity justification is that policy analysts who adopt an economic approach consider how to eliminate deadweight losses or capture unrealized gains from trade (i.e., improve efficiency).

ALTERNATIVES TO FOCUS ON MARKET EFFICIENCY

3. Policy analysis may deviate from the value-neutral efficiency paradigm due to the following four concerns: market failures and a technical command economy, interests groups and advocacy, analyst roles and resources, and the use of standards.
4. Some policy analysts argue that market failures call for an alternative form of economic organization. One possibility is a *technical command economy* where expertise is a substitute for a price system as a means of directing and valuing resources.
5. While many policy analysts ignore political considerations, *interest group advocacy* can skew regulation toward the regulated groups, thus decreasing overall efficiency.
6. The *roles and resources of policy analysts* may lead to deviations from the efficiency paradigm due to the following issues: loyalty conflicts, the need for certainty, and guild requirements.
7. The conflict between loyalty to *clients* and loyalty to *principles*

may affect the analysis of policy. Client conceptions of the appropriate problem formulation, set of alternatives, and criteria for evaluation may differ from the analyst's conceptions. Client goals usually dominate, given that the clients provide the funding and support for the analysis.

8. The trade-off between time and *the need for certainty* may cause the policy process to deviate from the efficiency paradigm.

9. The *guild*, or the profession of policy experts, may have norms and beliefs that affect the policy process.

10. Policy analysts are sometimes employed for the *legitimation* of policy choices.

11. Two types of *resource constraints* affect the policy process: economic and political resources.

12. An *incentives-based* approach to regulation employs taxes to produce the efficient or Pareto optimal level of production given the impact of externalities.

13. A *standards-based* approach to regulation imposes a uniform and acceptable level of activity on all producers or consumers. Fines are assessed to those who violate the standard.

14. *False specificity* is imputing a degree of exactness beyond the accuracy of the data.

15. Results may be *sensitive to the assumptions*.

PROBLEMS AND QUESTIONS

1. What should motivate an analyst? What goals should be most important to someone who works in service of public? List at least four, and provide a scale of relative importance, from most to least important.

2. What skills should an analyst possess? How can you differentiate between the goals of the analyst, and the neutral skills or training that the analyst has developed? Again, list at least four, and rank them from most to least important.

3. Now suppose you are going to hire someone for a job as a top-level policy analyst, someone who will be advising key decision-makers. What observable characteristics of the applicants would allow you to identify the motives you want (from question 1) and the skills you want (from question 2).

4. Put yourself on the other side of the interview table: suppose you are now the applicant for this very desirable position. What sorts of things can an applicant do to signal that he or she has the right motives, and the right training and talents?

5. Imagine that you are an analyst working for the Agency for Environmental Policy (AEP) on another planet. There are many coal-burning factories on the planet, some of which (100) are old, inefficient, and very smoky, and some of which (again, 100) are new and burn the coal in much hotter fires. An old factory produces about 16,000 pounds of airborne hydrocarbons per year, while each new factory produces about 7,000 pounds per year. The best available technology for such factories would result in annual emissions of 6,000 pounds per year per factory. Your boss, the governor, has ordered analysts to come up with alternatives to reduce the growing level of air pollution. The alternatives they come up with are these:

a. Pass a regulation that all factories have to produce no more than 6,000 pounds per year. The new factories all like this, since they only have to cut by 1,000 pounds per year, and all the old factories will have to shut down or be rebuilt from scratch.

b. Pass a regulation that all factories have to cut their emissions by 25 percent. The old factories favor this, since they can install scrubbers and other equipment to cut their emissions to 12,000 pounds per year, but the newer factories will have a very difficult time cutting out an additional 25 percent.

c. Pass a regulation that says each factory has the "right" to pollute as much as an "average" factory, or about 11,500 pounds per year. Starting next year, though, each factory has the right to pollute 25 percent less than that, or 8,625 pounds per year. These rights are tradeable on the open market, so that a new factory which produces less pollution can sell its rights to an older factory which is having a hard time changing to the new technology. The new factories like this, since it means they have a right to pollute more than they do, and they can sell these rights for lots of cash. The old factories don't like this much, but they like the flexibility of not having to change over to the new technology right away. The environmental activists in the community hate this policy, however: "Pollution *rights?* Aren't we trying to reduce pollution, not increase it?"

Write an analysis for the three alternatives, setting up a criteria-alternatives matrix. Include at least the following three criteria: (1) reducing pollution, (2) preserving jobs (keeping factories in business), (3) satisfying your *own* environmental ethics. Which of the alternatives is best?

6. Now suppose your boss, the governor, comes in and says, "You know, those old factories are owned by our political supporters. We have to help them out. Come up with an analysis that shows option b is best." Two questions: Is it possible to do this? Could you justify doing this, if you really liked your job?

7. Discuss the problem with interest group advocacy and regulation. Compare the Marxist solution to Stigler's solution to the problem.

TAKE IT TO THE NET!

Go to: http://www.wwnorton.com/college/polisci/analyzingpolicy for additional problems, data sets, and course materials.

NOTES

1. For a description of the "management" activities of the these three nations, including the Ugandan "Coffee Marketing Board," see Bates (1997), pp. 166ff.
2. See, for prominent examples of this work, Lerner (1944), or Leontiev (1941). The question that motivated economists in this area was whether the information on relative scarcity, and the consequent decentralized direction given to resources, could be duplicated using a hierarchy of command and control.
3. See, for example, "Russians Find Black Market Is Crucial for Survival," *Washington Times*, March 22, 1999, p. 4.
4. Consider the similarity in the premises of the following arguments.

> The Chicago students of regulation have usually assumed, explicitly as often as tacitly, that the players who count in regulation are the producers and consumers. Political intermediaries—parties, legislators, administrators—are not believed to be devoid of influence, but in the main they act as agents for the primary players in the construction and administration of public policy. (Stigler, 1988, xv)

The executive of the modern state is but a committee for managing affairs of the whole bourgeosie. . . . The ruling ideas of each age have never been the ideas of the government]. (Marx, 1848, 3)

When commercial capital occupies a position of unquestioned ascendancy, it everywhere constitutes a system of plunder. (Marx, *Capital*, Pt. II, chapter 3)

5. It might seem as if the firm doing the polluting is the chief beneficiary, but this is not true if the tax is accurately calculated. The firm's profit rate will be the opportunity cost rate of return, so there is no net benefit to the firm's owners.

6. As we will see in chapter 11, these calculations can be arrived at using the following equation:

$$P * \text{Cost}(i) + (I- P) * \text{cost}(i) = \text{expected value}$$

(a) $P = 1/5,000,000$, cost(not i) = 0, cost(i) = death or injury, EV = \$375 (assume you had a cheap ticket, and a car seat). Then the implied value of cost (i) = \$18 million.

(b) $P = 1/10,000$, cost(not i) = 0, cost(i) = death or injury, EV = \$25. Then the implied value of cost(i) = \$250,000.

(c) $P = 1/4$, cost(not i) = 0, cost(i) = stillborn, low-birth weight, or deformed child. EV = \$500. (If population can be targeted, this P is too low!) Then the implied value of cost(i) = \$2,000.

— 6 —

Democratic Decisions and "Government Failure": The Limits of Choice by the People

All voting is a sort of gaming, like checkers or backgammon, with a slight moral tinge to it, a playing with right and wrong.
—H. D. Thoreau, *On the Duty of Civil Disobedience* (1849)

So far the primary argument in this book has been that there are three very different ways to organize human activity: markets, expert analysis, and political choice by "the people," and that real policies emerge from the conflicts among these alternatives mechanisms for organization. In particular, conflicts between market processes and experts result in efficiency policies; conflicts between politics and the market result in equity policies; and conflicts between experts and politics give us political institutions, and institutional reform. The apparent incoherence or inconsistency of policies is an artifact of their diverse origins. An efficiency policy may contradict an equity policy, and a particular institutional reform may contravene both. But there is nothing illogical about this contradiction: efficiency policies are designed to satisfy one set of actors, and equity policies and institutional reforms two separate, and possibly very different, sets of actors.

Markets, at least at the level of analysis where I have been operating, have less to do with "deciding" than with many individuals' simply responding to incentives. People are making the "correct" choice, given their individual preferences, resource constraints, and the scarcity signals transmitted by prices. In this chapter, the problem of collective choice, by a group of people, is addressed. Political choices turn out to be very different from the decentralized, individual-centered decisions made by consumers in a market.

In fact, the problem of coming up with political choices that are never arbitrary (i.e., random) or imposed (i.e., dictatorial) is more than just *hard*. A famous result published by Kenneth Arrow (1963) shows that a general rule for using individual preferences to imply a unique choice for society's policies is actually *impossible*. We will discuss Arrow's theorem later in this chapter, and see how it presents a menu of choice for what defenders of political choices will have to accept as limitations. Just as with market failures and ethical problems for experts, political choices are not perfect.

The General Problem of Decision

People have to make decisions all the time. Some we make on our own, some in small groups, and others in large agglomerations of people. Sometimes the costs of these decisions, in terms of information gathered and thought given to weighing alternatives and choosing among them, can be very high. This cost of deciding may be one of the arguments against socialism, or technocracy, since the market process of "deciding" is so decentralized. As Oscar Wilde is reputed[1] to have said about socialism, "It sounds like a good idea, but it would take up far too many evenings."

In a less humorous, but substantively similar, vein, philosopher Wilhelm von Humboldt (1854) said:

> We must not overlook here one particular harmful consequence [of politics], since it so closely affects human development; and this is that the administration of political affairs itself becomes in time so full of complications that it requires an incredible number of persons to devote their time to its supervision, in order that it may not fall into utter confusion. Now, by far the greater portion of these have to deal with the mere symbols and formulas of things; and thus, not only are men of first-rate capacity withdrawn from anything which gives scope for thinking, and useful hands are diverted from real work, but their intellectual powers themselves suffer from this partly empty, partly narrow employment. (pp. 29–30)

Politics is expensive, because the costs of decision are high. It may be worth it, of course, if the quality of decisions is better. How would we know?

We will return to this notion of the costs of decision making when we cover "optimal" majorities later in this chapter. For now, though, let simply note that *all decisions* (as opposed to random choices, or "choices" where there is but one alternative) *are expensive*. The origin of the word "decide" tells us something about why this is so. "Decide" comes from two Latin words—*de* (off, from) and *caedere* (to cut).[2]

It takes effort to cut off, or separate, the "best" alternative from among several. One essential part of a good definition of "decision" is the existence of *options*. If there are no options, then of course there is no decision to make. The second key part of the definition is that criteria must be used to make selection: a decision is not random. Even if some random device (such as flipping a coin) is used to break a tie, it is only because the chooser has *decided*, through some prior process of analysis, that the "tied" alternatives are equally good and equally bad, though perhaps in different ways. This leads us to the definition of "decision":

> **decision** (noun): The result of applying judgmental criteria to a set of alternatives for the purpose of choosing a single course of action.

In this chapter, we will consider several types of decisions, as well as the problem of decision-making costs, that face citizens. We will also review some of the limits on a group's ability to make "good" decisions, or for that matter any real decisions at all.

Types of Decisions: Private, Public, Collective

So far, we have considered only purely private decisions, made in a market setting, or particular kinds of public decision, where an individual's choice may have implications for the welfare of other people. The only restrictions on private choices that have been considered so far are the regulations implied by "market failures," including informational asymmetries, economies of scale, and externalities.

But private decisions, even regulated private decisions, by no means exhaust the set of choices made by a group of citizens. There is a fundamental difference between private decisions (that is, decisions that I make, and that affect only me) and decisions that involve groups of people (either in making the decision or being affected by it). Earlier, Table 2.4 summarized the types of decisions that face a group of people, it is worth reproducing a simpler version of that table here.

TABLE 6.1
A Typology of Decisions

"Publicness": Number Affected

"Collectiveness": Number Choosing	*One Person*	*Many People*
One person	Private-noncoercive	Private-coercive
Many people	Collective-coercive	Collective-public

There are two important dimensions in the table; these two dimensions are also important in every decision that faces a society. Across the top of the table, the difference is in the degree to which the decision is "public," or that the choice of one person affects the welfare of others. The vertical dimension of the table is something very different, however: this is the degree of "collectiveness" of the decision. As the table suggests, there are two kinds of potential coercion inherent in group decision-making:

• A collective decision is, by definition, binding on all citizens whether they agree or not. If collective decisions are enforced on private choices, this is a "collective-coercive" outcome.
• A public decision, by definition, affects more than one person. If one person is put in a position to make a choice without regard for its impact on others, this is a "private-coercive" outcome.

The chief problem faced by people who would design political institutions is balancing the potential for these two types of coercion. As "Publius" (in this case, John Jay) pointed out in *Federalist* no. 2: "Nothing is more certain than the indispensable necessity of government, and it is equally undeniable, that whenever and however it is instituted, the people must cede to it some of their natural rights, in order to vest it with requisite powers." To rephrase in the terms of this chapter, the problem is to make government powerful enough to be able to control "private-coercive" actions such as pollution, theft, or violence, without endowing it with so much power, or placing so many decisions under government control, that individual freedoms are lost to "collective-coercive" rules and regulations.

What is the problem with "collective-coercive" decisions? In a democracy, collective decisions can be made simply by putting the matter to a vote. That is, "we" decide what "I" can do, often using majority rule. As P. J. O'Rourke put it:

> Now, majority rule is a precious, sacred thing worth dying for. But—like other precious, sacred things, such as the home and the family—it's not only worth dying for, it can make you wish you were dead. Imagine if all life were determined by majority rule. Every meal would be a pizza. Every pair of pants, even those in a Brooks Brothers suit, would be stone-washed denim. Celebrity diet and exercise books would be the only thing on the shelves at the library. And—since women are a majority of the population—we'd all be married to Mel Gibson. (O'Rourke, 1991, p. 5)

So, here is the problem that a society faces in making collective, as opposed to individual, choices:

- First, select the set of choices that will be *collective*, and the set of choices that will be protected as *private*.
- Second, select a *decision mechanism*. Disturbingly, the process of decision making may affect the outcome of decision: unanimity rule can produce different results from majority rule, which may have different results from decisions based on proportional representation.
- Only after the first two choices have been made can the society can start making decisions, or separating the best alternative from the others.

A society where citizens do not recognize the distinct, and hierarchical, nature of collective decisions will probably face problems. Let's consider a hypothetical example.

A Hypothetical Case: The Community Pool for Ruttenton

Suppose that the five citizens of tiny Ruttenton have met for their annual town meeting. This body is empowered to make decisions for the entire town, and all citizens have agreed in advance to abide by the collective decision. Notice that this doesn't mean that the citizens expect to *agree* on all policies. Instead, the citizens (Mr. One, Ms. Two, Ms. Three, Mr. Four, and of course the mayor, Mr. Fish) all have pledged in advance to *accept* the collective decision.

At a previous meeting, the five citizens agreed unanimously that decisions will be made by majority rule: if three of the five citizens favor one alternative, that alternative will become Ruttenton law. Any citizen can make any proposal he or she cares to introduce, but the time for making proposals or debating motions is restricted to a total of five hours. At the end of five hours, the citizens must vote to decide on the best policy.

The meeting this year has only one agenda item: the Ruttenton community pool. Mayor Fish, who very much enjoys swimming, now has to walk three miles to the pool in Blaineville. He wants to build an enormous, Olympic-size pool (expected cost: $100,000), both because it would be more convenient for him and because it would be a statement of Ruttenton civic pride (the Blainville pool is rather small). As Mayor Fish is fond of saying, "You can't attract a new Mercedes plant without a community pool!"

Ms. Three and Mr. Four also favor building a pool, because they like to swim for recreation and occasional exercise. Three and Four only want to build a medium-size pool (expected cost: $60,000), however, thinking that an enormous pool wouldn't be used enough to justify the expense. Furthermore, they don't believe Mercedes is going to locate a new assembly plant in the area anyway, since Ruttenton has no roads.

Mr. One and Ms. Two have no use for a pool, and vehemently oppose the proposal to build a community pool in Ruttenton. They claim that they should not have to pay for a pool if they are not going to use it, and object to Mayor Fish's plan to finance the pool out of property taxes. One and Two argue that if a pool is built at all, it should be run as a community "club," with the costs of building and operation coming from membership fees and charges at the door. The initial positions of the citizens are summarized in Figure 6.1. Notice that I have organized the differing points of view along a general "dimension": most favored spending on the Ruttenton pool.

Who is right? How could the Ruttentonians decide what to do, and what the "best" choice is for their little community? If you were hired by the town as an expert in policy analysis, what would you recommend? Remember, you have to help them decide whether this is a problem where collective choice should be used, and if so, to choose a collective choice mechanism, before an actual decision is reached.

Suppose you conclude that this is a problem that requires a democratic, or collective choice. Then you tell the citizens of Ruttenton that they face three (apparently) separate choices:

FIGURE 6.1
Five Citizens Register Their Preferences
for a Community Pool for Ruttenton

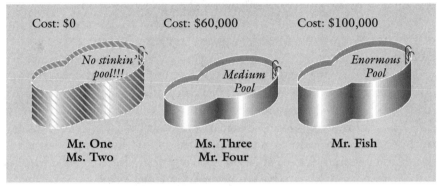

1. *Should we build a pool?* Alternatives:
   (a) Yes
   (b) No
2. *What size pool should we build?*
   (a) Medium
   (b) Enormous
3. *How should we pay for the pool?*
   (a) Finance through general property tax revenues (split cost five ways).
   (b) Finance through private club membership dues, and user fees (split cost *k* ways, where *k* is the number of people who join the club).

However, as is no doubt obvious to the reader, one cannot seriously recommend consideration of these three "choices" in isolation. Choice 1 (build) is clearly contingent on choice 3 (finance). For example, Mr. One might well favor the pool for civic pride reasons if he is sure he won't have to pay anything, but is likely to oppose any pool if financing will come from general revenues. After all, Mr. One doesn't swim, and never expects to use the pool at all.

Furthermore, choice 2 (size) might even be contingent on financing: Ms. Three might favor an enormous pool if the cost is to be split five ways (i.e., paid out of general revenues), but her honest evaluation is that a medium pool is best, especially if she expects the costs to be paid out of membership dues and user fees. Mayor Fish, who wants an enormous pool, might settle for a medium pool (or even favor no pool!) if he were the only one who signed up for the club, so that he would have to bear all the costs of the pool by himself.

Should these three issues be decided (build? size? financing?) collectively? Notice that this choice is not necessarily linked to the question of whether the pool is a public good. The "civic pride" (Mercedes plant) argument is certainly an attempt to make the pool seem public, but the primary use of the pool does not clearly fit the definition. If the pool is large, then the marginal cost of an additional user is very low, or even zero. But use of the pool is obviously excludable: it is possible to put a fence around the pool, and charge admission. If the pool is not a public good, what justification is there for making this a collective decision?

A Democratic Choice

Interestingly, the answer is that the choice can be collective if a majority of the citizens want it to be. Let's suppose that the citizens of Ruttenton accept your advice to split up the decision process, and decide to focus first on financing. Suppose further, for the sake of the example, that Ms. Three, Mr. Four, and Mr. Fish all want a pool enough that they will sign up for a private club, meaning that they would split the costs three ways if that is the outcome the town chooses.[3] To summarize the decision problem our citizens face, consider Table 6.2, which lays out the costs for the alternatives, broken down by the individual citizens' expected payments.

Let us imagine that the five hours for debate and proposals have elapsed. Now it is time for the citizens of Ruttenton to vote, and

TABLE 6.2
Cost Shares for a Community Pool for Ruttenton, Based on Financing Arrangement

		Alternative:		
Chooser:	No Pool	Medium, General Fund	Medium, Club-Financed	Enormous, General Fund
Mr. One	$0	$12,000	$0	$20,000
Ms. Two	$0	$12,000	$0	$20,000
Mr. Three	$0	$12,000	$20,000	$20,000
Ms. Four	$0	$12,000	$20,000	$20,000
Mayor Fish	$0	$12,000	$20,000	$20,000
Total Cost:	$0	$60,000	$60,000	$100,000

make the final decision. Given the discussion, and what we know about the five citizens, we can conclude that their "preferences," or evaluative rankings over alternatives, are described by Table 6.3.

TABLE 6.3
Preference Rankings of Citizens of Ruttenton

	Mr. One	Ms. Two	Mr. Three	Ms. Four	Mayor Fish
Best	No pool	Med., club	Med., gen.	Med., gen.	En., gen.
Next to Best	Med., club	No pool	Med., club	En., gen.	En., club
Middle	En., club	En., club	En., gen.	Med., club	Med., gen.
Next to Worst	Med., gen.	Med., gen.	En., club	En., club	Med., club
Worst	En., gen.	En. gen.	No pool	No pool	No pool

Key: Med.—Medium-size pool
    En.—Enormous-size pool
    Club—Financed by Community Club, cost paid by members
    Gen.—Financed out of general tax revenues

What this table implies (as you can quickly see with a little examination) is that the alternative "Medium pool, general financing" will be the outcome of any majority-rule decision process. The reason is that "Med., Gen." defeats all other alternatives in pairwise majority-rule contests. "No Pool" loses to "Med., Gen." by a vote of 3–2; "Med., Club" loses to "Med., Gen." 3–2; "En., Club" loses to "Med., Gen." 3–2; and "En., Gen." loses to "Med., Gen." 4–1.

It is possible to argue that this is the "correct" outcome, since it is chosen by majority rule. But wait. The outcome "Medium Pool," "General Financing" forces two people, Mr. One and Ms. Two, to pay for a pool they know they will never use. After the meeting, Mr. One and Ms. Two approach you (the outside consultant), angrily. "Some expert you are! All you did was help the others steal our money!" And they may have a point: it does seem tyrannical, or at least an abuse of power, for the majority to force its will on the minority this way. After all, the three pool aficionados could have gotten together and solved this problem on their own, with a private club. Why is the pool a *public* problem? The answer is a little scary: In political choice, the problem or activity doesn't have to be public. All it has to be is a *collective* problem, which is something that is often decided—here's the scary part—collectively!

Policy analysts have to deal with this sort of difficulty every day. Notice that the three parts of the decision (1. Build? 2. Size? 3. How pay?) require the analyst to solve many different problems, simultaneously. The hardest problem can be simplified, and restated like this: *What is the appropriate boundary between* public *and* private *decisions?* In the United States, this has been taken to be a question of individual rights versus public needs; but the boundary is not clearly, or permanently, drawn. The Bill of Rights in the U.S. Constitution, and the interpretation of individual rights found in the written opinions of the U.S. Supreme Court, provide only a partial answer. Nevertheless, the line between collective and individual choice is very important, and in any given case may be logically antecedent to the kind of policy analysis being considered in this book. In the example of the Ruttenton municipal pool, arguments can be made either way.

The remainder of this chapter is devoted to the second main task of the political process, the one that follows the conclusion that the problem should be decided collectively. This second task is the choice of a collective choice rule: how should we decide how to decide?

Institutions: The Choice of a Decision Rule

In the decision by the five citizens of Ruttenton whether the town should build a municipal pool, each person had an "ideal" conception of the appropriate amount to be spent, ranging from zero (for Mr. One and Ms. Two) to $60,000 (for Ms. Three and Mr. Four), all the way up to that natatic fanatic, Mr. Fish, who wants to spend $100,000. The outcome of a voting process, using majority rule, where all citizens can make proposals, was expected to be $60,000. A majority of the five citizens favor $60,000 to any other alternative pool budget, lower or higher than that number.

Is there some general principle at work here? Of course there is. The general principle is the power of the middle, or *median*, of the set of ideal budgets for citizens who get to vote. The prediction that "the median cannot be defeated" is quite general, so long as preferences are "single peaked," and the set of alternatives is a single dimension. In our case, spending on the pool meets the single dimension requirement, because no other issue is being considered. What does "single peaked" mean? Single peakedness has to do with how citizens evaluate alternatives different from their ideal points. Provided citizens dislike departures from their ideal budget, and dislike them more the larger the difference, we say their preferences are single peaked.

A person with single-peaked preferences finds each proposal better as the proposed spending level gets closer to her ideal budget. For example, Ms. Three likes the idea of spending $60,000 on the pool; she doesn't want to spend zero dollars, and would prefer spending $45,000 to spending just $30,000. So, for any comparison of two budgets,[4] Ms. Three prefers to one closer to $60,000, either from above ($65,000 is better than $70,000 is better than $75,000) or below ($50,000 is better than $40,000 is better than $30,000).

The principle that the median preference wins in majority rule elections was formalized by Duncan Black:

> **Median Voter Theorem** (Black 1958): If the issue space is a single-ordered dimension, and preferences are single peaked, a median position cannot lose to any other alternative in a majority rule election.

The median voter theorem implies that the middle of the distribution of citizen preferences in a society holds a privileged position in political competition. If the median position is unique (identified with just one voter), this very important person is called the "median voter."

But what if preferences aren't single peaked? Here a technical concept comes into play. That concept is "transitivity." Suppose a person is asked to rank three alternatives, A, B, and C, and he responds with a list that has two comparisons:

1. C is better than B.
2. B is better than A.

It is tempting to conclude that if a person likes C better than B, and likes B better than A, then that person must also like C better than A. But from a technical perspective, no such conclusion is justified, *unless the preferences of the person in question are transitive.*

> **Transitivity:** Preferences are *transitive* if, for three alternatives, C preferred to B preferred to A necessarily implies that A is not preferred to C (weak transitivity) or that C is preferred to A (strong transitivity).

Note that the concept of transitivity might be applied to a preference ordering of an individual or of a society choosing among alternative policies.

With this definition of transitivity understand, an important result in the theory of collective choice, often referred to as "Condorcet's paradox," can be stated.

Condorcet's paradox: Suppose all individual preferences are transitive, but not necessarily single peaked. Then the social preference ordering under majority rule may be intransitive.

The "paradox," or surprising finding, is that *the aggregation of* individually *transitive preferences leads to an* aggregate *intransitivity.*[5] The society faces an endless cycle of "best" alternatives, none of which commands a majority against all other alternatives.

Whether condorcet's paradox applies hinges on the notion of "single-peaked" preferences. What does this mean? Suppose as an example, that the only three foods in the world are apples, broccoli, and carrots. Each type of food is sold only in large crates. Three people get together and find they, if they cooperate, will have just enough money to buy one crate of food. The preference profiles of the three people, Mr. 1 (who loves apples), Ms. 2 (who loves carrots), and Mr. 3 (who loves broccoli), are listed in Table 6.4.

TABLE 6.4
Preference Lists of Three Voters over
Apples, Broccoli, and Carrots

Ranking	Person		
	Mr. 1	*Ms. 2*	*Mr. 3*
Best	Apples	Carrots	Broccoli
Middle	Broccoli	Apples	Carrots
Worst	Carrots	Broccoli	Apples

The premise of the example is that the choice is collective: if they cannot agree on a food, all will go hungry, because no one has enough money to buy a crate alone. But the three disagree about what to buy. After seemingly endless discussion, they realize they will never reach a consensus: no one is going to change their mind (if you don't like broccoli, you just don't like it). So, the three people decide to vote. They learned in ninth grade civics that voting is the only fair way to make collective decisions. Besides, they are all getting hungry.

Now the fun begins, because the preferences profiled in Table 6.4 do not admit of a single "best" alternative. By majority rule, apples are preferred to broccoli is preferred to carrots are preferred to apples, always by 2 to 1 margins. Say, for example, that apples are voted against broccoli first. Mr. 1 and Ms. 2 both prefer apples to broccoli, Mr. 3 vainly dissents, and apples are selected. Apples are then compared with the remaining choice, carrots: Mr. 1 votes for apples, Ms. 2 votes for carrots, and Mr. 3 votes for carrots.

If they don't think things through, the three may stop here. On the face of it, the "carrots preferred to apples preferred to broccoli" group preference seems fair enough. But in fact there is no unique choice that is defensibly the "general will" of this group. The general will does not exist, because the preferences of a significant proportion of the electorate are not "single peaked": no matter how you array the choices along a dimension, one of our three citizens thinks that the middle alternative is worst.

It turns out that Condorcet's paradox is a special case of a general class of paradoxes arising from using *any* social choice mechanism, except dictatorship, and regardless of whether preferences are single-peaked. The results are called "paradoxes" because the general problem seems so simple, yet turns out to be insoluble. Political scientists have concluded that there is no sure way of making a single, ethically defensible collective choice if a part of the definition of "ethically defensible" is that all citizens' preferences count.

This is true even under the best circumstances (perfect information, no manipulation), if no restrictions are placed on the form of individual lists. To object that these assumptions are unrealistic is to miss the point. If social choice is not tractable under idealized circumstances, then adding imperfect information and manipulation make the problem even harder.

I will briefly examine the best-known of these paradoxes, Arrow's (1963) impossibility theorem. Arrow laid out a set of properties or conditions that (arguably) are desirable features of a social choice mechanism. The impossibility theorem is a deduction that no social choice mechanism can possess all these features. In particular, all voting procedures must violate at least one of the conditions. Since Arrow's paradox applies to *any* nondictatorial aggregation mechanism, it encompasses all of what we might consider "democratic" decisions by societies. We will now consider briefly a variety of ways of choosing collectively and discuss some of their advantages and disadvantages.

Choosing How to Choose: The Optimal Size of the Decisive Set

Decisions may be made by one person, by some people, or by all the people. The set of citizens required to make a decision or choice is called the "decisive set."

> **Decisive set:** A set C of citizens is "decisive" if for two alternatives A and B the fact that all members of C like A better than B is sufficient to ensure that A is selected over B by the society, regardless of the opinions of citizens not members of C. We can call $S(C)$ the "size" of C, or the minimum number of people required to be decisive

An easy example of a decisive set is suggested by majority rule: C is any group of $(N/2) + 1$ citizens. Of course, there are many different potential Cs, each of which must have $S(C) \geq (N/2) + 1$ citizens.

Condorcet showed that majority rule may be intransitive even if each individual has transitive preferences over the alternatives. Intransitivity is a kind of breakdown, assuming that some choice is required. That choice may be to preserve the status quo, and do nothing, but the choice itself must be clear and determinate. Intransitivity means the society is incapable of choosing from among several mutually exclusive outcomes, without resorting to random or imposed "choice." One might ask whether this potential for incoherence extends to other collective choice rules. The definitive answer is less than fifty years old and dates to Arrow (1951; revised 1963).

That answer is upsetting for advocates of any particular form of collective choice. Before giving an overview of Arrow's technical result, it is worth summarizing the intuition.[6]

> **Arrow's paradox:** The only collective choice mechanism that is always transitive, allowing for any possible fixed set of pairwise preferences over alternatives, is dictatorship.

The "paradox" is that the only transitive collective decision rule that obeys the technical criteria Arrow sets out is dictatorship, or rule by one. But such a decision rule is not collective! Dictatorship resolves disagreements by restricting the decisive set to contain only one person. How did Arrow arrive at this conclusion?

The "Impossibility" Result

Let us consider a simplified paraphrasing of Arrow's theorem. (This discussion will not consider the technical aspects of the proof of the theorem; the interested reader can find an introduction to the literature in Mueller, 1989, especially chaps. 19–20 and a treatment in depth by Schwartz, 1986, and Kelly 1988). Arrow's result can be summarized this way:

1. Specify a set of desirable characteristics for an aggregation mechanism, or way of "counting" preferences registered by enfranchised citizens.
2. Determine the set of collective choice mechanisms that have all these desirable characteristics.
3. Ask how many of these choice rules are *not* dictatorial. The answer is: None! Any social choice mechanism exhibiting all the characteristics Arrow listed as desirable *must* be dictatorial.

Some scholars have questioned the validity of Arrow's list; others have suggested substitute axioms that are weaker or quite different. But Arrow's original set of desirable characteristics is not implausible. The version of these characteristics discussed here is adapted from Hinich and Munger (1997).

Consider three states of the world S_1, S_2, S_3, representing different policy vectors 1, 2, and 3, respectively. We can then describe the set of desirable characteristics as follows:

1. *Unanimity (also, the Pareto criterion)*: If all enfranchised citizens agree (for example) that S_1 is better than S_2, then S_1 is selected by the collective choice rule over S_2.

2. *Transitivity*: The collective choice mechanism is transitive, so that if S_1 is selected over S_2, and S_2 to S_3, then S_1 is selected over S_3.

3. *Unrestricted domain*: For any individual, and for any pair of alternatives S_1 and S_2, any of the following six preference orderings (from best to worst) is possible:

	1	*2*	*3*	*4*	*5*	*6*
Best	S_1	S_1	S_3	S_2	S_2	S_3
Middle	S_2	S_3	S_1	S_1	S_3	S_2
Worst	S_3	S_2	S_2	S_3	S_1	S_1

4. *Independence of irrelevant alternatives.* The social choice between any two alternatives must depend only on the individual rankings of the alternatives in question in the preference profile of the group. Thus, if S_1 is socially preferred to S_2, then it will still be socially preferred regardless of the orderings of the other alternatives, so long as the paired rankings of S_1 and S_2 are the same. For example, the following two sets of preference profiles of three citizens must yield the same social ordering for S_1 and S_2, if the social choice rule obeys independence of irrelevant alternatives.

Preference Profile Set A (for persons 1, 2, and 3)

	1	2	3
Best	S_1	S_2	S_1
Middle	S_2	S_1	S_3
Worst	S_3	S_3	S_2

Preference Profile Set B

	1	2	3
Best	S_1	S_3	S_1
Middle	S_3	S_2	S_2
Worst	S_2	S_1	S_3

Notice that the *relative* rankings of S_1 and S_2 are the same in profile sets A and B, even though the ranking of S_3 is different. For example, in set A, person 1 ranks the alternatives S_1, S_2, S_3. In set B, person 1 ranks them S_1, S_3, S_2. In both cases, person 1 likes S_1 better than S_2. Independence of irrelevant alternatives requires that this pairwise comparison of rankings does not depend on the position of another, "irrelevant" alternative (such as S_3 in our example).

The final "good" characteristic of mechanisms for the democratic aggregation of preferences is also the easiest: No one person possesses all power to decide.

5. *Nondictatorship:* There is no dictator. If person 2 (for example) is a dictator, then if person 2 ranks S_1 above S_2, then "S_1 better than S_2" is the social ranking, regardless of how anyone else, *or even everyone else,* ranks S_1 compared to S_2.

With these conditions established, a version of the "impossibility" theorem can be stated.

> **Impossibility theorem:** Consider the set of all collective choice rules that satisfy requirements 1–4 (unanimity, transitivity, unrestricted domain, and IIA). Every element of the set of collective choice mechanisms satisfying these requirements violates requirement 5, implying the existence of a dictator.

What does the impossibility result leave us? A menu of choice: Any mechanism for aggregating individual preferences must lack at least one of the desirable properties 1 through 4. I have considered non-dictatorship separately, because tyranny is incommensurable with democracy. To put it another way, nondictatorship is a starting point if the goal is to compare ideal forms of democratic government. A similar argument (for restricting the menu of choice for ideal forms of government) applies to the Pareto criterion, though on more practical grounds: it is hard to imagine adopting a rule that would prevent change if literally everyone favored the change. If nothing else, all members of society could unanimously change the rules![7]

If we insist on nondictatorship and the Pareto criterion in our social choice rules, we have three options: decision rules that allow *intransitivity*, rules that allow *independent alternatives* to affect pairwise choices of other alternatives, and rules *restricting the set of preferences* that will be allowed (i.e., violating universal domain). People have come up with many alternatives to simple majority rule. Each has some advantages and some drawbacks. The search for an "optimal" system of aggregating preferences is very difficult, however, because all systems have potential problems with fairness, and all systems can be manipulated. In its starkest form, that is what Arrow's theorem is all about.

Alternative Decision Rules

The difficulty with majority rule as a normative prescription for all members of society is that the majority's will must serve all, though it is only selected by most. Such a process must rely for its legitimacy on the majority's forbearance: "To be governed by appetite alone is slavery, while obedience to a law one prescribes to oneself is freedom" (Rousseau, 1973, Book I, chap. 8). If the majority does not act on "appetites," but rather enacts only good laws, *the same policy would be chosen by one person, by a group, or by the whole society*, provided the choosers are wise, well informed, and well intentioned. Such an approach begs the question of collective choice by assuming the problem away: The collective is organic, not composed of many individuals with potentially different ideas.

The moral force of unanimity can be achieved for majorities by artifice, as in Rawls's (1971) "veil of ignorance." Rawls posits a thought experiment: Suppose you didn't know what your position would be in the society. Then what laws, rules, and policies would you select? The answer, Rawls claims is that "Each is forced to choose for everyone" (p. 140). Since you don't know what your self-interest is, you must choose for society, rather than for your own "appetites." If each chooses for everyone, the distinction between private and collective choice vanishes.

But what if the majority decides to act on its appetites? Suppose, for example, most of the society wants simply to enslave the rest. Even on a smaller scale, it is possible that the majority may want to enrich itself at the cost of the minority, and ultimately at the cost of virtue and order for the society. One's view of the majority as moral arbiter comes down to what one sees as "human nature."

In two of the most famous political writings in American history, James Madison made two claims about the nature of people, and the place of government in society. First, we cannot count on *citizens* to forbear, and sacrifice their private interests for the greater good. Instead, Madison expected that people would act on their private appetites, and form interest groups, or "factions."

> By a faction I understand a number of citizens, whether amounting to a majority or a minority of the whole, who are united and actuated by some common impulse of passion, or of interest, adverse to the right of other citizens, or to the permanent and aggregate interests of the community. (*The Federalist*, no. 10, pp. 319–20)

Second, and just as important, we cannot count on *government*, or the people in it, to sacrifice their ambitions and love of power.

> The great security against a gradual concentration of the several powers in the same department consists in giving to those who administer each department the necessary constitutional means and personal motives to resist encroachments of the others. The provision for defense must in this, as in all other cases, be made commensurate to the danger of attack. Am-

bition must be made to counteract ambition. The interest of the man must be connected with the constitutional rights of the place. (*The Federalist*, no. 51, pp. 319–20)

Madison then neatly summarizes his philosophy of government structure, given that neither citizens nor governors can be relied on to act in any way other than simple self-interest:

> It may be a reflection on human nature that such devices should be necessary to control the abuses of government. But what is government itself but the greatest of all reflections on human nature? If men were angels, no government would be necessary. If angels were to govern men, neither external nor internal controls on government would be necessary. In framing a government which is to be administered by men over men, the great difficulty lies in this: you must first enable the government to control the governed; and in the next place oblige it to control itself. (*The Federalist*, no. 51, p. 320)

To summarize: citizens aren't angels, so we can't rely on pure democracy. Rulers aren't angels, so we can't rely on kings. Somehow, we have to do the best we can in choosing rules the allow government to control the polity, yet allow citizens to retain control, or at least accountability, over the officials who run the government.

These are daunting problems, because it means that the rules we choose matter; they *really* matter. How can we choose rules that determine how we select representatives, or policies, and have any confidence in the justice of the choice? In the long run, the choice of aggregation mechanism will determine the nature of the society itself, by advantaging certain alternatives and by affecting the citizens' perceptions of the legitimacy and responsiveness of government.

We will consider three major sets of alternatives to simple majority rule: (1) optimal majority rule, (2) the Borda count and approval voting, and (3) proportional representation.

Optimal Majority Rule

The first variation on majority rule is itself a form of majority rule, but one that allows the size of the required "majority" (i.e., decisive set) for an affirmative decision to be different from the simple majority $S(C) = (N/2) + 1$. After all, what is so special about 50 percent (plus one voter) as the minimum group in favor? In theory, as was discussed above, the size of the group making a decision can vary from one person to the whole society.

In practice, lots of normal collective business is done by majority rule. But even within the context of real-world collective decisions, the size of the proportion of enfranchised voters required to make a decision varies widely. In many legislative assemblies, unanimous consent is required to amend or waive temporarily the rules of procedure. To change the U.S. Constitution, two different supermajorities (two-thirds of a national assembly to propose, three-quarters of state assemblies to ratify) are required. There are examples of decisive sets smaller than even simple majority, including the U.S. Supreme Court's practice of accepting a case (technically, affirming a writ of *certiorari*) based on a vote of less than one-half of the seats on the Court (four out of nine). What is the "best" decisive set as a proportion of the polity? The answer, of course, like the answer to almost all important questions, is that it depends. But what does the answer depend on?

The classic treatment of optimal majority is Buchanan and Tullock's *The Calculus of Consent* (1962). Taking an economic approach, Buchanan and Tullock note that there are costs of widely shared decision power as well as benefits. The costs of including more people in the required majority entail defining and amending the proposal, explaining it to the voters, providing payoffs to solve strategic maneuvering of swing voters, and so on. These are called "decision costs," because the costs fall on those whose preferences count in the decision. The costs of excluding members of society from the required majority can be thought of as the costs of being forced to obey a policy that one opposes. We will call these costs "external costs."

The problem of optimal majority is depicted graphically in Figure 6.2. Decision costs rise dramatically as we near a rule of unanimity, because each voter becomes a potential swing voter. Anyone can threaten to withhold approval unless certain concessions or payoffs are made. Similarly, external costs fall as we near unanimity, because by definition there is less chance that a policy can be enacted without approval of everyone affected.

The optimal majority is $S(C^*)/N$, because at this choice of S the sum of the costs of inclusion and the costs of exclusion are minimized (the "asterisk" implies optimal cost level). Though hard to quantify these costs, clearly figure in how we choose how to choose, as public decisions fall into three categories.

FIGURE 6.2
Bauchanan and Tullock's "Optimal Majority" Analysis

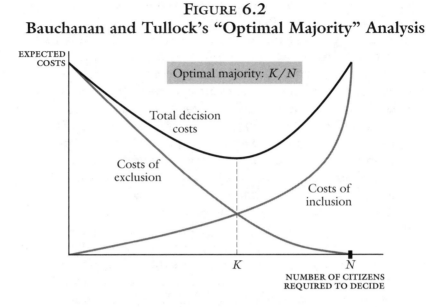

Access choices $0 < S(C^*) < (N/2) + 1$. One member of the U.S. House or Senate is required to introduce a bill. If no one introduces the bill, it is completely blocked. At least four members of the U.S. Supreme Court are required to grant a writ of *certiorari*, or petition for a case to be heard. In neither instance even an affirmative decision ensure success; all that is granted is access.

Routine choices $S(C^*) = (N/2) + 1$. The smallest strict majority is a very common value for the decisive set in democracies, from tiny private clubs to the U.S. Congress and Supreme Court. This value for the size of the decisive set $(S(C^*))$ is the smallest value that ensures no simultaneous passage of two directly contradictory measures. Thus, both inclusion and exclusion costs are moderate. For simple majority rule to have such wide real-world application, it must minimize the (perceived) costs of making routine collective decisions.

Rule changes $(N/2) + 1 < S(C^*) \leq N$. The rules of choice govern the kinds of outcomes that the choices represent. A decision to change the rules has more far-reaching and unpredictable effects than a decision made under a fixed set of rules. Consequently, the costs of excluding enfranchised members are higher for rule change decisions, and the optimal majority for rule changes is more than 50% + 1.

In most cases, no single decision rule is used for all choices. For example, in the U.S. Congress the introduction of a bill requires just one member; the passage of a bill requires 50% + 1 of the members present and voting; a resolution to propose an amendment to the Constitution requires a two-thirds majority; a motion to suspend the normal rules requires unanimous consent. Business in the Senate can be held up almost indefinitely by dilatory tactics or "filibuster," unless three-fifths of the membership vote for a resolution of "cloture," closing off further debate.

If a general rule exists, it is that we require larger majorities for larger questions, just as Buchanan and Tullock suggested. This conclusion is also quite consistent with some of Rousseau's thought, though his justifications are very different from those given by Buchanan and Tullock.

> A difference of one vote destroys equality; a single opponent destroys unanimity; but between equality and unanimity, there are several grades of unequal division, at each of which this proportion may be fixed in accordance with the condition and needs of the body politic.
>
> There are two general rules that may serve to regulate this relation. First, the more grave and important the questions discussed, the nearer should the opinion that is to prevail approach unanimity. Secondly, the more the matter in hand calls for speed, the smaller the prescribed difference in the numbers of votes may be allowed to become: where an instant decision has to be reached a majority of one vote should be enough. (Rousseau, 1973, Book 2, chap. 2, p. 278)

Multiple alternatives. One other consideration remains in our discussion of majorities. I have required that votes be conducted in a series of pairwise comparisons: that is, though the set of alternatives may be quite large, our consideration of majority rule has required that each new proposal be voted against the status quo, with the winner becoming the new status quo. It is possible to apply majority rule to more than two alternatives, but analysis becomes much more complex, and the existence of predictable, stable outcomes, or equilibria, is by no means assured. One solution is to have a modified form of majority rule over three or more alternatives: If any alternative receives more than half the vote, that alternative wins and becomes the status quo. Otherwise, the top two alternatives (in terms of vote received) are selected for a *runoff* election.

An apparently similar (but actually very different) procedure is *plurality rule*. In plurality rule systems, whichever party or candidate receives the most votes wins, regardless of whether a majority of the vote is received.

To see the difference, consider the following vote shares, for a four-candidate election: candidate 1, 27 percent; candidate 2, 26 percent; candidate 3, 24 percent; candidate 4, 23 percent. In a majority rule with runoff election, candidates 1 and 2 would have to stand for election again. The outcome is very much in doubt, since we have no idea how the 47 percent who cast ballots for candidates 3 or 4 will compare candidates 1 and 2. Importantly, the candidate who wins will be the one who appeals to more of the 47 percent of the voters who did not vote for candidates 1 or 2 in the first round. Under plurality rule, the leftover 47 percent are irrelevant: candidate 1 wins the election outright, and the other three candidates get nothing.

While majority rule with runoff and plurality rule are fairly widely used in the real world of politics, it is interesting to note that neither has quite the direct centralizing tendency so apparent in the two-alternative, majority-rule world of the median voter result. Plurality rule, in particular, may lead to a situation where no equilibrium exists if candidate entry or movement is free and unrestricted.[8]

Borda Count and Approval Voting

The various forms of majority rule rest on the premise that each person gets one, and only one, vote. Majority rule is simple, easy to understand, and technically defensible when the polity is seeking a choice of a single "best" outcome from among the set of alternatives. The bluntness and decisiveness of majority rule are disadvantages, however, if the goal is to select a *set* of alternatives, or to rank alternatives in a way that reflects voters' preferences from best to worst, rather than just to choose a single outcome or candidate.

In this section, aspects of two types of voting over "lists" of alternatives (or candidates) will be considered, with the presumption that the number of alternatives may be much larger than the two assumed so far. These two voting rules are the Borda count, and approval voting.

Borda count. Jean-Charles de Borda (1733–99) anticipated some of the observations of Condorcet, whose theorem was outlined earlier. Borda's objection to majority rule was different from Condorcet's, however (see Black, 1958, for discussion and background). Condorcet's criterion for value in elections was that if a majority preferred an alternative, that alternative should be selected. Borda was concerned that majorities might pick the wrong alternative, even if Condorcet's criterion was satisfied.

Suppose there are twenty-one voters, who must choose from three alternatives A, B, and C. Suppose further that the preference rankings of voters fall into three categories, as in Figure 6.3 below. If we use a majority (actually, plurality) choice rule, only first-place votes count. We don't know the second- and third-place preferences of voters in the first group. All we know for sure is that they like alternative A best, and they are the most numerous (eight first-place votes for A). Since B receives seven votes and C gets only six, A is the chosen policy.

FIGURE 6.3
Borda Count
Majority rule picks the "wrong" alternative:
A wins, but either B or C is better.

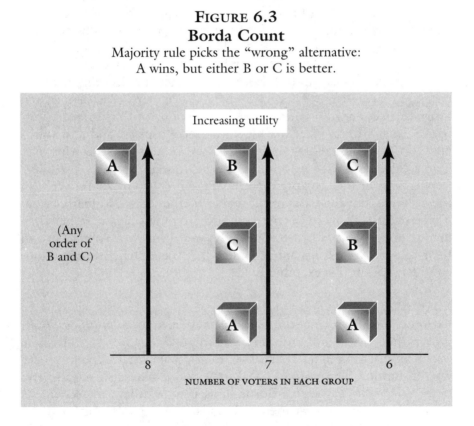

Borda pointed out that thirteen voters, more than a majority, may actually like alternative A *least*. The problem with plurality rule, he felt, was that it counted only first-place votes. Borda suggested several possible alternative decision rules, but the one most often associated with him is the "Borda count": Let each voter assign to each alternative a number corresponding to his or her ranking of that alternative.

Thus, each voter in the middle group in Figure 6.3 gives alternative B a rank of 1, alternative C a rank of 2, and alternative A a rank of 3. (If there were more alternatives—say, q of them—then the ranks would go down to the worst, or qth, alternative on each voter's ballot.) The authority conducting the election then adds up the scores, or "marks," for each alternative, and the alternative with the *smallest* number (for Borda, the most "merit") wins.

Borda left the exact distribution of preferences for C and B in the first group unspecified (again, see Black, 1958). For the sake of example, let us suppose that four of the eight voters like B better than C, and the others prefer C over B. What would be the result of using the Borda method? Alternative A has eight first-place marks, zero second-place marks, and thirteen third-place marks, for a Borda count of forty-seven. Alternative B has seven first-place votes, ten second-place, and four third-place, for a count of thirty-nine. Alternative C has six first-place marks, eleven second-place, and four third-place, for a count of forty. Using the Borda count, then, B wins over C in a close race, with A well back in the voting.

We might change the preferences of the first group for B over C in the example, but the basic result would be the same: No matter what preference for B over C is used, A always comes in *last*, rather than first as under majority rule. When the preferences of voters beyond their first-place rankings are considered, A is eliminated from serious consideration in this example.

Approval voting. The Borda count seems to require citizens to have too much information, because they have to *rank all the alternatives*, not just identify the single alternative they like best. If some voters do not rank every alternative, the outcome may depend on the way abstention is counted. The Borda count may also require too much character of citizens. Borda himself noted that "my scheme is intended only for honest men."[9] Because the Borda count provides opportunities for voting strategically, misrepresenting one's preference ordering to change the outcome.[10]

An alternative that preserves some of the qualities of the Borda count is **approval voting**: Each voter votes for as many of the candidates as he or she likes, and the candidate with the most votes wins.[11]

Another way to think of approval voting is to imagine that each voter ranks the list of candidates, from best to worst. The voter then draws a line somewhere between the worst acceptable candidate and the best unacceptable candidate. Every candidate the voter approves gets a vote, but those below the line get nothing.

Returning to the example in Figure 6.3, suppose that voters in the first group think that only candidate A is acceptable, and that voters in the middle and last groups consider both B and C acceptable. What will be the result under approval voting? Candidate A will receive eight votes, just as under plurality rule. Candidates B and C will each receive thirteen votes, so that the specific outcome will depend on how we assume ties are broken. The point is that A will not have a chance as long as A is judged not acceptable by a majority of voters, which is the spirit of Borda's example.[12]

Both the Borda count and approval voting violate one of Arrow's axioms, independence of irrelevant alternatives. The social choice under the Borda rule or approval voting may depend on the relative positions of two alternatives compared with other (irrelevant) alternatives. Violation of independence of irrelevant alternatives is the basis of the manipulability of the Borda count. This may be more of a disadvantage in small-group settings than for mass elections, of course. In any case, independence is violated for nearly all choice rules that require scoring an entire list of alternatives rather than making a single best choice.

Proportional Representation

A wide variety of collective decisions, in particular choices of political representatives in national assemblies for geographic districts, are made using "proportional representation" (PR) rules. There are many proportional representation rules, but they share the characteristic that *each party's share of seats in the assembly is approximately that party's share of votes in the last election.*

The ideal for a pure proportional representation system, then, would be:

$$\frac{\text{Party } s \text{ votes}}{\text{Total votes}} \approx \frac{\text{Party } s \text{ seats}}{\text{Total seats}}$$

In practice, this ideal is often violated, and for very practical reasons. One of the most common modifications made to pure PR systems is the *threshold*, or minimum vote required for a party to seat members in the assembly. For example, Greece requires that a party receive at least 15 percent of the votes; Israel has an "exclusion threshold" of only 1.5 percent (Sartori, 1994). Such rules have two effects: (1) There is a departure from the ideal of pure proportionality, since a party can receive up to the vote threshold, minus one vote, and receive no seats in the legislature. (2) Consequently, people may vote strategically, withholding sincere votes for small parties that have no chance and concentrating on one of the larger parties.

To contrast a proportional representation system with a plurality rule system, consider Table 6.5.[13] There we see a contrast between one-seat allocations under plurality rule and a pure proportional rep-

TABLE 6.5
A Comparison of Plurality Rule and Proportional Representation

Party	% Votes Received	Pluralities Won	Seats (Prop. Rep.)	Seats (Plurality)
Green	40	60	40	60
Red	35	40	35	40
Blue	25	0	25	0
Totals	100 percent	100 elections	100 seats	100 seats

resentation rule for three parties. The implications of plurality and PR rules, even given identical vote totals in either case, for the distribution of power in a one-hundred-seat assembly are strikingly different.

Notice that the table does not give individual election results, but only nationwide totals. The number of pluralities won was chosen arbitrarily, but represents a possible outcome: The Green party comes in first in sixty races, the Reds come in first forty times, and Blues don't win any races outright. Under a plurality rule, these are exactly the proportions of seats the two parties hold: Greens 60 percent, Reds 40 percent. (The Blue party is presumably outside, picketing in favor of new election laws.)

Under a pure PR system, the Blue party would get fully 25 percent of the seats, corresponding to its 25 percent of votes in the election. There is no clear majority party, since the largest number of seats is held by the Greens, who have only 40 percent of the assembly under their control. If they want to govern, the Greens will be obliged to form a coalition or face the possibility that a Blue-Red coalition government (the Purple)[14] will form and control 60 percent of the votes, a solid working majority.

The actual process of coalition government formation is complicated, and outside the subject of this book. The interested reader should consult Laver and Schofield (1990). For our purposes, the point to remember is that once a proportional representation election has been held, it may often occur that no government has been selected. In fact, the choice process may barely have begun. Any two of the three parties in our example are capable of joining and forming a government. On the other hand, no one party can govern. Consequently, the nature of the government is very much in doubt. Cycling over coalition partners simply moves the incoherence of democratic process from voter choice to bargaining among elites.

In some ways, the consideration of whether plurality/majority rule (sometimes called "first past the post" elections) or proportional representation is better raises the same issue as the earlier discussion on the optimal size of majorities. If a single decision among several mutually exclusive alternatives is required, then plurality rule, or majority rule with runoff, has clear advantages, especially when the polity needs to decide something *right now*. In such circumstances the costs of delay from deliberation and negotiation in proportional representation system may not be worth paying.

But questions of far-reaching consequence for all citizens may require representation of many points of view. In such decisions, representation may be an end in itself, since not only the decision but the decision's legitimacy is crucial to the survival of the society. For such decisions, voters may want to have a representative of their own choosing. Proportional representation systems are appealing because the deliberative process of the legislative assembly captures, in proportions of perspectives, the population as a whole.

Summary

This chapter described some of the procedures people have conceived, and used, to solve the problem of choosing collectively, or politically. Political choice is perhaps the most important type of choice by a society, because the way we choose collectively helps define the kind of society we are. Democratic societies, which allow their citizens to feel a sense of ownership of government, and participation in the process of decision, are more stable and more prosperous than societies with other forms of government. Since the middle 1980s, the world has seen a quiet revolution, with more and more nations embracing the idea, and in some cases the practice, of democracy.

But there are two problems with democracy, which I have tried to explain here. The first—the institutional design problem, which James Madison was addressing in *Federalist* nos. 10 and 51—is that neither citizens nor public officials can be counted on to act in the best interests of the larger society. Political systems that require such altruism, or other-regarding action, of its participants are open to manipulation by factions of voters or by coalitions of elected officials.

The second problem is the "collective choice" problem identified by Kenneth Arrow and other social scientists. Their results seem technical and abstract, but they are very important for the real world of policy analysis. One should not over interpret the results and conclude that we should abandon political, or collective, choice altogether. Rather, Arrow's theorem and the other apparent "paradoxes" of social choice represent a menu of choice: All forms of political choice processes, from majority rule to the Borda count to any other rule you can think of, must violate at least one of Arrow's axioms. We may be able to live with that, of course. After reading this chapter, I hope that the reader is more aware of the fact that political choice, like markets and expert-based choice, is useful but imperfect.

SUMMARY OF KEY CONCEPTS

1. A *decision* is the result of applying judgmental criteria to a set of alternatives for the purpose of choosing a single course of action.
2. *Collective decisions* are choices that are made by a group and are binding on all members of the group.
3. A *collective-coercive* outcome occurs if a collective decision is enforced on private choices.
4. A *private-coercive* outcome occurs if an individual makes a decision without regard for the effect on others.

INSTITUTIONS: THE CHOICE OF A DECISION RULE

5. If preferences are *single peaked*, then the farther the policy is from the individual's ideal policy point in a particular direction, the less that individual prefers the policy.

6. The *median voter theorem* states that the median preference in a majority rule election is the winner. Formally, if the issue-space is a single ordere dimension, and preferences are single peaked, a median position cannot lose to any other alternative in a majority rule election.

7. The assumption of *transitivity* is satisfied for three alternatives A, B, and C if the following condition is true: if A is preferred to B and B is preferred to C, then either A is preferred to C (strong transitivity) or C is not preferred to A (weak transitivity).

8. *Condorcet's paradox* states that the social preference ordering may be intransitive under majority rule if all individual preferences are transitive but not necessarily single peaked.

9. A group of individuals is a *decisive set* whenever, given two alternatives A and B, if all members of that group prefer A to B, then A will be chosen by the society, regardless of the opinions of members of the society.

10. *Arrow's impossibility theorem* states that dictatorship is the only collective choice mechanism that satisfies the following conditions: unanimity, transitivity, unrestricted domain, and independence of irrelevant alternatives.

11. *Unanimity*, or the Pareto criterion, is the assumption that if all enfranchised citizens prefer policy A to policy B, then policy A will be selected by the collective choice rule.

12. The *collective choice mechanism is transitive* for three alternatives A, B, and C if the following condition is true: if A is selected over B and B is selected over C, then A is selected over C.

13. *Unrestricted domain* is the assumption that all possible combinations of transitive preferences are permissible.

14. The *independence of irrelevant alternatives* assumption is that the social choice for any two alternatives depends only on individual rankings of the alternatives within the given preference profile

15. *Non-dictatorship* is the assumption that collective choices are made by more than one individual. In other words, all decisive sets have size ≥ 2.

ALTERNATIVE DECISION RULES

16. *Rawls's "veil of ignorance"* is a thought experiment that satisfies the unanimity principle by proposing that individuals select the rules and policies of society without knowledge of their own self-interest.

17. An *optimal majority* collective choice rule requires that the decisive set for an affirmative decision be different than the simple majority rule decisive set of $(N/2) + 1$. The optimal rule will be the one that minimizes the *costs of exclusion* and the *costs of inclusion*. The costs of exclusion fall as the size of the decisive set approaches unanimity because the chance that a policy will be enacted without the approval of everyone will decline. The costs of inclusion rise as the size of the decisive set approaches unanimity because the chance of any voter's becoming a swing voter increases.

18. Public decisions fall into three categories: *access choices, routine choices,* and *rule changes.*

19. *Majority rule* is a collective choice rule for two alternatives with the minimum decisive set, denoted $S(C)$, is $(N/2) + 1$, where N is the number of voters.

20. *Majority rule with runoff* is a collective choice rule useful for situations with three or more alternatives. All alternatives are voted on and if one alternative receives a majority of the votes, it is the winner. If no alternative receives a majority of the votes, then the top two alternatives participate in a runoff election. The alternative that receives the most votes in the runoff is declared the winner.

21. In a *plurality rule* system, the alternative with the most votes is the winner, regardless of whether that alternative receives a majority of the votes.

22. *Borda count* is a collective decision rule that is applicable in cases with more than two alternatives. Voters assign a number to each alternative equivalent to their ranking of those alternatives. These rankings are added for each alternative and the alternative with the lowest score is determined to be the winner.

23. *Approval voting* is a collective decision rule that requires voters to cast a vote for all acceptable alternatives. All votes are added and the alternative with the most votes is determined to be the winner.

24. In a system of *proportional representation*, the share of seats for a party in a legislature is proportional to the total number of votes received by that party.

PROBLEMS AND QUESTIONS

1. Suppose that there are five voters (1, 2, 3, 4, and 5), and three candidates (A, B, and C) seeking election. Assume that all citizens cast ballots, and that votes reflect honest preferences. Imagine that the preference, or ranking from best to worst, of each voter is as follows:

		Voter			
	1	*2*	*3*	*4*	*5*
Best	B	A	B	A	C
Middle	C	C	C	C	A
Worst	A	B	A	B	B

Which of the three candidates *should* win the election? That is, who is the best candidate? How would you know? Do an analysis of the candidates, and try to come up with a decision rule that would allow you to pick the "best" candidate, in this or any other situation. Give reasons why your rule is good, using the Pareto criterion or other criteria as you see fit.

2. Now, suppose our little five-citizen polity uses a "majority rule with runoff" decision rule. That is, if no candidate receives a majority on the first ballot, the top two vote-getters square off again in a final pairwise race. Which candidate would win?

3. Now imagine that the society uses a Borda count rule. Each voter assigns a score (3 = Best, 2 = Middle, 1 = Worst) to each candidate (again, assume that the assignment reflects sincere preference). The clerk adds up the scores for each candidate, and the candidate with the highest overall score wins. Which candidate is the victor?

4. Since the winner using majority rule with runoff is different from the winner using the Borda count, there has to be some way of deciding which decision rule is better. Apply the criteria you developed in answering question 1 to majority rule with runoff and the Borda count. Which decision rule is superior, according to your analysis?

5. Suppose you are in a time machine, hurtling back to Philadelphia in 1787. You find yourself at the front of the room in the State House (now Independence Hall) on May 25, the day of the opening of what will turn out to be the Constitutional Convention. This convention will create, between now and September 17, 1787, the text of the document we now know as the U.S. Constitution.

a. Explain the meaning of Arrow's impossibility theorem in terms that the delegates to the Constitutional Convention will understand.

b. In the first row of seats in the audience of delegates, you see James Madison. Do you expect his reaction to your presentation is:

(1) "Yes, yes, we know all that. Nothing really new there, except for a formal proof of our intuition about politics."

(2) "Nonsense. There is clearly a general will, a consensus of public minds. Arrow's theorem has nothing to do with real politics."

(3) "My, that is interesting. I will have to change the way I am thinking about the structure of the Constitution. The specific changes I will make are _____."

Which of these three is closest to the reaction you expect from Madison? Why? If you choose (3), make sure you fill in the blank.

6. What is a collective-coercive outcome and what is the normative issue? Explain Rawls's solution to collective-coercive outcomes. How would advocates of optimal majority rule respond to Rawls's solution?

TAKE IT TO THE NET!

Go to: http://www.wwnorton.com/college/polisci/analyzingpolicy for additional problems, data sets, and course materials.

NOTES

1. Quoted in King (1997); I found the reference in Moberg (1999), however.
2. *Webster's Third International Dictionary.*
3. Just to keep things simple, and eliminate concerns over strategic free-riding,

suppose that the other citizens can join the club later if they choose, but only if they compensate the founding members for the cost of initial construction.

4. Technically, of course, this should be "any two budgets on the same side of the ideal," since I have not assumed symmetry of the preference function. See Hinich and Munger (1994) for discussion and background.

5. It is possible to question whether the "individually transitive, collectively intransitive" contradiction is a genuine paradox. Buchanan (1954, 1975), Tullock (1970), and Plott (1972) argue that "paradox" simply results from an indefensible insistence on collective conception of societies. For a review, see Mueller (1989, pp. 388–92).

6. There are many statements of Arrow's paradox. This one is closest in spirit to that of Riker (1982, p. 18). An important general discussion, and some extensions, can be found in Sen (1970).

7. This statement is too strong. It is quite possible that societies are locked into conventions that nearly everyone knows are not Pareto optimal. See Schelling (1960), Lewis (1969), North (1981, 1990), Arthur (1989), and Denzau and North (1994).

8. More technically, "plurality rule" may also lead to equilibria that are "decidedly noncentrist" (Cox, 1987). Cox shows that some candidates (if there are several) will take positions outside the two central quartiles of the distribution of voter ideal points even in equilibrium. This point is elaborated, for a variety of voting systems, in Cox (1990).

9. Quoted in Black (1958, p. 182), quoting from J. Mascart (1919).

10. Strategic voting is generally beyond the scope of this book. See Cox (1997) on the importance and breadth of strategic action in politics.

11. For an in-depth treatment of approval voting, see Brams and Fishburn (1984), and Brams and Nagel (1991). For some interesting background on approval voting, see Cox (1984).

12. On the other hand, if each group selects only its first alternative as being acceptable, A will win, receiving eight votes compared with seven for B and six for C. Consequently, one might expect the middle and last groups to vote strategically, and include B and C in the acceptable category. This would ensure at worst a second-place rather than worst result for voters in those groups.

13. For a variety of comparisons between proportional representation and presidential systems, see Grofman and Lijphart (1992).

14. With apologies to John Zaller, who used the "Purple Land" metaphor in his 1991 book, in chapter 12.

Case 2: A Place of One's Own

This story is taken from an autobiographical account by Langdon Gilkey of events in 1943–45. Gilkey, his colleague Shields, and a number of other foreign citizens had been interned (imprisoned) by the Japanese in a camp in coastal China in 1943. They were forced to remain in this camp for the remainder of the war. Because they had very few economic resources, they had to organize their own food provision and sleeping arrangements, using meager supplies provided by the Japanese. For all practical purposes, there was no market of any kind for food, shelter, or other necessities.

This, then, is a story of *political* allocation of scarce resources. "Citizens" in the internment camp had to live in a setting with far less space, less and poorer food, and less personal freedom than they were used to. Since nearly all resources were held in common, far more choices were collective (i.e., made by the group, and imposed on individuals) than would be expected, or tolerated, in the sort of democratic societies where these people had grown up.

The internees set up a sort of civil government, with an elected executive council. This council created a number of working committees, one of which was the "Housing Committee," whose job it was to resolve disputes over allocations of space within the camp. While the Housing Committee (Gilkey was appointed a member) had no formal authority or weapons, they did have the full moral force of the freely chosen elected government of the camp behind them.

As you read, consider Gilkey's growing awareness of the importance of self-interest, and self-preservation. People in the camp found themselves with too little; how did they react to the attempts by their own civil "authority" to solve problems of resource allocation? How do you think you would have reacted in the same situation?

Chapter 6: A Place of One's Own

. . . Shields and I knew that great sections of the camp were terribly overcrowded. We also knew that our next task was to try to provide these people with more room. The difficulty, of course, was that nowhere in camp did anyone have any more space than he needed. Thus, if any extra space for our unfortunates was to be won at all, it had to be snatched

From *Shantung Compound: The Story of Men and Women Under Pressure*, by Langdon Gilkey, 1966, New York: Harper, Row, and Company. I want to thank my colleague Peter Feaver for calling this book to my attention.

from the person barely able to make himself comfortable and so, fair game. One or two brushes with the public had shown the difficulty of our task, and with both apprehension and excitement we began to talk about what we would do.

While we were pondering our first steps, a deputation of three single men appeared in the quarters office. When asked what they wanted, they replied a trifle aggressively, I thought: "Fair treatment from the Housing Committee."

Somewhat taken aback by this, I nevertheless said confidently, "Sure, and that's what you'll get! What's up, and how can we help you?"

"Our case is quite simple," said the elderly head of the group, an ex-soldier lamed by World War I and formerly the proprietor of a small bookshop in Tientsin. "We three," and he looked at the other two, a young American tobacco man and a British schoolmaster, "live in a dormitory room in Block 49. There are eleven men in our small room, and we have barely space to turn around, much less to stow our stuff in any comfort. Across the hall is a room exactly the same—isn't it, chaps?"

The other two nodded in agreement. Apparently two of them had measured it while the third held its unsuspecting inmates in conversation. "In that room there are only nine men—and in ours eleven. Now we suggest that you rectify this obvious injustice by moving one of our men in with them. Surely that's fair enough, isn't it, chaps?" The other two mumbled in grim agreement.

I must admit I felt elated. Here at last was a perfectly clear-cut case. Surely the injustice in this situation was, if it ever was in life, clear and distinct: since the rooms were next to each other, anyone who could (like Descartes) count and measure could see the inequity involved.

The solution was so easy: if we did move one man, then each room would have ten persons. "Are not people rational and moral?" I asked myself. "Does this not mean—if it means anything—that the average man, when faced with a clear case of injustice which his mind can distinctly perceive, will at the least agree to rectify that injustice—even if he himself suffers from that rectification? And besides, isn't it true that people are more apt to share with each other when they are in some common difficulty, like on a raft at sea, than they are in the humdrum pursuits of normal life?" So I argued to myself as I confidently accompanied the delegates confidently accompanied the delegates to Block 49. . . .

When I entered the dorm and said that I was from the Housing Committee, at once I could feel the inmates becoming wary. Their suspicions, I noted, did not decrease when they saw the three-man deputation from the next room behind me. Then, when I began to talk about the problem that had brought me there, their hostility came out into the open. One rather hard British engineer summed up the sentiments of the men standing there sullenly silent: "Sure we're sorry for those chaps over there. But what has that got to do with us? We're plenty crowded here as it is, and their worries are their tough luck. Listen, old boy, we're not crowding up for you or for anyone!"

In response, I argued with a good deal of passion the logic of this situation. I stressed as strongly as I could the sheer irrationality of nine men in one room and eleven in the other when both were the same size, and so the evident fairness of their taking in another man.

"That may be, friend. But let me tell you a thing or two. Fair or not fair, if you put one of them in here, we are merely heaving him out again. And if you come back here about this, we are heaving you out, too!"

Some of the others standing there wanted to be reasonable rather than emotional or threatening. So they argued the whole matter with me, expressing their doubts as to the wisdom of this particular course, or asking me, "Why do you pick on this particular dorm?"

In rebuttal, I found myself defending all the actions of the committee to date, explaining the present housing situation of the entire camp, and most of our future plans—and slowly realizing that these rational arguments were futile and would lead nowhere.[1] Clearly the driving force behind the reaction of these men was not their intellectual doubts as to the justice of our proposal but, on the contrary, the intense desire to hang onto their space.

This desire was at the root of the matter. It determined not only their emotional reactions but, to my wide-eyed surprise, it seemed even to determine the way they approached the issue in their minds. Thus, to try as I did merely to move their minds by rational or moral persuasion was to leave quite unaffected the fundamental dynamic force in the situation, namely the fear that if another man came in, each of them would be that much the more crowded. I almost laughed aloud when a queer thought struck me: Why should a man wish to be reasonable or moral if he thereby lost precious space? . . .

I came home that night confused and shaken. Everything that I had believed about "our sorts of people," about the ordinary civilized man, had said to me that his behavior would be fair and generous once he understood a situation. Most of our philosophers, educators, social scientists, and social psychologists had assumed this. For did not most of our modern culture hold that scientific knowledge and technical advance did lead to social progress? And did this not imply that the men who used this knowledge would be rational and just when they understood things clearly through organized inquiry?

But in Block 49 men understood—they understood fully. They understood that a "reform" meant their own loss, and so they fought that reform, whatever its rationality and justice, as if it were a plague, a poisonous thing. Self-interest seemed almost omnipotent next to the weak claims of logic and fair play.

Ironically, in this first and most logically clear of all our many cases, our committee, if justice were to be done, finally had to appeal to the least rational of all principles: the authority of force. We asked Mr. Izu [Japanese military commander] to tell this recalcitrant dorm to take one more man, which they did readily enough—and we heard no more from Block 49 . . .

Discussion Questions

1. Gilkey appeared to believe that human nature is fundamentally good, or at least reasonable. Would you say the people in the internment camp behaved "reasonably?"
2. Gilkey also expected a "we are all in this together" attitude to make solving problems of space allocation easier, but nearly the opposite happened. Is this inevitable in the face of severe hardship and scarcity? Can we count on voluntary group decision-making when people have such strong reasons to protect their own interests? Or must we, on any important question, resort to coercion and force, as the camp authorities found when they had to ask the Japanese military to step in?
3. One thing this excerpt makes clear is that the concept of human nature is central to one's conception of "politics." If people are basically good, or even potentially good, then a Rousseavian perspective may make sense. But if people are essentially self-interested, then a more Madisonian perspective may be necessary. Which view of human nature is more nearly correct? On what characteristics of the environment people find themselves in does the answer depend?

NOTES

1. It is worth pointing out that Gilkey, and all the other Housing Committee members, lived in the same dorms, and in the same conditions, as everyone else. Their membership on the committee brought them no special privileges.

~7~

The Welfare Economics Paradigm

This chapter presents the basics of the welfare economics paradigm of analysis. Welfare economics, as you have probably inferred, addresses what an economy *should* look like if the goal is to promote the welfare of the entire society. It is normative, and prescriptive. Often, welfare economics has taken the philosophical perspective of utilitarianism, or Jeremy Bentham's famous *telos*, "the greatest good for the greatest number." But there is nothing in welfare economics that inherently requires utilitarianism.[1]

There are two reasons to study this approach more deeply. First, everyone (or nearly everyone) starts with welfare economics if they want to "do" policy analysis. If you don't speak this language, you will be needlessly excluded from lots of important discussions. Second, welfare economics, for all its drawbacks, really is the best approach available for starting an analysis of policy problems. You will find the approach very useful for organizing your thinking about measuring the size of impacts of public policies, either in terms of costs or benefits.

In fact, the welfare economics approach has made significant inroads into the law of regulation and policy. Consider this excerpt from the "Report to Congress on the Costs and Benefits of Federal Regulations,"[2] published by the U.S. Office of Management and Budget, Office of Information and Regulatory Affairs:

> Both proponents and opponents of regulation have resorted to grand characterizations of either the benefits or the costs of regulation, without much substantiation and very little agreement on the underlying facts. In order to help further the debate on the nation's regulatory system, Congress adopted Section 645 of the Treasury, Postal Services and General Government Appropriations Act, 1997 (Public Law 104-208) on September 30, 1996. Section 645(a) directs the Director of the Office of Management and Budget to submit to Congress, no later than September 30, 1997, a report that provides—
> (1) estimates of the total annual costs and benefits of Federal Regulatory programs, including quantitative and nonquantitative measures of regulatory costs and benefits;
> (2) estimates of the costs and benefits (including quantitative and nonquantitative measures) of each rule that is likely to have a gross annual effect on the economy of $100,000,000 or more in increased costs;
> (3) an assessment of the direct and indirect impacts of Federal rules on the private sector, State and local government, and the Federal Government; and
> (4) recommendations from the Director and a description of significant public comments to reform or eliminate any Federal regulatory program or program element that is inefficient, ineffective, or is not a sound use of the Nation's resources.

Later, in the same report, we are told:

> An economic analysis cannot reach a conclusion about whether net benefits are maximized—the key economic goal for good regulation—without consideration of a broad range of alternative regulatory options. To help decision-makers understand the full effects of alternative actions, the analysis should present available physical or other quantitative measures of the effects of the alternative actions where it is not possible to present monetized benefits and costs, and also present qualitative information to characterize effects that cannot be quantified. Information should include the magnitude, timing, and likelihood of impacts, plus other relevant dimensions (e.g., irreversibility and uniqueness). Where benefit or cost estimates are heavily dependent on certain assumptions, it is essential to make those assumptions explicit, and where alternative assumptions are plausible, to carry out sensitivity analyses based on the alternative assumptions.

Here we have all the principles of welfare economics in action. The most useful measures of costs and benefits are monetized (stated in terms of dollars, a convenient unit for expressing costs and benefits, because it allows direct comparisons), but if monetized measures are impossible or unreliable, then other quantitative measures can be substituted. Finally, the sensitivity of the measures to assumptions should be made explicit.

It is difficult to recognize whether "estimates are heavily dependent on certain assumptions" however, unless we know what the assumptions are. Thus, this chapter identifies the assumptions, and the background, of the welfare economics approach. We will start with the representation of "preferences" that policy analysts use to capture the idea of **utility**, or satisfaction, of individual citizens. Next comes the graphical derivation of the demand curve for the individual, and the concept of consumer surplus, which is the single most important construct for monetizing impacts of policies and regulations.

We then consider the aggregation of individual demands, the market demand curve. It turns out that the market demand curve behaves very differently for private and public goods, in ways that are important for understanding how policies affect citizens' lives. The market demand curve, with its implicit aggregation across individuals, is the way that welfare economists "add up" individuals without making explicit assumptions about comparisons of individual utilities.

The other half of the analytical "scissors" of economics[3] is the supply curve. Prices of inputs and the technology of production combine to produce the marginal cost function, which implies a schedule relating price and quantity produced called the supply curve. Once again, individual supply schedules can be added up to obtain a market, or aggregate supply, curve. Together, market demands and aggregate supplies give us a way to explain the value of a commodity, where neither alone could do the job. The chapter concludes with a discussion of taxes and the financing of public goods, including some analysis of the fairness of tax systems.

The Representation of Preferences

Economists are fairly careful about what they claim can be accomplished through the analysis of preferences. We cannot go inside someone's mind and measure their psychic satisfaction from consumption of some good, or enjoyment of some service. Further, we cannot, in any scientifically valid sense, say that person A enjoys commodity Y more, or less, than person B enjoys it. Since we cannot measure satisfaction directly, there is no good basis for making interpersonal utility comparisons.

The Utility Function

But we can say *something*, by using the economists' construct of utility. Suppose that a person is faced with an infinite set of commodity bundles, made up of all possible combinations of available goods and services. *Utility* is a mathematical index function, designed to represent the unobservable preference relation P (which is read this way: $(X)P(Y)$ means "I like X better than Y"). It might seem that we are stuck, since P is unobservable, and therefore unmeasurable, and we can't analyze something we can't see. But the utility function is a clever way out of this apparently insoluble problem. The utility function is said to "represent" the person's preferences if the utility function has the following property:

> **Representation:** If the person likes bundle X as least as much as he likes bundle Y, then the utility function assigns an index number (called "**utility**") to bundle X that is greater than or equal to the number assigned to Y. More concisely: If $(X)P(Y)$, then $U(X) > U(Y)$. There are only three possibilities: $U(X) > U(Y)$, $U(X) < U(Y)$, or $U(X) = U(Y)$. The last case, where the utility function assigns the same index number to both commodity bundles, is very important, because it defines *indifference*. To put it another way, $U(X) = U(Y)$ if, and only if, $(X)\neg P (Y)$ and $(Y)\neg P(X)$ (where $\neg$ means "not").

In principle, nearly any kind of preferences are possible. The question immediately arises: Do there exist utility functions capable of "representing" these preferences? The answer is yes, under quite general circumstances.[4] For our purposes, a set of sufficient conditions for representability, stronger than is really necessary, is useful.

- Preferences are *complete*: Presented with any two alternatives X and Y, the consumer can immediately conclude "I like X better," "I like Y better," or "I am indifferent between X and Y." Complete-

ness is an informational assumption, because the consumer must
be able to link an alternative with an outcome, and evaluate how
satisfactory that outcome is.

- Preferences are *transitive*: If (X)P(Y), and (Y)P(Z) then we can
  conclude that (X)P(Z).
- Preferences are *insatiable*: More is always preferred to less. Consequently, if one alternative X has more of all commodities than another alternative Y, we know (X)P(Y), so U(X) > U(Y). This
  assumption is sometimes called **monotonicity**, and means simply
  that a bundle of four roses and four guns is definitionally preferable
  to three roses and three guns.
- Preferences are *not* (**necessarily**) purely *selfish*. The economic assumption of rationality really just boils down to goal-oriented behavior: given the desired ends, the citizens is assumed to choose
  the "best" means. It is possible to capture other-regarding goals in
  the notion of preference.
- Preference satisfaction exhibits *diminishing marginal utility* in
  each good or service consumed. This means that (for example) if I
  have four roses and four guns, I still like additional roses, holding
  my guns at four. But as I get forty roses, or four hundred roses, the
  marginal (i.e., additional) value I place on each one diminishes
  (though it never falls below zero, because of monotonicity).

These assumptions, when combined, allow us to depict utilities
graphically, using the **"indifference curve."** Indifference curves
seem complicated, but in fact are quite intuitive. Consider Figure
7.1, and focus on the starting point, A, with a consumption bundle
of four guns and four roses. Since guns are on the horizontal axis,
and roses on the vertical, we will follow convention and write the
bundle as (4, 4).

From the assumption of monotonicity, we immediately see that
there are points that are clearly worse, and points that are clearly better, than A. Any allocation with more of both guns and roses is better; any allocation with fewer of both is worse. Any point with the
same number of guns, and more roses (say, the point (4, 5)) is better
than (4, 4). Points with the same number of roses, and fewer guns
(for example, (3, 4)) are worse.

This sort of comparison allows us to evaluate with confidence all
the points above and to the right, or below and to the left, of A. But
what about the points where comparison is not so easy, where con-

FIGURE 7.1
The Slope of Indifference Curves
The marginal rate of substitution is the slope of the curve that divides the points that are "better" from those that are "worse."

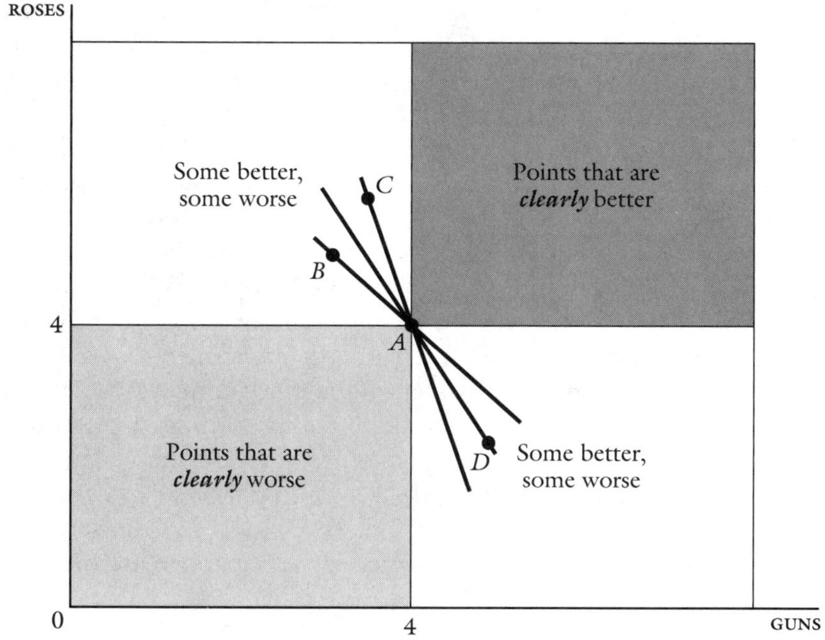

sumption bundles have more guns but fewer roses (like point *D*), or more roses but fewer guns (like points *B* or *C*)? The way to think about the problem goes like this: Since there are some points clearly better than *A*, and some points clearly worse than, there has to be a *boundary* between the better and the worse. This boundary, by definition, is the set of points the citizen likes just as well as *A*.

Marginal Rate of Substitution

The shape of this boundary captures the trade-off, at each point, between guns and roses, based on the citizen's preferences. The technical name for the trade-off is the *marginal rate of substitution*, but don't be put off: the marginal rate of substitution (MRS) is just the slope of the curve that forms the boundary between the better and the worse. The slope of a line, if guns are the horizontal axis and roses are the vertical axis, is Δ roses/Δ guns where Δ means change, or difference). Intuitively, the MRS tells us how many roses the citizen would want to receive to be willing to give up one gun, yet remain indifferent among the two consumption bundles.

We still haven't answered the question: Which points in the "some better, some worse" areas of Figure 7.1 are better, and which worse, than point *A*? Specifically, is point *B* better, or worse? What about point *C*, or point *D*? After all, by assumption we can't read the citizen's mind; what utility function represents his preferences?

To find out, we need to do a thought experiment. Suppose the citizen finds himself in an infinitely large warehouse, with all possible combinations of guns and roses, ranging in number from zero of each to arbitrarily many of each, scattered about in wicker baskets. The baskets are all the same, except for the amounts of commodities (if you'd like, the baskets can come in a rainbow assortment of delightful pastel shades; since it is a thought experiment, it might as well be pretty). The citizen considers all pairwise comparisons among baskets, ranking one or the other as better, or finding them equally preferable. An observer, without knowing the true preferences of the citizen, can still record all the pairwise comparisons and then come up with a function that "represents" the preferences in the sense defined earlier (provided the assumptions described above are met).

The Indifference Curve

Once this set of pairwise comparisons is completed,[5] the problem is solved: the **indifference curve** is simply the curve connecting all the consumption bundles the consumer likes just as well as point *A*. Every bundle below the indifference curve is worse, every point above the curve is better, at least as far as our mythical citizen is concerned. This allows, as Figure 7.2 illustrates, a concise way of recording all the laborious pairwise comparisons in our thought experiment. Instead of recording each pair $[(X)P(Y), (Y)P(X)$, or $(X)I(Y)]$, we can use the utility function to "represent" the citizen's preferences. This means we can recover the preferences of the citizen simply by analyzing the utility function: if $U(X) > U(Y)$, then it must be the case that $(X)P(Y)$.

For some of the comparisons in Figure 7.2, we don't need the utility function. For example, we know that $(A)P(B)$, just from the assumption of monotonicity (*A* has more roses, and more guns, than *B*). Similarly, $(C)P(A)$, by monotonicity. But to compare *A* to points *D*, *E*, or *F* we need to know the utility function. The dotted line in

FIGURE 7.2
Illustration of the Trade-Offs Implied by the Indifference Curve

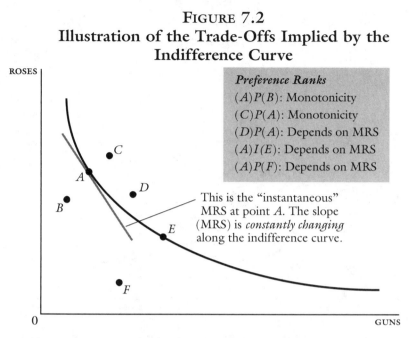

ROSES

Preference Ranks

$(A)P(B)$: Monotonicity
$(C)P(A)$: Monotonicity
$(D)P(A)$: Depends on MRS
$(A)I(E)$: Depends on MRS
$(A)P(F)$: Depends on MRS

This is the "instantaneous" MRS at point A. The slope (MRS) is *constantly changing* along the indifference curve.

0   GUNS

Figure 7.2 is the marginal rate of substitution, or the slope of the indifference curve at the point being evaluated.

Notice that the marginal rate of substitution changes at every point along the indifference curve, because of the assumption of diminishing marginal utility. More simply, the more roses I have, the less I value more roses; the more guns I have, the lower the marginal value of another gun. Given the particular MRS summarized by the indifference curve in Figure 7.2, and using "I" to mean "indifferent to," we know that $(D)P(A)$ $(E)I(A)$ and $(A)P(F)$. It is important to note, however, that things could be otherwise: the indifference curve (for another citizen, with different preferences) could be flatter, so that $(A)P(D)$, or steep, so that $(F)P(A)$.

Once we have the utility function, we can draw indifference curves for each "level" of utility. In principle this means that indifference curves pass through every point, every *possible* combination, in the graph. Of course, we can't draw *every* indifference curve (it would just be a black box, since there are no points through which a curve does not pass), but it is possible to illustrate a "family" of indifference curves, as in Figure 7.3.

Each indifference curve describes the locus of points among which the citizen is indifferent. Each curve is also the boundary between the set of points the citizen likes better, and the set of points the cit-

FIGURE 7.3
A "Family" of Indifference Curves

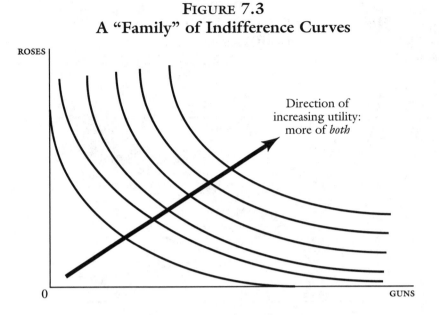

izen likes less, compared to the points on the curve. Curves above, and to the right, represent increasing utility. Curves below, and to the left, are less preferred. Having the "family" of indifference curves is an important step, because it means that demand curves can be derived.

Individual Demand and Consumer Surplus

The concept of demand, in economics, depends entirely on the idea of subjective utility developed in the previous section. The **demand curve** is the schedule of quantities purchased as price varies, holding all other factors constant. For simplicity's sake, I will consider the two commodities we have been using, roses and guns, but the analysis is capable of accounting for any number of goods at the same time.[6] Let's start with a verbal summary of how the demand curve for guns is derived, step by step.

1. Assume that the citizen is maximizing utility, and that he values both goods (roses and guns). The citizen faces a "constrained optimization" problem, of maximizing utility subject to the constraint that income is fixed, and the goods are not free.

2. Assume that the citizen takes as given two parameters: income I, and the price of roses P_R.
3. Assume that the map of indifference curves is derived from a utility function that accurately represents the citizen's preferences.
4. Vary the price of guns, P_G, and record the quantities G of guns purchased, with P_R and I held constant. The graph of these points, with G on the horizontal axis and P_G on the vertical axis, is the demand curve.

Budget Constraints and the Demand Curve

Now, let's follow these steps. First, let's nail down the "income constraint." Assuming that the consumer spends all his income (i.e., there is no saving), we can write:

$$I = P_G G + P_R R$$

Since we have put R on the vertical axis, and G on the horizontal axis of the "commodities" graph, we can put this identity into slope-intercept form.[7]

$$R = \frac{I}{P_R} - \frac{P_G}{P_R} G$$

If we graph the budget constraint, it is a line with vertical intercept I/P_R and downward slope P_G/P_R. This means that the citizen can spend all his money on roses, and get I/P_R, or can buy only guns, and get I/P_G, or any combination in between. The budget constraint is graphed in Figure 7.4.

The figure also depicts three indifference curves, IC_1, IC_2 and IC_3. As we have already established, a higher indifference curve implies higher utility; the consumer wants to allocate his income to ensure that the highest possible level of utility is achieved. Given the assumptions we have made about indifference curves, their shape is continuous, smooth, and concave (i.e., bowl-shaped) toward the upper right. Consequently, it is straightforward to identify the best feasible consumption bundle: it is the point of tangency between the highest indifference curve that touches the budget constraint and the budget constraint itself.

FIGURE 7.4
The Solution to the Citizen's Income Allocation Problem

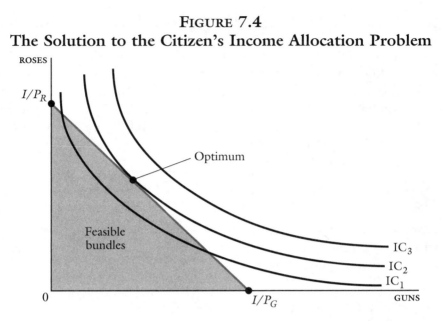

There are three ways that the budget constraint can change: Income could change; the price of roses could change; or the price of guns could change. In the real world, of course, all three of these parameters are likely to change constantly. But we want to construct an analytical device that allows us to consider the implications of changing just one parameter, the price of guns, holding everything else constant. For the sake of completeness, though, I will remind the reader of three things that seem obvious, but are worth being explicit about:

- Any change in relative prices (i.e., the ratio P_G/P_R) changes the slope of the budget line.
- Income changes shift the budget line: increases in income shift the budget line upward and to the right, and decreases move it back toward the origin, parallel to the original budget line.
- If both prices change, but the ratio P_G/P_R remains constant, the situation is exactly the same as a change in income: the budget line shifts in or out, parallel to its original position. Inflation, or a general rise in the price level, holding income fixed, moves the budget line toward the origin; deflation, a general decline in the price level, moves the budget line outward.

Now, for the demand curve for guns: all that is required is to let the price of guns in Figure 7.4 vary, and record the results. Suppose that the citizen's income in this example is $I = \$77$. Also, let $P_R = \$6$. That means that one budget constraint can be derived for any given price for guns. For the sake of example, I have put three different budget constraints in Figure 7.4, with the first associated with $P_G = \$11$, the second with $P_G = \$6$, and the third with $P_G = \$3$. Each separate budget constraint implies an optimal allocation of income for the citizen, yielding the following schedule:

Demand Price	Schedule for Guns Quantity
$11	2
6	6
3	10

The demand curve is the graph of the results of this procedure of varying price and recording the implied quantity demanded. In principle, this schedule could be calculated very finely, using price changes of only a penny, or even less, but for our purposes these three points are sufficient. Figure 7.5 depicts the three points in quantity-price space, with a curve connecting them. This curve, of course, is the demand curve.

If indifference curves are smoothly concave from above and to the

FIGURE 7.5
Deriving the Demand Curve for Guns

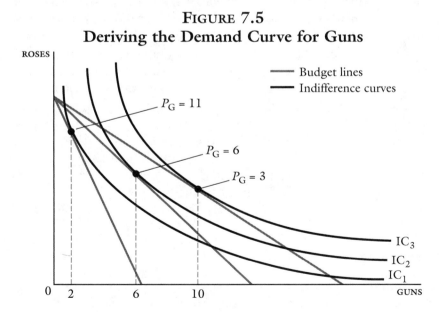

FIGURE 7.6

FIGURE 7.6
The Demand Curve for Guns, and Consumer Surplus for Single Price Market

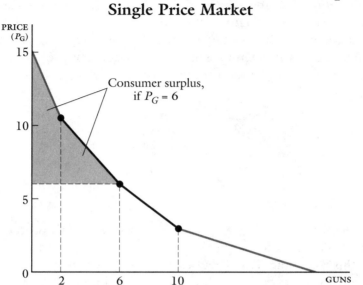

right, as I have drawn them, then the implied demand curve is generally *not* linear (i.e., the points derived using the technique in this section do not fall along a line). As you can see in Figure 7.6, the points fall along a curve, meaning the consumer is willing to pay a very high price for the first unit (if he has *none* of the commodity). Further, as the price falls to zero, demand for the commodity becomes infinite (because preferences are assumed to be insatiable, or monotonic). Nonetheless, for the sake of simplicity of exposition, I have extended the demand curve in Figure 7.6 as if it were linear, using dotted lines.

Demand curves record the *maximum* amount that the consumer would be willing to pay for an additional unit of the commodity on the horizontal axis. If a single price is charged in the marketplace, so that the consumer can purchase as many units as he likes at that price, then the consumer is very nearly indifferent between buying and not buying the last ("marginal") unit. But the first few units, obtained at a price of $6 (for example), yield very high utility for the consumer.

Consumer Surplus

Interestingly, knowing the demand curve means we know *exactly* how much (in monetary terms) the right to buy at the market price is

worth to the consumer. The value to the citizen of having access to
the market is the difference between the maximum he would be willing to pay (given by the demand curve) and the price he has to pay
(the price). Since this is true for each unit purchased, we have a measure of the total value to the citizen: It is the area (usually approximately triangular) underneath the demand curve but above the
horizontal line drawn at the market price. As we saw in chapter 4 this
area is called the *consumer surplus,* because it is the value of the transaction to the consumer, over and above the payments the consumer
has to make to complete the transaction.

In Figure 7.6, you can see this area marked "consumer surplus,"
and identified with diagonal lines. The idea that consumer surplus is
a triangle is based on the idea that the demand curve is linear. The
demand curve we derived in this section is not linear, and in fact any
demand curve based on smoothly concave indifference curves will
tend not to be linear. However, for the sake of simplicity, suppose we
could approximate the consumer surplus, or value of the transaction,
for the citizen at a price of $6, and assuming that the demand for
guns goes to zero at a price of $15 (i.e., that the vertical intercept of
the demand curve is $15). This gives a right triangle with height 9,
and width 6; such a triangle has an area of ½ × (9×6) = 27. What is
this number? What we have found is that the consumer would be
willing to pay up to $27 for the right to buy six guns at a price of $6.

Consumer surplus is a very important concept, because it can be
used to quantify the benefits of market actions, and the costs of government action to regulate markets. Consumer surplus also explains a
very old paradox, or puzzle, called the "diamonds and water paradox."[8] The paradox can be stated this way: Consumers need water,
but diamonds are a trifling luxury, of no real value other than as a
decoration. Yet diamonds are costly, and water is cheap. Is this not
clear evidence that the market is irrational, since it places objectively
false values on commodities?

The answer lies in the concept of consumer surplus. Consider the
two examples of demand curves in Figure 7.7. The demand curve for
water shows that people are fairly unresponsive to price: we need water, and would do almost anything we had to do to get it. The fact
that water is relatively cheap doesn't mean we don't *value* water! *In
fact, the consumer surplus for water is effectively infinite,* up to the
ability of the citizen to pay.

Diamonds, on the other hand, are a luxury. It may be true that
people are willing to pay a high price for diamonds, but it is equally

FIGURE 7.7
The Resolution of the Apparent "Paradox of Diamonds and Water"

High price and *low* surplus value for diamonds, but *low* price and *high* surplus value for water.

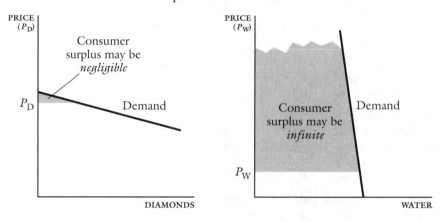

true that the "market" for diamonds is effectively a cartel led (at least at the turn of the century) by the DeBeers Corporation. This means that the price for diamonds is artificially high, much higher than the cost of production. The *surplus value* of buying a diamond (the diamond's consumer surplus) may be very small, because the price charged by diamond merchants captures much of the consumer surplus.

We can generalize this observation about the difference between price (the cost of a commodity to a consumer) and the consumer surplus (or surplus value—the value to the consumer of obtaining the commodity) by introducing a commonly used measure of the responsiveness of quantity demanded to the price level. That concept is **elasticity**. There are many different types of elasticity, but the one most commonly used is the **price elasticity of demand**, or **P.E.D.** Price elasticity measures the percentage change in quantity demanded, divided by the percentage change in price. In symbols:

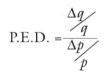

$$\text{P.E.D.} = \frac{\Delta q / q}{\Delta p / p}$$

We say that demand is elastic if the P.E.D. is very high; this means that demand is very responsive to changes in price. On the other hand, if quantity demanded hardly changes at all in response to a change in price, we say demand is *inelastic*. There is a silly, but useful, way to remember what elastic, and inelastic, demand curves look like the closer the demand curve is to a capital "I" (that is, the more vertical it is) the more *I*nelastic we say demand is. If the demand curve looks like the flat (horizontal) part of an E, on the other hand, we say that demand is *E*lastic.[9]

Here is the general observation about consumer surplus, which follows logically from the definition of elasticity. *Consumer surplus for commodities with elastic demands is relatively low. Consumer surplus for commodities with inelastic demands is large, and may be arbitrarily large, up to the total ability of the citizen to pay.* This observation, and the concept of elasticity, will prove very useful in later chapters.

We have very neatly resolved the "diamonds and water" paradox. Diamonds face an elastic demand curve, and therefore involve only a modest amount of consumer surplus. Water, on the other hand, faces a highly inelastic demand, with enormous consumer surplus. Consequently, though the *prices* may seem backward, the *values* the market system places on diamonds, and on water, are exactly in line with what one would expect: water is far more valuable. This illustrates a troubling aspect of using a price system to communicate about "value," however: prices are an accurate signal about value at the *margin*, not the total value.

Market Demand

Even though each person (presumably) faces the same price for the commodity being considered, and the same price for other commodities relevant to the consumption decision, two key factors still differ across people. Individual demand curves will differ (though they all slope downward![10]), perhaps significantly, as people's tastes and incomes differ. While we may be confident that, using the techniques of the previous section, we could come up with a demand curve for each individual, it seems clear that we need some way of aggregating, or adding up, the demands across people.

And it turns out that that is just what is required: adding up the individual demands. Of course, for the answer to make any sense, one has to do it in the right way. The "right way" is to add up the individual demands in such a way that the market demand is equal to the sum of individual demands for each price. Since the individual de-

FIGURE 7.8
Market Demand Curve

The market demand curve is the horizontal summation of the individual demand curves.

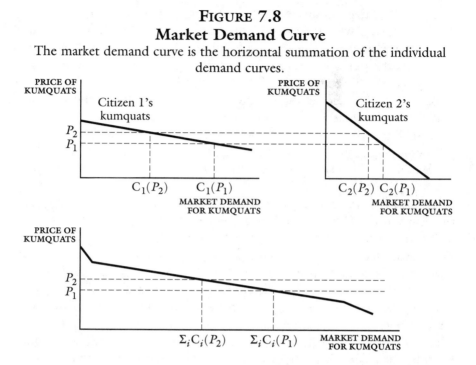

mand curves change at different rates (i.e., have different elasticities), this may seem complicated, but in fact there is a simple way of getting exactly the right answer, provided the commodities being analyzed are private goods. Just add up the individual demand curves *horizontally*, so that the total quantity demanded at each price is the sum of all individual demands. Figure 7.8 shows an example, with two individual demand curves, and the resulting market demand curve. The market demand curve passes through two points representing the sum of the individual demands at specific prices. I have used the summation notation "Σ_i," which means "sum over all items indexed by i." In this case, the index i can take on only two values, representing consumer 1 and consumer 2, but in principle the adding up can be over any number of people.

A quick look at Figure 7.8 will make two things immediately obvious; it turns out both are generally characteristic of market demand curves:

• Market demand curves are always more *elastic* (they are flatter) than individual demand curves.[11]
• If one consumer's demand curve intersects the vertical axis (zero

demand above that price) or the horizontal axis (no increase in demand, even if price is zero), then the market demand curve is "kinked" at that point. In our simple case of just two citizens, the slope of the market demand curve corresponds to the slope of the individual demand curve of citizen 2 at the far left of the diagram, and to the slope of the individual demand curve of citizen 1 at the far right of the diagram, for this reason.

Cost, Marginal Cost, and Prices

So far we have considered only the desire consumers have for products, directed by tastes and constrained by income. This focus is quite incomplete, however, for a reason that may never have occurred to you. Put it this way: What determines the price at which commodities are available in the market?

Your first thought might be that price is determined by demand, or how much people want the stuff. That would be wrong of course, since the supply of the commodity is also important. However, there is more to the explanation than this, and it may surprise you.

Two principles of operation in perfectly competitive markets make demand largely *irrelevant* to price. I will state the principles rather starkly, and then go on to explain them.

Static principle of market efficiency: In a perfectly competitive market, without scale economies, demand is irrelevant to market price. *Price at any point in time is determined solely by the cost of production.* Demand matters for determining the level of costs, if marginal costs are not constant.

Dynamic principle of market efficiency: In a perfectly competitive market, *technological innovation shifts costs downward*, resulting in declines in prices or increases in quality.

The concept of perfectly competitive markets was discussed in chapters 3 and 4. "Perfect" competition is the world of Adam Smith's "invisible hand," and entails three main claims:

1. All economic actors (both buyers and sellers, of both primary resources and consumer goods) are *price takers*.

2. There are *no market failures*, such as information asymmetries, natural monopoly, externalities, or public goods.
3. The *infrastructure*, or currency system and legal system for defining, transferring, and adjudicating disputes over property rights, operates smoothly and with minimal transactions costs.

This result of perfectly functioning markets gives us a notion of price which Adam Smith called the "natural price."[12]

> When the price of any commodity is neither more nor less than what is sufficient to pay the rent of the land, the wages of the labour, and the profits of the stock employed in raising, preparing, and bringing it to market, according to their natural rates, the commodity is then sold for what may be called its natural price. *The commodity is then sold precisely for what it is worth, or for what it really costs the person who brings it to market*, for though in common language what is called the prime cost of any commodity does not comprehend the profit of the person who is to sell it again, yet if he sells it at a price which does not allow him the ordinary rate of profit in his neighbourhood, he is evidently a loser by the trade, since by employing his stock in some other way he might have made that profit. (Smith, 1994, pp. 62–63; emphasis added)

In this passage, Smith identifies what are often called the factors of production, or "inputs" that go into the manufacture of commodities: labor, land, and capital. The cost of a commodity, then, is simply the total of the costs of the various inputs used in its production, including the opportunity cost of the investment made by the producer in equipment, office space, and so on.

The first step toward understanding the two principles above is to think about the way that the factors of production, which themselves have prices, are combined, given the most efficient available technology, to produce output. It is crucial to recognize that two very different kinds of "efficiency" are at work here. The first is **technological efficiency**, or the requirement that the production process does not waste inputs, and uses the best available techniques. The second is **factor cost efficiency**, which means that the productivity of factors is combined with their price per unit to arrive at an "optimal" (i.e., least cost) combination of inputs.

More precisely, the notion of "cost functions" starts with the **production function**, a purely technological relationship among combinations of inputs and the level of output produced. Using the convention that output is denoted q, inputs are l (labor), and k (capital),[13] the production function is conventionally written as:

$$q = f(l,k)$$

The cost function is then written as the dollar amount TC (for "total cost") associated with the combination of inputs that yield technological and factor cost efficiency. More simply, TC is the cost of the cheapest way of producing q:

$$TC = c(q)$$

It should be obvious to you that TC is nondecreasing in q: as q goes up, total cost cannot fall, and is expected to rise unless more q can be produced for free.

We need to define two other concepts of cost before proceeding. The first is *average* cost, or AC:

$$AC = \frac{c(q)}{q}$$

The second is *marginal* cost, or MC:

$$MC = \frac{\Delta TC}{\Delta q} = \frac{\Delta C(q)}{\Delta q}$$

Verbally, average cost is the cost per unit, for all units produced. Marginal cost is the cost of the next unit, given whatever has already been produced. Figure 7.9 illustrates the relationship between the AC curve and the MC curve.

As the figure shows, there are two important things to remember about the MC curve for an individual firm.

- MC is the slope of TC, because changes in total cost are the definition of marginal cost.
- MC determines the slope of AC, because if MC is below AC then average cost is declining; if MC is above AC then average cost is rising.

FIGURE 7.9
The Relation Between Marginal, Average, and Total Costs
The marginal cost curve is the slope of the total cost curve, and the marginal cost curve determines the slope of the AC curve.

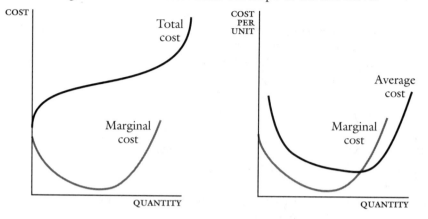

Now that we have developed the machinery of cost curves, the two principles of prices in perfectly competitive markets can be stated more succinctly. First, in a perfectly competitive market, *price equals both marginal and average cost*. Second, in the absence of resource constraints, in a perfectly competitive market, *average and marginal costs, and therefore prices, fall over time, or else quality rises*.

It is worth illustrating each of these two principles graphically. Figure 7.10 depicts the situation of a single firm, which acts as a price taker (i.e., faces a horizontal, or infinitely elastic, demand curve). Assuming no unique resources, or constraints on entry or exit firms, pursuit of profits will drive other entrepreneurs to start, expand, shrink, or abandon this industry. The point where new firms neither enter nor exit will be reached at the point where price (represented by the demand curve) is precisely equal to marginal cost (MC) at the minimum point on the average cost (AC) curve. If price were higher, more firms would enter. If costs were higher, firms would exit. This situation, called **market equilibrium**, represents a balance of quantity supplied at the market price and quantity demanded at that price. Market equilibrium corresponds precisely to the situation Adam Smith had in mind in the passage quoted earlier: "The commodity is then sold precisely for what it is worth, or for what it really costs the person who brings it to market."

Figure 7.10 allows the introduction of the most important concept in the economist's treatment of the firm: the *supply curve*. Just as the

FIGURE 7.10
Equilibrium

In equilibrium, the firm produces at the point where price
equals marginal cost and AC.

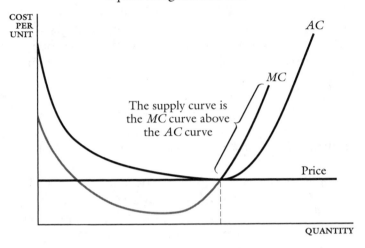

demand curve is the schedule of price and quantity purchased choices
by the consumer, the supply curve is the schedule of price and quantity produced choices by the firm. The definition of the supply curve
has two parts, corresponding to the two concepts of cost already derived above, the average and marginal cost:

Supply curve: The portion of the MC curve equal to or higher
than the AC curve.

The second principle of prices in perfectly competitive markets is
more difficult to depict simply, but the main point is that competitive
pressures on firms lead to innovations in the technology of production. These may be as simple as increases in the division of labor, and
simple machines which foster productivity, or they may take the form
of an entirely new form of production. In any case, the point of such
innovations is to reduce costs, or increase quality, as a way of making
the firm more competitive. Once again, though the firm is trying to
increase profits, the long-run effect (because of the first principle,
above) is to reduce costs, and therefore lower prices. In effect, in perfect competition, the supply curves of individual firms are made to
shift downward over time.

Market Supply and Equilibrium

Just as individual demands are aggregated, or added up, across consumers, the supply curves of individual firms can be added up to obtain the **market supply curve**. The process is exactly analogous to the derivation for market demand: market supply is the total quantity produced, and offered for sale, at any given price. In Figure 7.11, two separate firms are depicted with supply curves (i.e., upward-sloping marginal cost curves, higher than average costs) for kumquats. The market supply, if these two firms are the only suppliers and use marginal cost as their guide to prices charged, is the sum of the output of firm 1 at a given price and the output of firm 2 at that price.

Market supply curves have the same two properties that I listed for market demands: the market curve is always more *elastic* (flatter, more responsive to price changes) than individual supply curves, and may contain kinks as one or more firms drop out at very low prices.

Now that we have developed the logical structure underpinning

FIGURE 7.11
Market Supply

Market supply is the horizontal sum of the quantities produced
at each price.

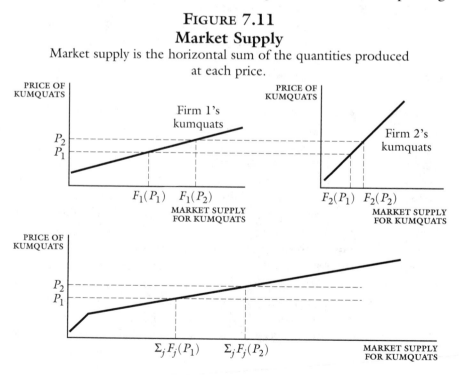

FIGURE 7.12
The Determination of Price

At the equilibrium price P_{EQ}, quantity produced by firms matches quantity demanded by consumers; away from the equilibrium price, surplus or shortage causes adjustment toward eqilibrium.

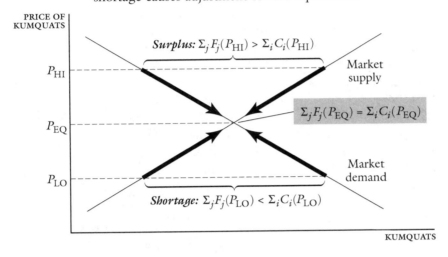

both market demand and market supply, we can consider what happens when the two types of behavior (consumption by citizens, and production by firms) are combined. This can be seen in Figure 7.12. Three possibilities for prices are listed in the figure: a "low" price (P_{LO}), and a "high" price (P_{HI}), as well as what I have called the "equilibrium" price (P_{EQ}). Let's start at P_{LO}: at this price, the quantity demanded (given by the intersection of the price line and the market demand curve) greatly exceeds the quantity produced (given by the supply curve). In the terms of our summation of individual behavior, $\Sigma_j F_j(P_{LO}) < \Sigma_i C_i(P_{LO})$, creating a shortage.

Of course, a shortage means that more consumers want kumquats, at the market price, than are available in the market. Prices of kumquats are consequently bid up; *then*, as price rises, more firms are willing to produce kumquats, and consumers substitute toward other fruits. Thus, the increase in price resulting from the shortage causes movements along both the supply curve and the demand curve, and the size of the shortage shrinks.

Now, let's consider the high price, P_{HI}. At this price, the problem of excess demand is reversed: firms produce too much in relation to demand, creating a surplus of inventories and overstocks of kumquats on store shelves. The size of the surplus is given by the difference between production, summed across firms, and consumption, added up across citizens: $\sum_j F_j(P_{HI}) > \sum_i C_i(P_{HI})$. Once again, however, there is a dynamic force in market processes which implies that the surplus cannot last: prices will fall as firms try to rid themselves of excess stocks of fruit. Falling prices mean firms produce fewer kumquats, and consumers buy more. The surplus shrinks, and finally disappears.

This brings us to the concept of **equilibrium**. The dictionary definition of equilibrium is "a state of balance or equality between opposing forces . . . a state of adjustment of conflicting desires or interests."[14] I have said that if the price is too low, then a shortage exists, and price adjusts upward, and that if the price is too high, then a surplus exists, and price adjusts downward. The equilibrium price is that price at which the quantity firms are satisfied to *produce* exactly equals the quantity consumers are satisfied to *purchase*. At the equilibrium price (P_{EQ} in Figure 7.12) all the kumquats produced are purchased, and either surplus nor shortage exists. Thus, we say that the market is in equilibrium, because $\sum_j F_j(P_{EQ}) = \sum_i C_i(P_{EQ})$.

Public Goods and Externalities

In the previous section, I claimed that equilibrium in private goods markets can be achieved by varying prices. Firms vary the quantities they produce, and consumers vary the quantities they wish to buy, in response to changes in price. The result is a price that exactly balances the production by firms and consumption by citizens.

Many things that are important to citizens are not purely private goods, however. I defined public goods in Chapter 4 as having two characteristics—zero marginal cost of production, and costly exclusion. There is a simpler defining characteristic of public goods, however: *all citizens must "consume" exactly the same quantities of pure public goods*. If a certain amount is spent on national defense, so that our nation has an army, air defenses, and ships to carry weapons and planes all over the world, then that amount is the same, by definition, for every citizen in the nation. Citizens may value national defense differently, of course, but the quantity produced and the quantity consumed are always identical. This leads to a problem: How are we to make adjustments in public goods? Is there anything like "equilibrium" in the decision to provide publicly financed public goods?

Lindahl Equilibrium

Well, yes, there is! We can't vary quantities consumed, so we have to vary price, or tax shares. The equilibrium concept most commonly applied to variable tax shares is "Lindahl equilibrium," named after the Swedish economist Erik Lindahl (see Lindahl, 1939, and Wicksell, 1958). Lindahl noticed a key difference between the aggregate, or market, demand for private goods (derived by summing *horizontally*) and the market demand for a public good (which must be derived by summing *vertically*). For public goods, the key is to choose a level of total output, and then discover whether the total taxes people are willing to pay exactly covers the cost of that output. If the hypothetical tax revenue is too high, then output of the public good needs to be expanded. If the hypothetical tax revenue is too low, then public good production needs to be cut back.

As Figure 7.13 shows, the Lindahl equilibrium really has two parts. The first part is pretty easy: Match total demand and the supply schedule of the public good. This is a little different from the private goods case, because the total demand curve is derived from the *vertical* sum of individual demands, but the idea that equilibrium output occurs at the intersection of total demand and the supply curve is the same.

The second part, the determination of the individual tax shares, is

FIGURE 7.13
Lindahl Equilibrium

Total cost equals the sum of individual willingness to pay for
the public good.

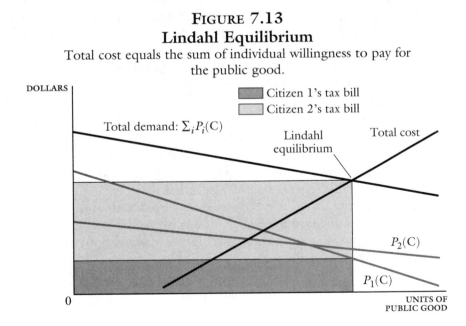

the step that is hard to understand, or to implement. Having established the total quantity it is optimal for the society to produce, we divide the total costs of production of that quantity among the citizens. One obvious way of doing this is to use the information in the individual demand curves, which are in effect "willingness to pay" schedules for each citizen. In Figure 7.13, the demand curve for citizen 1 is marked $P_1(PG)$, or the price citizen 2 will pay for a given level of public good. Citizen 2's demand curve is $P_2(PG)$.

Now, it seems that this is enough information to calculate the appropriate tax shares and make everything work out. After all, the construction of the total demand curve implies that the willingness to pay, for every point on the demand curve, represents the sum of the amount offered by citizen 1 and that offered by citizen 2. At the equilibrium output, we should be able to apportion the total costs as shown in Figure 7.3, with citizen 1 paying total taxes equal to the rectangle at the bottom, and citizen 2 paying a somewhat larger amount. After all, citizen 2 values the public good more, at least at the equilibrium point.

This analysis would go through, and the resulting production decisions would be optimal, if we could only get the information we need about individual willingness to pay for the public goods. But we generally can't. Reliance on self-reported willingness to pay, when citizens realize (as they quickly do) that their own valuations will determine their tax, is not going to work well. Each citizen is likely to free ride, by declaring a zero, or artificially small, willingness to pay. True, the result of such a fib is underproduction of the public good, but at a much lower tax bill. Many people might prefer this to the Lindahl equilibrium situation, where the honest high demanders also pay high taxes.[15]

One alternative is to share all collective costs equally, and collect tax bills using the coercive threats of government action (jail, seizure of assets, etc.). However, this choice is no more than second best, because all people will pay the same tax bills regardless of how much they value the public good. In this case, the incentives for misrepresentation go in the other direction: people who like the public good will misrepresent their preference in the positive direction, because they know that their statements about high demand for public goods will not raise their tax bills.

Conceptions of "Fairness" in Tax System

Most nations use a slight variant on equal tax shares. Generally, we have a government agency (in the United States, the Internal Revenue Service) which uses the threat of force, and financial penalties, to ensure compliance with the tax laws. Two fundamental principles of tax fairness, or equity, can be used to evaluate both individual tax provisions and the effects of the entire set of tax laws, or tax system:

Vertical equity: People with greater ability to pay contribute a larger share of the tax burden of financing public goods.

Horizontal equity: People with approximately equal abilities to pay contribute about the same share of the tax burden of financing public goods.

Tax systems that conform with vertical equity are "progressive," meaning that there is a stairstep marginal tax rate, with progressively higher taxes as income goes up. Tax systems that conform with horizontal equity treat all sources of wealth the same, so that ability to pay is the only consideration.

Let's consider an example where five people with different incomes are faced with the following (highly simplified) income tax system:

1. The first $5,000 of income is exempt from all tax.
2. Income between $5,000 and $50,000 is taxed at 15 percent.
3. Income over $50,000 is taxed at 25 percent.

To show how this mildly progressive tax system works, I have calculated the tax bills, and tax bill as a percent of income, for our five hypothetical taxpayers (ranging from poor George, to wealthy Pat) in Table 7.1.

TABLE 7.1
Five Taxpayers in a Mildly Progressive Tax System

Name	Income	Tax Bill	Tax Bill as Percent of Income
George	$11,000	$900	8.2
Sally	$24,000	$2,850	11.9
Tom	$49,000	$6,600	13.5
Alice	$78,000	$13,750	17.6
Pat	$436,000	$103,250	23.7
Total tax revenue:		$127,350	

George, who only makes $11,000 per year, has a tax bill of $900. George isn't saving any money, and is barely able to survive, with his wife and child, on this amount of money. The 8.2 percent of his income that George pays in taxes would appear to be a heavy burden. Sally, with more than twice as much income as George, pays only a slightly higher percentage (11.9 percent) in taxes. The very wealthy Pat, with an income of $436,000 per year, pays only 23.7 percent in taxes, or only about three times the percentage George pays. Since Pat's income is so much larger, shouldn't he pay even more?

Maybe, but it is not obvious. After all, in terms of total taxes, as opposed to percentages, Pat pays $103,250, compared to George's payment of $900. Pat is paying 115 times more taxes than George! Furthermore, Pat is paying 81 percent of the tax bill of the *entire* city of five people. Assuming that the money is used to finance the provision of public goods, then George, Sally, Tom, and Alice need Pat to be able to have a nice city. Pat is thinking of moving, though, to a place where he can pay lower taxes.

The point is that there are two ways of looking at fairness in tax systems. A focus on *percentage of income*, though legitimate in terms of measuring the burden or the purchasing power given up by different people, may mask the comparison of sizes of *total tax bills*. In even a mildly progressive tax system, or a neutral (constant percentage of income) scheme like the much-maligned flat tax proposal, wealthy people pay much more in taxes than poor people. Of course, the wealthy also may take advantage of tax loopholes, and use political power to distort the mix of public goods to favor themselves (fewer public parks, and more opera subsidies).

Distortions: Taxes and Subsidies

One problem with taxes, or with many other types of government action, is the distortion, or Pareto inefficiency, caused by the attempt to fix a problem, or raise revenues. There are four main types of distortions which are depicted in Figure 7.14.

Sales (ad valorem) taxes. To the extent that a tax changes relative prices, it distorts the price signal about relative scarcity in resources. The Pareto inefficiency results from having consumers willing to pay more than the marginal cost of the commodity or service, without the tax. With the tax, however, the cost of the good or service is artificially high, and these "marginal" transactions do not take place. The

FIGURE 7.14
Distorting Effects of Taxes, Subsidies, Ceilings, and Floors

Deadweight losses are cross-hatched.

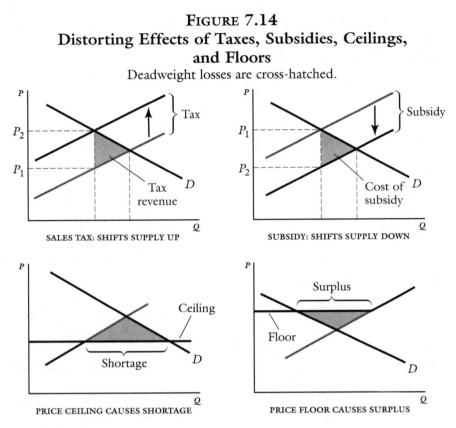

SALES TAX: SHIFTS SUPPLY UP

SUBSIDY: SHIFTS SUPPLY DOWN

PRICE CEILING CAUSES SHORTAGE

PRICE FLOOR CAUSES SURPLUS

size of the distortion can be measured by the loss of consumer surplus,[16] depicted in Figure 7.14 as a shaded triangle. The size of the distortion depends on the elasticity of the demand curve: the more inelastic the demand, the smaller the response of consumers to the change in effective price. Furthermore, goods facing inelastic consumer demand are the largest revenue sources, since people do not substitute away to other goods. Examples of this type of tax include general sales taxes, but the classic examples are taxes on cigarettes and alcohol.

Subsidies. Subsidies operate in exactly the opposite fashion of sales taxes: some portion of the price is paid by the government, effectively reducing the price paid by consumers. Unfortunately, this price reduction once again distorts scarcity signals, so that too many resources are devoted to producing the subsidized article. The size of the distortion is determined by the size of the shaded triangle, which again depends on the elasticity of the demand curve.

Ceilings. A ceiling is a policy prohibiting the charging of prices above a certain level (the price ceiling). Effective price ceilings are those below the equilibrium price. (Price ceilings don't matter if they are above the equilibrium price, because higher prices won't be observed anyway). Ceilings cause shortages, as a wedge is driven between the demand for the good or service (which is high, because of the artificially low price) and the quantity supplied (which is artificially low, as producers respond to the low price). The more "effective" the ceiling, the bigger the potential shortage. The distortion is, as always, a triangle shown as a shaded area in Figure 7.14. Examples of price ceilings include rent controls, often used to keep rents "affordable" in cities, but which actually have the perverse effect of reducing the total amount of affordable housing available. By definition, if the rent control "ceiling" is effective, it is less than the full opportunity cost of the unit. So no new units are built, and old units are not replaced.

Floors. A floor is a policy prohibiting selling at a price below a certain level. Again, floors are ineffective unless they change price, meaning that the floor must be set above the equilibrium price. Floors cause surpluses, because producers devote more effort and resources to this type of output, but consumers want less because of the high price. Examples of this type of government policy include milk price supports, or other agricultural support programs.

Summary

You have seen in this chapter that the approach to the welfare economics paradigm begins by deriving a theoretical model for representing the consumption behavior of individual consumers (the demand curve) and the production choices of individual producers (the supply curve). The next step is to add up, or "aggregate" this individual-level model to account for "market," or total, supply and demand. These tools allow us to illustrate the concept of equilibrium, and to make predictions about the effects of government policies such as taxes, subsidies, price ceilings, and price floors. Although welfare economics is hardly the last word, it is often the first, and most important, word in policy analysis.

It turns out, unfortunately, that the pure market model does not fare so well in describing a process by which optimal levels of public goods (i.e., those with zero marginal cost of production and high exclusion costs) can be determined, and taxes levied. This difficulty will make us fall back on political, or expert, choice mechanisms, as we will see in the next chapter.

SUMMARY OF KEY CONCEPTS

1. *Welfare economics* addresses the question of what the economy would look like if the goal were to promote the entire welfare of the society.

THE REPRESENTATION OF PREFERENCES

2. The *utility function* is a means to measure and rank a consumer's preferences over all possible consumption bundles.
3. The *completeness* assumption requires that an individual be able to compare any two alternatives.
4. *Diminishing marginal utility* for a good means that the additional satisfaction derived from the good decreases with an increase in the total amount of the good consumed.
5. *Insatiability* or monotonicity is the assumption that more of a good is always preferred to less, all else constant.
6. The assumption of *transitivity* is satisfied for three alternatives A, B, and C if the following condition is true: if A is preferred to B and B is preferred to C, then either A is preferred to C (strong transitivity) or C is not preferred to A (weak transitivity).
7. An *indifference curve* represents the set of consumption bundles that yield equal utility or satisfaction.
8. The *marginal rate of substitution* represents the trade-off between more of one good and less of other goods. Technically, it is the slope of the indifference curve at the point being evaluated.

INDIVIDUAL DEMAND AND CONSUMER SURPLUS

9. The *individual demand curve* is the schedule of quantities of a good or service for an individual purchased as the price varies, while holding other factors constant.
10. The *budget constraint* represents the total income available for purchasing goods and services.
11. *Consumer surplus* is the value of a transaction to the consumer above the payment the consumer has to make to complete that transaction.

MARKET DEMAND

12. The *market demand curve* is calculated by adding up the individual quantities demanded at each price. This is equivalent to summing the individual demand curves horizontally.
13. *Elasticity* is the measure of the responsiveness of quantity demanded to the price level. Elasticity is useful for conceptualizing differences between the price and consumer surplus.
14. *Price elasticity* is the percentage change in quantity demanded divided by the percentage change in price.
15. The *diamonds and water paradox* is a problem in value. Although consumers need water but don't need diamonds, diamonds are expensive and water is cheap. The paradox can be resolved through the concept of consumer surplus, since price is only the marginal value.

COST AND PRICES

16. The *static principle of market efficiency* states that in a perfectly competitive market at any given point in time price is solely determined by the cost of production.
17. The *dynamic principle of market efficiency* states that in a perfectly competitive market, technological innovations decrease production costs, resulting in either decreases in prices or increases in quality.
18. The *natural price* of a commodity is the price that will exactly cover the costs of production, or the price of the inputs of land, labor, and capital including the opportunity costs.

19. There are two types of efficiency involved in perfectly competitive markets. *Technological efficiency* is the requirement that the production process does not waste inputs and uses the best available production techniques. *Factor cost efficiency* is the requirement that the productivity factors be combined with the price per input to achieve an optimal combination of inputs.

20. The *production function* represents the technological relationship among combinations of inputs and the level of output produced.

21. The *cost function* represents the dollar amount or total cost associated with a combination of inputs that yields technological efficiency and factor cost efficiency.

22. The cost per unit produced is the *average cost*. It is calculated by dividing the total costs by the number of units produced. The cost of producing one more unit of a good is the *marginal cost*. In a perfectly competitive market, the price equals both the marginal and the average cost. The marginal (average) cost curve represents the level of goods produced and the corresponding marginal (average) costs.

23. A *price taker* faces an infinitely elastic (i.e., horizontal) demand curve.

MARKET SUPPLY AND EQUILIBRIUM

24. A *market equilibrium* is reached when the marginal cost is equal to price, which is the point where the average cost is at a minimum. It also represents the price at which the quantity supplied is equal to the quantity demanded.

25. The *individual supply curve* of a firm is the schedule of price and quantity production decisions. It is also defined as the portion of the marginal cost curve equal to or greater than the average cost curve.

26. The *market supply curve* represents the total quantity supplied at any given price. It is calculated by adding up the individual quantities supplied at each price.

PUBLIC GOODS AND EXTERNALITIES

27. A *public good* has zero marginal cost of production and costly exclusion. All citizens must consume the same quantities of pure public goods.

28. The quantity of a public good produced is always equal to the quantity consumed, which implies that it is difficult to make adjustments in public goods. The *Lindahl equilibrium* is a useful method for analyzing the supply and demand of public goods. The key is to match the total output with the total amount of tax revenue that consumers are willing to provide.
29. *Free riding* is the act of receiving the benefits of a good while not contributing to its provision.
30. *Vertical equity* in tax policy requires that people with larger ability to pay contribute a greater share to the tax burden of financing public goods.
31. *Horizontal equity* in tax policy requires that people with approximately equal abilities to pay contribute about the same share of the tax burden of financing public goods.
32. There are four types of *distortions* that alter price signals about the relative scarcity of goods and services: sales taxes, subsidies, ceilings, and floors.

PROBLEMS AND QUESTIONS

1. Imagine that a consumer has an income of $1,000, and must decide how to allocate her income between two commodities, pizza and caviar. The price of a slice of pizza is $3, and the price of caviar is $65, per ounce. (Our consumer is a discriminating eater of caviar, insisting on Caspian Sea Malossol Beluga, in the original blue tin!)

a. If our consumer spends all her month's income on pizza, how much could she buy? If she spends it all on caviar, how much could she buy? Give the equation for the "budget line" that connects these two endpoints, in slope-intercept form. Then graph the feasible set of consumption bundles, with pizza on the horizontal axis and caviar on the vertical axis.

b. Now draw indifference curves, assuming that the consumer has "normal" preferences, obeying transitivity, monotonicity, and diminishing marginal utility. Make sure you draw an indifference curve exactly tangent to the budget line. This tangency point represents the answer to the consumption problem: how many pizzas, and how

much caviar, does your consumer purchase in equilibrium, if she ex-
hausts her income and does not borrow?

2. Now let's see how your consumer reacts to price changes. Suppose the price of pizza falls to $2.50; how much more does she buy?
What if the price of pizza rises to $4; how much less does she buy?

3. Use these three price-consumption pairs (the consumption levels will depend on how you drew the indifference curves, but the
prices are $2.50, $3, and $4) to draw a demand curve for pizza. (No-
tice that, to derive the demand curve, we held both income and the
price of caviar constant). Plot the three points on a new graph, with
quantity of pizza purchased on the horizontal axis and price of pizza
on the vertical axis. Connect the points with a line (or two line segments, if they don't fall in a line). Does your demand curve slope
downward?

4. Imagine that, for a different consumer, over a small range of
variation in prices and income, the generalized demand for pizza is
given by the following equation:
$$P_p = a_1 Q_p + a_2 I + a_3 P_c$$

where:
P_p = price of pizza
$a_1 < 0$
Q_p = quantity of pizza
$a_2 > 0$
I = income
$a_3 > 0$
P_c = price of caviar

a. Suppose the slope terms in the demand function are as follows:
$a_1 = -1$, $a_2 = 0.1$, $a_3 = 0.4$. Then, start with $P_p = \$3$, $I = \$1,000$, and
$P_c = \$65/$ounce. What is the quantity of pizza demanded?
b. Imagine that the price of pizza goes to $2; what is Q_p? What if
P_p goes to $4.50?
c. Now suppose that the price of pizza is fixed at $3, and income
is fixed at $1,000, but the price of caviar falls to $50/ounce. Does
the demand for pizza go up, or down? Would you say that the consumer substitutes more caviar for less pizza?

ANALYZING POLICY

d. Finally, suppose that the prices of pizza and caviar are fixed at $3 and $65/ounce, respectively, but that income suddenly goes up by 50 percent, from $1,000 to $1,500. Does the consumer buy more pizza, or less? Do you think that this is normal?

5. Suppose that the following two equations are the simple demand for diamonds and for water respectively:

$$P_{diamonds} = 5,000,000 - 2 * Q_{diamonds}$$
$$P_{water} = 5,000,000 - 2,000,000 * Q_{water}$$

Now imagine that a consumer buys two units of diamonds and two units of water. What is the price the consumer pays for each commodity? What is the amount of consumer surplus the consumer receives from each purchase? Based on this measure of value, which transaction (purchase of diamonds, or purchase of water) does the consumer value more? Is the price paid a good measure of the maximum value to the consumer?

6. In terms of demand and supply curves, discuss the problem relating to the production and consumption of a public good. How is the Lindahl equilibrium a solution to this problem? On what grounds might someone reject the use of Lindahl's solution?

TAKE IT TO THE NET!

Go to: http://www.wwnorton.com/college/polisci/analyzingpolicy for additional problems, data sets, and course materials.

NOTES

1. This issue is beyond the scope of this work. For a discussion of many of the issues, and problems, in welfare economics, see Sen (1997).
2. From the url:
   http://www.whitehouse.gov/WH/EOP/OMB/html/rcongress.htm
3. The image is from Marshall (1920), on what factors determine value: "We might as reasonably dispute whether it is the upper or under blade of a pair of scissors that cuts a piece of paper, as whether value is governed by utility or costs of production." I found the reference in Fogarty (1996).

4. See Katzner, 1978, for details on the representability of preferences.
5. All right: if there are infinitely many baskets, it *never* would be completed. But this is a thought experiment.
6. I will ignore the problem of substitutes and complements, and "gross" substitutes, here because only two goods are being considered.
7. The slope-intercept form of a line is simply this:

(*Variable on vertical axis*) = Intercept + Slope *(*Variable on horizontal axis*)

8. The origin of the "diamonds and water paradox" is unclear, though the contrast between value in use and value in exchange is at least as old as Aristotle's paradox, as we discussed at the beginning of Chapter 3. Adam Smith wrestled with the problem but did not have the tools of marginal analysis required to solve it.

> The word value, it is to be observed, has two different meanings, and sometimes expresses the utility of some particular object, and sometimes the power of purchasing other goods which the possession of that object conveys. The one may be called "value in use;" the other, "value in exchange." The things which have the greatest value in use have frequently little or no value in exchange; and, on the contrary, those which have the greatest value in exchange have frequently little or no value in use. Nothing is more useful than water, but it will purchase scarce anything; scarce anything can be had in exchange for it. A diamond, on the contrary, has scarce any value in use; but a very great quantity of other goods may frequently be had in exchange for it (Smith, 1994 [1776]; pp. 31–32).

9. Be careful, though: the price elasticity of demand ranges from zero (at the top) to $-\infty$ (at the bottom) along a single linear demand curve, unless it is perfectly inelastic or perfectly inelastic!
10. As the reader may know, there are two possible counterarguments to the "demand curves always slope downward" claim. The first is that people are not, in the sense described here, rational, so that they value conspicuous consumption, or spending money for its own sake. The second is a technical possibility, the "Giffen" good, or a good so inferior that a decrease in price leads to a reduction in demand.
11. This is true even if the society is composed of exact clones. The reason is that each person buys more at a lower price. Consequently, adding up all the increases makes the aggregate demand schedule much, much flatter than any individual demand curve.
12. The idea of "natural price" is different from the "just price" discussed in the Radford case following chapter 3.
13. In Adam Smith's time, land was a much more important factor than it is now. I would not argue that land is valueless now, but it does not have the status of a separate and equal factor.
14. *Webster's New Universal Unabridged Dictionary*, 1986.
15. Examples of work on demand revelation mechanisms or ways to find out consumers' true preferences, include Tideman and Tullock (1976) and Groves and Ledyard (1977). For a review of many such attempts, and the limits of this type of analysis, see Mueller (1989), or Tideman (1997).
16. Actually, the size of the distortion is the sum of the consumer surplus and the "producer surplus," where producer surplus is defined as the excess of price over marginal cost.

─ 8 ─

Choice of Regulatory Form: Efficiency, Equity, or Politics?

The market failure approach to government action outlined in earlier chapters rests on the implicit premise that regulation, corrective taxes or subsidies, and redistribution of resources take market processes as a benchmark, and then manipulate the market to make it more efficient. The central concept in the measurement of the amount of satisfaction preserved, or wasted, by market processes is "consumer surplus." The notion of Pareto optimality as a means of choosing between two states of the world (say, one with regulation and one without) is closely related to consumer surplus.

The reason is that if a regulatory policy causes a loss of consumer surplus, that potential value is wasted, lost forever to the consumers and producers who might otherwise have captured the gains from trade through some foreclosed market activity. The first and second welfare theorems formalize this idea of cost, or value forgone, by identifying conditions under which market processes lead to Pareto optimal allocations, and proving that any Pareto optimum is feasibly obtained through the appropriate initial allocation of rights. As a consequence, we know that any distortion, whether through regulatory intervention or market failure, represents a waste of resources. The classical model of economic regulation takes as its objective the identification of that set of regulatory interventions which minimizes the total distortions, taking market failures and regulations together. The shorthand for this approach, the "efficiency rationale" for regulation, has been our study so far.

In real policy analysis, the choice of regulatory form is not driven primarily by the concern for economic efficiency. To put concern for efficiency in its proper perspective, let us go back to the diagram of policy conflicts among markets, politics, and experts in chapter 2, and consider how the conflicts are resolved. Note that in every case, the conflict between any two sources of wisdom and accountability is mediated, or even dominated, by the "out" group. Figure 8.1 shows the three pairwise primary conflicts in policy debates, and their mediators:

- *Markets* versus *experts* (mediated by *politics*)
- *Politics* versus *markets* (mediated by *experts*)
- *Politics* versus *experts* (mediated by *markets*)

Let's now consider some examples, and examine the differences in how the conflicts work out.

FIGURE **8.1**
**Three Conflicts: Conflicts Between Sources of Power,
Mediated by the Excluded Entity**

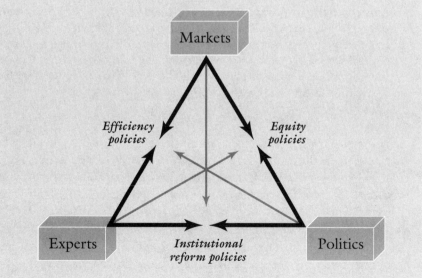

Markets versus Experts

I claimed the internal logic of operation for markets in fact is conditional on the institutional environment in which market activity takes place. Douglass North, winner of a 1993 Nobel prize in economics, makes a very important distinction between two levels of analysis: The level of *institutions*, or the humanly devised rules that constrain human action, and the level of *organizations*, or the set of contracts and agreements that constitute optimizing responses to the incentives and constraints fostered by institutional context.

> Institutions include any form of constraint that human beings devise to shape human interaction. Are institutions formal or informal? They can be either. . . . Institutions may be created, as was the United States Constitution; or they may simply evolve over time, as does the common law. . . . [Using a] sports analogy, taken together, the formal and informal rules and the type and effectiveness of enforcement shape the whole character of the game. Some teams are successful as a consequence of (and therefore the reputation for) constantly violating rules and thereby intimidating the opposing team. Whether that strategy pays off obviously depends on the effectiveness of monitoring and the severity of punishment.
>
> A crucial distinction [should be made] between institutions and organizations. Like institutions, organizations provide a structure to human interaction. Indeed when we examine the costs that arise as a consequence of the institutional framework, we see that they are a result not only of that framework, but also of the organizations that have developed in consequence of that framework. *Conceptually, what must be clearly differentiated are the rules from the players.* The purpose of the rules is to define the way the game is played. But the objective of the team within the set of rules is to win the game—by a combination of skills, strategy, and coordination. (North, 1990; pp. 4–5; emphasis added)

The "market" is not really a single institution, nor is it consciously created, as in the example of the U.S. Constitution. Rather, the market is what (sometimes) happens when individuals act *without any conscious or coercive central planning*. Consumers and firms are the "organizations" which act within the informal institution of a market. Under some circumstances, the outcomes we observe are clearly of mutual, and perhaps even universal, benefit, as the welfare theorems demonstrate. Under different circumstances, however, with different institutional features, the function of markets may be far from optimal. The organizations are quite likely behaving rationally, and optimally, in terms of their own goals. But the outcomes are inferior.

Let us now turn to a larger discussion of market failure, which considers institutions as well as organizations.

Market Failure and Expert Failure: Reforming Organizations

It is orthodox to claim, as was argued in chapters 3 and 4, that there are three kinds of market failure: information, externalities, and economies of scale. However, in some ways these are the least important "failures," of markets. As we have seen in the former Soviet Union, beginning around 1996, real market failures can be genuine disasters. The failure of markets causes an enormous loss of wealth, and reduces a society to chaos and perhaps revolution. Why this can happen is not obvious, at least from the perspective of economic theory, because economic theory assumes the existence, and acceptance, of a very specific set of institutions: without these institutions, markets must always fail.

Consider the discussion of Klein, Moore, and Reja (1997):

> The spontaneous order of free enterprise has been celebrated by Adam Smith, Friedrich Hayek, and other theorists. Following the teachings of Smith and Hayek, economists have explained how in normal market settings—the province of the butcher, the brewer, and the baker—the invisible hand of free enterprise performs better than do alternative governance arrangements. This comparative success is the result notably of two factors that find great vitality in free markets: competition and entrepreneurship. These two factors are often used to advocate deregulation and privatization of services that have slipped too far toward the [government by expert] end of the continuum.
>
> But a lesson of Smith and Hayek not so well learned is *that the success of a spontaneous order depends critically on the property rights framework within which it operates.* To call merely for deregulation and privatization *requires that the property rights framework for the free-market arrangement is self-evident and functional.* (Klein, Moore, and Reja, 1997, p. 2; emphasis added)

It is evident that the concept of "market failure" is rather more general, and more subtle, than the relatively simple notions of public goods, information, and economies of scale. In fact, there is a hierarchy of market failure, as I have argued elsewhere (Munger, 1997). In many ways, the failure of markets may turn out to be the failure of experts who do not learn the "lesson of Smith and Hayek" that Klein, Moore, and Reja highlight: unless the institutional environment is properly constructed, the organizations that give markets their dynamic power may do more harm than good. Briefly, the hierarchy is as follows:

1. *Markets fail if governments remove, or fail to create, what Hayek called the "infrastructure" of market processes.* Infrastructure includes a system for defining and trading property rights, a legal system for the adjudication of disputes, and a monetary system to facilitate exchange. In fact:

   > The functioning of a competition not only requires adequate organization of certain institutions like money, markets and channels of information—some of which can never be adequately provided by private enterprise—but it depends, above all, on the existence of an appropriate legal system . . . designed both to preserve competition and to make it operate as beneficially as possible. (Hayek, 1944, p. 38)

2. *Markets fail if governments create, or fail to remove, impediments to market processes.* Such impediments might include taxes, subsidies, regulations or standards that distort prices and information. Because the efficient transmission of information is the key advantage markets have over other forms of organization, persistent distortions may reduce, or even eliminate, the benefits of allowing markets to organize the activity of citizens. Hayek (1960, 1978) called the process of generating, and transmitting, accurate information "discovery." The problem is that incoherent price signals send economic discoverers off in the wrong direction, drawing resources and wealth after them.

3. *Markets fail to perform efficiently because of the classic list of inherent violations of the goal of Pareto optimality:* informational asymmetries, externalities in consumption or production, or large economies of scale in production.

To summarize: Type 1 market failure arises from inadequate infrastructure, type 2 market failure results from poorly designed policies, and type 3 market failures are caused by flaws irreducibly present in market processes themselves.

Clearly, these three levels of failure have dramatically different causes and implications. Blaming type 1 failure on markets is like saying your car is a lemon because there is no road. It is certainly true that the car won't go, but we can't use that immobility as evidence about the quality of the car itself. A car works well in a particular, very limited context: smooth roads, with wide lanes, and conventions about rights of way and directions of traffic flow.

Similarly, charging markets with type 2 failure is like blaming your car for breaking down after you put maple syrup in the crankcase and water in the gas tank. No matter how well constructed the machinery of the automobile, the way that you choose to maintain the car dramatically affects its performance. Even a first-rate car will quickly begin to perform poorly unless it is given the proper treatment, and the appropriate inputs for operation.

In short, then, only type 3 failures really represent failure of the *market*; type 1 and 2 failures are malfunctions of the *institutional infrastructure*, or the *informational inputs*, in which market organizations operate. To continue the automotive metaphor, there are just some things that a car can't do, even if the roads are good and maintenance is careful. Economies of scale, informational asymmetries, and externalities–public goods present problems for markets in the best of circumstances, and efficient performance will require extraordinary government action.

This leads to a very important point. The distinctions among types of market failure (infrastructure is bad, maintenance is bad, market is bad) may be difficult, or even impossible, to diagnose from a policy perspective. Most of the time, all we know for sure is that the car won't go! At what point should we conclude that the car is a lemon, and trade it in or get the motor rebuilt? A new engine won't help if the real problem is bad roads or bad maintenance; the new car will soon break down also, even if its machinery functions perfectly.

Likewise, if the only kind of market failure that expert analysts consider is type 3, then their recommendations will result in endless, and useless, tinkering with market processes when the real problem has to do with infrastructure or maintenance of inputs. The general problem can be put concisely, in North's terminology: Unless the institutional framework encourages optimizing organizational responses that lead to Pareto optimality, successful reform of those organizations is not just hard, but impossible.

In chapters 3, and 4, I argued that "efficiency" (i.e., Pareto optimality) is the guiding value for policy conflicts between experts and markets. This is clearly true for government interventions motivated by type 3 market failure, because economies of scale, information asymmetry, and externalities are all efficiency problems. Type 1 and type 2 market failures are also efficiency problems in some ways, but they are much harder to diagnose from a pure efficiency perspective. The reason is that property rights and law (type 1 failures) or redistributive taxation (distortions that cause type 2 failures) may have motivations other than efficiency alone: they affect the distribution of wealth, and consequently may have more to do with equity than most other market-expert conflicts.

More importantly, market failures are the entry point for the excluded, or mediating, power in policy conflicts. As we saw in Figure 8.1, conflicts between experts and markets over efficiency may be mediated by political concerns, where economic efficiency plays very little role. In a democracy, there are at least two sources of political power which may influence policy conflicts over experts managing markets: voters and organized interests.

Voters make decisions about taxation, regulation, and expenditures. They may do this directly, through the referendum or ballot propositions, where a policy question is be decided by majority rule. Voters also decide policy questions indirectly, through election or rejection of representatives who act in accordance, or in contradiction with voters' goals. This is not to say that voters always get what they want, since (as we saw in chapter 5) "they" disagree. But a politician who wants to stay in office may not care exclusively about efficiency, no matter what experts tell her. Voters' goal may not be the abstract, and aggregate, achievement of economic efficiency through minimizing distortions in tax policy. Instead, voters seem to want to follow the tongue-in-cheek dictum of Senator Russell Long of Louisiana: "Don't tax you; don't tax me; tax that man behind that tree."[1] Consequently, taxes may be levied on the politically weak, and expenditures targeted to benefit the politically powerful, quite separate from the goals of experts or the logic of market mechanics.

Policies designed to regulate, or improve the efficiency of operation of, markets have a special problem. In chapter 5, I quoted Adam Smith's observation that "People of the same trade seldom meet together, even for merriment or diversion, but the conversation ends in a conspiracy against the public, or in some contrivance to raise prices" (Smith, 1994, p. 148). I also earlier described portions of Stigler's (1971) "theory of economic regulation." Stigler's contribution was the recognition that "conspiracies against the public" are much more likely to be successful if the power of government can be enlisted on the side of the industry being "regulated." Stigler's argument takes on the question of politics intervening in markets quite explicitly. He is skeptical of the ability of experts to manage regulation in the public interest:

> The state—the machinery and power of the state—is a potential resource or threat to every industry in the society. With its power to prohibit or compel, to take or give money, the state can and does selectively help or hurt a vast number of industries. . . . As a rule, regulation is acquired by the industry and is designed and operated primarily for its benefit.
>
> . . . The industry which seeks regulation must be prepared to pay with the two things a party needs: votes and resources. The resources may be provided by campaign contributions, contributed services (the businessman heads a fund-raising committee), and more indirect methods such as the employment of party workers. The votes in support of the measure are rallied, and the votes in opposition are dispersed, by expensive programs to educate (or uneducate) members of the industry and other concerned industries.
>
> . . . The idealistic view of public regulation is deeply imbedded in professional economic thought. So many economists, for example have denounced the ICC for its pro-railroad policies that this has become a cliché of the literature. This criticism seems to me exactly as appropriate as a criticism of the Great Atlantic and Pacific Tea Company for selling groceries, or as a criticism of a politician for currying popular support. The fundamental vice of such criticism is that it misdirects attention: it suggests that the way to get an ICC which is not subservient to the carriers is to preach to the commissioners or to the people who appoint the commissioners. The only way to get a different commission would be to change the political support for the Commission, and reward commissioners on a basis unrelated to their services or the carriers. (Stigler, 1971, pp. 1, 11, 17–19)

It is worth remembering, then, that the conflict between pure market results and expert management to achieve efficiency does not occur in a vacuum. Instead, there may be substantial influence from political actors. And if Stigler is correct, then the attempt to manage what I have called type 3 market failures may actually do more harm than good, as regulations are distorted to the advantage of concentrations of economic power. If concentrations of economic power can be translated into concentrations of political power, then the interests supposedly being "regulated" may be able to distort the infrastructure and maintenance of the market system itself.

Markets versus Politics

In the previous section, I argued that the conflict between markets and experts over efficiency policy is often misunderstood, for two reasons. First, the nature of efficient functioning of market organizations may have more to do with the institutional setting than with the market processes themselves. Second, efficiency policies that take a naïve "public interest" view of regulation underestimate the ability of the excluded source of power (in this case, politics) to manipulate policy and distort its effects. Consequently, the conflict between experts and markets can be hard to understand, and the outcomes we observe are not always the ones we expected, or wanted.

But the next conflict, between markets and politics, is more difficult still. In the conflict over expert management of markets, there is at least agreement on the primary goal: efficiency, in the sense of ensuring that outcomes are Pareto optimal. In the conflict between markets and politics, the problem is that "solutions" require a trading off of two fundamental values: efficiency and equity.

Efficiency we have already defined, though the use of the Pareto criterion is not a very satisfactory way of narrowing down possible courses of action. After all, the outcome where I get everything and you get nothing, as well as the outcome where I get nothing and you get everything, are both Pareto optimal in a two-person exchange game. So is every allocation in between, provided we don't want to trade the goods we own. *Equity*, or the fairness of the distribution of resources, is a much more difficult concept.

Differing Conceptions of Equity

There are at least three conceptions of a "fair" distribution of resources:

1. *All should share equally.* Justice requires equality of treatment, and of opportunity. Deviations from an equal distribution of resources are unjust. Though this argument has been made by many, the best known modern proponent is Rawls, who articulated a "difference principle" (1971). The most vigorous, and passionate, defender of the notion of equality among humans is Rousseau (1988; 34):

> The first man who, having fenced off a plot of land, thought of saying, "This is mine" and found people simple enough to believe him was the real founder of civil society. How many crimes, wars, murders, how many miseries and horrors might the human race have been spared by the one who, upon pulling up the stakes or filling in the ditch, had shouted to his fellow men, "Beware of listening to this imposter; you are lost, if you forget that the fruits of the earth belong to all and that the earth belongs to no one.

This "property is theft" view of wealth is an important, if rather extreme, perspective on the distribution of wealth. After all, if "the fruits of the earth belong to all and the earth belongs to no one," it is hard to think of a *just* distribution of wealth that isn't an *equal* distribution of wealth.

2. *Each person should receive a share equal to the amount s/he needs.* A person with a disability, or special requirements, needs more resources just to achieve the same level of welfare as a healthy person. Further, each of us has a duty to help those who cannot help themselves. One origin for this idea may be found in the Christian *New Testament*: "And distribution was made unto every man according as he had need." (Acts, 4:35) There are some obvious practical difficulties with this position, of course: How can needs, as opposed to wants, be measured? How can one find a monitor for distribution who will not himself need to be monitored?

3. *Each person should receive a share proportional to the amount s/he produces.* The value of each person's output, in economic terms, is a measure of their contribution to the general welfare. For example, if you invent a new drug, or even if you just make really good bread, then you are making others better off. When you are paid more for these services than someone who produces very little, you deserve the extra wealth because you are serving others. This point of view has already been developed in earlier chapters: it is the implication of Adam Smith's "invisible hand" for the distribution of wealth.

All three of these ideas are used in political discussions, sometimes without an appreciation of the differences. Some people talk about inequality in the income distribution as if "not equal" and "not equitable" are interchangeable. On the other hand, we have a variety of programs, at the federal, state, and local levels, which focus on need, or on "underserved populations." And the de facto distribution of income, most of the time and in most countries, is related to the value of the output, or production, of the individual, or of the household.

Markets, of course, reward production. As I pointed out in chapter 4, your wealth at any time can be calculated as the sum of the product of the price (P) and the quantity (x) of all the productive, or otherwise valuable, resources to which you hold title:

$$\text{Wealth} = \Sigma_{i=1}^{n} P_i \chi_i$$

Consequently, if you own labor, or minerals, or land, or a factory, or if you just own diamonds or some really rare Beanie Babies, you are wealthy.

But do you deserve to be wealthy? After all, in a market economy, wealth entitles you to special treatment. At a minimum, you are able to provide more for your children, and to live a life of far greater luxury, than someone who is poor. Why should we (i.e., society) allow this? Why shouldn't we all have the same resources (an equality standard), or each get the resources we require to live (a need standard)?

Let's reprise the three primary points of view on equity, as well as three more concise statements of their justification:

- *Equality*: John Rawls, in *A Theory of Justice*.[2] "All social primary goods—liberty and opportunity, income and wealth, and the bases of self-respect—are to be distributed equally unless an unequal distribution of any or all of these goods is to the advantage of the least favored."
- *Need*: Karl Marx, in his "Critique of the Gotha Program,"[3] gives his rule for an idealized distribution of the "proceeds of labor": "From each according to his ability, to each according to his needs."
- *Production*: Adam Smith deftly summarizes an argument made at some length by the French economist Quesnay:[4]

> In what manner, according to this system, [is] the sum total of the annual produce of the land [distributed?]. . . . This distribution takes place, in a state of the most perfect liberty, and therefore of the highest prosperity; in a state where the annual produce is such as to afford the greatest possible net produce, and where each class enjoys its proper share of the whole annual produce. . . . Every violation of that

natural distribution, which the most perfect liberty would establish, must, according to this system, necessarily degrade more or less, from one year to another, the value and sum total of the annual produce. (Smith, 1994, pp. 729–30)

How Should Resources Be Distributed?

Given these three prescriptions for how resources should be divided, it is useful to consider the actual distribution of income in the United States. A standard, and intuitive, depiction of the extent of inequality of the distribution of income (the way we actually value resources) can be found in Figure 8.2. The vertical axis in the figure depicts percentiles of income (divided into fifths, or groups of 20 percent each), and the horizontal axis depicts percentiles of population (again divided into quintiles). Perfect equality of income distribution would

FIGURE 8.2
Inequality in Wealth Distribution in the United States

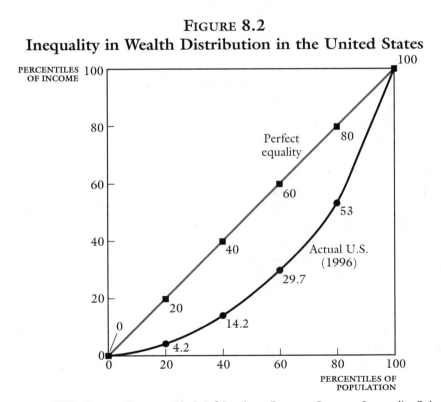

SOURCE U.S. Census Bureau, "A Brief Look at Postwar Income Inequality," by Daniel Weinberg, P60-191, June 1996, Table 1. Data are for percentiles of families/households.

be result in the bottom 20 percent getting 20 percent of the income, the bottom 40 percent getting 40 percent of the income, and so on. The perfect-equality benchmark is the 45 degree line through the origin.

Actual income is distributed in a way that is decidedly not equal, as the "actual U.S." curve in Figure 8.2 shows. The poorest 20 percent of the U.S. population receives only 4.2 percent of the income; the richest 20 percent receives nearly half (47 percent) of income every year. In general, an "income inequality" curve of the type shown in Figure 8.2 is a way of visualizing differences in the distribution of income: the vertical difference at each point between the two curves is the disparity between actual and equal distribution of income.

But so what? If you believe John Rawls, this is a disaster, since an unequal distribution of income is, prima facie, a sign of an unjust society. Likewise, if you believe Karl Marx, inequality of this magnitude is a problem, since the wealthy have far more than they "need," and poor people are starving. But if you believe Adam Smith, it is not clear that there is any cause for concern. In Smith's view, income is definitionally tied to productivity (more accurately, to the ownership of productive resources); consequently, there is no necessary relation between equity and equality. More simply, income differences may simply correspond to differences in work, in productivity, or in the value society places on a person's output.

Why would there be such large differences in income, and what, if anything, should society do about it? This second question is one of the most difficult questions any society faces. John Stuart Mill, although on most questions a libertarian, had second thoughts about the distribution of income. He claimed that there is a "proper distinction between the laws of the Production of Wealth, which are real laws of nature, dependent on the properties of objects, and the modes of its Distribution, which, subject to certain conditions, depend on human will" (Mill, 1873, chap. 7). For our purposes, this insight can be restated this way: The *functioning* of a market economy creates wealth differences, because some people work harder, are more productive, or are just luckier. But the choice of the final *distribution* of wealth is a policy choice; that is, it "depends on human will." How can we decide who gets what?

To see just how hard this choice can be, it is useful to consider a story, drawn from one of Aesop's fables.

Investment Requires Forgone Consumption: The Ant and the Grasshopper

In making choices today, a person or a society may determine the choices available next week, or next year. More specifically, *choosing to forgo consumption today can lead to more alternatives tomorrow.* Think what a radical concept "saving" really is. Put yourself in the place of a member of a primitive society, starving during a hard winter. Why not eat the seed corn? The simple answer, because we will need these seeds to plant in the spring, is a mental leap of awesome proportions. It would seem that this ability to plan, to abstract from current needs and "save" for the future, is the contribution of human cognition and mental power.

Such a conclusion is wrong, of course. All creatures have to solve this problem. For humans, the problem may be more complex, but only because it has a voluntary component: we trade off current consumption against future consumption consciously, while insects, fish, birds, and mammals do it out of instinct.

The moral of the story of "The Ant and the Grasshopper" in Aesop's Fables is: "It is thrifty today to prepare for the wants of tomorrow." Now, Aesop is trying to teach something about a good life, and a good society. But for guidance, we look to an *insect*, not to some law of human nature. As you may recall, the story goes like this: The grasshopper, who lived large all summer, starves in the first winter snow. The ant, on the other hand, lives snug in his hole under the snow, feasting on food stored up over a summer of hard work.

The same lesson is taught in what Christians call the Old Testament: "Go to the ant, O sluggard, study her ways and learn wisdom; for though she has no chief, no commander or ruler, she procures her food in the summer, stores up her provisions in the harvest" (*Proverbs*, chap. 6, verses 6–8). This is a powerful lesson: the present and the future are linked, whether we recognize it or not. Yet, though the ant can't possibly "recognize" the need to save, it does so immediately and unquestioningly. We point our children toward this lesson, and remind ourselves of it, when we raise the ant to a higher moral position than that "sluggard," the wastrel grasshopper.

Adam Smith describes human nature as if we were ants, or should want to be ants:

> . . . the principle which prompts to expense, is the passion for present enjoyment; which, though sometimes violent and very difficult to be re-

strained, is in general only momentary and occasional. But the principle which prompts to save, is the desire of bettering our condition, a desire which, though generally calm and dispassionate, comes with us from the womb, and never leaves us till we go into the grave. In the whole interval which separates those two moments, there is scarce perhaps a single in- stant in which any man is so perfectly and completely satisfied with his sit- uation, as to be without any wish of alteration or improvement of any kind. An augmentation of fortune is the means by which the greater part of men propose and wish to better their condition. It is the means most vulgar and the most obvious; and the most likely way of augmenting their fortune, is to save and accumulate some part of what they acquire, either regularly and annually, or upon some extraordinary occasions. (1994, p. 372)

Is this right? Are humans, by their nature, apt to save and accumu- late? Perhaps, but the manner and amount of accumulation is clearly conditioned on the incentives they face, and on their expectations about the future.

Today, of course, there are many ways of connecting present choices to future constraints on alternatives. Futures markets allow buyers and sellers to lay off risk; loans allow present consumption based on the expectation of future income. What should we do about people who guess wrong? What should we do about people who, like the grasshopper, fail to save for one reason or another and then make a claim based on "need"? It seems that there are only two responses: honor the claim based on need, recognizing that it changes both in- centives ("I don't have to work") and expectations ("I can take extra risks"), or reject it, letting the grasshopper starve in the snow.

What's Virtue Got to do with It? Marx and Okun. Karl Marx, in various writings (but see especially "The Secret of Primitive Accumu- lation," in *Capital*, vol, 1, chap. 26, pp. 461 and following), ques- tioned this parable. He claimed that *current* inequalities in income and resources can have only two possible sources: (1) fundamental unfairness in a capitalist system of production, depending on private ownership of the means of production, or (2) differences in "primi- tive" accumulation, or accumulations of wealth that occurred before industrialization occurred. Now, as is well known, Marx tried to argue that the answer is number 1: capitalism is unjust. But the meat of his argument (at least on this point) is that number 2 is im- plausible.

> Primitive accumulation plays in political economy about the same part as original sin in theology. Adam bit the apple, and thereupon sin fell on the human race. Its origin is supposed to be explained when it is told as an anecdote of the past. In times long gone by there were two sorts of people; one, the diligent, intelligent, and, above all, frugal élite; the other, lazy rascals, spending their substance, and more, in riotous living. . . . It came to pass that the former sort accumulated wealth, and the latter sort had at last nothing to sell but their own skins. (Marx, 1983, p. 462)

Marx rejected this claim, arguing that income inequality, and differences in ownership of the means of production that create wealth, are at best accidental, and at worst may result from outright theft. Since the "value of production" basis for wealth distribution is fatally flawed, Marx argued for a need-based system of distribution.

One does not have to be a follower of Marx to find truth in this conclusion. Consider Arthur Okun's celebrated argument in *Equality and Efficiency: The Big Trade-Off*.[5] Okun makes two claims for why government action is required to make the market-, or production-based, distribution of income more equitable. The first claim has to do with imperfections in the market; the second claim is that rewarding productivity is arbitrary.

In competitive markets, the distribution of income would precisely reflect the value of the product of all inputs, so that "workers and investors [would receive] the value of their contributions to output" (Okun, 1975, p. 61). In a *perfect* market setting, then, distribution of income based on productivity might very well be just, as Quesnay and Smith pointed out long ago. In Okun's view, however, markets are far from perfect.

Asymmetries in information, discrimination, differences in educational opportunity, and pervasive monopoly all distort the distribution of income, so that the pattern of wealth we see is already quite different from a genuine "to each according to his production" rule. Consequently, government needs to fight discrimination and monopoly, to provide education, and to make sure that citizens are informed about the consequences of economic actions.

These actions, in and of themselves, should reduce income inequalities by shifting the distribution of income to be more in line with potential productive capabilities of each citizen. It is very difficult to argue with this point, since it really just adds a step to the market failures justification for regulation. The difference is that here the "market failure" results in an inequitable distribution of income, which itself results from the more standard types of market failure (monopoly and information problems).

Okun's second argument is rather more radical. Suppose that it really is true that some people are more productive than others, because of differences in physical strength, energy, creativity, and intellect. Is there any just basis for claiming that these advantages in the market should attract greater wealth for their possessors? Okun claims that differences in natural abilities are like anything else one inherits from one's parents, or other ancestors: accidents! Genetic differences are not earned, and should not be differentially rewarded. If you are a better lawyer, or a better banker, than someone else, *you are just lucky*, and society should not base the distribution of wealth on what amounts to an arbitrary genetic lottery:

> Society should aim to ameliorate and certainly not to compound, the flaws of the universe. It cannot stop rain, but it does manufacture umbrellas. Similarly, it can decide to restrict prizes that bestow vastly higher standards of living on people with greater innate abilities. (Okun, 1975, p. 44)

This second argument is directed at the distribution of income itself, not at the causes of differences in income (as in Okun's first argument). If you buy this claim, then society should act to compensate those who did not get lucky, by taking wealth away from the winners and giving it to the poor and disadvantaged.

The difficulty with the argument is that there are at least three reasons why someone might be poor, and unable to provide for themselves. If you lack the ability to provide for your own needs, that is surely different than if you are just lazy, and would prefer that someone else provide resources without any effort from you. In this view, character isn't the result of some random draw where some win and some lose; rather, character is a response of a person to his or her environment, and it is capable of change. The income distribution policy you favor probably depends on your beliefs, selected from the list below, about the primary cause of income differences.

- *Effort.* People may be poor because of lack of effort, or because of irresponsible spending patterns. Rich people are thrifty and work hard; poor people waste their money and are lazy.
- *Skill.* People may be poor because they lack the ability to earn a liv-

ing, or lacked the chance to learn skills when they were young. So educated or well-trained people are rich, while poorly educated or untrained people are poor.

- *Market value of output.* People may be poor because the skills they possess, which once were valuable, have been devalued by changes in technology or the tastes of consumers. A highly skilled, energetic person may be poor if he manufactures buggy whips, because no one wants to buy those things anymore.

Simply put, you will be poor, in a market economy, if you are not productive. If you are productive, and if society values what you produce, you will be wealthy. But then wealth comes from a combination of effort, skill, and the value the market places on what you produce, or possess. So a poor person who is a skilled maker of slide rules or candle holders, or a hardworking day laborer with no skills valued by the market, is very different from a person who is poor because he is lazy.

Similarly, we might all agree that a person who works her whole life to invent a cure for cancer may deserve great wealth if she succeeds. But a person who inherits the ownership of many manufacturing companies is wealthy only because of what he owns, not because of any real productivity, or even effort. The scion of a wealthy family can live in the Bahamas on an enormous yacht, never working at all, and just cash the checks mailed by the firm he "runs."

What Standard of Decision Should We Use?

How can a market-oriented society decide about the "right," or just, distribution of income, if the sources of inequality of income can vary so widely?

The answer is that there is an *inevitable* conflict between the outcomes produced by the market (allocation) and the income pattern (distribution) that Mill said "depends on the will of men." Mill seems to have been assuming some universally agreed standard of fairness, but we do things a little differently. To decide whether, and how much, to change the allocation of income resulting from market processes, we use politics, not reason. Earlier, in Figure 8.2, we saw that the actual distribution of income in the United States is very different from equality: the top 20 percent of the population has 47 percent of the income.

It is equally true, however, that the actual distribution of income in the United States is dramatically different from the distribution that would be implied by a "pure" market society. The total amount of money spent on "transfers," or redistribution of money from the relatively wealthy to the relatively poor, exceeds $1 *trillion* per year in the United States. Some of this money goes into administration, some goes to people you might not really think are poor, or deserving of welfare benefits, but lots of it really does get redistributed.

To give you an idea of the total amounts of wealth and income redistributed in the United States, the data in Table 8.1 summarize the total amounts of income, in the form of direct payments, subsidies, services, or in-kind distribution of food or other commodities, provided to the poor in all fifty states and the District of Columbia.

TABLE 8.1
Total Annual Value of the Welfare Package (dollars), 1995

Rank	Jurisdiction	AFDC	Food Stamps	Medi-caid	Hous-ing	Utili-ties	WIC	Com-modi-ties	Total
1	Hawaii	8,544	5,064	3,689	8,219	310	1,730	180	27,736
2	Alaska	11,076	3,420	4,575	5,677	551	1,037	180	26,849
3	Connecticut	8,160	2,304	3,913	8,016	632	1,269	180	24,474
4	Massachusetts	6,948	2,664	4,533	8,446	417	988	180	24,176
5	District of Columbia	5,040	3,240	4,192	8,616	393	1,084	180	22,745
6	New York	8,436	2,412	3,824	5,677	357	1,237	180	22,124
7	New Jersey	5,088	3,312	3,824	7,960	583	1,021	180	21,968
8	Rhode Island	6,648	3,216	3,130	6,682	514	1,171	180	21,541
9	California	7,284	2,568	2,784	6,413	368	1,090	180	20,687
10	New Hampshire	6,600	2,772	3,473	5,520	460	959	180	19,964
11	Maryland	4,392	3,540	4,192	5,864	293	1,028	180	19,489
12	Virginia	4,248	3,480	4,168	5,608	584	1,117	180	19,385
13	Maine	5,016	3,252	4,232	5,089	260	989	180	19,018
14	Vermont	7,656	2,460	2,734	3,829	731	1,164	180	18,754
15	Washington	6,552	3,096	3,407	3,914	390	1,190	180	18,730
16	Delaware	4,056	3,540	3,870	5,437	368	1,035	180	18,486
17	Colorado	4,272	3,468	4,021	4,946	516	1,054	180	18,457
18	Nevada	4,176	3,504	4,021	5,173	421	981	180	18,456
19	Minnesota	6,384	2,832	3,843	3,491	718	993	180	18,441
20	Utah	4,968	3,264	4,021	4,102	343	960	180	17,838
21	Wyoming	4,320	3,456	4,021	4,314	455	1,034	180	17,780
22	Pennsylvania	5,052	3,240	3,275	4,364	394	1,068	180	17,574
23	Michigan	5,868	2,988	3,076	3,964	409	1,075	180	17,560

TABLE 8.1 (CONT.)
Total Annual Value of the Welfare Package (dollars), 1995

Rank	Jurisdiction	AFDC	Food Stamps	Medi-caid	Hous-ing	Utili-ties	WIC	Com-modi-ties	Total
24	Illinois	4,404	3,492	3,543	4,193	540	1,140	180	17,492
25	Wisconsin	6,204	2,892	2,837	3,539	615	1,122	180	17,389
26	New Mexico	4,284	3,468	3,988	4,181	145	1,122	180	17,368
27	Iowa	5,112	3,216	3,982	3,290	533	1,022	180	17,335
28	Florida	3,636	3,540	3,417	5,239	214	1,042	180	17,268
29	Indiana	3,456	3,540	4,642	3,991	440	943	180	17,192
30	Idaho	3,804	3,540	3,889	4,103	392	1,120	180	17,028
31	Oregon	5,520	3,516	3,108	3,360	325	950	180	16,959
32	North Dakota	4,908	3,276	4,241	2,482	579	1,146	180	16,812
33	South Dakota	5,004	3,252	3,748	2,897	613	994	180	16,688
34	Kansas	5,148	3,408	3,475	2,890	480	1,106	180	16,687
35	Oklahoma	3,888	3,540	4,789	2,926	227	1,092	180	16,642
36	Ohio	4,092	3,540	3,760	3,728	341	910	180	16,551
37	Georgia	3,360	3,540	4,099	3,822	388	1,016	180	16,405
38	Louisiana	2,280	3,540	4,891	3,702	530	1,167	180	16,290
39	North Carolina	3,264	33,540	3,921	3,905	211	986	180	16,007
40	South Carolina	2,400	3,540	4,192	4,512	266	863	180	15,953
41	Montana	4,812	3,312	3,228	2,756	422	1,104	180	15,814
42	Kentucky	2,736	3,540	4,209	3,637	433	1,072	180	15,807
43	Nebraska	4,368	3,444	3,412	2,800	437	1,084	180	15,725
44	Texas	2,208	3,540	3,459	4,180	1,000	903	180	15,470
45	West Virginia	2,988	3,540	3,568	3,628	258	1,041	180	15,202
46	Missouri	3,504	3,540	3,088	3,359	365	1,066	180	15,102
47	Arizona	4,164	3,504	1,171	4,331	240	1,212	180	14,802
48	Tennessee	2,220	3,540	3,583	3,504	480	1,075	180	14,582
49	Arkansas	2,448	3,540	2,984	3,766	196	975	180	14,088
50	Alabama	1,968	3,540	3,128	3,562	348	1,091	180	13,817
51	Mississippi	1,440	3,540	2,373	3,990	622	888	180	13,033

SOURCE Michael Tanner, Stephen Moore, and David Hartman, *The Work Versus Welfare Trade-Off: An Analysis of the Total Level of Welfare Benefits by State*, Cato Policy Analysis no. 240 (Washington, D.C.: Cato Institute. September 19, 1995). The table is adapted from Table 8. "AFDC" refers to Aid to Families with Dependent Children; "Food Stamps" are coupons redeemable for groceries and some other products; "Medicaid" is a medical benefit available to the poor; "Housing" and "Utilities" assistance encompass a variety of programs that offer subsidies, payments, and in-kind benefits; "WIC" is the Women with Infant Children program, which in some states provides food, nutritional counseling, and a variety of other services to women before and for a period after they give birth to children; "Commodities" benefits are made under the Temorary Food Assistance Program.

The total amount of the welfare "package" in some states appears quite generous, with nine jurisdictions offering benefits in excess of $20,000 per year for a family of four.

However, that these data are somewhat misleading. First, many of these benefits either are not available or are not understood by people who are eligible, so many poor people do not receive anything like the maximum package in their state. Second, the figures in the table represent the monetized value of services and commodities. Poor people don't get a check, but rather can take advantage of programs that provide useful items and services. Table 8.1 places a value on these services based on their *cost*, which may grossly overestimate the value that the poor family actually *receives*.

Third, and on the other hand, these figures represent what would be (for an employed person) the *after-tax* benefits available to the poor. If these services were provided to someone with a job, the pre-tax income required to achieve this level of income would be far higher, maybe as much as 25 percent. For example, suppose you lived in Hawaii. Given the taxes paid by employees in Hawaii, you would have to earn $36,000 or more to match the welfare benefits you could get for free![6]

The conflict between markets and politics comes down to this question: What system best ensures legitimate rewards to individual effort, while preserving the rights of everyone else? Tension inevitably arises between markets and collective decision-making from the nature of politics in a democracy. Markets are decentralized, operate with little central direction, and (most importantly) recognize power based on wealth. If you have more dollars than someone else, you have more "votes" in the market. Democratic politics operates on a much more egalitarian basis: each person gets only one vote, so that in the ballot box, at least, the poor person and the rich person have the same power.

Two observations together give an indication of how difficult the problem is.

Markets handle the allocation problem efficiently. This is simply an elaboration of Adam Smith's observation that the highest aggregate output results from the allocation of each productive resource to its highest-valued (in money terms) use. Smith was using only an intuitive argument, but economists in the intervening 225 years have shown that Smith's intuition was correct. Even with the caveats and qualifications to this conclusion introduced by the theory of market failures, the basic intuition is unassailable. The efficiency of prices as signals of relative scarcity cannot be matched by any other system of organization.

Politics in a democracy will be directed toward redistribution of market allocations of wealth. There are both practical and theoretical reasons why politics are more concerned with distribution than with allocation. The theoretical reasons have to do with equity, which is why I have labeled markets-politics conflict "equity policy." We apply theories of *justice* to the distribution of income. Whenever the allocation of wealth by markets conflicts with the distribution of wealth the society considers just, a redistribution of that wealth is likely to be implemented as policy.

The practical reasons for redistribution may, overall, be more important, than the theoretical reasons and they have different implications for how redistribution works. The argument can be made most clearly using a graphical depiction of the distribution of wealth, and a comparison of two measures of the "central tendency" of that distribution, the mean and the median. The *mean* of a distribution is the average value, or the sum of all the observed values divided by the number of observations. The *median* is the middle observation in the population, when that population is sorted from smallest to highest. Consider Figure 8.3, where the mean and median income levels for the United States in 1997 are highlighted along the overall distribution of family income.

Recall from chapter 5 that political power in a democracy rests with the "median voter"—in this case, the value of income associated with the median household. But the *average* (mean) income is higher than the income enjoyed by the median household. The mean and median incomes are almost always different in modern societies, because some people are very wealthy, and even the poorest people can't have incomes below zero!

In the United States, as you can see in Figure 8.3, average income for households was about $57,000 per year; median income was about $45,000 per year. That difference (mean income is nearly 27 percent more than median income) represents significant potential political pressure for redistribution of income.

But this means that it is tempting for politicians to offer the median voter a choice: "You like money, don't you? Well, how about if we gave you *more* of it?" Policies that tax the wealthy and give benefits to the middle class are the product of just this sort of political

FIGURE 8.3
Mean and Median Income
The mean income usually exceeds the median income,
creating political pressure for redistribution.

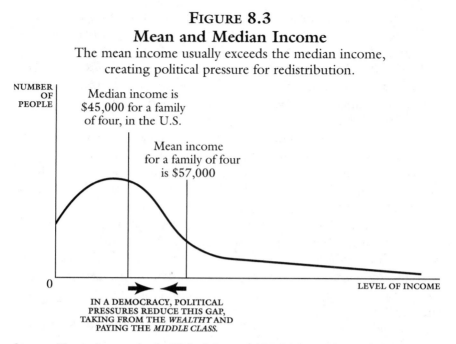

SOURCE Money Income in the United States, 1997, U.S. Department of Commerce
Current Population Reports, P60-200, Table B-4, "Families by Total Money Income, Race, and Hispanic Origin of Householder: 1967–1997."

pressure to close the gap between median and mean income. This
"practical" political reason for redistribution, of course, has an obvious flaw from a "justice" perspective of course: redistribution takes
place, but the chief beneficiaries are the middle class, not the poor!
This observation (a variant of "Director's law,"[7] named after Aaron
Director, the famous University of Chicago economist) presents a
real problem for those who favor redistributive policies. As Peltzman
(1980, p. 270) points out, "The very poorest may not have sufficient
[political power] to be included as beneficiaries" in politically motivated income redistribution programs.

So, to conclude: While conceptions of theoretical justice would require redistribution to the poor, practical political considerations may
lead to income redistribution that primarily benefits the middle class.
The conflict between market *allocation*, and political *distribution*, of
income is complex.

Experts versus Politics

The way we decide often affects what we decide. As we saw in Chapter 6, particular political "institutions," or ways of choosing, have very different implications for the nature of the choice. Charles Plott (1991) summarized the problem of policy outcomes very succintly, in his "fundamental equation of politics."

Preferences × Institutions = Outcomes

We might think of "preferences" as what individual voters want. "Institutions" are the rules and practices (such as majority rule or a legislative committee system) through which collective decisions are made. Plott's equation demonstrates that there are two very different sources of potential change in policy outcomes: change in what individuals want, and change in the rules for deciding. More simply:

- If preferences change, outcomes can change, even if institutions remain constant.
- If institutions change, outcomes can change, even if preferences remain constant.

One could easily argue, of course, that in the real world preferences and institutions are both changing almost all the time. And that's right. But keeping the two types, or sources, of change distinct analytically is fundamental to an understanding of politics. Further, as Plott's equation shows, changes of one type interact with changes of the other type. Relatively small changes in preferences, if multiplied by a change in the way those preferences are counted, may change policy outcomes dramatically.

For example, suppose I tell you that one type of policy will be observed if a particular nation uses majority rule, district-based elections to determine which representatives are selected for the legislature, but a quite different policy will result if the same nation uses a proportional representation system of election. How are we to decide which set of institutions, or ways of choosing, are better?

Choosing Institutions: Process or Outcomes?

One possibility too would be to look at the outcomes. This would mean, of course, that our preferences over *results* work their way back into our preferences over *institutions*. For example, suppose I like alternative A, and you like B. We both examine voting institutions, and I notice that majority rule is more likely to lead to A; you see that proportional representation leads to B. When it comes time to choose a voting rule, I argue for majority rule, and you argue for proportional representation, based not on a principled understanding of fairness or ethics, but simply on our guess about the likely outcome.

Such preferences are called **induced preferences**: my desired ends give me an instrumental reason to choose a means. None of this seems very satisfactory, of course: political choice mechanisms, if the process of choice is to be perceived as fair, should obey abstract norms of fairness and justice. Consequently, "experts" (in this case, people who have studied the technical consequences of different selection procedures as well as people who have studied political theory and its implications for the just society) and "politics" (the instrumental desire to choose voting rules based on outcomes) are in conflict.

Arguments for, or against, a particular institutional arrangement based on political theory are largely outside the scope of this book. Choice of voting rules, and of other institutions such as the rules of the legislature, or of dividing power between the legislature and the executive, is the subject of political science. Still, three points about this important area of policy conflict are worth making before this chapter closes.

First, there are two separate conceptions of "fairness," or justice, in the evaluation of political institutions. *Process* criteria highlight equality of opportunity to participate, equal access to the means of persuasion, and equal treatment of all citizens before the law. *Outcome* criteria focus on the fairness of the result: Does everyone get equal value, or equal service, when policy is actually implemented?

Clearly, this duality might lead to difficulties in evaluating a decision procedure: Suppose a particular decision rule satisfies all the process (i.e., just or fair procedure) criteria we can think of, but treats different groups in the society differently, even unfairly, in terms of outcome. Is that a "good" political institution? Some (Buchanan and Tullock, 1965; Buchanan and Congleton, 1997) would likely argue yes, claiming that only process criteria can be used to evaluate a process. Others (Rawls, 1971; Guinier, 1996) would dispute that conclusion, pointing out that it is only outcomes that really matter. There is no reason, this latter group would claim, to ignore outcomes, especially since the political reality (noted above) is that the choice of institution is really *driven* by outcome, regardless of the process criteria used to justify that choice mechanism after the fact.

Second, as was true with the other policy conflicts I have discussed, the policy conflict between politics and experts has an important role for the excluded entity: in this case, markets. Many people have argued (perhaps most famously, Walzer, 1983) that the legitimacy of political decision-making depends on its being insulated from other sources of power. In particular, most of us would object if it were clear that the power resulting from concentrations of economic power (wealth, ownership of property or resources) would be translated directly and routinely into concentrated political power. As Walzer points out:

> One can conceive the market as a sphere without boundaries, an unzoned city—for money is insidious, and market relations are expansive. A radically laissez-faire economy would be like a totalitarian state, invading every other sphere, dominating every other distributive process. It would transform every other social good into a commodity. . . . The exercise of power belongs to the sphere of politics, while what goes on in the market should at least approximate an exchange between equals (a free exchange). (Walzer, 1983, pp. 119–120).

On the other hand, it can be argued that there is no way to exclude money from the political process completely, if for no other reason than that running a modern campaign is expensive. It is naïve to conceive of politics as if it worked like a New England town meeting. In such a meeting, each citizen might be allotted an equal amount of time to speak, but all would recognize that some speakers are more articulate, and persuasive, than others. Citizens might willingly cede their time to the articulate few they agreed with, because persuasive people can make better use of the time, and even advance the interests of those who make the "contributions."

In modern politics, there are many kinds of "contributions" that make someone I agree with more likely to win the election. Continuing the town meeting metaphor, suppose I volunteer to help build a platform for the candidate to stand on, and be seen and heard better, or maybe to construct a system for amplifying her voice so that more people can hear her. By "bundling" resources, a group can improve its chances, and maybe even improve policy. The First Amendment to the U.S. Constitution admonishes that "Congress shall make no law

. . . abridging the freedom of speech, or of the press; or the right of people peaceably to assemble." If I own time in a debate, and give it to my candidate so she has more time to speak, or if I give her money or other resources to ensure her speech is widely heard, I am improving the quality of political choices, not harming them.

Problems arise, however, when large amounts of money can be used, not to inform or persuade, but to distract, confuse, or overwhelm. Suppose I built a sound system so powerful that it drowned out other voices, and then instead of broadcasting information I played music, appealing to emotions or people's baser impulses. Platforms could be erected, high and bauble-encrusted, not to make the candidate easier to see and understand, but to mesmerize the voters. As Richard Nixon said in rather different circumstances, "That would be wrong."

Third, there are two very different conceptions of the role of individuals, and of institutions, in society, which can lead to people talking past one another in policy debates. One conception of politics is associated with the thinking of Jean-Jacques Rousseau; the other is much closer to the conception of James Madison.

In the Rousseauvian view, the problem is to identify truths, or "best" policies, which actually exist but which are unknown. If citizens could just elect good people, and keep the different "interests" from having undue influence, government would do the right thing. Any organization, be it party, club, or trade association, that stands between the citizen and his government corrupts and distorts the process. Thus, reforms must focus on preventing organized interests from having any influence on elected officials.

The Madisonian view could not be more different. The key to controlling the evils of faction is to expand the scope of conflict, and to multiply the number of groups participating. The existence of many competing and conflicting interests circumscribes the ability of any one set of groups to dominate. Reforms designed to restrict influence can (almost) never make things better, because the relatively small set of interests advantaged by existing institutions distort politics to their benefit. If anything, "reform" is generally a pretext for consolidating power and protecting advantage. William Riker (1982) calls these two views "liberalism" (Madison) and "populism" (Rousseau). Riker claims:

> What is different between the liberal and populist views is that, in the populist interpretation of voting, the opinions of the majority must be right and must be respected because the will of the people is the liberty of

the people. In the liberal interpretation, there is no such magical identification. The outcome of voting is just a decision and has no special moral
character. (p. 14, emphasis in original)

To summarize: the question of the best (most just, most ethically
defensible, or just most practical and effective) system for making political choices is one of the most important conflicts in the policy
process, but it is largely the province of political science, and it is *antecedent* to policy analysis. Policy analysts generally start with a given
statute or regulation and don't go behind it to examine the institutions themselves.

One exception—and an important one of late—is the campaign
finance process. Almost by definition, campaign finance is the interference of the market in politics. The question of the legitimacy, and
effects, of allowing economic power to be used in the sphere of politics is one of the most difficult dilemmas societies face. On the one
hand, it seems clear that industries should not be able to manipulate,
and distort, regulations designed to govern and direct their actions.
On the other hand, the restriction on "interest" in politics would be
very hard to enforce. In our own way, each of us is a "special interest"
aren't we?

Summary

This chapter is the culmination of the main theoretical argument in
this book. To put it starkly, all policy debates contain elements of at
least one, and often more than one, of three types of conflict:

• *Efficiency* debates (conflict between markets and experts over the
  allocation of productive resources, with interference from the political forces in society)
• *Equity* debates (conflict between markets and politics over the
  distribution of wealth, with experts shaping the debate through
  theories of justice)
• *Institutional reform* debates (conflicts between experts and politics
  over how to decide political questions, with market forces interfer-
  ing)

The sense of bewilderment felt by most of the public, and even by
many policy analysts, over the apparently contradictory nature of pol-

icy choices stems from confusion over these three realms of policy conflict. Policies which represent "solutions" to one kind of conflict may appear misguided, or even bizarre, unless you recognize that the different answers are directed to very different questions.

For example, the complaint by people who study markets that redistributive tax systems distort incentives and hurt efficiency is really beside the point: redistribution is an equity policy. On the other hand, people who pursue equity policies single-mindedly should recognize that those policies really do have a cost, in terms of economic opportunities forgone because of perverse incentives. The simple framework laid out here should not be interpreted as a set of directions for reaching the ideal destination but rather as a set of guideposts to make it easier for you to find your way around.

SUMMARY OF KEY CONCEPTS

1. *Director's law*, named after Aaron Director, states that public expenditures are made for the primary benefit of the middle classes, and are financed with taxes which are borne in considerable part by the poor and rich.
2. Equity of income has at least three different conceptions in public policy, including *equality*, distribution according to *need*, and distribution according to the *value of output produced.*
3. The *fundamental equation of politics* is attributed to Charles Plott, and holds that outcomes equal preferences multiplied by institutions. Importantly, this means that outcomes may change if preferences change (institutions constant), or if institutions change (preferences constant). If both change even slightly, the change in outcomes can be large.
4. Even if people don't really care about how choices are made in the abstract, they may have strong *induced preferences over decision rules,* since (as Plott's "fundamental equation" shows) outcomes depend on decision rule. Consequently, if people have preferences over outcomes, they care about the decision rule because of the outcome it will select.
5. *Institutions* are the humanly devised rules that constrain behav-

ior, according to Douglass North. In the context of this chapter, institutions are rules for making decisions and guiding political choice.

6. *Investment and forgone consumption* are related in that the decision to invest is exactly equivalent to the decision to save, or to forgo consumption. To the extent that income is a return to investment, forgone consumption in an earlier period is a means of rationalizing income disparities: giving up consumption in one period justly increases the amount available to consume in a later period.

7. *Justice* has at least two sets of definitions, those that relate to the qualities of the process, in terms of fairness and procedural consistency, and those that relate to the qualities of outcomes, in terms of the equality and equity of the distribution of resources and power.

8. The concept of *market failures* includes classical problems such as inefficiency (information asymmetry, natural monopoly, externalities and public goods), but can be extended to account for failures to create and maintain *infrastructure* (a legal system, currency, well-defined alienable property rights), or the introduction of *impediments* and *distortions* (subsidies or regulations).

9. *Organizations* are the set of contracts and agreements that constitute optimizing responses to the incentives and constraints fostered by institutional context.

10. There are two fundamentally different conceptions of the *political process*: the *Madisonian* conception and the *Rousseauvian* conception. Madisonian politics are a process by which politicians and other government officials are made accountable to the public. Rousseauvian politics is the process of collective discovery of truth, or the unique best policy for the society.

11. *Primitive accumulation* is Marx's term to describe the supposed source of differences in wealth in pre-capitalist societies. This concept is similar to Smith's conception of "previous accumulation."

12. There are three *sources of income differentials*: differences in *effort*, differences in *skill*, and differences in *market valuation*.

13. George Stigler's famous *theory of economic regulation* holds that nearly all economic regulatory policies either are originally designed, or else are soon "captured," by the economic entities the

policies were supposed to constrain. More simply, regulation benefits the regulated group, and harms consumers.

14. *Transfers* are the pure handing over of wealth or property to another party, without any deadweight loss in the act of transference itself. The incentives created by transfers may cause deadweight losses, or loss of consumer surplus, but the transfer itself is efficient.

15. *Wealth* is the sum of the products of the value of the commodity, product, or talent possessed by the agent multiplied by the price of the commodity, product, or talent.

PROBLEMS AND QUESTIONS

1. What principles of justice should guide a society in allocating wealth and resources? In an ideal society, what would the distribution of income look like?

2. Which principles of justice are more important, principles of process (for example, equality of opportunity) or principles of outcome (for example, equality of incomes)? Are you confident that you can identify the differences between process and outcome criteria? What are the definitions?

3. Suppose that there are one hundred people in a society, who have to make a single choice among three mutually exclusive public alternatives. Let their preference profiles over the alternatives be as follows:

	Voter Type/Proportion of Population		
	Type 1–45%	*Type 2–35%*	*Type 3–20%*
Best	A	C	B
Middle	B	B	C
Worst	C	A	A

Now imagine that the first thing the society must do is choose a decision rule. The three alternatives are (i) plurality rule, (ii) majority rule, with runoff, and (iii) Borda count.

a. If each group is more interested in getting its most preferred outcome than in abstract considerations of justice, which decision rule does each like best? Construct a table of (induced) preference ranking for each group, like the one above, with the three decision rules above as the alternatives. (For example, a preference ranking for some group might be Best: plurality; Middle: Borda count; Worst: majority rule with runoff).

b. Suppose plurality rule is used. Which decision rule would be chosen, if people vote sincerely?

c. How should the society decide how to decide? That is, what is a fair way to choose the decision rule?

d. *Extra credit*: If you had to guess what this society would actually do, what would your guess be? Which decision rule would they pick, and what would be the outcome selected as a result? *Note*: In real politics, people would not necessarily vote "sincerely." If groups 2 and 3 formed a coalition, and voted strategically, how would the outcome be changed from your answer in b. above, even if the decision is still made by plurality rule?

4. Evaluate "Director's law." Is it always true, sometimes true, or never true? Consider the following policies: mortgage interest deduction, public schools, and social security. Do these tend to support, or prove false, the proposition that policies benefit the middle class, and are paid for by the wealthy and the poor? What is the relation between "Director's law" and the "median voter theorem" you learned in chapter 6?

TAKE IT TO THE NET!

Go to: http://www.wwnorton.com/college/polisci/analyzingpolicy for additional problems, data sets, and course materials.

NOTES

1. Quoted in Jones (1994), p. 211.
2. Rawls (1971), p. 303.
3. This "critique" was originally a letter, written in May, 1875, to the leaders of the Eisenach faction of the Social Democratic movement in Germany. Though the criticism Marx offered was sarcastic, even abusive, about the draft program, it was adopted anyway, in the Gotha Congress in late May of 1875. The letter was eventually published in *Neue Zeit*, a party organ, under the title "Critique

of the Gotha Program." The version referenced here is in Tucker (1972), p. 388.

4. Francois Quesnay was a "physiocrat," or one of the self-proclaimed economists, in France in the eighteenth century. His treatise, *Tableau économique*, was published in 1758, and is the source that Smith cites for his conclusions about income distribution and the level of production.

5. Okun (1975, pp. 43–44).

6. Tanner, Moore, and Hartman (1995), Table 1.

7. For background, and evidence, on Director's law, see Stigler (1970).

Case 3: Social Security Crisis?

This book has argued that the first and most important step in policy analysis is to move from a set of facts to an analytic problem definition. In this case,[1] we face the problem of arriving at a problem definition that people can agree on. The fact that social security has an equity basis, rather than an efficiency basis, makes the problem more severe.

In reading the case, keep the following questions in mind:

1. If social security is the answer, what is the question? Is there some other policy "answer" to this question which would cost no more, yet provide a better solution?
2. Who are the primary stakeholders in the social security debate? That is, who is affected (either positively or negatively) by social security in its current form?
3. Is there really a problem with the Social Security Trust Fund? How would we know? If there is a problem, what is the nature of this problem?
4. Is reform necessary?
5. Is the reform that would improve the program politically feasible?
6. Who will be the winners and losers if reform is undertaken?
7. What effect will the policy tools chosen have on other segments of the society and economy?

Introduction

Social security may be the single most popular public program in the United States. However, despite this widespread support, social security is one of the most hotly contested issues among politicians, experts, the media, and the public. One need look no further than President Clinton's January 1999 State of the Union address for proof of the primacy of social security. Despite his being only the second president of the United States to be impeached,[2] social security was main focus of the address. So what are the issues surrounding social security? What problems need to be resolved? How are they to be resolved?

The short answer to these questions is, it depends: on the perspective of the observer, and the criteria used to evaluate the program. Although there are technical disputes among policy makers and rep-

resentatives about social security, the major dispute is over *the definition of the problem*. The debate is about identifying what is wrong
with the current system and choosing which dilemmas to solve.

Social Security

The Old-Age and Survivors Insurance (OASI) Trust Fund is more
commonly known as social security. It has improved the living standards of the retired and elderly through a generous benefit structure.
Furthermore, there has been strong support to either maintain or increase the benefits provided through the program.

However, our ability to maintain this benefit structure is in jeop-
ardy. Demographic changes in the United States, in particular the
ratio of OASI recipients to workers, may make the current system
unsustainable. These demographic threats have sparked debates
about the need and possibility for reform of the system. Thus, while
there is strong support for providing a retirement safety net, there
is a widespread disagreement over how to manage this retirement
fund in a manner that protects current and future social security recipients.

Social Security Benefits and Financing[3]

Social security is a "defined-benefit" program that provides monthly
benefits to retired workers, as well as to their dependents and survivors. A defined-benefit program ensures in advance that workers'
contributions will entitle them to future benefits that are determined
by fixed-dollar formula based on their lifetime earnings record. However, while a worker's past earnings *influence* the benefits received,
there is not a one-to-one relationship between the benefits received
and past earnings, as would be the case in a private system or a government-run "retirement account" program. Instead, a progressive
benefit formula has been instituted which ensures that low-income
wage earners receive a greater percentage of their lifetime earnings.

Benefits are not solely determined by past earnings, however. To
ensure that the purchasing power of retired workers does not diminish, the benefit formula is linked to the rate of inflation through the
consumer price index (CPI). If the CPI increases, a benefit increase
equivalent to the CPI increase takes effect.[4] The benefit formula also
includes an automatic cost of living adjustment. In effect, then, OASI

is indexed, so that retired workers' purchasing power is held constant.

Social security's benefit structure is financed in three ways. The most important funding source is payroll taxes, either as defined by the Federal Insurance Contributions Act or the Self-Employment Contributions Act. The tax rate for employees in 2000 was 6.2 percent of the first $72,600 of taxable wages. Employers must match the amount paid by their employees. The revenues collected under FICA and SECA are used to pay for benefits and administrative costs.

Excess revenues from payroll taxes are invested in interest-bearing obligations, or special-issue securities, which earn interest at a rate equal to the average market yield on long-term U.S. government bonds. This is the second source of funding for social security. The interest earned from these obligations accounts for a growing share of the social security trust fund's income. In 1995, interest earnings accounted for 6 percent of total income. It is projected that by 2020, interest earnings will account for 24 percent of the trust fund's income (Stephenson, Horlacher, and Colander, 1995; p. 10). It should also be noted that if revenues were ever insufficient to cover current benefit payments, the obligations would be redeemed to fulfill the remaining expenses. The third and final source of funding is taxes on social security benefits themselves, paid by recipients.

Demographic Changes

Today, social security is the largest source of income for seniors in the United States. It is estimated that nine out of ten seniors receive social security benefits. Further, over two-thirds of seniors receive more than over half of their income from social security trust fund. But the program was not originally intended to be the primary source of retirement funds.[5] Instead, social security was to be one of three major sources of income for seniors, along with personal savings and private sector savings. To date, social security has been successful in reducing poverty among the elderly in the United States. The number of elderly has declined from 34 percent in 1960 to 10.5 percent in 1995. It is estimated that over 50 percent of the elderly would live below the poverty line if they did not receive their monthly social security benefits.

Given the success of the social security program, it easy to why it is so popular among the people and their elected officials. While the past of social security may be glowing brightly, the future of the program is not as clear. Many policy analysts have argued that in its current form social security will not be sustainable because of the changing demographics of the American population. In particular, the percentage of elderly over age sixty-five has been steadily rising due to increasing life expectancy. Further, looming on the horizon is the retirement of the baby-boom generation. In 1960, there were an average of 5.1 workers for every social security beneficiary. In 1998, there were approximately 3.3 workers for every beneficiary, and it is projected that there will be two workers for every beneficiary in 2030 due to the baby-boom generation retirements. With benefits for current retirees being financed by current workers, the declining ratio of workers to beneficiaries is projected to have profound effects.

In their 1998 annual report, the Social Security and Medicare Board of Trustees released estimates for the trust fund's future status.[6] The board releases two estimates: a short-range (ten-year) and a long-range (seventy-five-year) estimate. In order to project the future status of the trust fund, the board uses three alternative sets of economic and demographic assumptions. The intermediate set of assumptions (alternative II) provides the "best" estimate of future economic and demographic conditions. The board also uses a low-cost set of assumptions (alternative I) and a high-cost set of assumptions (alternative III). Alternative I provides a more optimistic projection of the trust fund's financial status, whereas alternative III provides a more pessimistic projection.

In the short range, the trust fund is considered "financially adequate" because revenues will be sufficient to cover all projected benefit payments and administrative costs, regardless of which of the three alternative sets of economic and demographic assumptions is used. The long-range projection, however, is not as promising. Under alternative II, it is estimated that the trust fund assets will be exhausted (i.e., the accumulated assets will be depleted) in the year 2034. The trust fund will still be supported by payroll taxes. It is estimated that payroll taxes will be able to cover three-fourths of the estimated benefit payments and administrative costs once the trust fund is exhausted and about two-thirds of estimated expenses at the end of the seventy-five-year period. Under alternative III (the pessimistic set of assumptions) the trust fund assets are expected to be exhausted in 2025, or approximately ten years earlier. However, under alternative I (the optimistic set of assumptions) the trust fund assets are not expected to be exhausted in the seventy-five-year period.

What Is the Problem?

OASI has functioned reasonably well by almost anyone's standards since its implementation in the 1930s. However, projected demographic changes in the United States may apply pressure that may strain the system beyond its capabilities. Comparing the system's current performance with its projected performance (assuming it is left unaltered) raises some interesting questions. Is there anything wrong with social security?

Policy analysts and politicians disagree about the answers to these questions, partly because of the complexity of the analysis, and sensitivity to assumptions, but mostly because they disagree about the nature of the problem itself. Some postulate that there is nothing flawed about social security, but instead that exogenous factors (i.e. demographic changes) have made the current system of distribution untenable in the short term. Therefore, the benefit and finance structures must be altered to fit changing circumstances. Others, however, would claim that the system is flawed, or more accurately, inefficient. What an analyst or politician believes the problem or issue is will shape whether he or she believes the system should be reformed and how to reform it.

Reform

Does social security need to be reformed? Using their "best" (i.e., alternative II) set of economic and demographic assumptions, the Social Security and Medicare Board of Trustees concluded that in the long term, social security is not secure.[7] In a message released with the 1998 annual report by the two public trustees from the board, they state:

> But while we devoutly hope that the recent strong performance of the economy continues for the next 75 years, we must in our fiduciary role as Public Trustees warn policymakers and the public that there are serious reasons at this point to project that it may not, and that action needs to be taken to ensure that Social Security can pay the retirement benefits the people expect. This also means that it is difficult to compare our projections for Social Security with the often optimistic forecasts of those who wish to promote a private investment approach. The financing problems facing Social Security is significant but could be solved by the small gradual changes IF those changes are enacted soon (emphasis in original).

While there appears to be a consensus that social security should be reformed, there is a wide range of disagreement over how to reform it. The basis of this disagreement hinges upon the answer to the question highlighted in the previous section: What is the dispute? In other words, if one believes that the current social security dilemma is concerned with the distribution of resources (i.e., income) in society, then this will imply a certain set of reforms. However, if one believes that the social security dilemma is about inefficiency, then this will imply a different set of reforms based on the notion of privatization.[8]

Redistribution and Reform

Those who argue that distribution is the fundamental problem with the current system advocate reforms that seek to adjust the defined-benefit format of social security. Recall that under a defined-benefit format, benefits are determined in advance by a fixed-dollar formula based on lifetime earnings. Thus, workers are promised benefits in advance. There are several policy mechanisms available to reform social security within the defined-benefit format. These policy mechanisms will enact incremental changes that may help secure the social security trust fund for the twenty-first century. Some possible alternatives are:

1. Increase the wage base and tax rates.
2. Reduce cost of living adjustments.
3. Increase the retirement age.
4. Means-test benefits.
5. Reduce initial benefits by changing benefit formula.
6. Include new state and local government employees in the system.

According to the Concord Coalition, a fiscal responsibility advocacy group, certain packages of these policy mechanisms will be effective in making social security viable well into the next century. It is important to note that all of these potential policy mechanisms would change the distribution of income by reducing benefits or increasing taxes. For example, increased payroll taxes would take money from current workers to fund the benefits of retirees; means testing (determining benefits based more on financial need, and breaking the link with contributions almost completely) would hurt wealthier retirees.

Inefficiency and Reform

Those who argue that social security is inefficient advocate reforms that are based on the virtues of the market as discussed in chapter 3. In short, a privatized or market-based system would make the social security trust fund more efficient by making the benefits higher and/or the costs lower.

One justification for a privatized system concerns the investment of trust fund assets. More specifically, it has been claimed that trust funds assets should be invested in private securities markets. Currently, the Secretary of the Treasury is required to invest revenues in special-issue securities from the U.S. government. The interest earned from these securities is becoming a larger part of the social security trust fund revenues. Perez and Hammerbacher (1993) have argued that the trust fund would have grown 22 percent larger (from $280 billion to $343 billion) in the 1980s if social security had invested in the same portfolio mix as private pensions plans in that time period.[9]

Further, some have suggested that a privatized social security system would increase incentives to contribute to the retirement fund. It has been argued that a defined-benefit program like social security can discourage work by making early retirement attractive. Early retirement has the obvious effect of decreasing the ratio of workers to retirees, which places greater stress on the system (Quadagno and Quinn, 1997).

Whereas the defined-benefit format creates negative incentives (e.g., early retirement), a privatized system could have a positive influence on incentives to contribute. Currently, social security functions on a pay-as-you-go (PAYG) basis, where the workers of today pay for the retirees of today, with the assurance that future workers will do the same for them once they retire. However, the attractiveness of the PAYG format is (arguably) being diminished by the projected individual rates of return. One of the main attractions of the PAYG format for today's workers is the increased rate of return that the system can provide. Increased rates of return are due to two factors: an expanding workforce and wage growth. An expanding workforce means that more workers will be contributing to the system for today's workers when they retire.

Growing wages provide an increased rate of return by expanding the revenues collected through wage and payroll taxes. Current projections on wage growth and workforce population, however, do not look promising. It is estimated that the average real rate of return for an individual is about 1 to 2 percent (Stephenson, Horlacher, and Colander, 1995). According to some, the increased rate of return from investing in private capital would be a more popular retirement program by substantially improving retirement benefits (Bosworth 1997).

Problems with Privatization

While there are compelling reasons for privatizing, there may also be compelling obstacles. One obstacle is that a pay-as-you-go format is an effective tool for dealing with uncertainty. For example, an unanticipated high rate of inflation might severely reduce the standard of living for retirees. A federal PAYG system allows the government to protect the purchasing power of payments (Thompson and Upp, 1997).

Likewise, a system based on private investment in equities is likely to cause significant pro-cyclical movements in spending by the elderly, increasing the severity and duration of recessions. If stock market prices fall, the income of retirees will also fall. Their reduced spending will further dampen the economy, increasing the procyclical tendencies of the business cycle. A federal PAYG system is clearly countercyclical, at least on the downside: the continued fixed injections of spending that come from predictable monthly benefits checks put a floor on how far down aggregate spending can be driven in a recession.

Conclusion

As things stand, at some point in the not so distant future, the OASI program will be unable to meet its financial obligations. Something has to be done. The alternatives that have been proposed range from minor (change funding and benefit formulas, push retirement ages back a year or two, and restrict cost of living adjustments) to major (create a universal government-run pension system which invests in private companies and earns a rate of return determined by the appreciation of the stock market). Others think we should scrap the whole thing, and either allow people to make their own provisions for retirement, or (less radically) allow people to direct their mandatory contributions to a private retirement fund of their choice, with only minimal licensing and oversight from the federal government.

What do you think? What is really the problem? What solutions does that problem definition suggest, and which does it rule out?

NOTES

1. The case was written primarily by Michael Ensley of Duke University.
2. Or, maybe because of the impeachment!
3. The following information regarding benefits and financing is drawn from Brain (1991), the Concord Coalition (1998) and Stephenson, Horlacher, and Colander (1995).
4. It is interesting to note that the opposite is not true: if the CPI decreases, it has no effect on the social security benefits.
5. See Paul Light (1984) for background on the passage and early history of social security.
6. The Board of Trustees is made up of six members: the secretary of the treasury, the secretary of labor, the secretary of health and human services, the commissioner of social security, and the two public trustees (appointed by the president and confirmed by the Senate to represent the public).
7. The information in this section is obtained from the Concord Coalition (http://www.concordcoalition.org).
8. It should be noted that there are reform proposals that advocate a "two-pillar" or a partially privatized system. The two-pillar programs are of two types: "carve-out" and "add-on" programs. Carve-out programs divert some of the current social security revenues to private retirement accounts. Add-on programs solicit more funds to invest in private retirement accounts.
9. Cited in Stephenson, Horlacher, and Colander, 1995, p. 10.

~9~

Discounting I:
Expected Values,
Probability, and Risk

This final section of the book teaches some skills that you will need to be able to understand (and in some cases even just to read!) policy analysis research. The two main topics covered are discounting and cost-benefit analysis. In general terms, "discounting" means to count at less than face value. Since there are two fundamentally different ways to "discount" values to be used for analysis, a separate chapter is devoted to each. This chapter considers discounting based on uncertainty, or risk, and introduces the concepts of probability and expected value. The following chapter, chapter 10, considers discounting over time, and introduces the concepts of discount rates and present value. The final substantive chapter, chapter 11, covers the various techniques known as "cost-benefit analysis," which put together the concepts of discounting and the indirect estimation of values for costs and benefits.

Risk Discounting Using Probability

Two examples can be used to illustrate expected value.

1. *A simple lottery.* Suppose I offer to play a game with you. The game looks like this: I will flip a coin, which is "fair" (i.e., it is equally likely to come up heads or tails), and then observe which side of the coin is up.[1] If the coin comes up heads, I will pay you $5; if the coin comes up tails, I will pay you $1. How much would you pay me to be able to play this game? Alternatively, if I offer to play this game with you for free, what is the value (in money terms) you should place on the gift?

2. *Russian roulette—Is there a "winner?"* You've probably heard of the game "Russian roulette," where one bullet is placed in a revolver (with six chambers, so that five chambers are empty, and one contains the live bullet). Each "player" then spins the chamber, and without checking the gun places the barrel against his temple and pulls the trigger. Suppose you play Russian roulette, and survive; did you win?

*Expected Value—The Central Analytic Concept
in Probabilistic Discounting*

To find the answer to the first question (the coin flip, with heads yielding $5 and tails yielding $1), one has to weigh, or *discount*, the potential outcomes. Discounting works this way: You define the expected value of an occurrence, which we will call by its technical name, an **event**. The **expected value** of an event is the value of the event, discounting by its likelihood of occurrence.

Expected value of heads = (value of heads)× (probability of heads)
                         = I pay you $5   × ½

Expected value of tails = (value of tails) × (probability of tails)
                         = I pay you $1   × ½

Now, we can determine the expected value of playing the game:

Expected value of game   = ($5 × ½) + ($1 × ½)
                         = $2.50 + $0.50
                         = $3.00

We have to be a little careful here, because the expected value of the game may not be the same as its value to any one individual. *You* might pay more, or less, than $3 for the privilege of playing the game. Some people love to take risks, and are willing to pay for the privilege. If you really enjoy gambling, you might be willing to pay more than $5, the largest amount you could expect to win in my game. Other people avoid risk whenever they can, and might be willing to pay no more than the $1 that is the minimum payment they can expect to receive from playing the game.

Then just what is expected value good for? After all, saying the game is "worth" $3 seems silly, since the only possible outcomes are either $1 or $5 payoffs. The answer is that expected value is the *average* value, or the amount you would win on average if you played the game many times. Suppose you played the game one hundred times, and that the fifty-fifty odds of heads or tails is exactly correct. That means that you would win $5 fifty times, and $1 fifty times. Your total winnings would be $300, and $300 divided by 100 is $3. So even though you never win $3 in any one play of the game, on average you win exactly $3. Consequently, one way to think of expected value is the amount of money that would make you *indifferent* between playing the risky game and taking the expected value as a sure payoff, assuming you neither like nor dislike risk.

Notice that expected value does not require that the coin is fair, or that the probabilities of "events" are equally likely. Imagine that I have a coin that is weighted in an extreme way, so that it comes up tails 60 percent of the time, and heads only 40 percent of the time. What would the expected value of my game be then?

$$\text{Expected value of game} = (\$5 \times 0.4) + (\$1 \times 0.6)$$
$$= \$2.00 + \$0.60$$
$$= \$2.60$$

Obviously, this tells us something about games of chance: If I tell you I am using a fair coin, and charge you $3 per turn to play, I can make money if the true expected value of the game is less than $3. That doesn't mean I will never have to make the $5 payoff; in fact, in this example, I have to pay you $5 40 percent of the time. But if we play the game one hundred times, your average payoff is only $2.60, meaning that you will have won $260 in the one hundred games. Since you paid me what you thought was the expected value of $3 per game, I can expect to make $40 ($3.00 taken in minus $2.60 paid out) every time someone plays my game one hundred times.

Now let's consider the second question, about Russian roulette. It may seem a macabre example (I am not suggesting anyone really should play this game, as an experiment: DON'T!), but it is surprisingly relevant to the study of public policy. When decisions are made under conditions of uncertainty, our evaluation of the decision may be very different from our preferences over outcomes. More simply, suppose you decide to play Russian roulette, so you pick up the revolver, place a bullet in one chamber, and then spin the cylinder. You close your eyes, put the gun to your head, and pull the trigger. SNAP goes the hammer on the empty chamber. Did you make a good decision? Of course not: you just got lucky! At the time you pulled the trigger, there was a one in six chance you would be killed. The fact that you dodged this bullet (the outcome was good) is irrelevant to the evaluation of the choice (the decision to play was bad).

False Reasoning in the Evaluation of Choice

Much of the point of risk discounting in policy analysis is to evaluate decisions based on probabilities before we know what is going to happen. After the fact, when it turns out that we avoided disaster through dumb luck, it is wrong to infer that the decision was a good one. Yet this sort of argument is made all the time, and it takes two forms:

- A leader pursues a strategy that places many people at risk. But after the fact it turns out that we got lucky, and the policy didn't cause the disaster that any reasonable person would have expected. The leader is praised, when it is quite possible he should be fired.
- A leader pursues a strategy that accurately captures the information he had at the time. In particular, given the probabilities of events and the policies the leader chose, any reasonable person would have expected success. But after the fact it turns out that disaster happened anyway, because of events beyond the leader's control. The leader is fired, when he should be praised.

Let's consider an example of each of these sorts of decisions, from the era of the civil rights conflicts in the late 1950s and early 1960s in the United States.

Example 1: Bad Decision, Good Outcome. In *Parting the Waters: America in the King Years 1954–63,* Taylor Branch tells a story about a decision by two civil rights leaders in Birmingham, Alabama, in 1961, to take an action that seemed obviously too risky. James Bevel and Charles Billups were at a mass meeting in a church in Birmingham. The civil rights advocates were growing restive under a self-imposed "truce," temporarily putting off confrontations with the Birmingham police chief, Bull Connor, and his policemen, firemen, and attack dogs. Suddenly, without warning or obvious provocation, several of the African-American activists were arrested on the front steps of the church.

> . . . The police were getting nervous, nasty, and unpredictable. Perhaps Bull Connor, interpreting the truce as a sign of weakness in the movement, was trying to intimidate the Negroes into submission. As the police hauled the [arrested activists] off to jail, an angry-looking James Bevel strode swiftly to the pulpit . . . "We're tired of this mess!" he shouted. "Let's all get up!" Waving his arms, he directed the packed congregation to march around inside the church and down to the city jail a few blocks away. They would encourage the movement prisoners inside, while showing the police that they were not afraid. . . .

> Off in the wings, [other leaders] huddled to argue. . . . Every circumstance [was] unfavorable: [Martin Luther] King was out of town; the congregation was mostly adults, in their Sunday clothes, unprepared for jail; and rough treatment by Connor's police might puncture morale before the [already planned] climactic jail marches the next day. (p. 66)

Because he could not afford to be jailed and miss the march the next day, Bevel could not lead the column now spontaneously walking toward downtown. Another volunteer preacher, Charles Billups, was selected. Billups hurried to the head of the march. In front of the city jail, police cars, paddy wagons, and fire trucks converged to block the way. As the first marchers reached the barricade, Bull Connor strode to a position to direct the counterstrike.

> Drawing close, Billups knelt on the pavement, and many of the two thousand behind followed his lead. . . . After a brief prayer, Billups stood up and shouted loudly enough for the distant reporters to hear, "Turn loose your dogs! We will stand here 'til we die!" Many of the Negroes within range trembled, and a woman keeled over in a faint, but after a few seconds some noticed that the fireman remained paralyzed at his tripod, unable to blast the preacher [with his fire hose] at point blank range. To

save face, Connor repeated his order to fire in a hushed, angry growl. Some heard him say "Dammit! Turn on the hoses" before the silence swallowed him up, too. (p. 67)

Now, Bull Connor had been particularly ferocious in the weeks leading up to this incident. When Billups issued his challenge, in a march that was unplanned and in fact poorly executed, from a tactical perspective, there was every reason to believe that the marchers would, in fact, be attacked and that some of them might even be killed. As it turned out, as Branch writes, "Nonviolence had touched the fireman's heart," and the unnamed man working the water cannon refused to follow the order to start the assault.

Was this a good *outcome*? Undoubtedly. The courage of the marchers, and the miracle of the symbolic victory, were recounted all over the civil rights movement. Was it a good *decision*? Absolutely not. First Bevel, and then Billups, courted disaster; they were brave, but they risked the bodies and lives of followers who had not expected, and had not consented, to face such a desperate situation. It is true that taking such chances may be the essence of what we call leadership, *if you win*. The two young preachers deserve our admiration, and they are justly remembered for their courage. But from the perspective of probabilities, they were also a little bit lucky.

Example 2: Good Decision, Bad Outcome. It is possible to make the right decisions, in terms of probabilities and the information the chooser has, and still have things turn out wrong. That is, even "good" decisions can lead to bad outcomes, in the face of uncertainty. There are things that are beyond the control of the chooser; one of the most obvious is the weather. Consider the account below, excerpted from Harold A. Winters (1998) of the *kamikaze*, or "divine wind." A bad (unlucky) draw from the distribution of possible weather conditions foiled the otherwise probably correct choices of Kublai Khan, leader of the Yuan dynasty of Mongol lords of China, in his attacks on the islands of Japan.

Kublai Khan first attempted to conquer the Japanese through diplomacy. In 1268 he sent envoys via Korea to deliver a letter to the Japanese emperor, explaining that subservience to the heaven-decreed emperor of Mongolia would avoid war. . . . By 1274, . . . having no satisfactory response to his demands, Khan, with possibly as many as 40,000 Chinese, Korean, and Mongol troops, gave orders to invade Kyushu. . . . Sailors may have been relieved to learn that the force would not sail until late

November 1274, *when the typhoon season was well over.* . . . On or about 20 November, Khan's force sailed for Kyushu, landing unopposed in Hakata Bay.

. . . On the first day of fighting the invading army forced the Japanese to withdraw into ancient stone fortifications. As evening approached the Japanese remained undefeated and in a favorable defensive position. In contrast, Khan's troops were exposed to the enemy and, possibly fearing a night counterattack, were ordered to withdraw first to the shore and then to the apparent safety of their ships in the harbor. This decision was disastrous for the invaders. That evening a large storm [either a very large mid-latitude cyclone or an even more powerful typhoon] moved northeastward into the Korea Strait and soon destroyed much of Khan's fleet now crowded with warriors who, ironically, had been ordered to board the ships for protection. . . .

. . . Many ships struck rocks and sank. Others foundered offshore. Before the storm had passed, as many as 300 vessels and 13,000 men, or about one-third of the Mongol army, were lost at sea. Meanwhile, the storm that destroyed much of Khan's force became reverently known as the Kamikaze, or Divine Wind, throughout Japan. (Winter, 1998; pp. 8–10; emphasis added)

Khan had done the prudent thing: he had put his forces out of harm's way, on the ships, only to have a freak storm (remember, "typhoon season was well over") blow up and wipe out his army. He had made the right decision, but lost anyway.

To understand how uncertainty discounting really works, we will need to step back now for an overview of the key concepts of probability theory.

Basic Concepts of Probability

The preceding examples showed how incorrect conclusions may be drawn about decisions made under uncertainty. In ordinary speech, we might call such conclusions false inferences. In the movies, detectives and lawyers make "inferences" by applying logic and deduction to a set of facts. As Sherlock Holmes said, in *The Sign of Four*, "When you have eliminated the impossible, whatever remains, *however improbable*, must be the truth" (Doyle, 1890, chap. 6; emphasis in original). The popular meaning of "inference," however, is rather different from its meaning in scientific applications.

In the world of policy analysis, Holmes's approach would be almost exactly backward. We rarely have enough facts to eliminate
alternatives, or policy choices, beyond the shadow of a doubt. Instead of deductive inference, policy analysts must use *statistical* inference, or conclusions based on probabilities. More simply, policy
analysts must focus on expectations about a future that is very uncertain, and probability is the tool used to handle the problem. The earliest interpretation of probability, the "frequentist" view, depended
on the assumption that all "events" were equally likely. This makes
sense if you are analyzing a card game, for example, where you are
trying to predict which card will be drawn from a fully shuffled standard deck of fifty-two cards. If we define an event as the drawing of
any particular card, the chance of drawing that one card is obviously
1 divided by 52, or 0.019. The *frequentist*, or percentage-based, interpretation is obvious: Suppose you shuffled the deck thoroughly,
and then drew the top card. Imagine that there is one card of interest, the ace of clubs. How often would you expect to draw the ace of
clubs? About 1.9 percent of the time, or once in every fifty-two
draws. If you played this little game (shuffle, draw, replace card, repeat) one hundred times, you would expect to draw the ace of clubs
about twice.

But this example shows the problem of uncertainty very clearly:
there is some chance (0.75×10^{-173}) that you might draw the Ace of
Clubs *every single time*! That is, of one hundred trials, you get one
hundred ace of club drawings. Alternatively, there is a pretty good
chance (15 percent, or probability of 0.15) that you won't draw the
ace of clubs even *once* in one hundred draws. How can I make these
calculations? Let's see.

First, the formal definition of probability, assuming all events are
equally likely:

$$P_x = \frac{\text{number of ways x can occur}}{\text{total number of events}}$$

In words, the probability *P* of an event *x* is the ratio of the number of
ways *x* can occur, divided by the total number of events that can possibly occur. In the card drawing example, there was only one way that
the event of interest (drawing the ace of clubs) could occur in any
given trial, and the "universe" of possible occurrences is the fifty-two
members of the deck, or set, of cards.

$$P_{\text{ace of clubs}} = \frac{1}{52}$$

Of course, probabilities can be calculated for less restrictive examples, also. Imagine that we are interested in the event of drawing an ace, of any suit (hearts, diamonds, clubs, or spades). Since there are four aces in the deck, there are four ways the event of interest (draw an ace) can occur. There are still fifty-two cards, of course, but the probability of drawing an ace of any suit is much higher than drawing the

$$P_{ace} = \frac{4}{52} = \frac{1}{13}$$

ace of clubs.

We can now summarize the basic properties of probabilities, and construct some rules for calculating and interpreting probabilities of more complex events.

The Three Basic Rules of Probability

Rule No. 1: *If an event is possible, it has a positive probability.* This seems simple. It is obvious that no probability can be negative, and the very definition of "possible" implies that there must be at least one way the event of interest can occur. Consequently, since both the numerator and the denominator in the probability ratio are positive, the probability must be positive.

But keep in mind that just because something is possible doesn't mean the probability of its occurrence is positive in a practical sense. Recall what I said earlier about the chance of drawing the ace of clubs from a thoroughly shuffled deck one hundred times in a row: it could happen. The probability, however, is only 0.0000 . . . (One hunded seventy-two zeroes in all) . . . 075! It is true that this number is positive, but for almost any purpose that matters it is indistinguishable from zero. This brings us back to the Sherlock Holmes quote about "eliminating the impossible": most things aren't *literally* impossible in policy. But we have to eliminate the extremely unlikely, and that means making an educated guess.

Rule No. 2: *The probability of any event is less than, or at most equal to, 1.* This really *is* obvious: at most, the event of interest constitutes the entire set of possible outcomes, in which case the probability of that event is 1.

Rule No. 3: *The sum of the probabilities of all possible outcomes must* *sum to 1.* We already know that the sum of probabilities can't be more than 1 (by rule no. 2). But then *something* has to happen, and it has to be one of the events that is possible (i.e., accounted for in the denominator of the probability ratio). So, the sum of the probabilities of all possible events can't be less than 1, either. Since it can't be more, or less, than 1, the sum of all probabilities must be *exactly* 1. In our playing card example, it is easy to see how this works. The probability of drawing any one card was $1/52$. If you sum up this probability across fifty-two cards, you get: $52 \times (1/52) = 1$.

We can summarize the three rules in mathematical language, now that we know what each means. For an arbitrary event x:

Rule no. 1: $P_x \geq 0$ for all x. If x is possible, then $P_x > 0$.
Rule no. 2: $P_x \leq 0$
Rule no. 3: $\sum_i^n P_{xi} = 1$, where "$i = 1$ to n" includes all conceivable events (whether event x_i is literally possible or not).

Counting Rules

The key to coming up with guesses about probabilities is to be able to use theoretical shortcuts to make predictions. In the examples so far, we have been able to count the number of events of interest, and to count the number of total events, so that the calculation of the probability ratio is easy. But that wouldn't have to be true. Suppose (sticking with our playing cards example) you wanted to know the chances of getting four of a kind in a standard five-card poker hand. That is, if I deal you five cards at random from a well-shuffled deck, what are the chances that you have four 2's, or four 3's, or four aces, and so on?

This problem is easy conceptually, but computationally very complex, or at least tedious. First, let's cut through the suspense: the answer is 0.00024. That means that, if you dealt yourself a million five-card poker hands, and didn't cheat or give yourself any "wild" cards, you would get (on average) 240 four-of-a-kind hands out of the whole lot. On a more intuitive level, we would expect a natural four-of-a-kind hand only once every 4,165 hands chosen at random.

Now, how did I do that? Did I deal myself every possible poker hand? No: there are 2,598,960 different possible hands (where a "hand" is defined as an unordered set of five cards, chosen randomly from the deck of fifty-two, without replacement). Dealing all those out would take all day, twenty-four hours a day, for more than fifteen months![2] Obviously, this is not what I did. Instead, I used **counting rules** to arrive at the answer. I will describe the basics of counting rules, and then show how the use of those rules transforms the "How many four-of-a-kind hands?" puzzle into a much more manageable problem.

The general point is that, as the number of possible outcomes increases, it would become tiresome to count all possible outcomes. Let's start with something simple: an experiment involving coin flips. If we flip three coins, we have eight possible outcomes. We can list all eight, using the convention that "H" means heads, "T" means tails, and the place in the order corresponds to the coin being flipped, 1, 2, or 3. In that case, the possible outcomes look like the list in Figure 9.1.

FIGURE 9.1
Possible Outcomes in a Three-Coin-Tossing Experiment

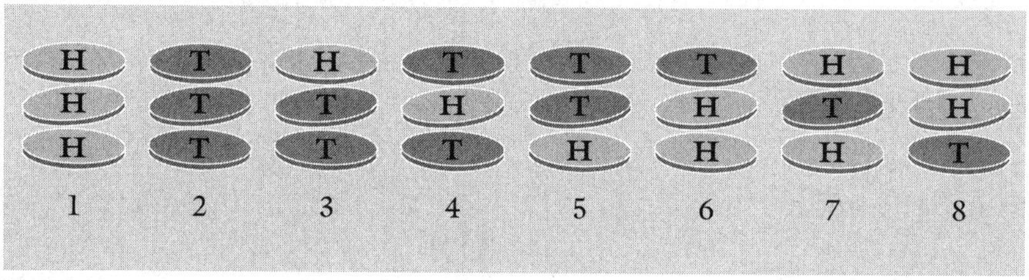

Now, suppose we add another coin to the experiment. Listing the possible outcomes gets harder, since each of eight outcomes with three coins now goes with "H" on the new coin, and each of the eight goes with "T" on the new coin. That means four coins give us 16 outcomes to list. It gets worse, real fast: five coins imply 32 different outcomes, six coins mean 64, seven coins result in 128 possible outcomes, and so on.

This approach (listing the possible outcomes, and counting them) is called the *posterior* frequentist approach. The alternative (using counting rules to calculate the number of events implied by a set of circumstances) is the *a priori* approach. A priori probabilities are just as accurate as posterior probabilities, provided you apply the right counting rule. And that is the hard part. The most important step in calculating probabilities using counting rules is the recognition of the appropriate rule. There are two main types:

• **Combinations:** Combinations problems are those where only the total number of objects, or occurrences, is of interest, and the order in which the objects are obtained, or events occur, is irrelevant to the problem.

- **Permutations:** Permutation problems are those where the order, or sequence, of events matters. Generally, there are more permutations than combinations in a given number of draws, or trials, because there are more ways an event can be defined if the order is part of the definition of the event.

The coin-flipping experiment from Figure 9.1 is obviously a "permutations" problem, because we were concerned with the value (H or T) on each of the coins in sequence, not the total number of H or T throws. It is possible to represent the combinations problem with three coins, of course, by defining an event as the number (not the order) of heads obtained. The possible events conceived as combinations are depicted in Figure 9.2.

FIGURE 9.2
"Combinations" Outcomes from Flipping Three Coins

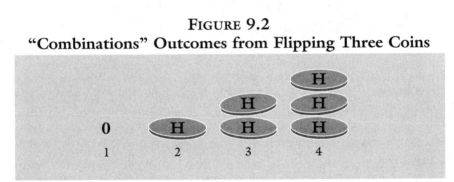

Combinations. In many situations, the order of selection is not important. Consider a simple example, with more alternatives than the H or T we get from flipping coins. Suppose we have four foods: apples (A), berries (B), cherries (C), and dirt (D). Imagine that there is exactly one can (all cans are identical as far as look and feel) of A, B, C, and D in a box. A blindfolded person draws one of these objects with each hand (which hand draws which can, doesn't matter). The problem is to calculate the probability that the person will be holding object A and object B, where the *order of the selection is not important.* Clearly, this is a combination problem. (Subjects who recognize this will get to eat the apples, berries, or cherries. Students who don't—well, I hope they like dirt.)

We could just count the number of possible outcomes to calculate the probability of selecting A and B, disregarding order (that is, the event "AB" and the event "BA" are indistinguishable). In fact, let's just go nuts . . . let's *do* that counting, just as a check. We can depict the complete set of possible outcomes as follows:

FIGURE 9.3
Outcomes of the Apples, Berries, Cherries, Dirt
Experiment (Combinations)

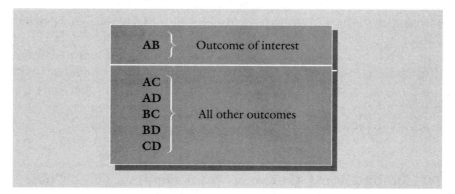

As Figure 9.3 illustrates, there are six possible combinations of the four food items, taken two at a time. It is important to remember that the experiment is not conducted in sequence, with one can selected, its contents recorded, and then replaced in the box so the second can be selected. This process would of course be very different, and is called *selection without replacement*: two cans are chosen, so that it is impossible to get an outcome of the sort "AA" or "DD."

For no particular reason, I have decided that the outcome "AB" (apples and berries) is the outcome of interest. It is pretty clear that the chances of this happening (assuming that all the six possible outcomes are equally likely) is:

$$P_{A\&B} = 1/6 = .167.$$

Of course, the whole point of this was to avoid actual counting. The fact that this is a combinations problem means that we can use the combinations formula to calculate the number of possible combinations. This formula is read "combinations of N, take k."

$$C_k^N = \frac{N!}{k! \, (N-k)!}$$

Where:

N equals the *total* number of objects in the set
k equals the number of objects to be *selected* (taken) from the set.
x! means "factorial," or the product of all the numbers from *x*
down to 1 in sequence, one at a time. For example, $4! = 4×3×2×1$.[3]
C is the "combinations" operator, so that you know what formula
to use.

In our example, $N = 4$ and $k = 2$. Therefore:

$$C_2^4 = \frac{4!}{2!(4-2)!} = \frac{4×3×2×1}{(2×1)(2×1)} = \frac{24}{4} = 6$$

Using one formula may not seem a lot easier than counting (the
formula seems intimidating), but for complex problems it is much
easier. For example, suppose you went into a small grocery store,
and selected five bar-coded items at random from the six hundred
items in the store. How many possible market baskets of food items
might you come up with? You might be tempted to answer, "A
whole lot!" but with the combinations formula we know the answer:
637,263,000,000! That *is* a whole lot, but that's the point: doing this
problem using a posterior counting technique would take the rest of
your life.

For the poker hands problem, the appropriate combinations formula is obvious:

$$C_5^{52} = \frac{52!}{5!(47)!} = \frac{(52×51×50×49×48)}{(5×4×3×2×1)} = 2,598,960$$

There are thirteen possibilities for the four of a kind (aces, 2's, 3's,
etc.), and for each of the thirteen pip values there are forty-eight possibilities for the "other" (i.e., the fifth) card. Consequently, the odds
of getting a randomly selected four of a kind is:

$$P_{\text{four of a kind}} = \frac{13 × 48}{C_5^{52}} = \frac{624}{2,598,960} = 0.00024$$

Permutations. In some problems facing analysts, the order of selection matters. Imagine that we have the same four foods—apples (A),
berries (B), cherries (C), and dirt (D)—available. A blindfolded per-

son draws one of these cans with her *right* hand, and then draws another one with her *left* hand: here, the hand holding the can does matter. Our problem is to calculate the probability that the person will be holding can A in her right hand and can B in her left. Getting B first, then A, doesn't count; that is the nature of a permutation: *permutations involve selecting the precise order of objects in the outcome of an experiment.*

As with combinations, we could simply count the number of possible outcomes to calculate the probability of selecting A in the right hand and B in the left. Thus, the total possible outcomes include the one item of interest (AB), and eleven other possible events, as listed in Figure 9.4.

FIGURE 9.4

**Outcomes of the Apples, Berries, Cherries, Dirt
Experiment (Permutations)**

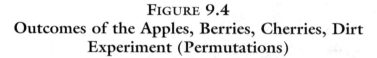

AB }	Outcome of interest
AC	
AD	
BA	
BC	
BD	
CA }	All other outcomes
CB	
CD	
DA	
DB	
DC	

Out of twelve possible (and equally likely) outcomes, then, we are interested in only one—AB. Therefore, the probability of selecting AB is:

$$P_{AB} = \frac{1}{12} = 0.083$$

But we wanted to learn the formula for permutations just so we could avoid counting. Here is the formula:

$$P^N_k = \frac{N!}{(N-k)!}$$

You probably noticed immediately that the difference between the formula for combinations and the formula for permutations is the presence of an extra term ($k!$) in the denominator of the combinations formula. Since this could be a fairly large number, you would conclude that there are more, maybe many more, permutations than there are combinations, for the same N and k. And you would be right: whereas the combination AB describes all the possibilities, there are two permutations for the same alternatives: AB and BA. Where ABC is the only combination we need to list, there are *six* permutations: ABC, ACB, BAC, BCA, CAB, and CBA.

In our present example, $N = 4$ and $k = 2$. Therefore:

$$P^4_2 = \frac{4!}{(4-2)!} = \frac{4 \times 3 \times 2 \times 1}{2 \times 1} = \frac{24}{2} = 12$$

Once again, we get the same answer (12) from the formula that we got by counting the whole thing out. But then, if we didn't, we probably wouldn't be talking about all this in the first place.

The Logic and Language of Probability

Probability logic concerns the ways in which events relate to one another, both in terms of definition and in the likelihood of their occurrence. The descriptions of "ways events relate to one another" has its own language. That language, and its rules, may seem intimidating at first. But as with any language, some study reveals conventions of grammar and syntax that make the language work.

The Probability of a Single Event

As you have already noticed, when we are concerned with the probability of only one event, we symbolize the event with a subscript, and use "P" to represent the probability "operator":

P_A = The probability that event A occurs

Example.[4] Suppose you take a first-year physics class, required for both pre-meds and engineering majors. The distribution of all sixty-five students in the class, regarding both whether they live in your dorm and whether they are pre-meds, is shown in Table 9.1.

TABLE 9.1
Events Describing Identities of All 65 Students in Physics 101

From Your Dorm?	Pre-Med Major?		
	Yes	No	Totals
Yes	10	1	11
No	19	35	54
Totals	29	36	65

What is the probability that another student in the class lives in the same dormitory that you do? Since there are sixty-five students in the class, and eleven are from your dorm, then the probability that a randomly selected student from the class will be from your dorm is:

$$P_{dorm} = 11/65 = 0.17$$

The Probability of Either of Two Events Occurring

Suppose we are concerned with the probability of either (or both) of two events occurring. Logically, we need a way to symbolize a concept you all know: "or." Mathematicians represent "or" with the symbol for **union**, which is $\cup$. It works like this:

$P_{(A \cup B)}$ = the probability that A occurs, or that B occurs, or both

Technically, the above expression is read "the probability of A union B."

Example. What is the probability that a student in your physics class is from your dorm *or* is a pre-med major? We know that twenty-nine of the students are pre-med, and eleven are from your dorm. Does this mean that there are forty students who meet one condition or the other? No—that would be double-counting. To get the union right, we have to add up the boxes in Table 9.1 that satisfy the conditions of interest: There are ten students who are both from the dorm and pre-med; there are nineteen more pre-meds who are not from the dorm; and there is one person who is from the dorm who is not pre-med. Consequently,

$$P_{\text{dorm}\cup\text{pre-med}} = (10 + 19 + 1)/65 = 0.46$$

The Probability of Two Events Both Occurring

When we are interested in the probability of two events occurring together, we are restricting the event of interest to the overlap, or "intersection," of two separate occurrences. This is the logical equivalent of "and," and we use the symbol $\cap$ for intersection:

$P_{(A\cap B)}$ = the probability that both A and B occur

This expression is read "the probability of A *intersection* B."

Example. What is the probability that a student in Physics 101 is both from your dorm and pre-med? This one is pretty easy: it is the overlap between the conditions "Dorm: Yes" and "Pre-med: Yes" in Table 9.1. There are ten students who meet this condition, so:

$$P_{\text{dorm}\cap\text{pre-med}} = 10/65 = 0.15$$

Conditional Probability

When we are interested in the probability of one event, given that another event has already occurred, we are interested in *conditional* probability. The fact that one event has already occurred is symbolized by a vertical line, like this:

$P_{(A|B)}$ = the probability of A, given that B happened already

More simply, this expression means "the probability of A *given* B."

Example. What is the probability that a Physics 101 student is a pre-med major, given that he is *not* from your dorm? Overall, the chance of a randomly selected student being pre-med is 29/65, or 0.45. But if you know the student is not from your dorm, you have more information. There are fifty-four students in the class who are not from your dorm, and of these nineteen are pre-med. So we know that:

$$P_{\text{pre-med | not from dorm}} = 19/54 = 0.35$$

Summary: Four Types of Probability Questions

We have considered four types of events, and four distinct notational conventions to indicate the type of probability question being asked.

Simple events: $P_{\text{pre-med}}$ = probability that student in Physics 101 is pre-med
Union of Events: $P_{\text{pre-med} \cup \text{dorm}}$ = probability that student in Physics 101 is pre-med and/or is from your dorm
Intersection of events: $P_{\text{pre-med} \cap \text{dorm}}$ = probability that student in Physics 101 is pre-med and is from your dorm
Conditional events: $P_{\text{pre-med | not dorm}}$ = probability that student in Physics 101 is pre-med given that the student is not from your dorm

We need to take a brief detour now to develop the logical machinery to deal with the compound events (unions, intersections, or conditionals). As you have seen, it is possible to make mistakes by *double-counting* in compound events. To solve this problem, and to identify the structure of calculating probabilities more accurately, it is useful to state some general rules.

General Rules of Probability

In this section, I will define four rules of calculating probabilities, and give examples of each. The four important concepts are independence, chi-square test, joint occurrence (intersection) and joint occurrence (union).

Independence

Two events are said to be *independent* if the occurrence of one event is unrelated to the probability of occurrence of the other. This intuitive definition can be made more precise.

Independence implies that both of the following are true:

$$P_{(A|B)} = P_A$$
$$P_{(B|A)} = P_B$$

One more time, because this is important: Two events are independent if knowledge about the occurrence of one does not help us (at all) predict the probability of the other.

Independence is tricky, but fundamental. It is worthwhile to think of an example of an event that is independent, as well as one that is not.

Example of independence. Suppose you want to know whether a card randomly selected from a standard deck is an ace. While you are thinking, I give you a hint: the card is red! After digesting this news, you mock me: "That isn't a hint! The fact that the card is red has no impact on the chance it is an ace!" You knew this because the probability of selecting an ace from a deck of cards is:

$$P_{(ace)} = 4/52 = .0769$$

But the probability of selecting an ace, after you get the "hint" that the card is red is:

$$P_{ace|red} = 2/26 = .0769$$

In terms of our definition, this means

$$P_{ace|red} = P_{red}$$

So, since the events are independent, information about one gives you no hint about the probability of the other.

Example where events are not independent. I have already given you an example; do you remember? Overall, the chance of a randomly selected student in our hypothetical Physics 101 class being pre-med was 29/65, or 0.45. But if you know the student is not from your dorm, this number was not correct. There were fifty-four students in the class who were not from your dorm, and of these nineteen were pre-med. But then we have:

$$P_{\text{pre-med | not from dorm}} = 19/54 = 0.35$$
$$P_{\text{pre-med}} = 29/65 = 0.45$$
$$P_{\text{pre-med | not from dorm}} \neq P_{\text{pre-med}}$$

In this case, knowing "not from dorm" really is a hint, because it gives you a more accurate guess about the probability that a randomly selected student is pre-med. More simply, then, "dorm" and "pre-med" are not independent.

A Test for Independence: The Chi-Square. What we have established is that if two events are not independent, then the conditional probabilities will differ from the overall probability of each event. But how "different" is different? To determine this, analysts use a "statistic" called the **chi-square** (χ^2) **statistic**. Recall the numbers from Table 9.1, reproduced as Table 9.2, with row, column, and cell proportions.

TABLE 9.2
**Distribution of Students, and Probabilities,
for 65 Students in Physics 101**

From Your Dorm?	Pre-Med Major?		
	Yes	*No*	*Totals*
Yes	10 (0.15)	1 (0.02)	11 (0.17)
No	19 (0.29)	35 (0.54)	54 (0.83)
Totals	29 (0.44)	36 (0.56)	65 (1.00)

There appears to be some pattern to the process of assignment of students to dorms. One possibility is that students have self-selected (lots of pre-meds hang out together, requested each other as roommates, and ended up in the same dorm). Alternatively, the college housing administrator may consciously assign students with similar majors to the same dorm. In any case, it is clear from Table 9.2 that the likely major of students in Physics 101 can be predicted based on whether they live in your dorm:

$$P_{\text{pre-med}} = 29/65 = 0.45$$
$$P_{\text{pre-med | not from dorm}} = 19/54 = 0.35$$
$$P_{\text{pre-med | from dorm}} = 10/11 = 0.91$$

To calculate the chi-square, what we need is a benchmark, something to compare with the actual numbers in Table 9.2. We need to answer the question, What would the proportions look like if "dorm" and "pre-med" were perfectly independent?" You can immediately see that the answer is this: Independence would require that the row (column) proportions do not depend on which column (row) the cell is in.

You could figure this out by hand, but once again we have a useful formula that will save you the trouble. The chi-square statistic measures the extent of the difference between the observed values in a table and the hypothetical values that would appear in the table if the data exhibited perfect independence. First, we need a formula for calculating the values in the table assuming independence:

$$\text{Expected cell value given independence} = \frac{n_r \times n_c}{n}$$

Let's call this "expected cell value" the ECV_{ij}, where the subscript i tells us what row we are in, and the j denotes the column. The formula allows us to add some ECV's (in parentheses) to Table 9.2, for the sake of comparison.

TABLE 9.3
Expected Cell Values (ECV's) and Actual Values for Distribution of Students in Physics 101

From Your Dorm?	Pre-Med Major?		
	Yes	*No*	*Totals*
Yes	10 (5)	1 (6)	11
No	19 (24)	35 (30)	54
Totals	29	36	65

At the risk of overstating the obvious, the actual and expected cell values are very different in Table 9.3. There are far "too many" premeds who are also from your dorm for these two characteristics to be independent. But we still have a problem, because we don't know how many "too many" really is. We are in danger of committing the fallacy of "interocular inference": the difference seems so big, it strikes you between the eyes!

The chi-square is the perfect cure for interocular inference. A difference that strikes one person between the eyes may look relatively small, and may seem to be the product of simple random variation, to someone else. But the chi-square is an objective, agreed-upon standard. It is calculated like this:

$$\chi^2 \text{ (table)} = \sum_i \sum_j \left[\left(\frac{ACV_{ij} - ECV_{ij}}{ECV_{ij}} \right)^2 \right]$$

where:

$\sum_i$ is the sum over all i rows

$\sum_j$ is the sum over all j columns

ACV_{ij} = actual cell value in the ith row and jth column

ECV_{ij} = expected cell value in the ith row and jth column

This means that if there are two rows and two columns, there would be four terms to add up:

$$\left(\frac{ACV_{11} - ECV_{11}}{ECV_{11}} \right)^2 + \left(\frac{ACV_{12} - ECV_{12}}{ECV_{12}} \right)^2 + \left(\frac{ACV_{21} - ECV_{21}}{ECV_{21}} \right)^2 + \left(\frac{ACV_{22} - ECV_{22}}{ECV_{22}} \right)^2$$

In words, you calculate the difference between the actual and expected (assuming independence) cell values as a percentage of the ECV's, square them, and then add them up. To use the chi-square statistic, once upon a time you needed a book with a chi-square table, but now the easiest thing to do is use Excel™, or some other spreadsheet program. For Excel™, you will need two pieces of information: the value of the chi-square statistic, and the "degrees of freedom," where degrees of freedom for a table like this can be calculated using the following formula:

Degrees of freedom for χ^2 statistic: (number of rows − 1) × (number of columns − 1)

Let's see what the chi-square statistic is for Table 9.3:

$$\chi^2 \text{ (table)} = \left[\frac{10-5}{5} \right]^2 + \left[\frac{1-6}{6} \right]^2 + \left[\frac{19-24}{24} \right]^2 + \left[\frac{35-30}{30} \right]^2$$
$$= 1 + 0.7 + 0.04 + 0.03 = 1.77$$

The degrees of freedom for the table is:

$$DF = (2-1) \times (2-1) = 1 \times 1 = 1$$

If you look up this number using Excel's™ "CHIDIST (value, DF)" function—what you type is: "CHIDIST (1.77,1)"—you will get a number: 0.183. This means that the difference between the expected and actual values in the table would be observed about 18 percent of the time in an arbitrarily chosen class, *even if the underlying relationship were simply random*. Now, 18 percent is a small number, but not beyond all doubt. Thus (and this is the surprising part), the data in Table 9.3 imply that "dorm" and "pre-med" are *probably* independent, but you can't be sure. The reason this is surprising is that "interocular inference" makes it look like independence fails for sure. The problem is that there aren't enough students from the dorm to make much of a difference; with such small numbers (11 out of 65), strong statistical conclusions are hard to draw. The moral: Don't trust your eyesight; run the test.

Joint Occurrence (Intersection)

The probability that two events both occur is a product of the chance that each occurs. The pun is intended: "Product" means multiplication, and we calculate joint occurrence probabilities with the *multiplication rule*. The general rule is this:

General rule: *The joint probability of two events is equal to the product of the probability of one event and the conditional probability of the other event, given that the first event has occurred. Formally:*

$$P_{(A \cap B)} = P_{(A)} \times P_{(B|A)}$$

If (but only if!) the two events are independent, we can use the definition of independence to simplify matters. The reason is that for independent events:

$$P_{(B|A)} = P_B$$

This would mean that, for independent events, we have a very simple rule:

Specific rule (independence): *The joint probability of two independent events is equal to the product of their separate probabilities. Formally:*

$$P_{(A \cap B)} = P_{(A)} \times P_{(B)}$$

A note of caution: You can use the specific rule (assuming independence) only if you are sure that the two events really are independent. The best examples are simple ones, like this: What is the probability of drawing an ace from a standard deck and then rolling a four on a standard die? The chance of drawing an ace is 4/52; the chance of rolling a 4 is 1/6. So the probability of the joint event is:

$$P_{(4 \cap Ace)} = P_{(4)} \times P_{(Ace|4)} = P_{(4)} \times P_{(Ace)} = 1/6 \times 4/52 = 0.013$$

In all other cases, however, you need to use the general rule. And remember: In the case of independence, the general rule simplifies to the specific rule, so you can't go wrong starting with the general rule every time.

Joint Occurrence (Union)

The intersection rule implies "and": You have to find out how likely it is that one event occurs *and* another occurs. An alternative set of problems, as we have already seen, is presented when one has to deal with "or": the probability that one event occurs, or that another occurs, or that both happen. Such problems are solved with the *addition rule*.

There is a condition on the addition rule, as there was on the multiplication rule. Here, the condition is whether the events are, by definition, mutually exclusive. The general rule is for circumstances where events are not mutually exclusive; the specific rule requires that there be no overlap between the two events.

General rule: *The probability of either of two events is equal to the sum of the probability of one event and the probability of the other event, minus the probability that both occur. Formally:*

$$P_{(A \cup B)} = P_{(A)} + P_{(B)} - P_{(A \cap B)}$$

If (but only if!) the two events are mutually exclusive, we can use the definition of "mutually exclusive" to simplify the problem. "Mutually exclusive" implies that if one event occurs, the other cannot:

$$P_{(A \cap B)} = 0$$

Consequently, if events are mutually exclusive, the rule is simply to sum the probabilities of the individual events.

<u>Specific rule (mutually exclusive):</u> *The probability of two (or many) mutually exclusive events is equal to the sum of their separate probabilities. Formally:*

$$P_{(A \cup B)} = P_{(A)} + P_{(B)}$$

This rule is very intuitive, but it is important to watch for overlaps in the definition of events. For example, suppose you want to know the probability of getting values of 1, 2, 3, or 4 on a standard die thrown on a flat surface. Ignoring the chance of landing in a corner, and assuming the die is fair (each face has a 1/6 chance of turning up), then the probability is:

$$P_{(1 \cup 2 \cup 3 \cup 4)} = 1/6 + 1/6 + 1/6 + 1/6 = 0.67$$

But there are other possibilities. Suppose you are interested in either of the following two events: *even,* or the event that an even number (2, 4, or 6) turns up on the die; and *low,* or the event that a number 3 or smaller (1, 2, 3) turns up on the die. Obviously, even and low are not mutually exclusive, since the event "2" appears in both events. We have to use the general rule:

$$P_{(even \cup low)} = P_{(even)} + P_{(low)} - P_{(even \cap low)}$$
$$= 3/6 + 3/6 - 1/6 = 0.83$$

If we had neglected to subtract the overlap in the two events, we would have concluded that the probability of even or low was 6/6, or 1; that can't be right, since the event "5" is not contained in either the set of even numbers or the set of low numbers on the die.

Now it should be clear why we had to recalculate the probability of being either a pre-med major or a resident in your dorm in the earlier Physics 101 class example. Remember that we had to subtract out the number of students who were both pre-med and from your dorm; these students are exactly those in the intersection of the two events:

$$P_{(pre\text{-}med \cup dorm)} = P_{(pre\text{-}med)} + P_{(dorm)} - P_{(pre\text{-}med \cap dorm)}$$
$$= 29/65 + 11/65 - 10/65 = 0.62$$

A Parable of Warning

Complex problems of conditional probabilities simplify to problems of single events if, but only if, the events are independent. It is easy to misunderstand independence, as some public managers have discovered to their dismay.

There is a story, perhaps apocryphal, about a city manager in a midwestern town who had to make recommendations about rentals of snow removal equipment for the coming year. Historically, the chance of a mild winter was about 0.2, so that one of every five years turned out to be mild, with little snow. The forecasts all called for a mild winter, so she decided to allow the leases to lapse on salt trucks and snow plows. It turned out the winter was, in fact, very mild, and the city saved more than $150,000 by having avoided the unnecessary lease payments. The mayor smiled when he passed the manager in the hall, and asked her, "How's the husband? How are your kids doing?" The mayor and the manager played golf together. Life was very good.

The following year, the chance of a mild winter was the usual 1/5, and there was a debate over whether the city should sign a new lease on snow removal equipment. But the city manager had studied probability a little, and knew that in the region where she lived the probability of two consecutive mild winters was only 0.04. To put it another way, if there was a mild winter, it had been followed by another mild winter in only one of twenty-five previous times. Consequently, she purchased all the lease options she could get her hands on, committing more than $300,000 to ensure that the coming harsh winter could be dealt with by the city.

Of course, the winter turned out to be mild, and the $300,000 (twice the usual expense the city had incurred) was wasted. The mayor snarled in the hall, and scheduled a special meeting of the city council on a "pressing personnel matter." Life was not good at all. The city manager argued that she could not possibly have known, since there was only a 1/25 chance that one mild winter would be followed by another.

Do you see the city manager's mistake?

It depends on the nature of independence. The calculation of the probability of two consecutive mild winters is easy enough:

$$P_{(\text{mild 1} \cap \text{mild 2})} = P_{(\text{mild 1})} \times P_{(\text{mild 2} | \text{mild 1})}$$

The city manager misunderstood the conditional probability. If each winter's weather is an independent event, then the probability of a mild winter is 0.2, regardless of what happened the previous year. One cannot use the product rule to adjust the conditional probability in the middle of the two years. Yet this is just what the city manager did, when she concluded that

$$P_{(mild\ 2|mild\ 1)} = 0.04$$

This is wrong, of course. All the formula means is that:

$$P_{(mild\ 1 \cap mild\ 2)} = P_{(mild\ 1)} \times P_{(mild\ 2|mild\ 1)} = 0.2 \times 0.2 = 0.04$$

More simply, the probability of two consecutive mild winters is 0.04, *before either of the two winters occurs*. After a mild winter, the probability of another mild winter is $1/5$ (just like after a severe winter!) because the severity of each winter's weather is an independent event.[5]

The city manager was fired, of course, and rightly so. One can't blame her for not predicting the weather accurately, but she should have understood the concept of statistical independence. You should, too.

Risk Aversion

Recall from chapter 4 the concept of "preference," based on the comparison of outcomes given certainty about the implications of those outcomes. Now we will extend the notion of preference to incorporate uncertainty. This approach is usually referred to as "risk preferences" or the extent of "risk aversion."

In the classical treatments of risk aversion (von Neumann and Morgenstern, 1947; Luce and Raiffa, 1957), axioms are developed that allow a rigorous treatment of the incorporation of risk into preferences. The axiomatic treatment is more advanced than is required for our purposes, though the interested reader is referred to these readings. I will simply define[6] the three qualitative possibilities for capturing preferences toward risk, with reference to the comparison of "expected value" and "certain value" for the chooser.

Risk neutrality: The chooser is indifferent between a sure payoff *x* and a gamble (lottery) whose expected value is equal to *x*.

Risk acceptance: The chooser is indifferent between a sure payoff *x* and a gamble (lottery) whose expected value is *less*

than x. Alternatively, the chooser always prefers a gamble
with expected value *x* to a sure payoff *x.*

Risk aversion: The chooser is indifferent between a sure payoff
x and a gamble (lottery) whose expected value is *more than*
x. This means the chooser always prefers a sure payoff *x* to a
gamble with expected value *x.*

It is easy to see how these definitions fit into the example I used to
start this chapter. I flip a fair coin, and then observe heads or tails. If
the coin comes up heads, I will pay you $5; if the coin comes up tails,
I will pay you $1. How much would you pay me to be able to play
this game? It depends on your preferences toward risk. The expected
value of the game is $3 (0.5 × $5 + 0.5 × $1); obviously, a risk-
neutral chooser would be willing to pay exactly $3 to play. A risk ac-
cepter would be willing to pay more than $3 to play. The difference
between $3 and the willingness to pay of the risk accepter is an em-
pirical measure of the extent of that person's risk acceptance. Conversely, a risk-averse person would not be willing to pay the expected
value of the game, and would be indifferent between paying some
amount less than $3 and the expected value of $3 from playing.

It is possible to summarize the three categories of attitudes toward
risk in a graph, Figure 9.5. Suppose we define "willingness to pay" as
the amount of money *y* that makes a chooser *precisely indifferent* between playing and not playing, a gamble with expected payoff *x.* If *y*
is less than *x,* the chooser is risk averse. If *y* equals *x,* the chooser is
risk neutral. If *y* exceeds *x,* the chooser is risk accepting.

Two things are worth noting about these concepts, before we

FIGURE 9.5
Expected Value and Risk
The amount a chooser is willing to pay for a game with payoff *x*
is a measure of preferences toward risk.

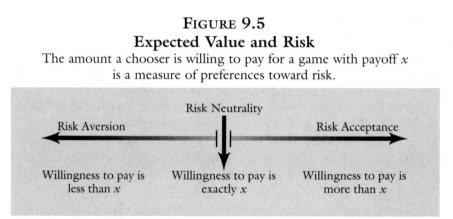

move on. First, if there are many independent trials, it doesn't make much sense to have any "preference" other than risk neutrality. After all, the expected value is the "average" payoff over many trials. Preferences toward risk are more usefully thought of as the attitude of the chooser toward one gamble, or a small number of gambles.[7] Second, it is important not to confuse preferences toward risk with the subjective perception of probabilities. Suppose someone who is normally risk averse "feels lucky." In the language of probability, this statement has no meaning unless the "lucky" person has some way of changing the probabilities of the roulette wheel, the dice, or the sequence of cards in the blackjack deck. Nonetheless, as psychologists have demonstrated,[8] (mis)perceptions of objective probabilities play an important role in determining human behavior in the face of risk. Whether it is possible to model this aspect of choice is an open question, because it would require a theory of systematic errors.

Decision Analysis

We have gone to the trouble of laying out the basic logic and formulaic shortcuts for calculating probabilities because we want to make good decisions. Think back to the comparison of evaluations of *outcomes* and evaluations of *decisions* at the beginning of this chapter. The evaluation of outcomes has to do with preferences, or the aggregation of preferences, a topic which, as I noted above, was covered, or at least introduced, in earlier chapters.

What we are working on now is the problem of making decisions, under uncertainty. All the work we have done to develop your intuition about probabilities is simply a way to evaluate, or "discount," the likely consequences of different courses of action. Stokey and Zeckhauser (1978; 201)[9] use the metaphor of mapmaking to describe decision analysis: "Decision analysis in effect provides us with a road map for picking our way through confusing and uncertain territory. Equally important, it gives us a technique for finding the best route." This metaphor is not just a verbal flourish. Decision analysis is, in most cases, literally the drawing of a map, or "decision tree," to illustrate the consequences of choices and to help identify the best choice.

Before we proceed, we need to make a distinction that has both theoretical and practical consequences. This distinction is the difference between risk and uncertainty. Consider the following two statements:

- I have no idea what the weather will be tomorrow. (Uncertainty)
- There is a 40 percent chance it will be cloudy, and rain, and 40 percent chance it will be cloudy but won't rain, and 20 percent chance of sunshine. (Risk)

In both cases the speaker doesn't know what the weather will be like tomorrow. But in the first case there is no basis for choice, if choices ("Should we go on a picnic?") have different values depending on the realized value of the weather. In the second instance there is enough information for a choice, because we know the distribution of possible outcomes. As Weimer and Vining (1992; 83) put it, "In standard terminology, risk involves contingencies with known probabilities and uncertainty involves contingencies with unknown probabilities."

Outline of the Decision Analysis Process

It is conventional[10] to summarize the "process" of decision analysis as involving multiple steps. For our purposes, we will think of the process as having five steps:

1. *Convert from "uncertainty" to "risk," by assigning probabilities to outcomes, or to the results from intermediate steps between choices and outcomes.*

There are two problems with this step: (a) We generally don't know enough to assign exact probabilities and be confident they are correct, and (b) some "uncertainty" is in fact the result of a lack of *strategic,*[11] rather than *probabilistic,* information.

2. *Identify a set of outcomes that (a) are mutually exclusive, (b) exhaust the set of possibilities, and (c) correspond to the model of cause and effect to be employed in the decision analysis.*

Deciding what outcomes are possible, and determining which courses of action lead to which sets of outcomes (branches of the decision tree), is the key to drawing the "map" of decision analysis.

3. *For the policy being evaluated, or the decision being considered, estimate the value of the outcome if it came to pass.*

There are several possibilities for "valuing" outcomes, but the most obvious ones derive from the willingness of consumers to pay for a benefit. The value of an outcome is then measured by the quantity of consumer surplus that it captures.

4. *Assign probabilities to each of the mutually exclusive outcomes, using the appropriate "intersection" or "union" of events to specify the sequence of intermediate steps which lead to that outcome.*

This step is fairly straightforward, provided that the dependence of probabilities of future events on current choices can be accounted for. In principle, the rules of probability outlined in the first part of this chapter ought to do the trick. In practice, things may be a little more difficult, because the nature of the dependencies among outcomes may be hard to gauge.

5. *Multiply the estimated values of each outcome by the probabilities of the sequence of events which could lead to that outcome to obtain an "expected value" for each feasible course of action.*

It may be possible simply to choose among alternatives based on expected values, but this ignores potential risk aversion in the preferences of the people the analyst is serving. If preferences are risk neutral, the highest expected value should always be chosen. If preferences are risk averse (or, for that matter, risk accepting), then another alternative may be selected.

An Example of Decision Analysis Under Risk

For the sake of simplicity, I will assume risk neutrality in this example. There are arguments about whether risk neutrality is the correct approach for public sector decisions, as we will see in chapter 11, but using it here makes the process easier to understand.

Imagine that a government agency has to choose a disposal technology[12] for "low level radioactive waste" (LLRW). LLRW is defined as radioactive waste which is low in curies (intensity of radioactivity), or relatively short in half-life (duration of the radioactivity). Nonetheless, it can still be quite dangerous, and must be handled with care. The government agency must be concerned with both the safety and the cost of the chosen technology. Let us assume that the government will spend whatever is necessary to ensure safe disposal, but that there is some uncertainty about the consequences of different choices, with the resulting potential for costs of remediation if the disposal technology fails to contain the waste.

There are three choices available to the government agency:

- *Shallow land burial:* Trenches, each ten to twenty yards deep, are dug in geologically stable land, on an impermeable clay basin. Concrete is poured to form engineered barriers to prevent water seepage. When a trench is filled to within ten feet of ground level, an impermeable "cap" is placed on the waste, rocks and dirt are graded over the site, and grass is planted to prevent erosion.
- *Aboveground vaults:* Large concrete structures are erected, with cranes for lifting waste into the vaults. When a vault is filled, it is covered with a waterproof roof.
- *Augured holes:* With a steel drill, holes thirteen feet in diameter and thirty-five yards deep, are made in geologically stable land. Waste is placed in the hole, up to ten yards from the surface. The waste is then covered with an impermeable cap, and soil, and grass is planted to prevent erosion.

It is useful to draw a "map" of the decision problem, as a way of organizing our thinking. We depict alternatives as branches, encompassing both costs and probabilities of events. I should emphasize that the figures and the probabilities I am about to give you are completely made up. The comparison is fairly realistic, but nonetheless real policy decisions in this area (as described in Coates and Munger, 1992) are much more complicated. The decision map, or "tree," can be depicted as shown in Figure 9.6.

Suppose that the government faces a choice among three alternatives, each of which has a known cost of construction. Furthermore, each alternative disposal technology has a known probability of failure (leaking, or requiring repairs). The "remediation" costs will be incurred if, but only if, the disposal facility fails. We can ignore differences in safety, because I will assume that remediation will fully restore the facility, and that no permanent leakage is allowed to occur. Finally, because the facility types are very different in their materials, and forms, the costs of remediation, if required, differ dramatically. The problem, from the agency's perspective, is that the cheapest alternative to construct is the most expensive to repair. But the repairs will be necessary only in the case of failure, so we must calculate the expected values of total cost for each facility type to make a decision.

FIGURE 9.6
Simplified Decision Analysis for LLRW
Disposal Technology

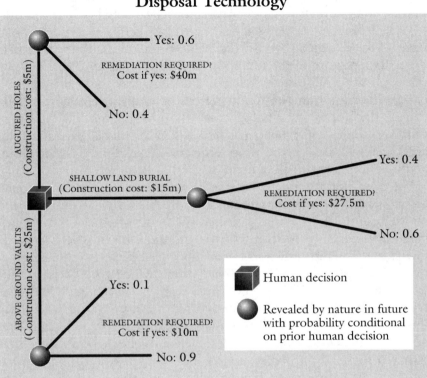

Expected values for costs. As is no doubt obvious, the expected value of total cost will be the sum of construction expense plus the expected cost of remediation. The three alternatives then look like this:

Cost (millions of dollars)

Technology	Construction	Expected Remediation	Total
Augured holes	$5	0.6 × $40m + 0.4 × $0 = $24	$29
Shallow land burial	$15	0.4 × $27.5m + 0.6 × $0= $11	$26
Aboveground vaults	$25	0.1× $10m + 0.9 × $0 = $1	$26

So the cheapest alternative to construct is the most expensive alternative in expected total costs. The other two alternatives, shallow land burial and aboveground vaults, are indistinguishable in expected value, even though their construction and remediation costs are very different. This comparison, on first glance, may seem odd, because the total cost figures never will actually be spent! After all, the cost of augured holes will either be $5m (no repairs) or $45m (if remediation is required). How can we represent its expected cost as $29m?

Well, from a pure budget perspective we can't. If augured holes were selected, our agency would have to set up a contingency plan for an expenditure of the full $45m in case the facility fails. But from the perspective of decision making, the $29m expected value figure is exactly the right number. Assuming risk neutrality, the agency should choose the disposal technology with the lowest expected total cost. On average, and if many such decisions were made over time, this approach will ensure the most efficient allocation of public funds among competing possible uses.

We have not yet made a recommendation about which disposal technology the agency should choose. Both shallow land burial and aboveground vault have an expected total cost of $26m, but shallow land burial costs less for construction and more for possible future remediation. Interestingly, this impasse between these two "finalists" is exactly the sticking point in real-world technology decisions for LLRW disposal.[13] Shallow land burial really is cheaper, and is probably safe, but remediation is expensive because any leakage or leeching into groundwater occurs deep underground. Aboveground vaults really are expensive to build, both because of the support structures required to build reinforced concrete bunkers aboveground and because of the necessity to build cranes to lift the materials into the vaults, but remediation is unlikely to be necessary, and would be relatively cheap if it were required.

There are two possible recommendations, and it is very difficult to make a choice between them. What many state LLRW disposal authorities have done is to recommend some version of shallow land burial, because it is a proven technology and because it is cheaper to build in the short run. Many public safety and environmental activists have fought for the other alternative, some version of aboveground vaults. The hope is that a relatively short-term solution, with a higher degree of safety, will allow the development of new and even more effective disposal technologies. And there is no question that it would be easier to remove waste from an aboveground vault in the event that an even better technology were to be developed.

The argument of proponents of aboveground vaults comes down to an argument for risk aversion, instead of risk neutrality: better to pay more up front for certain than to take the chance of incurring large costs in the future. In the actual decision process faced by state LLRW disposal authorities, this may be an important consideration. Real remediation costs have often been grossly underestimated, and failure rates have been higher than expected.[14] Clearly, if we raised the estimates of the probability of failure, and the cost of remediation, for shallow land burial in Figure 9.8, the "tie" would be broken.

Summary

In this long, hard chapter, we have covered the basic intuition, and formal logic, of probability and expected value calculations, and gone over the basics of "decision analysis," and the value of drawing a map of the decision process and the consequences of choosing one alternative over another. Probability is used to discount, or count at less than face value, the consequences of decisions, because at the time the decision is made we are not certain what the future holds. Discounting for "risk," by assigning probabilities to outcomes, or sets of outcomes using the multiplication or addition rules for aggregating probabilities, is a big advance over simple "uncertainty," where no specific values for the likelihood of outcomes can be assigned.

It is worth making one more pitch for the concept of expected value as an analytic device for representing the value of an outcome or the consequences of a decision. Students often resist the notion of expected value, because it has no apparent basis in objective reality. In the LLRW example, I claimed that there are only two possible outcomes for a technology choice: if augured holes were chosen, the expense for the agency would be either $5 million (if no repairs are required) or $45 million (if the darned thing leaks), but we use the expected value of total costs, $29 million, as the basis for comparison even though *there is no possibility* that exactly $29 million will be spent. How can we do that?

The answer can be seen in the example at the start of this chapter. If I offer to play a game with you, where I flip a fair coin and then pay you based on the outcome, then that game has an expected value. This value is an objective, real-world number, and represents the payment which would make you indifferent between playing and not playing my little game, if your attitude toward risk were neutral. If the coin comes up heads, I will pay you $5; if the coin comes up tails, I will pay you $1. The expected value of this game is $3, even though there is *never* a play of the game where you would receive exactly $3.

The amount you would pay more (less) than $3 is an indication of how risk accepting (averse) you are. Presumably, you would pay at least $1 to play (that is the lowest payoff, so even an extremely risk-averse person would take the bet), and no more than $5 (that is the most you could hope to win), regardless of the probabilities involved. Thus the expected value is an important benchmark for the sake of comparison in individual decisions. Further, if an agency faces a large number of decisions, which it must get right on average, the expected value is a very useful tool for comparing different outcomes. It is precisely the fact that expectation gives us an average—a mean—between extreme outcomes that makes it useful.

SUMMARY OF KEY CONCEPTS

1. A *chi-square statistic* is used to test the null hypothesis of independence. To interpret a chi-square, remember that the probability estimate is the answer to the following question: "What is the likelihood of finding so large a difference due only to chance, assuming the null of independence to be true?"
2. *Conditional probability* is written as "$P_{(A|B)}$", which is read "the probability of A, given that B happened already."
3. *Counting rules* are used to compute the number of events with specific definitions, including both the events of interest and the larger population of all possible events. There are two main kinds of counting rules: those used to compute the number of *combinations* (where order within the event group does not matter), and those used to compute the number of *permutations* (where different order implies a different event).
4. *Degrees of freedom* are extra, or "free," pieces of information, over and above the minimum required to compute a parameter value. To compute a mean, one needs only one observation, but since there are no extra observations ("degrees of freedom"), this is a mean largely without meaning.

5. *Decision analysis* is a structured organization of a problem, focusing on the likelihoods that alternative courses of action will lead to a desired outcome. Decision analysis seeks to account for choices under conditions of uncertainty or risk, and can account for either a single or multiple objectives.

6. An *event* is the occurrence of a particular set of outcomes.

7. The *expected value* is the sum of the products of likelihood of events multiplied by the probability of occurrence of each event. More intuitively, the "expected value" of a gamble or choice is the average payoff if you played the same gamble, or made the same choice, a large number of times in exactly the same setting.

8. The *factorial* sign "!" is an operator which "operates" on a number *n*. The definition of *n*! is the product of all of the positive integers from 1 up to *n*. In symbols, $n! = 1 \times 2 \times 3 \times \ldots \times n$:

9. The definition of *independence* requires the concept of conditional probability. We say two events A and B are "independent" if the knowledge that one has occurred does not change the probability estimate that the other will occur. In symbols, this means that if $P_{(A|B)} = P_{(A)}$, then A and B are independent.

10. *Inference* is the process of drawing a conclusion from a set of facts. In statistics, "inference" is usually taken to mean using a sample to draw conclusions about the value of some unknown parameter of a population.

11. A *lottery* is a set of mutually exclusive events, each of which has a known probability of occurence, and each occurence of which is associated with a fixed payoff.

12. In addition to having preferences over outcomes, we often assume that people have *preferences toward risk*, so that they also evaluate lotteries in terms of probabilities, not just the expected values. *Risk-accepting* preferences mean that a person prefers A (a gamble with expected payoff $x) to B (an offer of $x for sure). A person with *risk-neutral* preferences is indifferent between A and B. A *risk-averse* preference profile implies B is better than A.

13. *Probability* is the likelihood of the occurrence of an event. The classical interpretation of probability is called the "frequentist" view. Frequentists define probability as the ratio of the number of ways that an event of interest can occur, divided by the total number of events possible. One can conceive of probabilities either in *posterior* (empirical) terms arising from measurement and

observation, or as *a priori* (theoretical) constructs derived from counting rules or analytic formulae.

14. To call a process *random* is to imply that it operates without aim or purpose. Randomness might be used to describe the order of cards in a well-shuffled deck; the cards are in some *arbitrary* order, resulting from the process of shuffling, but there is no discernible pattern or sequence in that order.

15. *Risk* exists when there is incomplete information of a particular kind in a decision problem. If one is not sure what is going to happen, because there are several possible outcomes, none of which can be ruled out completely, then this is a setting of incomplete information. If the chooser can attach (accurate) probabilities to the relative likelihoods of the outcomes, then this is a situation with "risk." If the chooser does not have this much information, but can only guess at which outcome is most likely, then the situation is more difficult. Lack of knowledge of the probabilities needed to assess risk implies fundamental *uncertainty*.

16. It is possible to manipulate sets, or collections of elements, in much the same way that it is possible to perform various operations, such as multiplication or subtraction, on numbers. The two basic *set operations* described in this chapter are *intersection* (the elements shared by both sets) and *union* (the elements contained in either of the sets).

PROBLEMS AND QUESTIONS

1. An educational policy expert was asked to advise a school board on how to improve the students' achievement test performance. She provided three plans: one would cost the district $1,000 per pupil, one would cost the district $500 per pupil, and one would require no additional expenses. Her assessment was that the chance of success for the first, $1,000 plan, was 50 percent; for the second plan, it was 20 percent; and for the third plan it was 10 percent. On the basis of her discussion with the school board, she was sure one of the three plans would be adopted. Her best guess was that there was a 10 percent chance of their adopting the first plan, a 40 percent chance of their adopting the second plan, and a 50 percent chance of their adopting the third plan. Two years later she learned that the school had been successful in improving achievement test scores. Assuming that her probability assessments were correct, what is the chance the school board adopted the third plan, which cost them no additional money?

2. Consider the table below, which summarizes the relationship between income level and taxpayers' willingness to have their taxes raised in order to spend additional money on local schools.

Income level	Willingness to Raise Taxes		
	Yes, *a lot*	*Yes,* *a little*	*No,* *not at all*
High	.12	.12	.06
Mod	.12	.24	.04
Low	.03	.15	.12

   a. What is the probability that someone selected at random would be willing to have a large increase in taxes?
   b. What is the probability that a person with high income would be willing to have a large increase in taxes?
   c. What would this table have looked like if income and attitudes toward increased taxation were independent?

3. A committee consists of twelve Democrats and nine Republicans. How many subcommittees of eight containing five Democrats and three Republicans can be formed? (You may leave your answer in symbolic form.)

4. In how many different ways can you get exactly three tails in eight flips of a coin?
   a. *CALCULATE* your answer, by counting relative frequencies.
   b. Now apply the correct formula. Show all your work.

5. Suppose that you bought Christmas presents for your three nephews in a January sale and had them wrapped. By the time Christmas came you had forgotten who should get which present. What is the probability that: no one gets the correct present; one nephew gets the correct present; two nephews get the correct present; and all three nephews get the correct present?

6. What is the probability of a "full house" if you are dealt a five-card hand? (For those unfamiliar with poker, a full house is three cards of one kind, e.g., three tens; and two cards of another kind, e.g., two fours. Remember that there are thirteen different cards in four different suits for a total of fifty-two cards.) (You may leave your answer in symbolic form.)

7. Suppose that the probability of one lightning strike in any one-acre area in central Oklahoma (lightning capital of the world) in a given year is .1. Let the probability of more than one strike per acre per year be negligible. Suppose further that lightning strikes are independent events.

a. Draw a graph of the probability distribution of lightning strikes in an arbitrary acre over a five-year period taking as "events" zero strikes, one strike, two strikes, three strikes, and more than three strikes.

b. Evaluate the claim that "lightning never strikes twice in the same place," assuming that a "place" is a one-acre area. In other words, what is the probability that lightning strikes two or more times in the same place over a five-year period?

TAKE IT TO THE NET!

Go to: http://www.wwnorton.com/college/polisci/analyzingpolicy for additional problems, data sets, and course materials.

NOTES

1. No, it can't land on its edge. Seriously, have you ever seen one do that? Get out.
2. I am assuming fifteen seconds to deal each hand, with no breaks, twenty-four hours per day. Don't try this at home, please.
3. It is important to remember that 0! = 1, which seems odd but is a useful mathematical convention.
4. The example that follows is similar to an example used by David Lowery and myself in a long series of classes at UNC-Chapel Hill, in the Master of Public Administration Program. I thank David for originating the problem, and helping to identify difficulties with the examples over the years.

5. It is not quite true that winters are independent, because there are long-term trends in mean temperature. But the variance of temperatures does appear to be independent, or close enough to independent that the dependencies cannot usefully be used to make forecasts.

6. In fact, these "definitions" are overly simple. The reason is that they ignore the variance in the payoffs as a positive good for the risk accepter, or a bad for the risk averter. It would be more accurate to say that the definitions given here are implied by the theory of preferences toward risk, rather than being complete definitions in themselves. Again, see von Neumann and Morgenstern, 1947, and Luce and Raiffa, 1957.

7. Again, this is a simplification. If the "payoff" includes death, or bankruptcy, or some other large negative outcome, even a large number of trials won't make risk aversion go away. Further, someone who enjoys gambling for its own sake might pay for many games where the net payoff (pay the money, play the game) is negative in expected value.

8. See, for example, Tversky and Kahneman, 1981, and Kahneman and Tversky, 1985.

9. There are hundreds of sources for decision analysis, and entire academic departments devoted to educating students in its nuances. Besides Stokey and Zeckhauser (1978), two other classic readings are Raiffa (1968), Behn and Vaupel (1982), and Weimer and Vining (1992).

10. See, for example, Raiffa (1968), Stokey and Zeckhauser (1978), Behn and Vaupel (1982), or Weimer and Vining (1992).

11. For example, if I say I am uncertain about what move my opponent will make in a chess game, or a political campaign, there is no easy way to convert this problem to a "risk" problem, with probabilities describing the relative likelihood of the opponent's choices. Strategic choice is best modeled using game theory, a subject outside the scope of this book.

12. For background on LLRW, and details about the disposal technologies being discussed in this example, see Coates and Munger, 1991, and Murray, 1989.

13. See Texas LLRWWDA, 1987, Burns, 1988, and English, 1991.

14. See, for some background and details, Bartlett and Steele, 1985.

～ 10 ～

Discounting II: Time

I'll give you a dollar on Tuesday for a hamburger I eat today.
—Wimpy, friend of Popeye, on many occasions.

Discounting means counting at less than face value. Chapter 9 described techniques for discounting outcomes based on risk, or *expected value*. As you recall, to calculate expected values, we discounted possible outcomes based on their likelihood of occurrence. The present chapter describes a very different discounting technique, which values outcomes based not on their likelihood of occurrence, but rather on the time when they occur. The key concept in time discounting is **present value**. Just as expected value makes events with different likelihoods comparable, present value makes events that occur in the future comparable with events that occur today.

Present value allows the comparison of a benefit today and a cost incurred in the future, or a cost today and a stream of benefits spread out over many years in the future. At first blush, this might seem easy: all you have to do is add up the benefits, or the costs, and there you are! Of course, that is wrong, as Popeye's friend Wimpy knew well. Wimpy would always offer a dollar for a hamburger, which should have worked. But Wimpy didn't want to give a dollar now; he always wanted to pay the *next Tuesday* for a hamburger received, and eaten, *today*. The reason is what we might call "Wimpy's principle."

Wimpy's principle: A dollar tomorrow is worth less than a dollar today.

Consider two states of the world:

a. I give you a dollar today, and you give me a hamburger today.
b. I promise to give you a dollar tomorrow, and you give me a hamburger today.

For most people, b. is preferable. You get the hamburger, and you get use of the dollar for another day. In fact, you may not even *have* the dollar yet; you can wait until tonight, or tomorrow morning, and do something to earn the dollar. By eating the hamburger now, you are borrowing against your future earnings.

From Wimpy's principle, we can derive a corollary:

Corollary to Wimpy's principle: A dollar in the distant future has very little value, even though when you get it it will be "worth" a dollar.

The corollary is obvious, of course: every tomorrow is itself followed by a tomorrow. If a dollar tomorrow is worth less than a dollar today, then a dollar lots of tomorrows from now is worth *much* less than a dollar today.

But how much less? How much does each tomorrow, or "unit" of time, reduce the value of a promised payment, or service? The difference between the value of a dollar in one period and the value of a dollar in the following period, is defined as the **discount rate**, or the **rate of time preference**. Three things should be pointed out about discount rates:

• If you have a *high* discount rate, you value payments or services today much more than anything that happens in the future. In other words, you "discount" the future heavily, and prefer to consume today. Wimpy was like this, of course. He wanted to eat lots of hamburgers today, even though that meant that he had to starve for the next few days as he tried to find a way to pay for his eating binge.

• If you have a *low* discount rate, you consider payments or services today to be only slightly (or not at all) more valuable than what happens tomorrow, or next year. People with a low discount rate consider events over a long time horizon, and forgo consumption today.

- If discount rates, or preferences about the time pattern of consumption, differ within a population, then there are potential gains from trade. If I have a low discount rate, I may be willing to loan Wimpy some money, because consuming now is more valuable to Wimpy than it is to me. Of course, I want some compensation for this loan: even if I have a zero discount rate, I am only *indifferent* between a dollar today and a dollar tomorrow.

People with a low discount rate are probably willing to loan money to people with high discount rates, but only if the low discount rate person gets more consumption in the future. In other words, if I loan you a dollar, I want the dollar back, plus a little extra. This "extra" is called **interest**, and it is the rental price of money.

Interest and the Rental Price of Money

Imagine that your college allows students to paint their dorm rooms any color, so long as they repaint it in a neutral color at the end of the year. The dorm rooms aren't that big, but it would take a long time to paint by hand. So, you go to a hardware store, hoping to rent one of those air-powered sprayers that will allow you to paint your whole room flat black (hey, you are a literature major!) in about an hour.

You get to the store, and you notice that the rental price is $20 per hour, or $100 for twenty-four hours. You stop and think: *How do they decide how much it costs to rent something?* This is obviously different from buying something, because the price paid to purchase a commodity is the total average cost of producing that commodity, at least most of the time.

Two components of a rental price occur to you immediately:

1. Compensation for depreciation and normal wear and tear. The paint sprayer is mechanical, and won't last forever. Misuse, or even lengthy proper use, will eventually wear the sprayer out. The owner obviously needs to recover this value if he wants to rent out the machine for a profit. The larger the likely damage, or wear, on the machine per use, the larger the rental price.

2. Risk that you won't return the sprayer, that you will simply run off with it. The owner can take a deposit, but there is still some risk that the sprayer won't be returned. The greater this risk, the greater the implied rental price.

Satisfied you have solved the problem, you get ready to sign the rental papers. But then something occurs to you: Depreciation, and risk of theft, are just costs that get you back to the original sprayer in good condition. There has to be something else: There has to be some compensation for the *opportunity cost* of the sprayer itself: If you have it, that means that it cannot be used for anything else, or by anyone else.

This may seem like a small concern (after all, the hardware store owner is working today, so *he* can't use the sprayer!), but it is actually the heart of the matter. The hardware store owner invested money in the paint sprayer, in the hopes of making money. It is the investment of money that has an opportunity cost, because the hardware store owner could have used the $1,300 invested in the sprayer to buy stocks, or bonds, or some other investment that yields a return. Alternatively, he could have bought himself plane tickets to Bermuda and consumed goods and services instead of forgoing consumption and investing the money in the paint sprayer.

To summarize, then, you have come up with the three components of rental price:

- Compensation for loss of value from normal wear and tear
- Compensation for risk of loss from not being returned
- Compensation for opportunity cost of investment in the asset

Interestingly, exactly the same three components of rental price would be operating no matter what you wanted to rent—even if you wanted to rent some money, by taking out a loan from your local bank. Of course, you wouldn't literally wear out the money, but it is still possible that you would return a dollar that was worth less than when you borrowed it. That is called "**inflation.**" There is also a risk that you could default, or that you might not return the loan at the time you promised to in the loan agreement. Finally, there is the actual opportunity cost of money, the "real" **interest rate.** The determination of total interest rate as broken down into components is credited to Irving Fisher, and is often expressed in the form of "Fisher's equation":[1]

Total Interest rate = inflation rate + risk premium + real cost of money

Consequently, the **rental price** of a dollar has the same three components as any other rental price:

- Compensation for expected loss of value resulting from use (for money, inflation)
- Compensation for risk the asset will not be returned (for money, people use credit history or information on the riskiness of the venture proposed)
- Compensation for opportunity cost of the use of the asset (for money, this is the real risk-free rate)

There is quite a bit more to be said about interest rates, of course, than the few basics that this little section provides you. Interest rates are at once a matter of policy, with important implications for the way government is able to finance debt and encourage investment, and the price of money, which responds primarily to market forces and represents an equilibrium among the many groups willing to loan, and others wanting to borrow, money. For our purposes, the point to bear in mind is that there is no one "interest rate" in an economy. As Fisher's equation shows, rates might differ dramatically across borrowers with different risk profiles, or over loans of different duration, because the risk of inflation or nonpayment is cumulative.[2]

Forecasting Value One Year in the Future

Once we know the interest rate, we can take a dollar today and calculate its value in the future, assuming that the dollar is "earning" the *annual* rate of interest r:

$1 invested at interest rate r = $1 \times (1 + r)$ one year from today

For example, if you had $7, invested at 10 percent interest, one year from today you would have $7.70, because:

$$\$7 \times (1 + 0.10) = \$7.70$$

Of course, there is a generalization of this one-year-at-a time evaluation of an investment. Suppose you had $7, invested at 10 percent interest. What would the $7 be worth nine years from today? It is tempting to think that the answer should be nine times the amount of interest earned, or:

$$\$7 \times [1 + (0.10 \times 9)] = \$13.30$$

What is wrong with this formulation? Well, what about the interest earned in the first year, and the second year, and so on? What did you do with it? If you reinvest that interest, at the same rate, then you will earn interest, not just on the $7 you started out with, but also on the interest. This "earning interest on interest" is called **compounding**. The correct formula accounts for compounding by applying the interest rate to the interest that has already been earned, plus the original amount, called the **principal**.

Forecasting Value t *Years in the Future*

$1 invested at interest rate $r = \$1 \times (1 + r)^t$ t years from today, provided the interest earnings are reinvested

Expanding this, we get:
$$\$1 \times (1+r)^t = \$1 \times (1+r) \times (1+r)\,(1 + r) \times \ldots \times (1+r)$$

Interest rate applied
t times

Going back to the example ("What would the $7 be worth nine years from today?"), the answer is $16.50, because:

$$\$7 \times (1 + 0.10)^9 = \$7 \times 2.358 = \$16.50$$

The $16.50 has three parts:

• $7 is the original "principal."
• $6.30 is interest on the principal.
• $2.20 is interest on the interest, resulting from compounding.

Using this formula, we can go as far into the future as we want. Let's do some time travel: How much will the $7 be worth one hundred years from now?

$7 \times (1 + 0.10)^{100} = \$7 \times 13780.61 = \$96,464.28$

Once again, this sum has three parts:

- $7 is the original "principal."
- $70 is interest on the principal.
- $96387.28 is interest on the interest, resulting from compounding.

Whoa! The $7 is worth nearly $100,000, and almost all of it came from compound interest. Obviously, the future looks pretty strange unless you understand compound interest, the mechanism that takes us from a value now to a value many periods from now.

Discount Rates: Getting Back from the Future

If interest rates are the means by which we travel into the future to measure the value of investments, we need a way to go in the other direction. We need an answer to this question: If we expect a payment, or a benefit, or a cost, in the future, what is it worth today?

Clearly, that question is important. Consider an example: Which of the following public works projects (assuming they all cost the same!) should be chosen to be built by the government?

Project 1: Build a road. Delivers benefits valued at $1,000 per year for twenty years.
Project 2: Build a dam. Delivers benefits valued at $500 per year forever.
Project 3: Fix up a "brownfield"[3] site, and sell it immediately Delivers one-time benefit of $15,000.

Comparison without Discounting

Suppose we didn't know about the need for discounting future benefits. Then the three projects can be compared pretty simply, based on the amount of monetary benefits they will yield:

Project 1: $1,000 \times 20 = \$20,000$
Project 2: $500 \times \infty =$ infinite benefit
Project 3: $15,000 right away

Based on this "analysis," project 2 is the clear winner. Of course, if you make this recommendation, the City Council will fire you.

The reason is that benefits in the distant future have negligible value. Let us consider the procedure for discounting future benefits, and then return to the comparison of the three projects.

Discounting a Benefit One Year in the Future

Each $1 expected one year from today = $1/(1 + d) today

The d in this formula is the **rate of time discount,** the flip side of the interest rate. Empirically, the discount rate may be quite different from the interest rate, however, for reasons I will discuss in the next section. For now, just notice that it works the same way, except that we are "discounting," or reducing the value of benefits promised in the future, instead of using interest to add to value of investment starting today and extending into the future.

For example, suppose you expected to be paid $7 one year from today, and that (for you) $d = 10$ percent. You would value that payment at $6.36, because:

$$\frac{\$7}{1+0.10} = \$6.36$$

Once again, there is a generalization of this "one year at a time" discount of a future benefit. Continuing our previous example, suppose that nine years from now you expect to be paid $7. How much is it worth to you now?

Discounting a Value Anticipated t Years in the Future

$1 expected t years in the future = $1/(1 + r)^t$ today

So, the value of $7 nine years from today is $2.97, because:

$$\$7/(1 + 0.10)^9 = \$7/2.358 = \$2.97$$

Back to the Three Projects

We are now in a position to evaluate the three projects described earlier, using what is called the **present value** formula:

$$\text{Present value} = \frac{\text{Value in year } t}{(1+d)^t}$$

Project 1. This road project will yield \$1,000 per year for twenty years, after which the road will have to be replaced. Consequently, the present value for the project is:

$$PV_1 = \frac{\$1,000}{1+d} + \frac{\$1,000}{(1+d)^2} + \frac{\$1,000}{(1+d)^3} + \frac{\$1,000}{(1+d)^4} + \ldots + \frac{\$1,000}{(1+d)^{20}}$$

Project 2. This dam project will yield \$500 per year forever (dams last a long time). ("Forever" may be an exaggeration, but we will use that assumption.) Consequently, the present value for the project can be represented as the following infinite series:

$$PV_2 = \frac{\$500}{1+d} + \frac{\$500}{(1+d)^2} + \frac{\$500}{(1+d)^3} + \frac{\$500}{(1+d)^4} + \ldots$$

Project 3. Cleaning up the "brownfields" site and selling it yields an immediate benefit of \$15,000. Since the benefit occurs today, the size of the benefit and the present value of the benefit are identical: \$15,000.

The present value for project 3 is easy, but the others require a bit of work. You could do the calculation for project 1 by hand, calculating each separate present value and then summing from years 1 to 20. But it is easier (and more accurate, given the chances for mistakes in writing all those numbers down!) to use a spreadsheet function such as Excel's™ "PV" function, where you enter the discount, the number of periods, and the amount of the payment per period.[4] The result of calculating the sum of separately discounted annual benefits (i.e., the first benefit of \$1,000 is discounted once, because it will be received one year from now, all the way up to the twentieth benefit, which is discounted twenty times because it will occur twenty years from now) is:

$$PV_1 = \sum_{t=1}^{20} \left[\frac{\$500}{(1+0.10)^t} \right] = \$4,256.78$$

The fact that a stream of payments totaling $20,000 is "worth" only $4,256.78 may seem surprising, but it is obvious once you understand discounting. The simple general rule is this: The higher the discount rate, the more we "discount" benefits in the future. Consider Table 10.1, which presents values for project 1 with different assumptions about the appropriate discount rate. The only way that the full $20,000 in benefits "counts" is if the discount rate is zero. More simply, *the **most** a stream of benefits can be worth is the sum of the benefits, assuming a zero discount rate. Any positive discount rate reduces the present value of the stream of benefits.*

TABLE 10.1
Present Values for Project 1 ($1,000 benefits per year, for 20 years) and Project 2 ($500 benefits per year, forever), under Different Assumptions for Discount Rates

	Project (Shaded Means "Best")		
Discount Rate	1	2	3
100%	$1,000.00	$500	$15,000
50%	1,999.40	1,000	15,000
25%	3,953.88	2,000	15,000
10%	8,513.56	5,000	15,000
5%	12,462.21	10,000	15,000
3.52649%	14,178.40	14,178.40	15,000
3.33333%	14,429.15	15,000	15,000
2%	16,351.43	25,000	15,000
1%	18,045.55	50,000	15,000
0%	20,000.00	∞	15,000

We could *start* the calculation for project 2 the same way, but of course we would never finish: the stream of benefits from project 2 is infinite in time, and is therefore infinite in benefits. We can safely ignore benefits in the distant future, of course: a promise of $500 in one hundred years, discounted at 10 percent, is worth less than a nickel today. But that still leaves the question of how much the stream of benefits is worth! Should we stop at sixty years? at seventy-five years? at one hundred?

Fortunately, there is an answer to the question that is both computationally simple and mathematically accurate. It is well known that the following statement about an infinite series is true:

$$\text{If } 0 < \rho < 1, \text{ then } \text{Lim}_{N \to \infty} \sum_{t=1}^{N} \rho^{i} = \frac{1}{\rho}$$

In this formula, ρ (the Greek letter rho) represents any number strictly less than 1 and strictly greater than zero. The summation sign Σ means that we add up all the values from the lower number (in this case, one) to the larger number (in this case, N). And the "Limit" operator implies that the formula is evaluated only as the value of N goes to the limit, in this case infinity.

Why does this rather abstract and forbidding formula help us with the practical problem of discounting for time? The reason is that the discount factor, $1/(1 + d)^{t}$, takes the role of ρ in the equation. Here is what we can do with this result:[5]

$$PV = \sum_{t=1}^{\infty} \left[\frac{\$B}{(1+d)^{t}} \right] = \frac{B}{d}$$

So, it turns out that calculating the present value of the benefits from project 2 is actually very easy. All we need to do is plug the value of the annual benefit (\$500) into the formula above, and then come up with a value for the discount rate. If we use 10 percent, we get:

$$PV = \frac{B}{d} = \frac{\$500}{0.10} = \$5,000$$

Of course, many other values for the discount rate are possible, as Table 10.1 shows.

It is time to make our recommendation. Like any policy analyst, we answer the question of which project is best with, "It depends!" Like *good* policy analysts, however, we are able to tell the client *what it depends on*: In this case, the answer depends on the discount rate. Project 3 has a clear advantage if the appropriate discount rate is high, because it delivers an immediate \$15,000 benefit. Project 2, by contrast, is the best if the discount rate is very low.

The information in Table 10.1 allows us to be very specific, and let the client make a choice based on good information.

- Project 1 should *never* be chosen. At all possible discount rates, at least one of the other projects delivers larger benefits in terms of present values. Project 1 is better than project 2 at very high discount rates, but project 2 (because of its longer time horizon) increases in present value very quickly. The two projects have equal value at a discount rate of 3.52649 percent, but at that discount rate their present value ($14,178.40) is still less than the project 3 benefit ($15,000).
- Project 2 should be built only if the discount rate is *less* than 3.33 percent.
- Project 3 should be built at any discount rate *greater* than 3.33 percent.
- If the discount rate is *exactly* 3.33 percent, projects 2 and 3 are equally desirable.

An Aside on the Present Value of an Infinite Series

Two formulae were derived in the preceding section. The first, the general formula for present value, is complex, but useful; you have probably seen it before. The second, the specific formula for the present value of an infinite series of payments, is astonishing, and depressingly few people know it. If you think about what the formula implies, it should make the hairs on your head stand straight up. The formula was originally derived to compute the value of a type of British bond, the "consol," which pays interest *forever* at specified periods on an amount borrowed by the government. The reason this is so cool is that you can compute, in your head, the upper bound on a series of payments or benefits that would otherwise require complex and time-consuming calculations.

Suppose someone tells you that he is going to do you a favor, because he likes you. He offers you a piece of land with a rental value of $12,000 per year for a "low price" of $240,000. Your new best friend tells you that the land will pay for itself in twenty years (20 × $12,000 = $240,000), and after that you will make money forever. "So," he says, putting his arm around your shoulder, "the price is a bargain!" How much is that land worth? Hard to say, because that depends on what someone will pay for it. But the formula for the present value of an infinite series gives you an easy immediate benchmark: Suppose that the $12,000 per year continues *forever*, and your discount rate is 10 percent. Then that land is worth something around:

$$\frac{B}{d} = \frac{\$12,000}{0.1} = \$120,000$$

Maybe this is not such a bargain after all. Of course, your discount rate could be lower, at 5 percent. In that case, the value of the land would be:

$$\frac{B}{d} = \frac{\$12,000}{0.05} = \$240,000$$

Not a bargain, but not an unfair price, either. In fact, $240,000 is exactly the right price if the annual rental payment is $12,000 and your discount rate is 5 percent.

This suggests a way to rearrange the formula $PV = B/d$:

$$B = d \times PV$$

You would need to put $PV in the bank at interest rate d in order to earn B dollars in interest each year, forever. The formula is therefore very intuitive indeed. But this intuition also suggests a potential problem in deciding what "your" discount rate should be. Suppose that to buy the land, you have to borrow the money from a bank. Suppose further that the bank wants you to pay an interest rate of 7 percent, a pretty good rate for unimproved land. That means that for the price of $240,000 to make sense, the rental "benefit" B would have to be:

$$B = d \times PV = 0.07 \times \$240,000 = \$16,800$$

Since the rent you anticipate is much less than this ($12,000), you could not afford the interest payments. *So, your discount rate should be at least equal to the cost of money used to finance the project,* unless you expect increased revenues from some other source in the future. The bottom line here is that your "friend" is not offering you a very good deal, and you should respectfully decline.

You may find that you can use this formula every day. If you are considering buying a piece of machinery that you expect will produce $100 per month in revenues, net of repair costs, and your discount rate is 10 percent (a very plausible, and easy to figure, rate), then you immediately know that the most you could possibly consider paying to rent the machine is $12,000 (12 months × $100 per month/0.10).[6] If the machine costs less than that, you should consider signing the lease. But if it costs more than $12,000, don't give it another thought, because your decision is made: no.

Net Present Value: Combining Future Costs and Benefits

Both costs (future budget commitments, or future penalties that "count" in valuing a project) and benefits (either money savings, or values attached to goods and services) may occur in the future, of course. Suppose we are considering building an engineered, limited-access four-lane highway from our city (Ruttenton) over the intervening four miles to reach cosmopolitan Bakersfield. The current road is a narrow, winding stretch of cracked pavement which is both embarrassing and unsafe.

Our engineers have studied the project, which will take three years to complete, and have come up with the following schedule of costs and benefits from building the road:

Year	Benefits	Costs
1	0	$2,000,000 (construction, $1m/mile)
2	0	$2,000,000 (construction, $1m/mile)
3	$500,000	$50,000 (maintenance)
4 and after	$100,000	$50,000

To summarize: The road would cost $4 million, over two years, plus $50,000 per year forever to maintain. There is an initial $500,000 benefit when the road is completed, from new investment and prestige for Ruttenton ("Hey . . . nice road! Let's build a factory!"), and then $100,000 per year as long as the road is maintained. The question then becomes a present value problem: How do we bring all these costs and benefits back from the future into a single number that will let us evaluate the road project?

All we need to do, of course, is compute the discounted costs, and benefits, and add them all up, like this:

$$\text{Net PV} = \underbrace{2m + \frac{2m}{1+d}}_{\substack{\text{Construction} \\ \text{costs}}} + \underbrace{\frac{500k}{(1+d)^2} - \frac{50k}{(1+d)^2}}_{\text{Year 3}} + \underbrace{\left|\frac{100k-50k}{d} - \sum_{t=0}^{2}\frac{(100k-50k)}{(1+d)^t}\right|}_{\substack{\text{Permanent benefits} \\ \text{and maintenance costs, after} \\ \text{years 1-3 (subtracted)}}}$$

We want to know if the road project has a positive net present value, taking into account all the costs, present and discounted, as well as all the discounted future benefits. The result of this calculation obviously depends on d, which is the only unknown in the expression for net present value. Table 10.2 calculates net present value for the road project, assuming discount rates from 20 percent (obviously too high) down to 1 percent (obviously too low).

TABLE 10.2
Net Present Values for Ruttenton Road Project, under Different Assumptions for Discount Rates

0.2	−1494444.444
0.15	−1306458.727
0.125	−1180864.198
0.1	−1016942.149
0.075	−780845.5021
0.05	−371995.4649
0.03750471	0
0.025	710261.749
0.01	3763155.573

At a discount rate of 20 percent, the road project has a net present value of about −$1.5 million. At a discount rate of 1 percent, the road project has a net present value of more than $3.5 million. It reaches a zero value at a discount rate of about 3¾ percent. The meaning is apparent: If the appropriate discount rate is more than 3¾ percent, the road project is nothing but "pork barrel," public spending for the sake of political gain, without a real net return to the public. If the appropriate discount rate is less than 3¾ percent, however, the road project is a good one.

How would the citizens of Ruttenton know? What is the right discount rate for public sector projects?

The Internal Rate of Return and the "Public" Discount Rate

The previous example focuses attention on the discount rate at which the net present value of the project equals zero, once all the costs and benefits are appropriately discounted for time and then gathered up in comparable, current dollars. There is a special name for this discount rate: the *internal rate of return* (IRR).

> **Internal rate of return:** The discount rate at which the net present value of a proposed project or activity becomes zero.

As Stokey and Zeckhauser (1978) point out, the internal rate of return would appear to have the advantage of offering a clear choice: "For a yes-no decision on a single project, the choice criterion associated with [IRR] is: 'Undertake a project if its internal rate of return is greater than the appropriate discount rate.' "[7] Stokey and Zeckhauser also point out, however, that internal rate of return is a misleading, and possibly useless, criterion for making good choices, in spite of its apparent simplicity and ease of application. Let's see why.

Example 1: Comparing two projects; IRR is no guide. Suppose you are comparing two projects, project 1 and project 2. (For our purposes, it doesn't matter what the projects are.) All their net present values are accounted for in Figure 10.1, for discount rates ranging from 0 to 20 percent.

The first thing to notice is that project 1 has a much higher internal rate of return, 17.5 percent, than the IRR of 8 percent for project 2. Does that mean that project 1 is a better project? Well, you can't tell! The real question is: What is the appropriate discount rate? Once you have decided that, the comparison of the projects is easy: *Build the project with the higher net present value, given the discount rate you have chosen.* Implementing this decision rule would lead to the following choices:

- If $d < 6\%$, build project 2.
- If $d = 6\%$, both projects are equally good.
- If $6\% < d < 17.5\%$, build project 1.
- If $d = 17.5\%$, you are indifferent between building and not building project 1.
- If $d > 17.5\%$, don't build either project.

FIGURE 10.1
Two Projects—The Higher Internal Rate of
Return Is No Guide

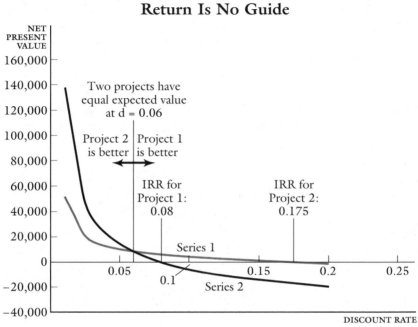

Notice that the IRR for project 2 is not relevant to any part of this decision, and the IRR for project 1, 17.5 percent, is relevant only for deciding whether *any* project should be begun at high discount rates.

Example 2: Project with up-front benefits but long-term costs. The internal rate of return can be misleading in the event the project(s) being evaluated have immediate benefits but long-term costs. To take a very simple example, consider a project with an immediate, one-time benefit of $1 million, but a permanent cost of $100,000 per year. Obviously, the net present value for this project is:

NPV = $1 million − ($100,000/d)

For large values of d, of course, we can "discount" the future costs. However, for smaller values of d, the net present value of this project will be very negative. I have graphed the NPV for this project against discount rate d in Figure 10.2.

If we tried to implement the "If the internal rate of return is

FIGURE 10.2
Project with Up-front Benefits and Long-term Costs

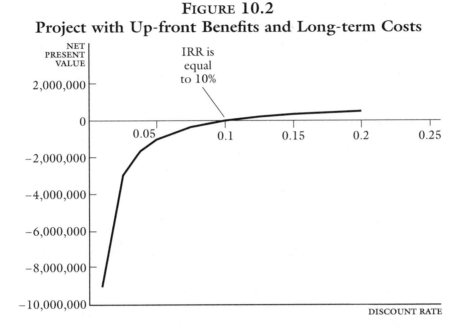

greater than the discount rate, then build" rule, we might make a disastrous mistake! The IRR for this project is 10 percent. Suppose our discount rate is 5 percent; it is obvious from the figure that the NPV with $d = 5$ percent is negative. In fact, it is pretty large: –$1 million. So, as this example shows, the internal rate of return should *never* be used unless the project takes the form of initial costs, followed by long-term benefits. If the project has short-term benefits and long-term costs, then IRR will actually give the wrong answer.

Example 3: The IRR may not be unique. Not all projects produce NPV curves that are consistently increasing or decreasing. It is possible to get a U-shaped curve, opening either up or down. Imagine that we have a project with immediate benefits of $900,000, significant costs ($2 million) in the middle term (five years from now), and then enormous benefits ($5 million) in the distant future (fifty years from now). This would produce a bowl-shaped NPV curve like the one in Figure 10.3.

Which of the two possibilities, 4 percent or 17.5 percent, should we pick for "the" IRR? The answer obviously is neither. It would be just as easy to get an inverted bowl-shaped NPV curve, if the costs

FIGURE 10.3
A Project with 2 IRR's

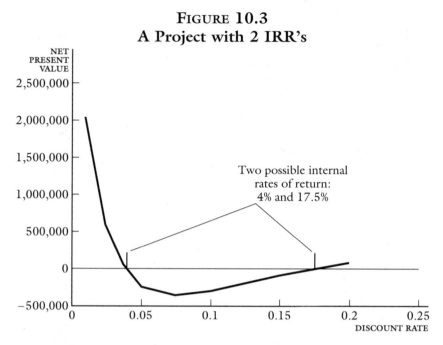

were both immediate and distant and the benefits were expected in between. Likewise, in that situation, the IRR criterion would have no meaning.

To summarize: The choice of discount rate is much more important than the calculation of the internal rate of return for projects. We can extend the **single project decision rule** ("Choose the project with the highest present value") to multiple projects. Stokey and Zeckhauser (1978: 167) state the appropriate rule most clearly:

> It is now widely (but not yet widely enough) realized that the present value criterion and the internal rate of return criterion lead to accepting and rejecting the same projects only if there are no budgetary limitations, if projects do not preclude one another, and if streams of net returns are first negative and then positive. . . . The proper criterion is: "Choose the mix of projects that offers the highest present value."

We are still left with the problem of choosing the "right" discount rate. The preceding examples have shown that the most important single consideration in deciding among public works projects is the net present value, given the correct discount rate. But if we can make the right decision only if we have the right discount rate, then the discount rate is really the heart of the matter.

FIGURE 10.4
Project 2 Dominates Project 1—The Discount Rate Doesn't Matter

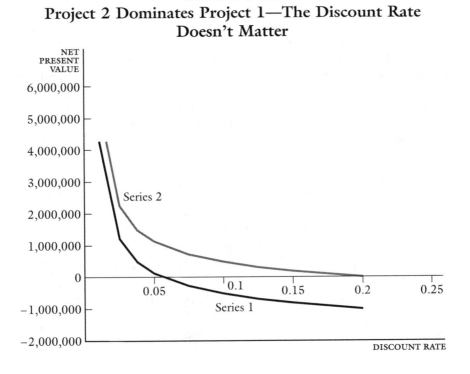

There is one easy situation, where the correct choice is obvious. This is the instance where one project dominates another, with higher (or equal) net present values at every conceivable discount rate. This concept of dominance can be extended to encompass situations where one project yields a larger net present value for any plausibly occurring discount rate: if one project dominates another for discount rates from 0.01 percent to 40 percent, we probably don't need to worry about rates higher than 40 percent. An example of this sort of dominance can be found in Figure 10.4.

When we compare the projects in Figure 10.4, the choice of discount rate doesn't matter, since project 2 "dominates" (offers a higher NPV) for every discount rate. The only question is whether project 2 should be built or nothing should be done. For this choice, the appropriate discount rate may still matter. Stokey and Zeckhauser (1978: 170) give a succinct explanation:

The funds expended for a government project are not funds that would otherwise stand idle. They are obtained by the government from the private sector, either by taxation or borrowing, or from the government itself by diverting funds from other purposes. If left in the private sector, they will be put to use there, and in that use will earn a rate of return that measures the value that society places on that use of the funds. If the funds are diverted to government use, the true cost of the diversion is the return that would otherwise have been earned. This cost . . . is known as the opportunity cost. The opportunity cost is the correct discount rate to use in calculating the present value of a proposed project. If the present value is positive, the project uses the funds to better advantage than they are currently being used in the private sector. If the present value is negative, it doesn't. It's as simple as that.

This observation, that the discount rate must embody the correct opportunity cost of funds diverted from other uses in order to be useful, is not as simple as it seems. There are three points to remember. First, the discount rate reflects the opportunity cost of the resources used in the project. Second, accounting for risk in public projects is complex, and there is no obvious correct way to compute the discount rate. Third, frequent elections may create improper incentives for the use of correct public discount rates (the appropriate discount rate for public projects), because politicians have artificially short time horizons (and so artificially high discount rates).

Discount Rate Reflects Opportunity Cost

Money is an abstract claim over goods and services. The desire to hold money, therefore, is a measure of the willingness of consumers and investors to forgo current consumption, or investment. This desire is *variable*. An "excess demand" for money is the same as a *shortfall* in aggregate demand for goods and services.

Consequently, the interest rate that manages to balance the quantity of money against the summed-up desire to hold money is hard to predict. It must represent both the rate of time preference of consumers and what J. M. Keynes called the "marginal efficiency of investment," or the return to investing.

A word of caution: It is surprisingly easy to say foolish things about interest rates and the money supply. One way to avoid doing so is to remember that money is in some ways simply a "veil"—a unit of account that allows us to measure how much private activity is displaced by public spending, and vice versa.[8] More simply, a public works project doesn't cost *money*; it costs the private resources that would be available, or other public projects that would have been built, if those resources had not been diverted.

Discount Rate May Reflect Risk

There is a very important question that public managers and political leaders have to face: What is the correct public discount rate? The classic statement of the problem is found in Arrow and Lind (1970: 364).

> It is widely accepted that individuals are not indifferent to uncertainty and will not, in general, value assets with uncertain returns at the their expected values. Depending upon an individual's initial asset holdings and utility function, he will value an asset at more or less than its expected value. Therefore, in private capital markets, investors do not choose investments to maximize the present value of expected returns, but to maximize the present value of returns adjusted for risk. The issue is whether it is appropriate to discount public investments in the same way as private investments.

On one hand, it seems that ignoring risk in the public sector will lead to (relative) underinvestment in private projects, because private projects will be discounted for risk and public projects will not. Consequently, the required stream of net benefits for public projects will not have to be as large as the net benefits of an otherwise similar private project for the NPV calculated (using different discount rates) for the two projects to be seen as equal.[9] On the other hand, the public sector is larger, and invests in more projects. Remember: The expected value is, over the long term and across many projects, the *actual average value* of investments. Doesn't it make sense for the public sector to ignore risk,[10] and focus solely on expected value?[11]

Disturbingly, there is no consensus on the answer to this question. Arrow and Lind (1970) conclude that the appropriate discount rate may differ for costs and benefits, and may depend further on the distribution of those costs and benefits. Others have argued that the appropriate discount rate for public projects is the "cost of borrowing," but this will differ for different government units based on (you guessed it!) risk. A municipal government which stands at risk of defaulting on its debt (as New York City did in the 1970s) has a much higher cost of borrowing money than a jurisdiction with an AAA bond rating. The "risk" accounted for in the cost of borrowing is very different from the risk of the project, because the cost of borrowing mostly reflects the market's perception of the likelihood of repayment of the debt, not the quality of the project.[12] Nonetheless, in practical terms the interest rate at which the government can borrow is the de facto discount rate for many public projects, if for no other reason than that discount rate represents the "break-even" rate for the project.

Elections May Cause Artificially High Discount Rates

In his 1995 book, *The Agenda,* Bob Woodward describes the reaction of an incredulous President Clinton in 1993 when he was told that the reforms he was working for would have no important benefits for several years. The next election was scheduled for 1996; the next congressional election was 1994. The president said, "You mean we won't see any benefits for three years?" The problem the president faced was clear: in the near term, the tax reform and budget reduction measures he was proposing were very painful. The benefits were expected (by advisors, who turned out to be quite correct) to take the form of a much stronger economy, and lower real interest rates. But these benefits would not be felt until after the 1994 congressional election (which, as it turned out, was a disaster for the Democrats), and maybe not until after the 1996 presidential election (which, of course, President Clinton won rather handily).

Elected officials may have very short time horizons, because they feel the need to confer immediate benefits on voters to win relection. If this is true, then the discount rate implied by frequent elections is distorted. The direction of the bias is not clear, however. In the case of public works projects, with immediate "benefits" in the form of contracts and pork barrel payments to local districts, the discount rate is probably too low, so that questionable (on an NPV basis) projects are funded anyway. For projects with up-front costs and long-term benefits, on the other hand, such as President Clinton's 1993 deficit reduction measures, the discount rate may be too high, because benefits expected after the next election don't count politically at all.

In any case, it is clear that politicians face incentives to have a very short time horizon, meaning that two kinds of projects may be mis-evaluated in democracies:

1. Projects with immediate costs but long benefit streams are re-jected for bad reasons.
2. Projects with immediate benefits but long streams of costs are accepted for bad reasons.

Summary

This chapter began whimsically, with a statement of "Wimpy's prin-ciple": A dollar tomorrow is worth less than a dollar today. The *amount* of this difference in value, for a time period determined by the problem being analyzed (an hour, a day, a year, a century) is called the *discount rate*. These differences in value accumulate over longer periods, because the calculation of the discount for time is *compounded*.

Discounting for the time value of resources is a little like time travel. Traveling forward in time, or valuing a current asset in the fu-ture, requires the use of an *interest rate*, or rental value for money. I claimed that the interest rate actually charged in the market is the sum of three components: (1) the pure opportunity cost of funds, (2) the anticipated inflation rate, and (3) the risk of nonpayment of the loan.

But once we are in the future, we need a way to get back. Travel-ing back in time from the future to the present requires the use of a discount rate. There are special problems with calculating an appro-priate discount rate. First, and perhaps most importantly, the dis-count rate reflects the *opportunity cost* of the *resources* used in the project, not the money invested. In this context, money is just a mechanism for facilitating exchange, and for representing the relative price of one physical resource in terms of others.

Second, accounting for risk in public projects is difficult, because people disagree about the very nature of risk in public finance. The usual discount rate used for public projects is the cost of borrowing, which has obvious practical advantages but may not capture the true opportunity cost of the resources being used.

Finally, we live in a democracy. In a system of government with fre-quent and recurrent elections, the time horizon for delivering benefits to a constituency may be artificially shortened. Politicians looking ahead only one or two years may distort the process of selecting public projects, by either undercounting future costs or overcounting current benefits.

SUMMARY OF KEY CONCEPTS

1. **Compound interest** is the repeated application of the rate of return, or "interest rate," to the accumulated value of an investment or asset. The return is "compounded," or computed as each time period elapses. Compounding can occur over any period, from centuries to decades to years, months, weeks, or days. The advantage of compound interest is that one earns interest not just on the original asset value, or principal, but also on the accumulated interest.

2. The **discount rate** is the precise rate by which a payment in the future is "discounted," or reduced in value, for each time period it is deferred. The discount rate is the mathematical compensation for the rate of time preference.

3. **Fisher's equation** is the formula for estimating the components of the total nominal, or observed, interest rate. The components are the risk premium, the real cost of money, and the expected inflation rate. The actual equation is:

   Nominal rate = Risk premium + Cost of money
   + Expected inflation rate

4. **Inflation** is a general increase in the price level, or a decline in the amount of goods and services that a unit of money can command. The inflation rate is strongly associated with changes in the rate of growth of the money supply.

5. The **interest rate** is the "rental" cost of money. Where the discount rate is used to discount values in the future, the interest rate represents the charges which must be paid on money borrowed now, and which must be paid every period until the loan is repaid.

6. The **internal rate of return** is the calculated "rate" of discount that exactly balances expected expenditures and expected revenues for a particular project. It is misleading as a basis for comparing multiple prejects.

7. The **present value** of a cash payment or benefit in the future is the value of the payment discounted for the number of time periods by which the payment is deferred. The present value is lower as the number of periods is greater, or the discount rate is higher.

8. The **principal** in a financial computation is the original value of the asset, or the base value on which interest payments are to be figured in any given time period.

8. The **"rate of time discount"** is the flip side of the interest rate. People with high discount rates do not consider the future to be very important, while people with low discount rates consider the future to be very nearly comparable with the present.

9. The **single project decision rule** is used to choose among projects with approximately the same cost. The rule is "choose the project with the largest present value." Interestingly, it is very difficult to choose a rule that outperforms this simple rule in all cases, even if multiple projects are to be ranked using the "largest present value" criterion.

PROBLEMS AND QUESTIONS

1. Imagine you are faced with three alternatives, each of which cost $1,000. Which would you decide to build, assuming the discount rate is 15 percent?

a. A bridge which takes five years to build, then yields $500 benefit per year for next ten years.

b. Temporary classrooms for schools yielding $500 benefit per year for three years.

c. Tax breaks to a foreign auto manufacturer for a new auto plant, yielding $200 benefit per year forever.

2. Would your answer to problem #1 change if the discount rate were 5 percent? How about if it were 55 percent; would any of the projects be worth building?

3. Rank the following ten projects, using the criterion of the internal rate of return. Rank those projects which are worth building from highest to lowest priority. Also identify those projects which are not worth building at all.

	Cost of Projects	Returns from Project
Project 1	$1,000 now, then $100/year forever	$200/year forever
Project 2	$2,000 now, then $500/year forever	$300/year forever
Project 3	$2,000 now, then $10/year forever	$200/year forever
Project 4	$100 now, then $40/year forever	$20/year forever
Project 5	$1,000 now, then $100/year for 2 years	$200/year for 5 years
Project 6	$100 now, then $10/year forever	$2,000/year for 3 years
Project 7	$10,000 now, then $100/year forever	$5,000/year for 20 years
Project 8	$600 now, then $25/year forever	$1,500/year for 10 years
Project 9	$100 now, then $1,000/year forever	$700/year for 2 years, then $2,000/year forever
Project 10	$4,000 now	$1,000/year for 6 years

4. Using the same projects as in problem 3, assume a discount rate of 15 percent, and rank the projects in terms of priority (including identifying those projects which should not be built). Is your ranking different or the same as in problem 3? Would you always expect this result, or do the projects in this example have some special features?

TAKE IT TO THE NET!

Go to: http://www.wwnorton.com/college/polisci/analyzingpolicy for additional problems, data sets, and course materials.

NOTES

1. The actual "Fisher equation" comes from Fisher (1911), and is correctly stated as:

$$1 + r = (1 + d) \times (1 + i) = 1 + d + i + (d \times i)$$

where:

r = the total rate *offered* in the market—that is, if you want to borrow, and there is no risk of default, the best rate you can find

d = the discount rate, or the underlying real *opportunity cost* of money

i = the anticipated rate of *inflation*

For low rates of inflation the interaction term ($d \times i$) can be ignored, though of course it makes a difference if inflation rates are large, or the compounding is performed over many time periods. The elaboration for risk differences presented here is a later addition, though the whole thing is still commonly referred to as "Fisher's equation."

2. Like most statements about interest rates, this is only true *often*, and is certainly not true always. It is quite possible for the "term structure" (the pattern of rates graphed against time on the horizontal axis) to be flat, or even downward-sloping. Remember: Interest rates are a price, and therefore reflect both demand and supply considerations.

3. A "brownfield" site is a contaminated area which has been condemned for health reasons. It is a blot on the urban landscape, because it cannot be developed, even through the land itself might be quite valuable. Companies may fear the contamination, but more likely they are unwilling to accept the potentially unlimited liability claims resulting from taking responsibility for this property.

4. There are many different formulas for calculating present values in spreadsheet programs. PV is the simplest Excel™ "formula; you should also look at the NPV formula, or even XNPV if the periodicity of payments is not constant.

5. Those interested enough to want to see a proof can no doubt do the proof for themselves. However, here is a sketch for the value of a finite series of payments of $1, with a discount rate of d:

$$PV = \frac{1}{1+d} + \frac{1}{(1+d)^2} + \frac{1}{(1+d)^3} + \frac{1}{(1+d)^4} + \ldots + \frac{1}{(1+d)^N}$$

Now, multiply this expression (on both sides) by $1/(1 + d)$:

$$\frac{1}{1+d} PV = \frac{1}{(1+d)^2} + \frac{1}{(1+d)^3} + \frac{1}{(1+d)^4} + \ldots$$

Subtract the second expression from the first:

$$\left(1 - \frac{1}{1+d}\right) PV = \frac{1}{(1+d)} \left(1 - \frac{1}{(1+d)^N}\right)$$

Divide both sides by the term in parentheses on the left, so that we get back the "clean" PV:

$$PV = \frac{\frac{1}{(1+d)}\left(1 - \frac{1}{(1+d)^N}\right)}{\left(1 - \frac{1}{1+d}\right)}$$

Rearranging, we find that:

$$PV = \frac{1-(1+d)^{-N}}{1+d\left(\dfrac{1+d-1}{1+d}\right)}$$

But this can be simplified to:

$$PV = \frac{1-(1+d)^{-N}}{d}$$

It is clear that the limit of this expression, as N grows large, is:

$$Lim_{N\to\infty}\ PV = \frac{1}{d}$$

For an annual payment of any arbitrary size B, the present value is:

$$Lim_{N\to\infty}\ PV = \frac{B}{d}$$

6. I do not mean to say that this is the correct value of the machine. Rather, it is an easy approximation of the upper bound of its value.
7. Appropriate here means a rate that accounts for both rate of time preference and risk of failure.
8. The use of "veil" to describe money dates from Keynes (1936). The problem, as Gurley (1961: 308) pointed out, is that "When the veil flutters, output s putters." For a broad discussion of "The Fluttering Veil," see Yeager (1997).
9. Consider an example. Imagine that two entities, one private and one public, are considering building the *same* project. The privately built project and the publicly built project both have up-front costs of $25,000. Suppose the private project is expected to pay $5,000 per year forever and the public project is anticipated to pay $3,000 per year forever. Imagine the two projects are equally risky (that is, there is the same chance the construction will fail, or the returns will be less than expected). If the private project's properties discount rate is 20 percent, the private project has a net present value of −$25,000 + ($5,000/0.2), or $0. If the public project discount rate is 10 percent, however, the public project has a NPV of −$25,000 + ($5,000/0.1), or $25,000. The conclusion is obviously that the project is "better" if it is built by the public sector.
10. By "risk," what is meant here is that the project has uncertain returns, and the expected return is chosen to represent the project. I do not mean that there is a risk to public health or safety, which is another question entirely. For two views on this point, see Weiner (1995) and Van Doren (1999).
11. As Arrow and Lind (1970: 364) also point out: "Many of the uncertainties which arise in private capital markets are related to what may be termed moral hazards. Individuals involved in a given transaction may hedge against the possibility of fraudulent behavior on the part of their associates. Many such risks are

not present in the case of public investments and, therefore, it can be argued that it is not appropriate for the government to take these risks into account when choosing among public investments."

12. There are exceptions to this rule, as in the case of "revenue bonds," where repayment is directly tied to the performance of the project to be funded.

~ 11 ~

Cost-Benefit Analysis

I t has taken us a long time to get here, but here we finally are: cost-benefit analysis! Cost-benefit analysis (CBA) is the most commonly used form of decision analysis. It unites three ideas, or assumptions, each of which we have already covered separately:

1. The costs and benefits of a public activity can be measured in dollars.
2. The risks of failure, and the chances of success, can be captured through probability discounting.
3. The future value of an asset, and the present value of a future cost or benefit, can be measured using time discounting—compound interest and discount rates.

Let us take another look at each assumption so that we can better see how they fit together.

Assumption I: Costs and Benefits Can Be Measured, and Added Up, in Dollars

For cost-benefit analysis to work, it has to be possible to measure costs and benefits of public actions by reducing the effects of those actions to the amount of consumer surplus gained or lost. The gains and losses can therefore be **monetized** or expressed in dollars (or the monetary unit appropriate to the jurisdiction). The obvious advantage is that these units are comparable across individuals; the not-so-obvious underlying assumption is that a dollar's loss to one person is offset by a dollar's gain to another. This Kaldor-Hicks criterion, which was mentioned briefly in chapter 4, is the normative, or ethical, underpinning for cost-benefit analysis. To make the logic clearer, I will break down the development into three parts.

First, remember the Pareto criterion: Given a status quo state of the world "S", the decision whether to implement an alternative policy "A" must be based on unanimous consent. That is, for each and every person i, the following inequality must be true:

$U_i(A) > U_i(S)$ (utility of A is greater than utility of S)

The weaker form of the Pareto criterion allows that some people are only indifferent, so that for all people:

$U_i(A) \geq U_i(S)$

and for at least one person j:

$U_j(A) > U_j(S)$

Second, we saw that the Kaldor-Hicks compensation principle was an extension of the Pareto criterion that allowed for disagreement, rather than always requiring at least weak Pareto comparisions (i.e., allowing for indifference). The extension is intuitive enough, because it simply allows for what economists call **side payments**.

Suppose we compare alternative A with status quo S, and find that while some people strongly prefer A, others would rather stay with S. We could simply add up votes, and count the number of people who want A and the number who want S. But voting asks only the direction of preference ("Do you like A, or S, better?"), not the intensity

("How much do the alternatives differ?"). What is needed is some way of adding up the *intensities*, or the differences in the gains and the losses, for all the gainers and all the losers.

Imagine we have five people, three (1, 2, and 3) who prefer S, and two (4 and 5) who prefer A. Suppose that persons 4 and 5 really, *really* prefer A, but that persons 1, 2, and 3 only mildly prefer S. Clearly, it might be possible for persons 4 and 5 (the gainers) to compensate persons 1, 2, and 3 (the losers), provided the total gains exceed the total losses. If it is possible, then the use of side payments transforms a situation of disagreement into unanimity. More simply, allowing the gainers to compensate the losers means that the Pareto criterion could, in principle, be satisfied.

Suppose we surveyed the five people, and (importantly) they all told the truth about the amount they would be willing to pay to have A win, or to have S win. In effect, this number is simply the quantity of dollars required to make each person indifferent between alternatives A and S. The results of our hypothetical truthful survey are presented in Table 11.1.

TABLE 11.1
Side Payments Required to Make People Indifferent Between Alternative A and Status Quo S

Person	Alternative A	(Status Quo) S	Vote
1	−$1,000	$1,000	S
2	−$400	$400	S
3	−$250	$250	S
4	$3,000	−$3,000	A
5	$5,500	−$5,500	A
Total side payments: (implied choice)	$6,850 (A wins)	−$6,850 (A wins)	$0 (S wins)

The way to interpret Table 11.1 is this: The entries in the columns are monetized differences in the citizens' evaluations of the two alternatives. A negative number means a citizen likes the alternative less. Notice that the numbers in each row are mirror images of each other, with one number negative and the other positive. The reason is that if person 1 likes S $1,000 more than A, it must be that person 1 likes A $1,000 less than S.

To find out which proposed policy, "Stay with S" or "Switch to A," will be chosen, we can compare two choice procedures. The first procedure, voting, is easy to figure out, because the positive numbers in each row show which alternative that person prefers. As I said above, persons 1, 2, and 3 like alternative S better, and persons 4 and 5 prefer alternative A. The size of the number doesn't matter, because voting is asking a very simple question: Which is better? With voting, *how much* better is irrelevant.[1]

So we know what voting would tell us. We also know that the pure Pareto criterion is inapplicable, because it is not true that everyone prefers alternative A, or that everyone prefers alternative S. The Kaldor-Hicks criterion is a different mechanism for suggesting a choice,[7] by registering intensity of preference not the number who prefer A. If we add up the number of dollars persons 1, 2, and 3 would pay to preserve alternative S as the policy, we find that they would pay $1,650. If we add up the dollars persons 4 and 5 would pay to switch to alternative A, the answer is $8,500. The difference is $6,850, meaning that a move from alternative S to alternative A would produce a net increase in value, for the society, of $6,850. Exactly symmetrically, staying at alternative S would create a deadweight loss to the society of −$6,850. So, where voting chooses A, Kaldor-Hicks selects S.

It is possible, in principle, for persons 4 and 5 to offer persons 1, 2, and 3 the $1,650 required to make them indifferent between the two policies, and still come out $6,850 ahead. It might be that persons 1, 2, and 3 would want more than that, and some settlement might be reached for a different amount, but the point is that the move from alternative S to alternative A creates net surplus value. *Once the side payments are made, we can apply the Pareto criterion*, because (with the losses to the losers compensated from the surplus gains to the winners) now everyone prefers alternative A to alternative S. For this reason, one might think of the Kaldor-Hicks approach as the *potential* Pareto criterion: "A policy can be adopted, despite opposition by the losers, if the winners can hypothetically compensate the losers to create a situation in which no one has lost and some have gained" (MacRae and Whittington, 1997, p. 89). Interestingly, this means that the outcomes of voting and Kaldor-Hicks are identical, if side payments are possible and costless.

This suggests the general procedure for applying the Kaldor-Hicks "compensation principle:"

- Consider all n feasible alternatives A_k ($k=1$ to n), compared to status quo S.
- For all individuals in society, compute the **net gains** (in dollars) for each A_k:

$$\text{Net gains} = \underset{\text{gainers}}{\Sigma \text{ gains}} + \underset{\text{losers}}{\Sigma \text{ losses}} = \underset{i}{\Sigma} \ (\$U(A_k) - \$U(S)$$

- Choose the best alternative A_k, or stick with alternative S, based on highest net gain to society.

There are some good things, and some bad things, about the Kaldor-Hicks approach. The clear advantage is that we have a basis for choice in situations where the Pareto criterion gives us no guidance. Also, it is interesting that Kaldor-Hicks gives us a way of choosing that can lead, at least in principle, to different outcomes than would be expected under voting procedures that ignore intensity.

But some potentially troubling questions also arise about using the Kaldor-Hicks approach, as many scholars have pointed out. The first is the question of **standing**[2]: Which gainers, and which losers, "count" in the calculation of net gains? As we saw earlier, the idea of externalities is a complicated thing to put into practice. If something you do upsets me, that is a loss. If it upsets me a lot, it might take millions of dollars to "compensate" me for the loss. But should we credit subjective, self-reported losses, or gains, with all the potential for irrationality and strategic misrepresentation they imply? Should we instead rely on "objective" measures of gains and losses, made by a third person? And does it matter whether the compensation is actually paid?

The second problem is the question of **distribution**: The reason that the Kaldor-Hicks approach is often called the compensation *principle* is that there is no requirement that the compensation actually be effected! So long as the compensation is *possible*, in principle, because the net gains are positive, that is enough to identify the correct policy action. As Stokey and Zeckhauser (1979; 279) characterize this approach, "Make a change when total income increases; don't worry about how it is distributed." This accords with a standard axiom of policy analysis that I first pointed out in chapter 6: Focus on efficiency, because distribution is a separate question ignored in cost-benefit analysis. The Kaldor-Hicks approach simply *separates* the creation of the surplus, or net gain, created by a policy choice, from the distribution of that surplus. Distributional questions are relegated to the larger question of equity within the entire system of taxes and subsidies, and inequities created by the choices of particular policies should be addressed in that context, not in pairwise comparisons of the policies themselves.

I am not taking a position in this debate; rather, I want you to recognize that cost-benefit analysis rests on the ethical foundation laid by Kaldor and Hicks. If you have problems with the Kaldor-Hicks compensation principle, you may have some questions about cost-benefit analysis more generally. The problem is that cost-benefit analysis is often presented as an objective, purely scientific mechanism for making policy choices, and that is not true. Cost-benefit analysis is the simplest kind of utilitarianism, and much of its apparent power for making "choices" derives from the way it simplifies the problem it is trying to solve.[3] Although this may not have been the intention of either Kaldor or Hicks, the fact is that "[The Kaldor-Hicks compensation principle] has evolved into the basic criterion of benefit-cost analysis: when the monetary gains/losses for all concerned parties are summed, a positive sum justifies adoption of the policy" (MacRae and Whittington, 1997; p. 89).

A number of mechanisms have been proposed for reforming the Kaldor-Hicks approach, but the most provocative is the "constitutional political economy" approach.[4] In many respects, the constitutional political economy view might be called "neo-Wicksellian," after the work of Knut Wicksell,[5] because of its emphasis on a **social contract** and the need for unanimous consent, either for decisions or for inclusion of a policy choice within the public sector. From the perspective of constitutional political economy, the apparent difference between voting and Kaldor-Hicks comparisons is not real, or at least it should not be. If the idea is to apply the Pareto criterion, then it should be applied straightforwardly. In fact, all voting should employ unanimity rule, or a decision rule so close to unanimity that the difference will simply prevent one, or a few, people from holding up the process for strategic purposes. Following this logic, if the gains to the gainers exceed the losses to the losers, then the gainers should be able to transform the vote from being split to being something close to unanimity. Of course, *requiring near unanimity would mean that the compensation would actually have to be negotiated, and paid.* For this reason, the constitutional political economy approach is quite radical. Consider the differences:

- *Kaldor-Hicks/cost-benefit analysis.* Identify the gainers and the losers from a policy change, and use objective measures to monetize and then sum up the gains and losses. If gains to gainers exceed losses to losers, implement the policy change, regardless of whether compensation from gainers to losers is actually effected.
- *Constitutional political economy.* Government has no role in policy choice, other than to implement the unanimously (near unanimously) selected alternative from the set of choices. Those who expect to gain from a policy change must find a way to compensate, and *credibly* commit to making that compensation, to secure the consent of nearly all the affected parties. It will still be true that the gains to gainers must exceed the losses to losers, but *the surplus in gains must be distributed, rather than taken from the losers.* The compensation could be in the form of side payments on the issue in question, or it could be concessions in another policy area (that is, a "logroll").

This brief discussion hardly begins to address the complex ethical and practical issues involved in distributing and redistributing the net gains of policy choice. The interested reader should consult MacRae and Whittington (1997), or other recent work on the ethical foundations of cost-benefit analysis. We now turn to the nuts and bolts of the benefit and cost calculation: the measuring of consumer surplus.

Review of Consumer Surplus

You recall from chapter [7] that consumer surplus is the value to the consumer of a transaction, over and above the value he or she actually has to pay for the commodity or service. Graphically, consumer surplus is the area under the demand curve but above the price the consumer has to pay. Because we often draw demand curves as lines, consumer surplus is represented as a triangle.

As an example, suppose the city of Ruttenton is trying to decide whether to build a parking garage. Right now, there is not enough parking in Ruttenton; when there is a football game at Ruttenton High School, people have to park in a muddy field on the city limits and walk into town. For the sake of simplicity, assume that all of the people who would like to use the parking garage (were it built) have identical demand curves for parking, and that the aggregate demand curve for parking in Ruttenton looks like the one depicted in Figure 11.1.

FIGURE 11.1
Demand Curve of a Representative Ruttentonian
for Parking

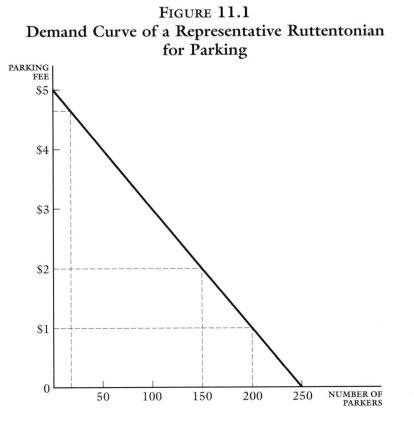

One measure of the value of the parking garage to the citizens of Ruttenton is the revenue it would bring in. But that is not a very good measure, because the revenue depends on the price the city decides to charge. For example, at a price of $5 per car, there are only twenty parkers, for a total revenue per week of $100. One hundred dollars is a gross underestimate of the value of the parking garage. What we need to do is take advantage of the fact that the demand curve organizes uses of the garage from most valued (the people who would pay $5.25) to least (those who would pay only a nickel). In fact, at a price of zero, we can see from Figure 11.1 that the number of people would park, per week, is 250.[6]

From Figure 11.1, we can conclude that the total (gross) value of a parking garage is the area under the demand curve, bounded by the horizontal and vertical axes. Since this is a right triangle (the legs meet at a 90-degree angle), we can use a simple formula to calculate its area:

Area of a right triangle = ½ × (base) × (height)

The base of the triangle is 250; the height is $5.25. One-half the product of these two is $656.25. So the largest value the parking garage could have, to the Ruttentonians, is about $34,125 per year. If we assume that the garage will last forever, that nothing will change about demand for its services, and the appropriate discount rate is 10 percent, we can do a quick calculation of its total present value to the city:

$$PV = \frac{\text{annual value}}{\text{discount rate}} = \frac{\$34,125}{0.10} \approx \$341,250$$

That is, the absolute maximum the garage could be worth is about $350,000, assuming it got maximum use and its services were provided for free, so that even the most marginal demanders consumed parking services.

If the parking garage costs $250,000 to build, it is probably a good deal. But suppose the garage costs $500,000 to build. Not a good deal. The discount rate would have to be less than 7 percent to make such a project break even, and that is assuming that the $500,000 could be paid out of general funds. Most parking garages don't work that way, of course. Instead, the city builds a parking garage and then charges a fee to get back some of those costs. For example, suppose the city charges a flat $2 fee to use the parking garage. Surely now the project is much more doable, financially, right? Doesn't charging money for the service obviously make the project more justifiable in terms of cost-benefit analysis?

Not so fast, sharp pencil person. Charging a $2 fee does two things: (1) It raises revenue for the city, by transferring $2 per use of the consumer surplus from the parker to the polity. (2) It prevents people who value the parking spot less than $2 but more than zero from using the parking garage, even when there are no other cars in the lot and the marginal cost is zero.

The consumer surplus triangle if there is a $2 fee is quite a bit smaller, as you can see in Figure 11.2. The base of the triangle is 155,[7] and the height is the difference between the maximum price anyone would pay ($5.25) and the price charged ($2): it is $3.25. Applying our formula, one-half times the base times the height is

FIGURE 11.2
Consumer Surplus Divided into Three Components

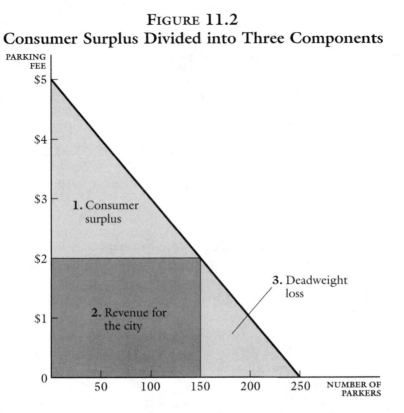

$252 per week. Over a fifty-two-week year, this would mean total consumer surplus is $13,104. About ninety-five people per week are not parking in the garage who would be using it if it were free.

You can see this clearly in Figure 11.2. The consumer surplus in Figure 11.1 was the entire area under the demand curve. If we charge a fee, that triangle (which represents the maximum amount the services could be worth) is divided into three parts, numbered here as in the figure:

1. Consumer surplus: The triangle beneath the demand curve, bounded by the vertical axis (zero parking) and the price line ($2), has an area of $252 per week.
2. Revenue for the city: The number of parkers (155) times the price ($2); the area of the rectangle is $310 per week.
3. Deadweight loss: The triangle beneath the demand curve corresponding to people who value parking but do not use the service ($\frac{1}{2} \times 95 \times \$2$) has an area of $95 per week.

This means that the total area under the demand curve per week ($252 + $310 + $95 = $657) is still just as it was when there was no fee (the $0.75 difference is due to rounding error). But the total present value of the project is actually less, because (by definition) *the deadweight loss is not being captured by anyone*. Deadweight loss is value that just escapes into the atmosphere. If a $2 fee is charged, then the present value (again, changing the weekly totals to annual totals by multiplying by 52) of the parking garage is:

$$PV = \frac{\text{Consumer surplus} + \text{tax revenue}}{\text{Discount rate}} = \frac{\$13104 + 16120}{0.10} = \$292240$$

The present value of the parking garage will depend a lot on the discount rate chosen (lower discount rate, higher value), of course, as you know from the previous chapter. For our present purposes, the example is meant to illustrate two points:

First, the concept of "value" is slippery. The fact is that if government provides a service for free the citizens will "value" it. However, in the example there is no discussion of alternatives—no mention of the possibility of private parking provision.

Second, it is easy to fall into the trap of believing that a service should be provided for free. In this case there may be something to that argument—in the example, the way to maximize "value" (i.e., minimize deadweight loss) was to charge a zero price. But that argument is true only if (a) the financing comes from the general fund, and (b) all citizens really do have the same preferences for use of the parking garage. If, on the other hand, the situation is like that in chapter 5, where the citizens of Ruttenton were deciding whether to build a pool, then the majority of high-demand parkers can impose their will on the low-demand parkers (also known as "bicyclers"). In that case, all prior claims about deadweight loss go out the window. Forcing people who don't use cars to pay for "free" parking for those who do use cars creates much larger deadweight losses.

So be careful not to overinterpret this little example. Consumer surplus is a measure of value, but only if you buy the Kaldor-Hicks argument that value can be added up across citizens without regard to the actual *distribution* of gains and losses on individuals. Otherwise, it is possible to manipulate, or at least to confuse, the actual size of the deadweight losses that accrue to policy decisions. The attribution of "value" to amenities is fraught with opportunities for apparently innocuous assumptions to change the estimates of values dramatically.

Assumption II: Risks of Failure and Chances of Success Can Be Captured through Probability Discounting

The problem of discounting for risk is computationally complex, because it requires both an understanding of the theory of calculating probabilities and an accurate knowledge of the true distributions of likely outcomes of policy alternatives. The theory one can learn fairly easily, by studying chapter 9 in this book, or by going deeper and taking a course in probability. The problem is knowing the true distributions: we usually have to settle for an estimate, or even a guess, and the results can depend crucially on just what that guess is.

A common distinction in the literature is the contrast between uncertainty, where no one knows what will happen, and risk, where we at least know the distribution of likely outcomes. Perhaps the simplest example is weather: Tomorrow, either it will rain or it won't. I am uncertain, because I don't know the relative likelihood of the elements of this set of mutually exclusive (both can't happen), exhaustive (it's summer; it won't snow) alternatives. I could try to transform my uncertainty into a risk assessment, by guessing that the two events are equally likely, so the chance of rain is 50 percent and the chance of no rain is 50 percent, or by doing research, looking up the history of rain/no rain at this time of year, and concluding that on June 12 there has been measurable rain 55 percent of the time in the past fifty years. Or I might rely on someone else's research, such as watching the weather report on television, and learning that a high pressure area over my state will stay in place, reducing the chances of rain to less than 10 percent.

The probability estimates we use in policy analysis are generally derived from our own estimates, or someone else's research. The thing you have to watch out for is the "probability estimate" that is really just a guess, or (worse) a value chosen to serve an advocacy mission, rather than an objective answer to the question, "What is the probability distribution over possible outcomes?"

Assumption III: Future and Present Values
Can Be Measured Using Time Discounting

The third assumption of cost-benefit analysis is the rate of time discount, or the relative values of costs and benefits in the future, compared to costs and benefits today. The rate of time discount can be used as a trick if you want to support or oppose a project: High discount rates overvalue the present, and low discount rates overvalue the future. In the debate over the value of a tree in a national forest, a low discount rate serves the advocates of the tree, while a high discount rate serves the advocates of the lumber. Who is right? That depends on the correct discount rate.

Consequently if, in a policy analysis study or elsewhere, someone quotes you a value of an asset, you should immediately wonder about their discount rate assumption. It is easy to be fooled by an apparently authoritative argument about "value" that quotes a specific number as the basis for the claim. Anyone who wants to value the future is smart enough to choose a low discount rate, and anyone who wants to value the present will quote a high discount rate. Obviously, this is *backwards*: their use of a low, or high, discount rate is a consequence of their desire to reach a particular conclusion. The fact that they can "prove" their claim is a sham, unless you think the discount rate they are using is the correct one.

Cost-Benefit Analysis in Action

Now that we have reviewed the assumption, it is time to do some cost-benefit analysis. The following two examples illustrate cost-benefit analysis in action.

An Individual Example: A State Lottery Ticket

Suppose a friend tells you he is going to enter the state lottery, which has a possible payoff of $10 million. You ask, "Why? Why today, and not last week?" He tells you, "Oh, the payoff last week was only expected to be $2.5 million."

It strikes you that you ought to be able to decide whether the lottery ticket is "worth" its price of $1, using cost-benefit analysis. What you need is three pieces of information:

- Dollar-denominated *values* for the costs, and possible benefits, of participating
- The *probabilities* of all possible future streams of costs and benefits of lottery ticket purchase
- The *discount rate* appropriate to transform future costs, or benefits, into current dollars

The fine print on the lottery ticket says that there are two ways to win: (1) There is a 1/250,000 chance the ticket will win a $10,000 "instant" prize. You scratch off the gray chalky stuff on the bottom corner, and if you won, it says "winner!" Otherwise, it says, "Sorry, try again!" This prize is paid immediately, by check, from the state if you turn in the ticket. (2) There is a 1/15,000,000[8] chance you will win the grand prize, the $10,000,000 your friend was so excited about. If your number is drawn on the selection day, the state will pay you $500,000 a year for twenty years, which adds up to $10 million.

Before we do the cost-benefit analysis, it is worth pointing out a few things. Clearly, a grand prize of $500,000/year for twenty years is a lot different than a lump sum of $10 million, which is what your friend has in mind. To figure out the "value" of a ticket, you are going to have to discount the possible values of participation, both by the probabilities of winning and by the time discount value of the payments. Finally, a ticket can (in principle) be both an instant winner and a grand prize winner, because those are two different contests. Since the two events are not mutually exclusive, but are independent, you will need to use the product rule (from chapter 9) to figure out their relative likelihoods.

The easiest way to depict the decision problem is in a **decision tree diagram**, as is shown in Figure 11.3. The nodes in this tree are not human choices, but rather are results revealed by chance. We know for sure all the possible values of each outcome, since a ticket can (a) not win, (b) win an instant $10,000, (c) win the grand prize, or (d) win both an instant and a grand prize. Since at the time of buying the ticket we don't know which outcome will occur, we use the concept of *probability discounting* to arrive at *expected values*, and the concept of *time discounting* to arrive at *present values*.

As the figure shows, the four possible outcomes can be grouped according to whether the ticket holder wins the instant prize and the grand prize, the instant prize only, the grand prize only, or no prize at all. The figure gives the present values of each outcome (that is,

FIGURE 11.3
Cost-Benefit Analysis for Buying a Lottery Ticket

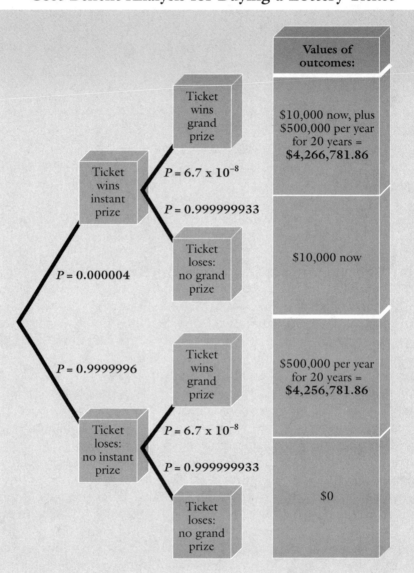

discounted for time as appropriate) in the box on the right side. Of course, we must still discount for probability, using the product rule to evaluate the probabilities of each set of events. The results of applying this procedure can be found in Table 11.2, which presents both the probability of each "branch" of the tree and the expected

TABLE 11.2
Table of Probabilities, and Expected Present Values, for Lottery Ticket

Outcome	Probability of Outcome	Expected Present Value
Win both	2.68×100^{-15}	$0.04
Win instant only	0.0000039999997	$0.039999997
Win grand prize only	6.7×10^{-8}	$0.29
Win Neither	0.999999533	$0.0
Totals:	1.00	$0.37

present value (that is, discounted by time and probability) of that outcome.

The bottom line, figuratively and literally, is that the lottery ticket, with its appropriately discounted chances of winning an instant $10,000, or $500,000 per year for five years, or both, is "worth" about 37 cents in expected present value. Is it really worth paying the $1? Quite possibly, provided that one of these two conditions is met:

- The buyer is risk-loving, and will pay 63 cents for the privilege of betting.
- The buyer enjoys the chance to dream about what he or she would do with the winnings, and the lottery ticket makes it fun.

These two conditions may seem the same, but they are not. The "risk-loving" condition is a specific requirement on the concavity of the citizen's evaluation of risk and return. The citizen need not be *truly* risk-loving, in the sense that he or she wants more risk everywhere; rather, the lottery must have aspects of a "Friedman-Savage" (after Friedman and Savage, 1948) game, where poor people rationally risk small amounts of money for large possible, but unlikely, returns. The "chance to dream" condition is simply consumption: the enjoyment of daydreaming is an end in itself, for which the expected value of the ticket is nearly irrelevant. If I throw a coin in a wishing well, it may not be for any specific return. Instead, my coin, or my 63 cents over and above the expected value of the lottery, is the cost of a ticket to daydream.

Neither of these considerations (Friedman-Savage games or tickets to daydream) are important to my friend, however. He was going to buy the ticket as an investment, because he stood to gain so much if he won. What you have shown, however, is that from a cost-benefit analysis perspective this "investment" makes no sense: even the "grand prize" of $10 million once you have discounted for the time value of the payments and discounted for the probabilities of winning, is a poor investment.

A Public Sector Example: Does Andrews Street Need a "Dead End" Sign?

Now come with me to a town council meeting, where the solons of Ruttenton are making a decision, using cost-benefit analyses. Here is the situation: Andrews Street, a pretty little street off of Main Street in Ruttenton, goes about one hundred yards and then curves enough so that you can't see past the large oak trees on both sides of the curve. Visitors to Ruttenton often drive down Andrews Street, only to find that there is a dead end just past the curve. Sometimes three or more cars will be waiting to turn around, and inevitably some person in a hurry will pull through Grandma Smith's rose garden.

Grandma Smith has petitioned the council to put up a Dead End sign at the corner of Main Street and Andrews Street, so that people won't turn onto Andrews by mistake. She lists several benefits that would result from the erection of the sign:

1. People will stop driving through my rose bushes! Of course, there is still a fifty-fifty chance some errant driver will hit the bushes when they turn around, but the chances now are 100 percent.
2. There will be less traffic and congestion on Andrews Street, where a number of children play in yards right by the street.
3. Out-of-town visitors will save time, and frustration, by not taking a wrong turn trying to find the road they want.

Several of the council members nod; Grandma Smith is a respected member of the community, and her argument seems to make sense. But then old Mr. Andrews (the street was named after his grandfather), who has a large house on the corner of Main and Andrews, stands up and offers a different view:

1. If you put up a Dead End sign, it would be right in the middle of my azaleas! Surely my azaleas are as important as Grandma

Smith's roses. Furthermore, there is only a chance that people are going to drive through the roses, whereas the sign will ruin the look of my azaleas for sure. I don't want a sign on my property, and my property extends all the way past the curve in the road.

2. Those kids shouldn't be playing out by the street in the first place. Young ruffians!
3. Who cares about the out-of-town people? The taxpayers of Ruttenton shouldn't have to use their tax money to improve the convenience, and save the time, of people from outside.

Once again, the town council members nod in agreement. Mr. Andrews has some good points, except for the ranting about kids. One person wonders aloud about how to break the apparent impasse. You stand up and say, "We could do a cost-benefit analysis."

Immediately, the meeting dissolves into an uproar. Mr. Andrews, who is hard of hearing, thinks you have said, "I'm cross, on how banal this is!" Sure that he has been insulted, Andrews picks up his chair and tries to hit you with it. Grandma Smith wants to know if anyone is going to act on her proposal. Everyone else is talking at once, trying to figure out who you are and why you came to a Ruttenton town meeting.

Once things settle down and everyone learns you are a trained policy analyst, they ask you to prepare an evaluation, using cost-benefit analysis, of the proposal to build to Dead End sign. Here is what you come up with.

Costs

1. Materials (sign, post, concrete for base): $150
2. Labor (1 hour at $22 rate for public works employees): $22
3. Actual damage to Mr. Andrews' azaleas (1 plant must be killed): $7
4. Visual harm to the look of Mr. Andrews' azalea bed, and property: $??

Benefits

1. 50 percent chance people will stop driving through Grandma Smith's roses (replacement cost of six plants, at $25 each, discounted by ½): $75.

2. Reduced chance of child being struck by car. Suppose that the value of a child's life is $100,000. If the chance of being struck before was 1/10,000, it would now be reduced to 1/100,000. Net benefit: savings of expected value of $100.[9]

3. Saving of time/inconvenience for visitors. Assume that fifteen cars per day will be turned away by the Dead End sign. The road is one-fourth mile long (for a round trip of one-half mile), saving a driving distance of 7.5 miles and time of about fifteen minutes (it takes sixty seconds to drive the quarter mile, turn around, and drive back) per day. Net benefit: savings of expected value of $10,000.[10] All of these cars belong to visitors to Ruttenton, because the Ruttentonians themselves all know the road is a dead end.

After writing these figures on the blackboard, you say you need two more pieces of information to complete your analysis. "First, the benefits from erecting the sign are at least $175, in terms of expected present value. There is a very large additional value of $10,000, but that will all go to outsiders, so we face a question of 'standing': Do the outsiders count in our calculation of the benefits?"

Several of the people at the meeting mutter "Yes," or "No," but no one is sure how to handle the problem. The large size of the benefits to outsiders, who don't pay taxes in Ruttenton, is confusing to the citizens. It is hard to know whether they should take these benefits into account. They decide they will have to give the matter more thought.

Then you say, "And here is the second issue. I don't have a value for the damage to the appearance of Mr. Andrews' azaleas. I need to know how to value that." Mr. Andrews says, "one million dollars!" Others say, "He should get something, because those are darned pretty azaleas. The yellow sign will clash with the pink flowers." Grandma Smith, at the back of the room, yells "What about my property? I don't like looking at all those cars. How come that doesn't count in your analysis?"

Hoping to bring people back to the subject, and make a decision, you point out that the decision is really a close one, if the people of Ruttenton truly don't want to count benefits to outsiders. It comes down to this:

Benefits: $175 + [benefits to outsiders]
Costs: $179 + [damage to view of property]

The costs are slightly larger than the benefits, and that is before we consider the loss of beauty of the azaleas. Mr. Andrews is still insisting that he wants $1 million, and people are starting to look at their watches.

Suddenly you remember that the key to cost-benefit analysis is the Kaldor-Hicks compensation principle. You walk to the back of the room, and have a whispered conversation with Grandma Smith. She is reluctant at first, but then agrees to try your suggestion. You walk back to the front of the room, and say, "Mr. Andrews, I have a proposal. Suppose that Grandma Smith offered you $500 in cash to accept the sign in your azaleas. Would that be enough to get you to say okay?"

Mr. Andrews, who up until now had just been trying to block the sign, and hadn't actually considered the prospect of being paid, breaks into a big smile. Everyone looks back at Grandma Smith, expecting an operatic protest. But she just stares at the floor, expressionless. Mr. Andrews, thinking he is going to get $500 out of this, says, "Well, I suppose I could live with a sign in my yard. Sure, $500 would be enough to make me say okay."

"Yahoo!" Grandma Smith shouts, startling everyone in the room as she leaps to her feet. "You outfoxed yourself this time, you old coot! I'm not going to pay that old fraud a penny! This young person was just trying to find an honest figure for the value; it *doesn't matter* whether the compensation is actually made. Right, policy analysis person?" You nod. "We just wanted to show what a liar Andrews is. A million dollars! Ha! He would accept $500." Mr. Andrews picks up the chair again, but Granny Smith stares him down, hands on hips.

Now that you have a figure for the value of the azaleas, you are almost finished. All that remains is settling the question of standing, or placing a value on the savings in time and money to visitors to Ruttenton from not having to travel down the dead end road and then turn around and come back out. "Should we consider them at all," you ask, "or just ignore them?"

Grandma Smith wants to count the full $10,000 benefit. Mr. Andrews, still smarting from his embarrassment about the value of the azaleas, shouts "To heck with outsiders! Don't count them at all." After lots of discussion, it is decided to count benefits to outsiders, but at a greatly reduced rate. Benefits to outsiders will "count" at only 10 cents on the dollar. This is the last piece of the puzzle to fall into place; you are now ready to make a recommendation.

"The total benefits are $1,175, and the total costs are only $679. The sign should be built." Relieved, everyone gets up to leave. Mr. Andrews, looking like he wants to bite someone, says that he deserves to be paid. "Tell me again, young person: This Condor-Hickey thing says I can't get paid for damage to the value of my property?"

"Oh, no, that is not true!" you say. Now Grandma Smith starts to look sick. "All the Kaldor-Hicks criterion requires is that the compensation is possible; it can be made or not made, depending on the choice of the political group making the decision. The Kaldor-Hicks criterion *only* tells us whether to do the work, not who should pay for it. You don't have to have compensation, but there is nothing to say you *can't*."

Mr. Andrews triumphantly waves his arms, but Grandma Smith says, "Wait a minute!" "The total benefits to me are only $75; all the other benefits go to children on the street and to the drivers from outside. Even if we decide to pay Andrews, I don't see why I should be the one paying. The benefits to me aren't that big."

"I've got it!" howls Mr. Andrews. "We put up a booth in the middle of the road, charge a quarter, and then tell the person the road is a dead end!"

Grandma Smith stares, open-mouthed. "Let me get this straight: instead of a sign, you want to build a *dead end toll road*?"[11]

"Of course," says Andrews, sure he has the answer now. "The problem is that most of the benefits go to outsiders. For those of us in the city, and especially to me, the costs of building the sign greatly outweigh the benefits. What we have to do is capture some of those gains. The information that the road is a dead end is valuable to the driver. We can charge for that information!"

Looking out the window, you notice that the sun is starting to come up; the meeting has lasted all night. You've had enough. As you walk out to your car, with the citizens of Ruttenton arguing away behind you, you realize that cost-benefit analysis is harder than you thought. The issues are complicated, even for so simple a decision as whether to put up a Dead End sign.

Here are four things you resolve to find out next time, before you even get started on one of these cost-benefit analysis problems.

• **Standing** of those affected. You have to decide who counts. For example, in the decision on whether to install burglar alarms and locks at a musuem, one effect is a reduction in the value of the museum as a target to thieves. Alarms reduce the income of thieves. This effect, no matter how real, should probably not be counted. The question Ruttenton's citizens face is harder: it is hard to justify ignoring benefits to "outsiders," because unlike criminals they are not disobeying the law. On the other hand, they don't pay taxes in Ruttenton, so the benefits and costs of the policy are guaranteed to fall on different groups. The general problem is this: You need to decide who counts before you start counting.

• **Discounted values** of outcomes, accounting for risk and time. In many cases, you will have to make assumptions, based more on good guesses than on hard facts.

• **Sensitivity analysis.** Consider the implications of bad assumptions for your decision. Did the choice of probabilities, or discount rates, drive the conclusion? Did the particular values you chose force a conclusion, when a slightly different set of values would have led to the opposite conclusion? This is called **sensitivity analysis** because it tests to see whether your results are "sensitive," to, or dependent on, specific values or assumptions. The opposite of "sensitive" (here, a bad thing) is a *robust* result, which does not depend on assumptions.

• **Compensation.** Not withstanding Kaldor and Hicks, the issue of compensation is central to most real world cost-benefit analysis. For one thing, there is the practical political question of getting support. In some cases, the size of the compensation package is crucial to achieving the desired outcome. People who aren't compensated for losses can defect from the agreement, and may be able to block passage of a policy choice which, from a pure policy perspective, is worth implementing. Second, there is a genuine legitimacy issue. The Fifth Amendment to the U.S. Constitution is quite clear: "No person shall . . . be deprived of life, liberty, or property, without due process of law; nor shall private property be taken for public use without just compensation." So, while compensation may be unimportant from a policy analysis perspective focusing on efficiency, it is central to a legitimate and fair system of public policy. Due process and just compensation are legal concepts whose definition is beyond our scope here. The important thing for you to remember is that there must be compensation for "takings," or the use of private resources for public purposes, no matter how legitimate the underlying public purpose may be.

ANALYZING POLICY

A Real Example: The Army Corps of Engineers

One of the main practitioners of cost-benefit analysis, in several different forms, is the United States Army Corps of Engineers. Traditionally, the Corps of Engineers has used cost-benefit analysis techniques to arrive at judgments on the merits of projects (especially rivers, harbors, and flood control projects). Using assumptions about values of projects, and discounting both costs and benefits of those projects over time using a discount rate, the Corps of Engineers has arrived at a "benefit-cost" ratio for the projects. A value of 1 for the benefit-cost ratio means that the project is expected to break even. Choosing a benefit to cost ratio of 1 as the cutoff between fundable and nonfundable projects is (the reader should see immediately[12]) exactly equivalent to using the internal rate of return criterion from chapter 10.

So, in addition to the assumptions listed above (value, risk, discount rate, and distribution), the Corps of Engineers faces another important assumption: the extent to which benefits must exceed costs before a project is viable. This is different from the classic two-step approach to CBA, in two ways: (1) The projects are ranked, either by the excess of benefits over costs or by the ratio of benefits divided by cost; and (2) projects are funded one by one, starting at the "best" projects at the top of the list, until the budget is exhausted. By law,[13] the Corps of Engineers must give advice on the total number of projects that are technically fundable, or (more practically) must evaluate the "recommendation" from Congress that a project's benefits justify its costs.

To give you an idea of how many conflicting goals the Corps of Engineers must juggle, consider the wording of just *one* (of seven), "strategies" listed for fulfilling its mission:

> We will improve effectiveness by using best business practices, revamping processes, and leveraging technology integrated across traditional functional and geographic boundaries. We will produce products and services that fully meet customer expectations of quality, timeliness, and cost effectiveness, within the bounds of legal responsibilities.[14]

The "cost effectiveness" part of this is a nod to cost-benefit analysis, but the Corps has gotten in lots of trouble trying to apply the logic of cost-benefit analysis to projects where the benefits and costs may be widely separate, both in time and space.

Consider, for example, a sharp critique by Senator Max Baucus, from Montana:

Few people here in Washington know this, but the Fort Peck Reservoir in eastern Montana is one of the largest flood control projects in the country. In the 1930's, Montanans sacrificed over 240,000 acres of prime farm land to build Fort Peck. For decades the reservoir has *provided flood control benefits for Montanans' downstream neighbors* with *few benefits for Montanans* and *many burdens accruing to Montana residents.*

With this budget, the Administration proposes to put the Corps out of the local flood control business. . . . This would signal an almost total withdrawal by the Federal Government from a mission with mostly local benefits. (Statement of Max Baucus, Senator from Montana, Senate Hearing 104–42, February 14, 1995, before the Subcommittee on Transportation and Infrastructure of the Committee on Environment and Public Works. Emphasis added)

Is it any wonder that Corps of Engineers has resorted to "Dilbert-speak," or the use of cliches about "customer service," and "revamping processes, and leveraging technology"? The fact that benefits go to one group, and costs to another, is simply *irrelevant* in the context of cost-benefit analysis. The Corps of Engineers was simply following the logic of the model, and the letter of the law. Yet members of Congress find little reason to accept the results, and who could blame them? From the perspective of the citizens of Montana, whom Senator Baucus represented, the division of costs and benefits seemed unfair. The obvious solution is to go to local funding, so that the people benefiting are also the people paying.

Along these lines, in the same hearings, the new Corps procedure was described by John Chafee of Rhode Island:

In an effort to find spending reductions in the outyears, the Administration will propose legislation to reduce Federal involvement in the construction of new water resources projects. As I understand the forthcoming proposal, new Army Corps' flood control projects would not be carried out for local flood prevention efforts. Moreover, the benefit-to-cost ratio of a project will have to be at least two to one; and, the local funding match for new projects will rise from 25 percent to 75 percent. These would indeed be real changes representing a clear departure from traditional Army Corps' policy. . . .

It seems the Corps is taking it on the chin here, and probably unfairly. It is easy to criticize cost-benefit, but the reality is that we cannot do without it. Cost-benefit analysis is the only way of arriving at a starting point for analyzing projects and coming up with priorities. It is easy to criticize assumptions, but the fact is that the assumptions can be clearly identified, and the sensitivity of the results to particular assumptions analyzed.

Summary

Cost-benefit analysis is one of the most commonly used techniques for making, or assisting, policy decisions. When you think about it, it is fairly obvious why this is so: cost-benefit analysis offers a hard number, or estimate, of the net value of an investment, project, or activity. If the benefits exceed the costs, there would appear to be a plausible argument for pursuing that project. If funds are scarce, then cost-benefit analysis offers a technique for ranking projects, or putting them in order of priority.

But there are four important issues that make this approach tricky at best, and at worst downright misleading or dangerous. These four assumptions are:

- *First*, that the costs and benefits of a public activity can be measured in dollars. Generally, this means we must rely on consumer surplus, or some other mechanism for measuring value. These estimates are notoriously inexact.
- *Second*, that the risks of failure, and the chances of success, can be captured through probability discounting. But the resulting expected values are very sensitive to the specific probabilities used, and these probabilities are usually just rough estimates. Uncertainty in the probability estimates translates directly into uncertainty in the expected values, but it is difficult to represent the degree of uncertainty accurately.
- *Third*, that the future value of an asset, and the present value of a future cost or benefit, can be measured using compound interest and discount rates. Unfortunately, the present value estimates are, if anything, even more sensitive to the discount rate used than the expected value estimates are to the probabilities. Even small changes in discount rates can make huge differences in the total benefits, or the value of costs, over long periods. Often, the result obtained depends entirely on what turns out to be an arbitrary assumption about risk or inflation.
- *Fourth*, that compensation need not be effected for a policy to be selected as optimal. This idea has some plausibility in the academic world of cost-benefit analysis, but in politics questions of distribu-

tion and equity are at least as important as, and may even dominate, questions of efficiency.

The idea that the *compensation principle,* or *potential Pareto comparisons,* are useful is not going to go away. It is primarily an efficiency-based approach, and helps to resolve policy conflict over differences between markets and experts. But the question of distribution, or the conflict between markets and politics, is at least as important in understanding real policy decisions. Cost-benefit analysis, because it is an apparently neutral tool, is often criticized for ignoring distribution. But the logical basis of cost-benefit analysis is an abstraction from equity concerns. That is its power and its weakness.

SUMMARY OF KEY CONCEPTS

1. **Consumer surplus** is the sum of the differences between the prices actually paid by consumers and the maximum price that each consumer would be willing to pay if there were no alternatives.

2. **Cost-benefit analysis** is the process of evaluating policy alternatives by comparing the advantages and disadvantages, based on the appropriate discounts for risk and rate of time preference.

3. **Deadweight losses** are the opportunity costs of the consumer surplus forgone by distortions in prices, incentives, or as a result of regulatory policies.

4. **Decision tree diagrams** are devices for organizing the impacts of different courses of action, with nodes representing choices among alternatives; values are computed based on discounts for risk and time preference. Decision trees are one important way of organizing cost-benefit analysis.

5. **The discounted value** is the end result of the process of counting assets, costs, and other values at less than face value, based either on risk (expected value), or on rate of time preference (present value).

6. **Distribution** is the allocation of wealth, ownership, and income in an economy. *Redistribution* is the process of changing the distribution as a matter of policy.

7. The **Kaldor-Hicks Compensation Principle** is an extension of the Pareto criterion which allows for comparisons even if there is not unanimous preference for one alternative over another. Ap-

---

plication of the Kaldor-Hicks criterion involves monetizing, or putting into some other comparable units, all the gains to the gainers, and the losses to the losers, from some policy action. If the total gains exceed the total losses, the Kaldor-Hicks criterion would imply that the policy should be pursued, independent of whether the compensation is actually paid.

8. **Monetization** is the process of converting different units of value into dollars, or some other unit of money, so that they can be compared directly.

9. **Net gains** represent the advantage of a policy, or course of action, after accounting for the costs, or drawbacks. More precisely, net gains are the benefits minus the costs.

10. The **Pareto criterion** is a mechanism for comparing two alternatives A and B. Pareto comparison requires that each individual prefers A to B (in the strong form), or that everyone either is indifferent between A and B or prefers A to B, with at least one person strictly preferring A (in the weak form), before the society could decide that A is socially preferred to B.

11. It is common to point out that an analysis is "sensitive" to the assumptions that lead to a conclusion. As **sensitivity analysis** is an attempt to gauge just how sensitive the conclusion may be, and what the implications of changing assumptions are. By modifying assumptions, singly and then in groups, it is possible to consider the implications of using inaccurate assumptions, and to learn how robust the conclusions of the analysis are likely to be.

12. In applying the Kaldor-Hicks compensation principle, **side payments** refer to the amount of compensation required to make each person indifferent to the outcome.

13. The notion of a **social contract,** or collective agreement to give consent to transfer power to a ruler, and for the creation of a government, is the basis of the application of the Kaldor-Hicks principle. The social contract is often invoked to explain, or to justify, decisions which benefit most people at the expense of a few.

14. The ability to have a voice, or to be "counted," in law, is called **standing.** The issue of standing is very controversial, since the size of gains or losses is irrelevant unless it is decided first that the person or organization has standing.

PROBLEMS AND QUESTIONS

1. Judgments about "standing" may be the single most important aspect of cost-benefit analysis. Yet for many policy problems, standing is considered almost as an afterthought. Give a judgment about standing for each of the following situations: should the person's values or welfare count?

a. An herbicide called paraquat was sprayed by American drug agents on marijuana fields in Mexico in the late 1970s. Arguably, at least some of the paraquat-laced marijuana was later (illegally) smoked by people in the United States. Should the consequent respiratory problems, and increased cancer risk, have been foreseen, and considered in the decision to use the herbicide?

b. Citizens in Canada have noticed that rain in the Maritime provinces has grown steadily more acidic since the 1950s, killing fish and denuding trees in many areas. It seems likely that pollution from coal-burning plants in the midwestern United States has had at least some influence on the acid rain problem in Canada. In deciding whether to modernize the plants, should officials of private utility companies in Michigan, Ohio, and Pennsylvania include potential benefits to Canadians?

c. In his famous pamphlet "Proposal to Give Badges to Beggars," Jonathan Swift argued that beggars who lived in Dublin, Ireland, should be given badges to identify their right to beg within the city limits. Other beggars should be run out of town, if need be by the "native" beggars themselves. Swift believed that the Dublin parishes were being forced to support more than their share of impoverished people who poured in from the countryside in times of famine. In evaluating this proposal, how should the welfare of the country beggars be addressed?

2. Suppose you are a freshman and are trying to decide what kind of portable stereo (boom box) to buy now, so you have one for the four years you are in college. The inexpensive model has all the features that you want (super "woofer," CD player, and detachable speakers), but there are two problems: (1) The sound quality is not great, and (2) the cheapo stereo is more likely to break down. If it breaks down within two years, it will be covered under warranty, but you will have to pay $20 to send it to the factory to be repaired. If it breaks down after two years, you will have to buy a whole new inexpensive stereo. Assume that the expensive model has a lifetime warranty, and free packaging and mailing for service. For your decision (which stereo to buy?), the information you have is as follows:

- The inexpensive stereo costs $50.
- If you buy the inexpensive stereo, there is a 50 percent chance it won't break, and will last the whole four years. There is a 25 percent chance it will break down in the warranty period (assume that the breakdown occurs at exactly the one year point!), and it will cost you $20 to send it to the maker's factory. There is a 25 percent chance it will break down the day after the warranty expires, and you will have to pay $50 for another inexpensive stereo, which you can assume lasts the rest of the time you are in college.
- Your discount rate is 10 percent per year.
- Just in terms of sound quality, the expensive stereo is worth $50 more to you.
- The expensive boom box $110.

a. Draw a decision tree, and use it to analyze the problem. Be sure you include probabilities, and calculate the expected present values of the expenses.

b. Which stereo should you buy, assuming that you are risk neutral? Support your answer with evidence from the decision tree.

3. Imagine that you are asked to help make a decision between two policies, the status quo S, and proposed alternative A_1. The distribution of monetized preferences is as follows:

Person	Alternative A	Status Quo S	Vote
1	-$1,000	$1,000	S
2	$400	-$400	A
3	-$400	$450	S
4	$300	-$300	A
5	$300	-$300	A
6	-$250	$250	S
7	$500	-$500	A

a. Which alternative would win if you decide to apply the Pareto criterion?

b. Which alternative would win if you decide to use majority rule?

c. Which alternative would win if you decide to use the Kaldor-Hicks criterion?

d. Suppose that you have decided to use the Kaldor-Hicks criterion; who should pay compensation, and how much? Who should receive compensation, and how much? Give an explanation that is grounded on some principle of distributive justice.

TAKE IT TO THE NET!

Go to: http://www.wwnorton.com/college/polisci/analyzingpolicy for additional problems, data sets, and course materials.

NOTES

1. In actual voting procedures, this stark contrast is probably not right. One way for voting procedures to register intensity of preference is through interest group competition. Bentley (1908) and Truman (1951) argue that interest groups "weight" the expression of preferences in voting, since more intensely felt preferences make people work harder. This general conclusion was questioned by Olson (1965), but the basic argument that intensity can be registered by interest groups still holds. For a review of this literature, see Mitchell and Munger (1991).

2. The issue of standing is quite complex. For a review of this issues, and some important arguments about who should "count," see Whittington and MacRae (1986).

3. For three different, but well-informed, views on this question, see Anderson (1979), MacIntyre (1977), and MacRae (1976).

4. The constitutional political economy school has had many important contributors, but its founder is James Buchanan. For a review, see Mueller (1997), and Buchanan and Congleton (1997).

5. See, for example, Wicksell (1958).

6. This is a linear demand curve, as seems to make sense. A zero price should not imply infinite parking. It is fun, but it is not *that* much fun.

7. Rounding up, that is. The correct number is 154.76. Using 155 is easier, but the numbers don't quite add up.

8. I am assuming no ties, to make the calculations simpler. In real lotteries, of course, if two people hold the winning number, they split the winnings equally. The number who can hold the winning number is unlimited, which makes the problem hard to represent graphically.

9. The expected value of danger to a child is $1/10,000$ now, for a cost (assuming the value of a life is $100,000) $10. The present value of this benefit, assuming it accrues forever, using a 10 percent discount rate, is $100. For simplicity, I am ruling out the chance that more than one child might be hit in a given year. No child has ever been hit in Ruttenton, since the town started recording traffic statistics.

10. The fifteen minutes per day, over 365 days, at $10 per hour time value, would

mean an implicit saving of $91.25 per year. The 7.5 miles per day, over 365 days, at 33 cents per mile, means a saving of $903.38. Together, the benefit is about $995 per year. If this benefit continues forever, we can assume a total benefit to outsiders of $10,000.

11. If you think this suggestion is too ridiculous ever to be made at a city council meetings, you haven't been to many city council meetings.

12. The internal rate of return is the discount rate at which the present value of costs and benefits are equal. So, a benefit-cost ratio of 1, given the assumed discount rate, is exactly the same as the requirement that the IRR must equal, or exceed, the discount rate.

13. The most recent statute specifying the use of cost-benefit analysis as a policy tool for the Corps of Engineers is the 1986 Water Resources Development Act.

14. From the "Satisfy the Customer" portion of the "Seven Sub-Strategies" part of the "Mission Statement" of the U.S.A.C.E.

12

Conclusion

You walk through a grocery store putting a bunch of food and household products into your cart. At the checkout line, you realize you have too many items to carry everything back to your car in one trip. You will need a . . . *a bag*!

The young man standing on the other side of the register asks you the fateful question: "Paper . . . or plastic?"

You freeze up. What is the right thing to do? What model of decision making should you apply? You are a trained student of policy analysis; your mind is a finely tuned, dangerous weapon, ready to render judgments on complex matters. Why can't you decide?

Of course, you *can* decide; each of us makes this decision very quickly, all the time. But do we get it right? What does getting it "right" even mean? What values do we apply to the problem? Do we take account of the costs and benefits to everyone affected by our decision, or do we consider only our own interests?

Our minds contain a little "model" of the policy world that enables us to decide questions like this every day—often several times a day. Actually, "decide" may be putting it too strongly. What we do is make the same choice we have always made, unless there is a reason to change, or unless a change in costs, preferences, or income comes to our attention. Of course, we can also change our minds because we have encountered a new idea, or a new way of thinking about a problem.

The point is that there are many inputs to decisions, at both the individual level and the government level, that don't fit well into the "policy analysis" perspective. In this final chapter, I will first review some of the essential features of the policy analysis approach we have covered in the eleven previous chapters. Then I will contrast these with two additional, and very different, perspectives: the "ideological" model of policy decisions and the "agenda shift" model.

Review of the Policy Analysis Approach

Policy analysis can be viewed as a collection of techniques and approaches that attempt to reconcile three types of conflicts:

- *Politics versus markets*—debates over the *equity* of distribution and compensation for public takings or restrictions on property
- *Markets versus experts*—debates over the *efficiency* of the function and direction of market processes of production, investment, and use of scarce resources
- *Politics versus experts*—debates over the *institutional* function in the process of selection of public officials, and the representation of citizens in the political process

The apparent inconsistency in public policies, without the differentiation implied by the above categories, could lead one to conclude that there is no coherence, or logic, in the process of policy formation. This is not necessarily true. What is true is that different policies, at different times, are designed to solve just one of these three conflicts. A compromise between any two of the three sources of power and legitimacy (experts, politics, and markets) is likely to contradict the goals of the excluded entity. That is, efficiency policies conflict with equity policies, and political institutions may appear to serve neither efficiency nor equity. Yet each policy conflict is real, and the process of policy formation does have considerable logic, when taken on its own terms.

The "classic" model of public policy analysis divides the process of decision into five steps:

1. *Problem formulation:* This is a combination of pattern recognition and creative insight. The analyst must recognize a problem that is analogous to something she has seen before, or else must understand the nature of the policy problem, given a very complicated set of facts in the problem situation.
2. *Selection of criteria:* The analyst must choose dimensions of evaluation, identifying all those who "count" in the decision, and deciding *how much* they should count, on each criterion.
3. *Comparison of alternatives:* The alternatives are suggested by the problem formulation, in step 1. But the actual listing of alternatives, and evaluating their performance on each of the criteria of interest, can be an enormous task. The analyst may need to rely on published work, or even informed guesses, from other experts.
4. *Consider political and organizational constraints:* The analyst's ability to consider a wide variety of alternatives will depend on whether she has enough economic resources to conduct an in-depth study, and enough political latitude to suggest radically different policy alternatives.
5. *Evaluation:* The analyst must select measures, and a research design, capable of revealing whether the policy has had the desired effects.

This outline of policy analysis will stand you in good stead, in a variety of jobs or activities in the policy community. But it is important to recognize that some parts of this outline are suspect in the eyes of social scientists. I will consider two other models of policy process: the theory of political ideologies, and a psychological model that poses two psychological objections to the "rationalism" built into policy analysis.

Ideology as a Template for Policy Decision

In real politics, alternatives don't always come along one by one. Instead, choices come in clusters, called "candidates." We have names for the different clusters of policies that candidates most often represent. "Liberals" tend to advocate an identifiable set of policy positions, favoring a strong social safety net, support for individual civil liberties and abortion rights, and more restrictive environmental regulations on private action. "Conservatives" take the opposite view on each of these apparently separate issues. Consequently, one might argue that there are not really three issues (welfare, civil liberties, environment) at all; there is only one—liberal versus conservative ideology.

A theory of policy making and political decision based on ideology is quite different from the approach we have taken throughout this book, in two important ways. First, if ideology is paramount, then it doesn't make much sense to think of decisions being made one at a time. Instead, many decisions are made using the same set of rules, or general principles. Environmental policy, antitrust regulation, and tax policy may seem to be unrelated but in an ideological environment they are linked, and may all be decided together. As Thomas Sowell pointed out:

> One of the curious things about political opinions is how often the same people line up on opposite sides of different issues. The issues themselves may have no intrinsic connection with each other . . . yet the same famil-iar faces can be found glaring at each other from opposite sides of the po-litical fence, again and again. It happens too often to be a coincidence, and it is too uncontrolled to be a plot. (Sowell, 1987: 6)

Any attempt to conceive of issues purely from the perspective of pol-icy analysis focusing on efficiency, will miss the point that politics are decided politically. More simply, *ideology constrains choices,* in the sense that only the available parties, and politicians, are part of the system of political decision.

Second, the way that ideology constrains choices into small clusters is variable, both across times and in different nations. Coalitions and alliances form and then evaporate. The meaning of "conservative" has changed today compared to what it meant fifty years ago in the United States. The meaning of "liberal" is completely different in the United States today from what it means in the former Soviet Union, where it means support for markets and elimination of government intervention in the ownership of productive resources. Ideological dimensions are *latent,* in that they emerge from the rhetoric that politicians use to describe, and that voters use to think about policy conflicts, rather than being fixed and constant. Consequently, it makes sense to think of political debate over policy issues in the con-text of the larger ideological conflicts that divide the society.

Ideologies organize policy conflict. People use ideologies to sim-plify (often, to *over*simplify) policy problems, because they are unable, don't want, or don't have time, to think about each problem separately and to analyze it objectively. Politics doesn't take place in the arena of policy, where facts and arcane arguments matter. Politics happens in an arena where simple arguments and principles are powerful in persuading people about what is the right thing to do.

A useful definition of ideology is that of Hinich and Munger (1994, p. 11): An ideology is

> an internally consistent set of propositions that makes both proscriptive and prescriptive demands on human behavior. All ideologies have implications for (a) what is ethically good, and bad; (b) how society's resources should be distributed; and (c) where power appropriately resides.

In other words, ideologies tell people what is good, who gets what, and who rules. But make no mistake: the simplifying nature of ideologies does not imply that political choice based on ideology is divorced from issues completely. To the contrary, ideologies provide a set of "linkages" with issues. These linkages can be highly uncertain, however, and may differ across voters and over time. Confronted with a hard decision on a new policy, people may not start over and do policy analysis. Rather, they are likely to use their ideologies, or beliefs about the principles that organize political conflict, to judge which course of action is best.

A depiction of policy decision based on ideology is fundamentally a theory of party politics.[1] Ideologies that have a large number of adherents are likely to be associated with a party, an organization that tries to popularize their point of view with the public and to advance their goals in the legislature. The cleavages between parties fall along simpler, more predictable lines than an issue-by-issue approach would imply.

Why Are Issues Linked?

Issues are linked within ideologies for at least three reasons: *communication, commitment,* and *budgets.* These are not mutually exclusive, so that more than one may apply in any given political context.

- *Communication.* Ideologies give voters a message they can understand and use to make choices. Ideologies come into everyday politics through parties. The voters themselves may not be "ideological," but they are constrained to choose among the alter-

natives presented at the polling booth. Because only broad statements of principles can be used in advertising and position-taking,
the latitude for complex distinctions and differences is highly circumscribed.

- *Commitment.* Parties, in order to persuade voters that they can be
  trusted to do as promised after the election, can't just take positions. Instead, they must give reasons and explanations. But explanations require an overarching system of justifications, as well as
  the advancement of values that can be applied to a variety of issues.
  Parties trade on their reputations for consistency. If parties act on
  their ideologies when such actions do not appear self-interested,
  their reputations are enhanced.[2]
- *Budgets.* An increase in spending in one area of the budget forces
  either a decrease elsewhere or increased taxes or deficits. Thus, any
  change from the status quo forces a linkage to other issues, if only
  in terms of what is given up.

Consider an example. Suppose there are two parties, Right and
Left, which support candidates who stand for election in a variety of
offices. Each party uses an ideological message to communicate with
voters, and commits to that ideological position by building a reputation for consistency, both in its actions over time and with the logic
of the ideological message. Imagine that the Right's ideology is this:
"Government should maintain law and order." The Left's ideology,
by contrast, is "Government should help people who cannot help
themselves."

Now, imagine that I am a voter who doesn't care about ideology,
but I do care about one specific issue: prison overcrowding. Knowing
the simple aphorisms that the parties use to communicate their core
values, I can guess what their "solution" to the policy problem (too
many prisoners, too few beds) will be. The view of the Right is that
there are not enough prisons, and that conditions should be made
harsher to deter criminality. The position of the Left is that there are
too few economic opportunities and too little training in job skills for
people already in prison.

Does either of these ideological "positions" have anything to do
with policy analysis? The answer is no. The policy solution is implied
by the ideological perspective of the party, not discovered through an
objective process of selecting among alternatives. This drives policy
analysts crazy, of course, but it is the way that many real-world decisions are made. In this kind of policy debate, ideologies are conflict-

ing visions of governance, or contradictory templates that are used to frame every problem, whether the "answer" addresses the question or not.[3]

In 1997 I appeared on a conservative-leaning television talk show in New Jersey, debating solutions to the problem of low-level radioactive waste disposal. Each guest gave detailed explanations for why particular ways of organizing waste disposal would be financially, or technically, infeasible. As I tried to "out-wonk" the other guests, the host became glassy-eyed and seemed to be daydreaming, or on the verge of falling asleep.

Then I did it: I said that the federal government would be obliged to take over certain aspects of the management of radioactive waste disposal, because the states couldn't manage the externalities involved. The host's head snapped around, and he glared at me, now fully awake. "You can't be serious!" he shouted.

Taken aback, I stammered the definition of externality. The host interrupted, "One of the key tenets of the Republican revolution is *devolution*! The power to regulate must be given back to the states." I tried to answer. "Yes, but in this case . . ."

"There are no *cases*; the states can perform the regulatory function better than the federal government," said the host, nearly shouting. He was really upset, not just posing for the camera.

I had run up against an ideology. One of the key tenets of the conservative ideology, from the election of Ronald Reagan in 1980 on, has been the devolution of spending power and regulatory authority from the central government back toward the states. Because devolution is a simple principle, it can be applied to most policy areas without any detailed understanding of the workings of the policy are in question. In some cases, it may be true that devolution improves policy, but the universal application of the principle amounts to an *assumption*, not a *conclusion*.

Still, the talk show host had a point. It may be better to implement an entire program, even one that is sometimes the wrong answer, than to make case-by-case decisions on all policy dimensions. The reason is not necessarily that policy is better—in fact, the policy outcomes will almost certainly be different from those implied by an "ideal" selection process. Rather, ideological consistency pays political dividends. Besides, it is hard to figure out whether the policy changes have worked or not.

To summarize: No matter how much the fact may upset policy analysts, there are good political reasons why policy debates are tinged, and may be suffused, with ideology. A politician who has reached a conclusion about a policy for ideological reasons is not interested in "analysis." All he or she wants is a study to hold up as evidence for a conclusion reached before any analysis was conducted. Policy analysts, in this world, are simply hired guns, hired or used to support positions implied by an ideology. Some policy analysts accept this, and work within the system. The rest of us become professors.

Here are the "good political reasons": Ideology transmits information to voters, and creates enthusiasm for political action. These two features alone are enough to give ideology a powerful competitive advantage in political discourse and in electoral politics. But there is an additional feature of ideology that makes it crucial for candidates and parties. This is its capacity to constrain the positions which political actors can take. The need to preserve a reputation for ideological consistency strengthened commitment to follow through on actions that will be taken long after the campaign, and the election, are over.

To put it a little differently, there are two things that successful campaigns must do. First, they must establish a candidate's, or a party's, position on many different policies. Second, and no less important, they must persuade citizens that, once in office, the candidate or party will support or enact policies close to the policies they promised. Elections reflect the aggregation of individual voters' assessment of the candidate's or party's success in both of these endeavors.

The primary goal of real campaigns is to persuade voters that the candidate or party will *not* move under any circumstances, and is deeply committed to the promised platform. In fact, if voters evaluate candidates based on their reputations for consistency, it may be quite "rational" for a candidate to choose the "wrong" policy in all those decisions where ideology and policy analysis conflict.[4] "Look, Senator Joe always votes the same way! We can trust him." Voters are more likely to pay attention to deviations from ideology than they are to policy errors (since more than likely they will never understand anything about the policy), and elected officials may worry more about their reputation than about getting policies right.

This is frustrating for policy analysts, but it is reality. Ideologies are templates, or pre-cut "solutions" for complex problems. The fact that the template does not fit well in all problem settings is beside the point. In the long run, for the politician, the ideology is more important than the policy problem.

Priming, Framing, and Attention: The Psychological Model

Another view of policy decision-making, different from both the policy analysis view and the theory of ideological constraint, is the "psychological" model. The basis of this model of policy formation is a question about the nature of preferences. The original work in this area was done by psychologists, who demonstrated experimentally that the claim of "fixed," exogenous preferences often used in the policy analytic approach is empirically questionable.[5] It was shown that it was possible to obtain preference "reversals," or apparent contradictions, depending on how the issue was "framed," or conceived in the subjects' minds.

Subsequent work asked why this might be so. After all, if the preferences about which analysts can elicit information are incoherent, there is little basis for building a science of policy analysis. One needn't conclude, however, that preferences are *literally* incoherent, in the sense that people don't know what they want, or that there are contradictions in those wants. Rather, there may be a difference between *preferences* and *survey responses*, reflecting a problem in measurement more than a problem of cognition.[6] One compelling piece of evidence for this claim is the finding that "priming,"—the problem definition given, or the statements preceding a question, can influence answers to the question. More disturbingly, there may be a fundamental indeterminacy in the very nature of survey response, as people use different parts of their short-term memory to answer. The order in which questions are asked may influence how the questions are answered.[7] Even the appearance of the questioner may influence the "preference" expressed. These results raise significant problems for policy analysts, since even if citizens are really trying to report honest, rather than strategic, preferences on policy issues, obtaining usable preference measures through survey instruments is at best tricky, and may be impossible.

Another view of the policy process, also owing its origins to psychology but with a slightly different focus, is the set of studies which focus on the effects of variable attention on the public agenda.[8] A general review of this literature is beyond the scope of this book, but it is worthwhile to state two general conclusions. First, the things that people care about may be those policies or issues to which they have been led to direct their attention, by the media by or elite opinion-makers. If this conclusion (see, for example, chapter 12 in Zaller, 1991) is correct, then surveys asking citizens to ranks of issues by importance may not elicit citizens' objective views. Instead, answers may simply reflect the relative importance assigned to each issue in the media.

Second, instability of the policy agenda need not reflect a fundamental instability of policy preferences. Instead, a change in the policy "agenda" may result either from a change in media attention or from a change in the public conception of the policy problem (Baumgartner and Jones, 1993; Jones, 1994). This point of view offers an important critique of the classic policy analysis model.

> A design decision precedes an actual choice: it involves imposing structure on a situation so that alternative solutions may be listed. Any design decision can be factored into two components. The first component encompasses the dimensions of evaluation that are used to structure the decision. These evaluative dimensions are actually *goals*; they are what the decision is supposed to contribute to. . . . All participants in politics have multiple goals, and the alternatives that can be listed once the situation is structured are likely to affect these goals differently and not necessarily in the same direction. Hence trade-offs are necessary.
>
> The second facet of design is the structure of attention; the aspects of the problem situation that the decision-maker attends to. That is, many evaluative dimensions may be relevant to a particular decision, but the decision-maker has no ready way of making comparisons among these dimensions. Hence one of the great heuristics of decision-making is the elimination of evaluative dimensions that do not seem to be relevant at the moment. (Jones, 1994; pp. 60–61; emphasis in original).

According to this critique, the decision maker, by definition, does not have enough information to perform the classic policy analysis described earlier. The choice of evaluative dimensions structures the problem. But a knowledge of problem structure is required to make the right choice of evaluative dimensions. The way out policy makers actually choose is to apply the heuristic of *salience*: focus attention on those dimensions that seem important at the time.

But constraints, and the true structure of the problem, may emerge only after the process of analysis has begun. "It may be noted that ill-structured problems with emergent constraints focus the attention of decision-makers on a limited number of attributes of the problem. Indeed, one characteristic of suboptimal solutions that can emerge in solving ill-structured problems is the ignoring of essential dimensions of evaluation that later appear to be important." (Jones, 1993; p. 52).

To put it more simply: Hard problems, or new problems, are diffi-cult to structure. Such "ill-structured" problems present policy ana-lysts with difficulty, because no one knows how to start the analysis. The initial problem definition may, by sheer good fortune, be appro-priate and accurate. More likely, however, it will ignore important constraints, costs, or complexities. Once a particular conception of the problem is chosen, then that understanding of the problem, even if it is not appropriate, is built into future discussion of the problem. The short name for this phenomenon is *path-dependence*: where we can go from here depends on how we got here.

Final Remarks

Having read this book, you may be tempted to conclude that policy analysis is too hard. Nearly all the conclusions I have offered, or in-struction I have given, have been qualified or diluted. If you were hoping to find out the simple way to "make" good policy, you are no doubt disappointed.

But this reveals something about the nature of policy analysis, something that shouldn't surprise you much if you think about it. You can't make chicken salad out of chicken feathers. The idea that there must be, or even should be, a single "best" policy in every dif-ficult situation is a conceit unique to people who know more about mathematics than they know about politics. The overselling of policy analysis, as a guide to policy rather than just as a tool, has made a lot of people frustrated and disillusioned with the policy process. I have talked to many people, people I considered friends, who were con-vinced that they (and maybe only they) knew the truth about good policy—everyone else either was being bought off by interest groups or was too confused to understand the truth.

I guess I am one of the confused ones, then. (I certainly never got bought off by interest groups, though I keep looking in my mailbox for the check!) As David Truman pointed out fifty years ago:

There is a political significance in assertions of totally inclusive interests within a nation. . . . This assumption is close to the popular dogmas of democratic government based on the familiar notion that if only people are free and have access to "the facts," they will all want the same thing in any political situation. It is no derogation of democratic preferences to state that such an assertion flies in the face of all that we know of the behavior of men in a complex society. (Truman, 1951; p. 50)

Each of the three sources of power in policy processes that I have identified—experts, markets, and politics—has peculiar features. Each is a significant and legitimate player in the proposing, formulation, implementation, and monitoring of policies. Being a playing partner, rather than taking a position of dominance, seems frustrating to policy analysts. Hank Jenkins-Smith, in a provocative book on the tension between democratic politics and policy analysis, put it this way:

> The proponents and critics of policy analysis seem more often than not to talk *past* one another, generating images of analytical perfection (wherein all citizens' preferences are accurately measured and reduced to a single comparable metric of benefits and costs) that compete with specters of *analysis from hell* (in which analysts usurp political power, mangle preferences, or reduce venerable political institutions to ruin by the very weight of the analytical complexity they generate). It is no wonder that new entrants to the debate ignore their adversaries, or that many students and practitioners of policy analysis ignore the debate altogether. But that is a tragedy, for analysis has become, for better or worse, an integral part of the workings of our political institutions. (Jenkins-Smith, 1991; pp. 1–2; emphasis in original)

The debate over the proper place of analysts and interest takes place with nearly theological fervor in the academy and the halls of federal departments. But I am an agnostic. The objections made against policy analysis seem to me as overblown as the claims made for it. The techniques for measuring, evaluating, and analyzing policy in this book are nothing more than tools. Like any tool, these techniques can be used well or poorly. Used correctly, they can be as valuable as their proponents claim. Used incorrectly, these tools are every bit as misleading, or simply wrong, as their opponents argue. Try to use them correctly.

One thing: Should you choose paper or plastic? The answer is revealed here, for the first time. It is the same as the answer to thousands of other important questions in policy analysis—in fact, this answer should be applied to *any* problem that is hard or interesting. The answer is: *It depends!*[9] More specifically, it depends on the values you choose and the assumptions you apply. A good policy analyst can show you how different answers can come from different values and assumptions. The idea that policy analysis has all the answers is chimerical. At best, analysis has all the questions. If you always answer a question with "it depends," and think hard about "On what?" you will be on the right track.

NOTES

1. This view of the relation between party platforms and ideologies has complex origins, and could easily be identified with Marx, or in this century with Duverger (1951). But the particular perspective taken here on the linkages between ideology and issues begins with Downs (1957), as extended by Hinich and Pollard (1981), Enelow and Hinich (1984), and Hinich and Munger (1994). The empirical evidence for the regularity of a small number of organizing dimensions in the American Congress is most strikingly presented in the pioneering work of Poole and Rosenthal (1985; 1997). Other significant works on the nature of ideology as a constraint on, or guide to, policy decisions include Kau and Rubin (1981) and Higgs (1987).

2. The problem of commitment is long recognized in analytical politics. Three important treatments are Barro (1973), Ferejohn (1986), and Banks (1991). On the question of ideology as a filter and commitment device in particular, Kau and Rubin (1981) is the seminal work. Two other papers that follow this perspective are Lott (1987) and Dougan and Munger (1989).

3. This view of ideology has much in common with the view that voters use "heuristics" (Simon, 1977; 1981) to economize on the cost of gathering information about candidates or policies. The difference is that ideologies are shared heuristics, whereas in the more typical conception, heuristics are idiosyncratic.

4. Dougan and Munger (1989) make this point with two examples. First, "conservative U.S. senators tend to return a larger proportion of their allowances for expenditures on staff than their more liberal counterparts" (p. 126). Later, they point out that twelve senators who had taken isolationist positions on World War II in 1942 had a success rate of only 33 percent in their next election, compared to a 71 percent overall success rate during the period.

5. Tversky (1972), Tversky and Kahneman (1981; 1986).

6. See, for example, Zaller and Feldman (1992).

7. One interesting answer to this objection is that preferences really are fixed, but are "nonseparable" (Lacy, 1996). Even if this is true, then attempts to measure issue preferences using survey instruments which proceed one issue at a time are likely to provide misleading or even contradictory results.

8. Kahneman (1973), Simon (1981), Fiske and Taylor (1984), Zaller (1991); Baumgartner and Jones (1993); and Jones (1994).

9. Plastic grocery bags were introduced in 1977, by the Mobil Chemical corporation, in a few supermarkets around the Mobil Technical Center in Rochester, New York. The advantages of the bags were their durability, wet strength, and the strap handles, which meant you could carry lots of bags at once. At first, however, the bags were nearly twice as expensive as paper bags, were not strong enough to carry canned items, and were so much smaller than paper bags that acceptance was slow. Twenty years later, however, the bags are nearly universal, and the cost of one bag is less than a penny, while paper bags cost 5 to 8 cents, depending on their strength. The problem is this: Plastic bags cost less to make, but paper bags cost less to throw away. The plastic, under nearly any reasonable

circumstance, will never decompose. The paper bag would return to simple organic compost, with an additional acid content in most cases from the paper-making process. Further, the "cost" may be deceptive: The main input into plastic bags is petroleum, which is not renewable. Forest products, of which paper is one, may not be perfectly renewable, but they are nearly so. Thus, a key feature is the discount rate assumed in the comparison. For high discount rates, plastic bags are clearly better. For low discount rates, paper bags are better. For very low discount rates, and people with long-term concerns about the environment . . . well, you should use washable cloth bags! The information above comes from several news stories, including an article by Rich Hein in the Chicago *Sun-Times* (January 24, 1999), and the study published by the Council for Solid Waste Solutions (1990).

References

~⁓~

Anderson, Charles. 1979. "The Place of Principles in Policy Analysis." *American Political Science Review.* 73: 711–23.

Aristotle, 1979. *Politics and Poetics.* Translated by Benjamin Jowett and S. H. Butcher. Norwalk, Conn.: Easton Press. Greek original c. 350 B. C.

Arrow, Kenneth J. 1963. *Social Choice and Individual Values.* Reprint. New Haven, Conn.: Yale University Press. First published by John Wiley, 1952.

Arrow, Kenneth J., and Robert C. Lind. "Uncertainty and the Evaluation of Public Investment Decisions." *American Economic Review* 60 (June 1970): 364–78.

Bartlett, Donald, and James Steele. 1985. *Forevermore: Nuclear Waste in America.* New York: W. W. Norton and Company.

Baumgartner, Frank, and Bryan Jones. 1993. *Agendas and Instability in American Politics.* Chicago: University of Chicago Press.

Behn, Robert, and James Vaupel. 1982. *Quick Analysis for Busy Decision Makers.* New York: Basic Books.

Bergson, A. 1938. "A Reformulation of Certain Aspects of Welfare Economics." *Quarterly Journal of Economics* 52: 314–44.

Birnbaum, Jeffrey, and Alan Murray. 1987. *Showdown at Gucci*

Gulch: Lawmakers, Lobbyists, and the Unlikely Triumph of Tax Reform. New York: Random House.

Bingham, Richard, and Claire Felbinger. 1989. *Evaluation in Practice: A Methodological Approach.* New York: Longman Press.

Brehm, John, and Scott Gates. 1997. *Working, Shirking, and Sabotage: Bureaucratic Response to a Democratic Public.* Ann Arbor, Mich.: University of Michigan Press.

Burke, Edmund. 1961. *Reflections on the revolution in France [by] Edmund Burke. The rights of man [by] Thomas Paine.* Reprint. Garden City, N.Y.: Doubleday.

———. 1982. *A Vindication of Natural Society, or a View of the Miseries and Evils Arising to Mankind from Every Species of Artificial Society.* Reprint. Edited by Frank Pagano. Indianapolis, Ind.: Liberty Fund. First published 1756.

Burns, Michael E., ed. 1988. *Low-Level Radioactive Waste Regulation: Science, Politics and Fear.* East Lansing, Michigan: Lewis Publishers, Inc.

Coase, Ronald H. 1960. "The Problem of Social Cost," *Journal of Law and Economics,* October: 1–44.

Coates, Dennis, and Michael Munger. 1992. "Guessing and Choosing: A Multicriterion Decision on a Disposal Technology for Low Level Radioactive Waste," *Journal of Public Policy* 11: 275–89.

Council for Solid Waste Solutions. 1990. "Resource and Environmental Profile Analysis of Polyethylene and Unbleached Paper Grocery Sacks." Kansas City, Kans.: Franklin Associates, Ltd.

Demsetz, Harold. 1968. "Why Regulate Utilities?" *Journal of Law and Economics* 11: 55–65.

Dougan, William, and Michael Munger. 1989. "The Rationality of Ideology." *Journal of Law and Economics* 32: 119–42.

Doyle, Arthur Conan. 1975. *The Sign of the Four.* Reprint. Edited by Dennis Rosa. New York: Dramatists Play Service. Orginally published 1890.

Easton, Allan. 1973. *Complex Managerial Decisions Involving Multiple Objectives.* New York: John Wiley and Sons.

English, Mary. 1991. *1990 Update: Summary of Low-Level Radioactive Waste Disposal Facility Siting Laws.* January, Knoxville, Tennessee: Energy, Environment and Resources Center, University of Tennessee.

Fisher, Irving. 1912. *The Purchasing Power of Money.* New York: Macmillan.

Fiske, Susan T., and Shelly Taylor. 1984. *Social Cognition*. New York: Addison-Wesley.

Fogarty, Martin. 1996. "A History of Value Theory." Trinity College, Dublin. Internet reference: http://www.economics.tcd.ie/ser/1996/mfogarty.htm

Friedman, Milton, and James Savage. 1948. "The Utility Analysis of Choices Involving Risk. *Journal of Political Economy* 56: 279–304.

Gurley, John G. 1960. "Review of *A Program for Monetary Stability*, by Milton Friedman." *Review of Economics and Statistics* 43: 306–309.

Groves, Theodore, and John Ledyard. 1977. "Optimal Allocation of Public Goods: A Solution to the 'Free Rider' Problem." *Econometrica* 41: 617–31.

Harberger, Arnold. 1954. "Monopoly and Resource Allocation." *American Economic Review* 44: 77–87.

Hayek, Friedrich. 1944. *The Road to Serfdom*. Chicago: University of Chicago Press.

———. 1960. *The Constitution of Liberty*. Chicago: University of Chicago Press.

———. 1978. "Competition as Discovery Procedure," in Friedrich Hayek, *New Studies in Philosophy, Politics, Economics, and the History of Ideas*. London: Routledge, pp. 119–30.

Hicks, John. 1939. "The Foundations of Welfare Economics." *Economic Journal* 49: 696–712.

Hobbes, Thomas. 1968 (first published 1651). *Leviathan*. Edited by C. B. McPherson. New York: Penguin Books.

Humboldt, Wilhelm von. 1993. *The Limits of State Action*. Reprint. Edited by J. W. Burrow. Indianapolis, Ind.: Liberty Fund. Originally published 1854.

Jenkins-Smith, Hank. 1988. *Democratic Politics and Policy Analysis*. Pacific Grove, Calif.: Brooks-Cole Publishers.

Kahneman, Daniel. 1973. *Attention and Effort*. Englewood Cliffs, N.J.: Prentice-Hall.

Kahneman, Daniel, and Amos Tversky. 1985. "Prospect Theory: An Analysis of Decision-Making Under Risk." *Econometrica* 47: 263–91.

Kaldor, Nicholas. 1939. "Welfare Propositions of Economics and Interpersonal Comparisons of Utility." *Economic Journal* 49: 549–52.

Keynes, John Maynard. 1936. *The General Theory of Employment, Interest, and Money*. New York: Harcourt Brace Jovanovich.

King, A. 1997. *Running Scared: Why American Politicians Campaign Too Much and Govern Too Little*. New York: Free Press.

Klein, Daniel, Adrian Moore, and Binyam Reja. 1997. *Curb Rights: A Foundation for Free Enterprise in Urban Transit*. Washington, D.C.: Brookings Institution.

Lacy, Dean. 1996. "A Theory of Nonseparable Preferences in Survey Responses." Typescript, Department of Political Science, Ohio State University, Columbus, Ohio.

Leontief, Wassily W. 1941. *The structure of American economy, 1919–1929; an empirical application of equilibrium analysis*. Cambridge, Mass.: Harvard University Press.

Lerner, Abba P. 1944. *The Economics of Control: Principles of Welfare Economics*, New York: Macmillan.

Lichfield, Nathaniel, Peter Kettle, and Michael Whitbread. 1975. *Evaluation in the Planning Process*. Oxford: Pergamon Press.

Lindahl, Erik. 1958. "Just Taxation—A Positive Solution." Translated by S. H. Frowein in R. Musgrave and A. Peacock, eds., *Classics in the Theory of Public Finance*. London: Macmillan. 168–76. Originally published in Swedish, 1919.

MacIntyre, Alasdair. 1977. "Utilitarianism and Cost-Benefit Analysis: An Essay on the Relevance of Moral Philosophy to Bureaucratic Theory." In Kenneth Sayre, ed., *Values in the Electric Power Industry*. Notre Dame, Ind.: Notre Dame University Press.

MacRae, Duncan. 1976. *The Social Function of Social Science*. New Haven: Yale University Press.

MacRae, Duncan. 1993. "Guidelines for Policy Discourse: Consensual vs. Adversarial." In Frank Fischer and John Forester, eds., *The Argumentative Turn in Policy Analysis and Planning*. Durham, N.C.: Duke University Press.

MacRae, Duncan, and Dale Whittington. 1997. *Expert Advice for Policy Choice*. Washington, D.C.: Georgetown University Press.

MacRae, Duncan, and James Wilde. 1979. *Policy Analysis for Public Decisions*. Belmont, Calif.: Wadsworth, Inc.

Marshall, Alfred. 1920. *Principles of Economics*. London: Macmillan.

Marx, Karl. 1972. *Capital*. Reprint. In Robert C. Tucker, ed., *The Marx-Engels Reader*. New York: W. W. Norton and Co. Originally published 1867–1883.

Mascart, Jean. 1919. *La Vie et les Travaux du Chevalier Jean-Charles de Borda (1722–1799)*. Lyon, France: Pamphlet.

Meade, J. E. 1964. *Efficiency, Equality, and the Ownership of Property*. London: George Allen and Unwin.

Mill, John Stuart. 1944. *Autobiography of John Stuart Mill.* New York: Columbia University Press. Originally published 1873.

Moberg, Erik. 1999. *Democracy: Constitutions, Politics, and Welfare Effects.* Unpublished. Lovestad, Sweden.

Munger, Michael. 1997. "Kicking Competition to the Curb." *Regulation* 20: 69–72.

———. 1998. "Pangloss Was Right: Reforming Congress Is Useless, Too Expensive, or Harmful," *Duke Environmental Law and Policy Forum* 9, no. 1: 133–42.

———. 1999. "Five Questions: An Integrated Research Agenda in Public Choice." *Public Choice.* In press.

Mueller, Dennis. 1989. *Public Choice II.* New York: Cambridge University Press.

Murray, Raymond L. 1989 (3rd edition). *Understanding Radioactive Waste.* Columbus, Ohio: Battelle Press.

Okun, Arthur. 1975. *Equality and Efficiency: The Big Trade-Off.* Washington, D.C.: The Brookings Institution.

O'Rourke, P. J. 1991. *Parliament of Whores: A Lone Humorist Attempts to Explain the Entire U.S. Government.* New York: Atlantic Monthly Press.

Ostrom, Elinor. 1990. *Governing the Commons: The Evolution of Institutions for Collective Action.* New York: Cambridge University Press.

Patton, Carl V., and David Sawicki. 1986. *Basic Methods of Policy Analysis and Planning.* Englewood Cliffs, N.J.: Prentice Hall.

Peltzman, Sam. 1980. "The Growth of Government." *Journal of Law and Economics* 23: 209–87.

Pigou, A. C. 1932. *The Economics of Welfare.* 4th ed., London: MacMillan.

Plott, Charles. 1991. "Will Economics Become an Experimental Science?" *Southern Economic Journal* 57: 901–20.

Posner, Richard. 1975. "The Social Costs of Monopoly and Regulation." *Journal of Political Economy* 83: 807–27.

Quade, Edward S. 1982. 2d ed. *Analysis for Public Decisions.* New York: Elsevier. First edition published 1975.

Raiffa, Howard. 1968. *Decision Analysis.* Reading, Mass.: Addison-Wesley.

Rawls, John. 1971. *A Theory of Justice.* Cambridge, Mass.: Harvard University Press.

Rousseau, Jean-Jacques. 1988. *On Social Contract or Principles of Political Right.* Translated by Julia Conaway Bondanella. In Alan

Ritter and Julia Conaway Bondanella, eds., *Rousseau's Political Writings*. New York: W. W. Norton and Company. Originally published 1762.

Samuelson, Paul. 1947. *Foundations of Economic Analysis*. Cambridge, Mass.: Harvard University Press.

———. 1954. "The Pure Theory of Public Expenditure." *Review of Economcs and Statistics* 36: 387–9.

———. 1967. "Arrow's Mathematical Politics." In S. Hook, ed., *Human Values and Economic Policy*. New York: New York University Press.

Sen, Amartya. 1997. *Choice, Welfare, and Measurement*. Cambridge, Mass.: Harvard University Press.

Simon, Herbert. 1977. "The Logic of Heuristic Decision-Making." In R. S. Cohen and M. W. Wartofsky, eds., *Models of Discovery*. Boston: D. Reidel.

———. 1981. *The Architecture of Complexity*. 2d ed., Cambridge, Mass.: MIT Press.

Smith, Adam. 1994. *An Inquiry Into the Nature and Causes of the Wealth of Nations*. Reprint. New York: Modern Library. Originally published 1776.

Sowell, Thomas. 1987. *A Conflict of Visions*. New York: William Morrow Publishers.

Stigler, George. 1956. "The Statistics of Monopoly and Merger." *Journal of Political Economy* 64: 33–40.

———. 1970. "Director's Law of Public Income Redistribution." *Journal of Law and Economics* 13: 1–10.

Stockman, David. 1986. *The Triumph of Politics: How the Reagan Revolution Failed*. New York: Harper & Row.

Stokey, Edith, and Richard Zeckhauser. 1978. *A Primer for Policy Analysis*. New York: W. W. Norton and Company.

Stone, Deborah. 1988. *Policy Paradox and Political Reason*. Glenview, Ill.: Scott, Foresman, and Company.

Texas LLRWDA. 1987. *Low Level Radioactive Waste Disposal Facilities: Conceptual Designs and Assessments*. Vols. 1–5. Austin, Tex.: Texas Low Level Radioactive Waste Disposal Authority.

Tideman, Nicholas. 1997. "Voting and the Revelation of Preferences for Public Activities." In D. Mueller, ed. *Perspectives on Public Choice: A Handbook*. New York: Cambridge University Press.

Tideman, Nicholas, and Gordon Tullock. 1976. "A New and Superior Process for Making Social Choices." *Journal of Political Economy* 84: 1145–59.

Trisko, Karen Sue, and V. C. League. 1978. *Developing Successful Programs*. Oakland, Calif.: Awareness House.

Tucker, Robert, ed. 1972. *The Marx-Engels Reader*. New York: W. W. Norton and Company.

Tversky, Amos. 1972. "Elimination by Aspects: A Theory of Choice." *Psychological Review* 79: 281–99.

Tversky, Amos, and Daniel Kahneman. 1981. "The Framing of Decisions and the Psychology of Choice." *Science* 211: 435–58.

———. 1986. "Rational Choice and the Framing of Decisions." *Journal of Business* 59: 251–78.

Whittington, Dale, and Duncan MacRae. 1986. "The Issue of Standing in Cost-Benefit Analysis." *Journal of Policy Analysis and Management* 5: 665–82.

Wicksell, Knut. 1958. "A New Principle of Just Taxation." Translated by S. H. Frowein, in R. Musgrave and A. Peacock, eds., *Classics in the Theory of Public Finance*. London: Macmillan. 72–118. (Originally published in Swedish, 1896)

Wildavsky, Aaron. 1979. *Speaking Truth to Power: The Art and Craft of Policy Analysis*. Boston: Little, Brown.

Winters, Harold A. 1998. *Battling the Elements: Weather and Terrain in the Conduct of War*. Baltimore: The Johns Hopkins University Press.

"The Worst of 1998 Scandals." *Time* (International Edition). December 21, 1998, p. 59.

Yeager, Leland. 1997. *The Fluttering Veil: Essays on Monetary Disequilibrium*. Edited by George Selgin. Indianapolis: Liberty Fund.

Zeleny, Milan. 1982. *Multiple Criteria Decision Making*. New York: McGraw-Hill.

Zaller, John. 1991. *The Nature and Origins of Public Opinion*. Chicago: University of Chicago Press.

Zaller, John, and Stanley Feldman. 1992. "A Simple Theory of Survey Response: Answering Questions versus Revealing Preferences." *American Journal of Political Science* 36: 579–616.

Answers to Selected Problems and Questions

Chapter 1

1. One possible policy problem may be that standardized test scores among high school students in the United States are low compared to students in other advanced industrial countries. Three possible problem formulations are: 1) classrooms are too large; 2) teachers are inadequately trained; and 3) schools are inadequately funded. To determine which problem formulation is better, a policy analyst could compare how standardized test scores vary with classroom size, quality of teachers, and funding.

3. The additional information needed would assist in assigning weights for the different criteria. For the cost criteria, you would want to know the probability of being hospitalized. For the quality criteria, you would want to know the impact of quality on your health. For example, you would want to know the impact of quality on the likelihood of being cured or on the likelihood of negative side-effects that would require further medical attention. For the waiting period criteria, you would want to know whether the illnesses contracted would require immediate care.

4. An example of a policy variable that could be measured categorically is race of an individual. The numerical value assigned to each individual is not interpretable; it is only a short-hand representation for the category. You need more information about the data on the trees in order to form expectations about what kind of trees you would see in the park.

Chapter 2

2. a. An efficiency policy is designed to improve the functioning of the market or to correct market failures, where the market is a set of institutions designed to facilitate the exchange of goods and services in an efficient manner. An example of such a policy is the requirement that pharmaceutical companies reveal the side effects of the drugs they produce. An efficiency policy is characterized by the tension between experts and markets. Policy debates are focused on whether the efficiency policies will produce a more desirable allocation of resources.

b. An equity policy is designed to adjust or correct for the outcomes of market processes. An example of this type of policy is unemployment benefits. An equity policy is characterized by the tension between markets and politics. Policy debates focus on whether the allocation of resources generated by the market are just and fair.

c. An institutional reform policy is designed to improve the process by which political decisions are made. An example of such a policy is the line-item veto of the president. An institutional reform policy is characterized as the tension between experts and politics. Policy debates focus on whether the current method of political decision making is fair.

Chapter 3

1.

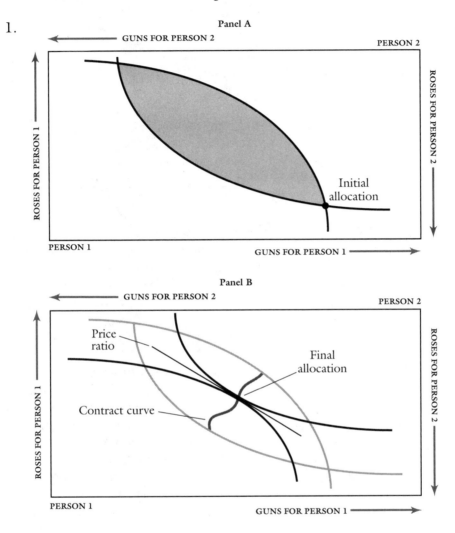

2. See the diagram in answer to problem 1.
3. See the diagram in answer to problem 1.
4. See the diagram in answer to problem 1.

5.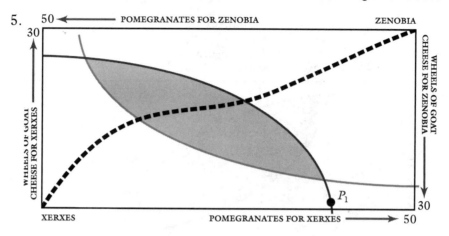

6. An example where queuing is used for allocating scarce resources is organ donations. Queuing is used because it prevents the discrimination based on particular characteristics, such as celebrity status, wealth, race, and age. The ethical criteria at the base queuing in this case is that all lives should be valued equally. A lottery would also satisfy this criteria for organ donations, whereas price and authority as a method of allocation would most likely violate this criteria.

7. Money helps reduce the transactions costs of exchange by providing its holder abstract command over goods and services. This abstract command eliminates the effort required from the producer of a particular good to find a producer of another good she needs, while having that producer want her good as well. Instead, she can sell her good to any buyer and then use the money to purchase her desired good from another producer. Money also allows a producer to delay the purchase of desired goods. This may be crucial to a producer such as a farmer whose product needs to be sold at the same time (i.e., harvest time) but whose consumption must be spread out over the course of a year. In the case of the farmer needing to delay consumption, it is evident that requiring money to be durable is an important characteristic of good money.

Chapter 4

1. a. For the road to be built without government intervention, each individual would have to be charged the value that she places on the road.
    b. Given that the marginal cost of provision is 0, the road could be publicly financed if the costs of collecting tolls did not exceed the revenue from the tolls.
2. The road that maximizes the net gains.
3. Under the assumption of full information and a genuine desire to do the least cost alternative, there is no difference between the Kaldor-Hicks criterion and the Coase theorem. Both perspectives imply efficiency and the only difference between them is who builds the road.
4. a. 16.
    b. 72.
6. A common pool resource is a good that is difficult to prevent others from consuming and has a high marginal cost of production. Many natural resources such as fisheries and forests are common pool resources. The problem with common pool resources is that consumption of the resource by an individual depletes the supply available to others, and no individual unilaterally has the incentive to curb her consumption in order to achieve a Pareto optimal allocation of resources. Pigou's conjecture states that an efficient or Pareto optimal outcome can be achieved in the use of common pool resources through a system of taxes and subsidies.

Chapter 5

7. The problem is that interest group advocacy may lead to the entrenchment of economic power in the form of industry protection instead of correcting market failures. Stigler argues that the solution to the problem is to abandon regulation whereas Marx suggested we should eliminate private interests.

Chapter 6

2. The winner is candidate A.
3. The winner is candidate C.
6. A collective-coercive decision is a collective decision that is enforced on private choices. The normative issue is that collective decisions limit the behavior of the individual whether they agree with the decisions or not. Rawls's solution to the problem is that all should go behind the "veil of ignorance" where the individual would be blind to one's self-interest. From behind the veil of ignorance, just decisions could be made about which set of institutions should be used to decide matters of policy.

Chapter 7

1. Approx. 15 oz. caviar; approx. 333 slices of pizza; amount of caviar = $(1000/65) - (3/65) \times$ amount of pizza
4. a. 123
   b. 124; 121.5
   c. 119; The consumer substitutes more caviar for less pizza.
   d. 173 pizzas
5. $P_{diamonds}$ = 4,999,996; P_{water} = 1,000,000; Consumer surplus for diamonds = 4; Consumer surpluse for water = 4,000,000; The purchase of water is valued more.
6. The supply curve is flat, implying that all citizens must consume the same amount of the public good regardless of how much they value the good. Lindahl's solution was to vary the price or tax share for each individual.

Chapter 8

3. a. Type 1 prefers plurality rule; Type 2 prefers majority rule, with runoff; Type 3 prefers Borda count.
   b. plurality rule.
4. Both Director's law and the median voter theorem state that the constitutents or voters in the middle are the main determinant of public policy.

Chapter 9

1. Approximately 28 percent.
2. a. 0.27
    b. 0.40
    c.

$(30 \times 27)/100 = 8.1$	$(30 \times 51)/100 = 15.3$	$(30 \times 22)/100 = 6.6$	30
$(40 \times 27)/100 = 10.8$	$(40 \times 51)/100 = 20.4$	$(40 \times 22)/100 = 8.8$	40
$(30 \times 27)/100 = 8.1$	$(30 \times 51)/100 = 15.3$	$(30 \times 22)/100 = 6.6$	30
27	51	22	100

3. $(12!)/(5! \times (12 - 5)!) \times (9!)/(3! \times (9 - 3)!)$
4. b. $8!/(3!(8 - 3)!) = 56$
5. $1/3; 1/2; 0; 1/6.$
6. $\{[13 \times (4!)/(3! \times (4 - 3)!)] \times [12 \times (4!)/(2! \times (4 - 2)!)]\} / [52 \times /(5! \times (52 - 5)!)]$
7. a.

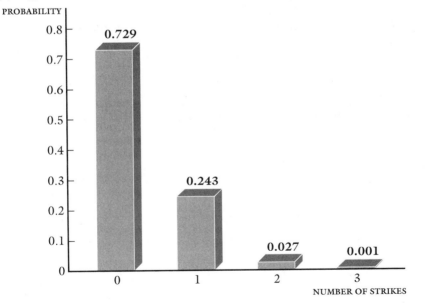

b. $P(0) = (0.9) \times (0.9) \times (0.9) = 0.729$
$P(1) = 3 \times (0.9) \times (0.9) \times (0.1) = 0.243$
$P(2) = 3 \times (0.9) \times (0.1) \times (0.1) = 0.027$
$P(3) = (0.1) \times (0.1) \times (0.1) = 0.001$

Chapter 10

1. a. $247.61
   b. $1,141.61
   c. $1,333.33
2. With a discount rate of 0.05:
   a. $2,025.09
   b. $1,361.62
   c. $4,000.00
   With a discount rate of 0.55:
   a. $–899.66
   b. $664.97
   c. $363.64
3. Projects ranked from highest to lowest discount rate: 6, 8, 9, 7, 10, 1, 3, 5, 2, 4. Projects 5, 2, and 4 are not worth building at all.
4. Projects ranked from highest to lowest present value with a discount rate of 0.15: 7, 8, 9, 6, 10, 4, 1, 5, 3, 2. Projects 10, 4, 1, 5, 3, and 2 are not worth building. The rankings are different than problem 3. This result is expected because the rankings will change with different from discount rates. Therefore, the IRR does not provide a universal ranking criterion for projects.

Chapter 11

2.

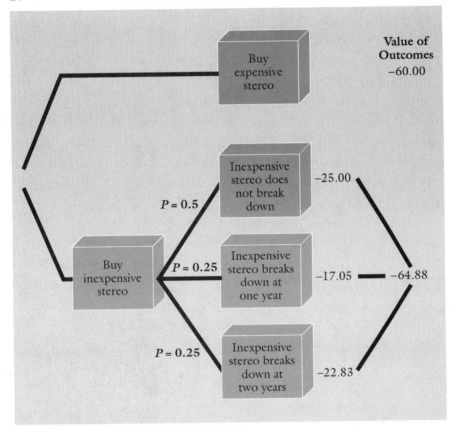

3. a. Status quo
    b. Alternative A
    c. Status quo

Index

∽ ∼

Page numbers in *italics* refer to illustrations. Those in **boldface** refer to definitions of terms.